STAKEHOLDER THEORY

edited by
ABE J. ZAKHEM, DANIEL E. PALMER,
AND MARY LYN STOLL

STAKEHOLDER THEORY

ESSENTIAL READINGS

IN ETHICAL LEADERSHIP

AND MANAGEMENT

FOREWORD BY NORMAN E. BOWIE
Elmer Andersen Chair in Corporate Responsibility
Carlson School of Management, University of Minnesota

 Prometheus Books
59 John Glenn Drive
Amherst, New York 14228-2119

Published 2008 by Prometheus Books

Inquiries should be addressed to
Prometheus Books
59 John Glenn Drive
Amherst, New York 14228–2119
VOICE: 716–691–0133, ext. 210
FAX: 716–691–0137
WWW.PROMETHEUSBOOKS.COM

12 11 10 09 08   5 4 3 2 1

Library of Congress Cataloging-in-Publication Data

Stakeholder theory : essential readings in ethical leadership and management / ed. by Abe J. Zakhem, Daniel E. Palmer, Mary Lyn Stoll.
    p. cm.
  Includes bibliographical references.
  ISBN 978–1–59102–526–9
    1. Corporate governance. 2. Business ethics. 3. Social responsibility of business. I. Zakhem, Abe J. II. Palmer, Daniel E. III. Stoll, Mary Lyn.

HD2741.S7615 2007
174'.4—dc22

2007011478

Every attempt has been made to trace accurate ownership of copyrighted material in this book. Errors and omissions will be corrected in subsequent editions, provided that notification is sent to the publishers.

Printed in the United States of America on acid-free paper

CONTENTS

PART 4. STAKEHOLDER IDENTITY   **163**

PART 5. APPLICATIONS 1: STAKEHOLDER THEORY AT WORK IN THE CORPORATE DOMAIN   **219**

8   Contents

FOREWORD
Norman E. Bowie

S takeholder management theory has a curious history. Given the popularity of the term "stakeholder management," one might think that the concept of stakeholder management is clear and that all that needs to be done is to convince managers to give up the notion of exclusively serving stockholders and instead to focus on addressing the interests of the various corporate stakeholders. However, as this volume of essays on stakeholder management theory shows, nothing could be further from the truth.

First there is a problem of identification. Who is to count as a stakeholder? The father of stakeholder theory, R. Edward Freeman, has consistently distinguished between a wide definition of stakeholder and a narrow one. For example, in a *California Management Review* piece in 1983, Freeman and his coauthor, David L. Reed, distinguished the wide and narrow definitions as follows:

> The Wide Sense of Stakeholder: Any identifiable group or individual who can affect the achievement of an organization's objectives or who is affected by the achievement of an organization's objectives.

> The Narrow Sense of Stakeholder: Any identifiable group or individual on which the organization is dependent for its continued survival.

Several things stand out in these two definitions. There is an issue as to the appropriate level of analysis. Do we look for individuals or do we look for groups when we seek to identify stakeholders? As Freeman and Reed do here, stakeholder theorists often move back and forth between the two levels of analysis. Thus, a stakeholder is any person affected by the business or, alternatively, the stakeholder is any group affected by the actions of the business. If we switch to a narrow sense of stakeholder, a stakeholder is any group or any individual necessary for the survival of the firm. Is stakeholder theory of management a theory of the management of individuals or of the management of groups?

Why worry about the level of analysis? Because, as Freeman and his students have always maintained, stakeholder theory is really a theory of management. If it is a theory of management, then it seems to me we must ask the pragmatic management question: should management focus on individuals or should it focus on groups? For the most part, I would argue that stakeholder theory is about how to manage groups. If the focus were to be on individuals, it would be too difficult to implement in practice.

To focus on groups is only a start, however. Almost from the beginning critics challenged Freeman's distinction between the wide sense and the narrow sense of stakeholder. The wide sense was too wide; too many would count as stakeholders under that description. The narrow sense was too narrow. "Necessary to the survival of the firm" would capture too few stakeholders. In 1997 Mitchell, Agle, and Wood provided a finer theory of stakeholder identification that uses power, legitimacy, and urgency as identifying marks. Their theory of identification has been accepted by many, especially by those who attempt to apply stakeholder theory. However, as the papers in this volume indicate, other theories of stakeholder identification have been developed. Moreover, research on this issue of stakeholder identification continues. Papers that seek to reform the Mitchell et al. account are in circulation. More than a quarter of a century after stakeholder management was developed, the struggle to decide who counts as a stakeholder continues.

A second controversy surrounds what stakeholder theory is a theory of. Indeed, is it a theory at all? In their classic article, "The Stakeholder Theory of the Corporation," Donaldson and Preston recognize that stakeholder theory is descriptive, instrumental, normative, and managerial. Many have separated these components then conducted scholarly research and investigation into one aspect. Descriptive stakeholder theories and instrumental stakeholder theories are easily conceptualized. Thomas M. Jones has one of the more developed instrumental stakeholder theories.

While a descriptive stakeholder theory and an instrumental stakeholder theory present few conceptual difficulties, a normative stakeholder theory presents real conceptual and justificatory issues. Some write as if stakeholder theory is an ethical theory the way utilitarianism, Kantianism, or virtue theory are ethical theories. But these writers are not correct. One can see this if one takes the perspective of a manager. From a management perspective, stakeholder theory, in contrast to stockholder theory, instructs managers of an organization to pay attention to the interests of the stakeholders. The immediate question is: why?

Those who defend the classic stockholder model have a ready answer, or set of answers, to the question: how should the firm be managed? It should be managed in the interests of the stockholders. Why? Because the stockholders are the owners of the firm, and the managers are agents of the stockholders and have a fiduciary obligation to manage in their interests. Or, alternatively, because the firm is a nexus of contracts and the interests of all the contractors can be covered in written contracts while the interests of the stockholders cannot be protected by contracts. Since stockholders bear the risk, they are entitled to the residual (profit). Whether these defenses are adequate is not the issue here. Rather, the point is that the stockholder theory of management has ready answers to the question: why should managers manage for the interests of the stockholders?

Freeman has resisted the attempt to make sharp distinctions among descriptive, instrumental, and normative stakeholder theories. He has insisted that stakeholder theory is managerial. Freeman firmly rejects what he calls the separation thesis: the separation thesis puts business on one side and business ethics on the other. Freeman insists that business and ethics are tied together and that the normative aspect of managerial stakeholder theory is the normative core. Freeman argues that there can be many normative cores. In some of his writings, Freeman proposed a "redesigned contractual normative core based on autonomy, solidarity, and fairness." Some have provided feminist cores (e.g., Burton and Dunn) or fairness cores (e.g., Phillips). These normative cores are represented in the readings in this volume. For a pluralist like Freeman, further research in managerial stakeholder theory would lead to the development of different normative cores.

I would come at this controversy in a slightly different way. I am with Freeman and the editors of this volume who look at stakeholder theory as a theory of management. I accept the central moral obligation of a stakeholder theory of management: that the firm should be managed in the interests of the firm's stakeholders. Thus, rather than a moral core, I would maintain there is a core moral obligation. To be complete managerial stakeholder theory needs a moral justification for this core moral obligation. What have been called normative cores are really justifications for the core obligation. The justification can come from a Rawlsian perspective, a feminist perspective, or, in my case, from a Kantian perspective. I have spent much of my career emphasizing and developing the Kantian justification for stakeholder theory—so much so that few would count me as a stakeholder theorist. But that is not correct. Let me make explicit what has been implicit: I am a managerial stakeholder theorist who seeks to justify the core moral obligation of managerial stakeholder theory on Kantian grounds.

One can now summarize what is perhaps the central debate in business ethics. Should the firm be managed exclusively for the stockholders or should it be managed in the interests of all the stakeholders? Both the stockholder theory of management and the stakeholder theory of management have moral obligations at the center. The stockholder theory is a normative theory just as stakeholder theory is. Indeed, as Freeman has pointed out, stockholder theory could be understood as a kind of stakeholder theory with a distinctive normative core. I am in total agreement with Freeman here. The question then becomes which managerial theory provides the best theory of management? Using some of the distinctions of Donaldson and Preston, one can ask which theory best accounts for how firms are actually managed. What many claim is that only if one adopts the stakeholder theory of management, will the interests of the stockholders be best protected. The empirical evidence is not explicitly addressed in this book. However, this volume provides many examples of stakeholder theory in practice and that is one of its strengths. Moreover, this volume provides many good accounts of those who defend the stockholder theory of management and some responses by those who hold the stakeholder theory of management. Inevitably in a long and contracted debate of this kind, each side accuses the other of misinterpretations and misunderstandings. Readers of this volume will find the article by Phillips, Freeman, and Wicks, "What Stakeholder Theory Is Not," stipulating what stakeholder theory is not, to be instructive in this regard.

Yet another issue for managerial stakeholder theory is the question of balance. If the firm is to be managed in the interests of the stakeholders, and the interests of the stakeholders conflict, how are managers to achieve that balance? Michael Jensen, in his *Business Ethics Quarterly* article from 2002, "Value Maximization, Stakeholder Theory, and the Corporate Objective Function," argues against the possibility of the balanced scorecard. Jensen's main argument is that you cannot maximize conflicting values. Of course, as a matter of logic, that is correct. But managerial stakeholder theory is not arguing for the maximization of competing values; it simply argues that there is a moral obligation for managers to take into account the interests of the relevant stakeholders. You will note that managerial stakeholder theory does not require that the interests of the various stakeholders need to be treated equally.

The strongest argument against managerial stakeholder theory might appear to be a practical one. How is the manager to manage if he or she is always balancing all these stakeholder interests? Management under stakeholder management theory creates paralysis—or so the argument goes. But a look at actual management practice shows the failure of that argument. Suppose one adopts the stockholder management theory, that a manager is obligated to manage in the interests of the stockholders. But to accomplish that the manager must take into account the interests of the stakeholders. Recall the narrow definition of stakeholders: those groups necessary to the survival of the firm. Failure to address their interests would obviously undermine stockholder profits. To some extent managers must take into account the interests of at least certain stakeholders, and they do.

Perhaps the most developed application of stakeholder management is in those firms that are managed as sustainable firms or as firms that practice corporate social responsibility (CSR). Sustainability or CSR is the official policy of the European Union. A sustainable firm is one that is financially successful, environmentally friendly, and socially responsible—especially with respect to human rights. How does a firm achieve sustainability? A key element is to adopt stakeholder management. In many firms, stakeholder management is achieved in part through stakeholder dialogues. As the officials of one major European international company have said, "We have gone from 'trust me' to 'show me' to 'engage me.'" The relation between stakeholder theory and corporate social responsibility is a concern of several articles in this volume. Suffice it to say that managerial practice shows that managerial stakeholder theory is practical and financially viable.

Discussions in business ethics focus on managerial stakeholder theory in corporations or business firms. But as a number of articles in this volume show, managerial stakeholder theory works successfully in government, nonprofits, and nongovernmental organizations (NGOs) as well. Also, stakeholder theory is not culture bound in the sense that stakeholder management can work in all, or nearly all, cultures. What might vary from culture to culture would be who counts as a stakeholder, and the techniques by which stakeholder management is achieved. Papers in this volume explore some of the international aspects of managerial stakeholder theory.

Managerial stakeholder theory presents a rich stew. I urge readers of this volume to have a hearty appetite and to enjoy the morsels herein.

Norman E. Bowie
University of Minnesota

INTRODUCTION

The term "stakeholders" has become widespread in contemporary discussions of business ethics and corporate responsibility both inside the academy and within the business community itself. Indeed, stakeholder theory represents one of those rare instances in which philosophical ideas have transcended the realm of academic discourse and taken hold amid a much broader population as well. Today it is not uncommon for business managers and executives to speak openly of their obligations to their stakeholders, and not just their stockholders, and the scholarly research in business ethics has been dominated in recent years by the stakeholder approach to analyzing and reacting to ethical issues in business. In part, the emergence of stakeholder theory merely reflects the growing interest in business ethics in recent decades—an interest partly sparked and sustained by some of the prominent and much-discussed instances of unethical business behavior, such as those found in the Enron, WorldCom, Tyco, and Arthur Anderson cases. What these cases illustrate is the definite need, both theoretical and practical, for a paradigm in which the ethical problems and concerns of business can be discussed and evaluated. To a large extent stakeholder theory now provides that paradigm, and offers both academics and businesspersons a means of analyzing and deliberating about ethical issues in business—a paradigm that is theoretically grounded, but that provides a readily accessible idiom to apply to the ethical issues of the corporate world as well.

Given the present influence of stakeholder theory on the literature of business ethics and in the business community itself, we believe that a larger view of the sources, controversies, and emerging directions of stakeholder theory is particularly imperative. This volume serves to realize this goal. By offering a comprehensive and thematically organized reader on stakeholder theory, we hope to provide a valuable aid to students, teachers, researchers, and businesspersons interested in stakeholder theory in at least three respects. One, the readings in this work provide a solid introduction to the main elements of stakeholder theory for readers who are seeking a basic introduction to the nature of the theory. Two, this work provides a historical overview of the development and expansion of stakeholder theory, from its origins in business literature to its contemporary applications. Three, the thematic arrangement of the readings provides a guide to the major issues within stakeholder theory for those readers who are interested in specific aspects or applications of the theory. As the readings cover nearly every aspect of the literature on stakeholder theory, readers with diverse interests can profitably use them as a starting point for their own research. In addition, the extensive bibliography provided at the end provides further suggestions to guide those readers who are interested in continuing their research into various aspects of stakeholder theory.

While the readings contained in this volume provide the most telling story of the development of stakeholder theory, in the remainder of this introduction we would like to map out a few of the most salient aspects of the history and development of the theory. In doing so, we will argue that there have been three primary, though sometimes overlapping, phases in the development of stakeholder theory. First there was the development phase, in which stakeholder theory emerged as a response to the then-dominant managerial models. The focus in that early phase was largely on formulating an alternative theoretical framework that would allow the incorporation of certain business externalities into management models. As the new "stakeholder" model began to gain traction, business ethicists sought to clarify its normative foundations. As such, the second phase in the development of stakeholder theory tended to focus on its theoretical and normative underpinnings. Finally, as the stakeholder model of management began to find a foothold in business schools and the corporate world, there was a greater need for understanding on the part of businesspersons as to how to utilize the model in corporate management. As such, the third phase in the development of stakeholder theory has emphasized the concrete application of the theory, with a further emphasis on specifying how stakeholder management operates in practice.

Although specific reference to "stakeholders" in management literature dates back to the early 1960s, it was not until R. Edward Freeman's monumental *Strategic Management: A Stakeholder Approach*, published in 1984, that the concept evolved into a comprehensive and formal management theory. Prior to the stakeholder concept, the dominant "managerial" description of the firm characterized business organizations as being comprised of various production processes through which raw materials are converted into sellable products. Presiding over production processes, managers could reach ownership-specified objectives and goals by simply attending to organizational roles and relationships on simple input-process-output terms. That is, suppliers provide necessary raw materials; employees process, transform, and add value to supplied inputs; and customers ultimately purchase production outputs. Thus constituting the recognized "environment" of a firm, the managerial model and its associated strategies and economic tools offered a rudimentary but successful framework through which managers could measure, analyze, and improve organizational performance.

Alongside traditional descriptions of business organizations is the classical theory of the firm that narrowly equates business's social responsibility with maximizing profits for shareholders. According to Milton Friedman, one of the most vocal proponents of the classic view, to act in any other way is tantamount to subverting our "free" society, unjustly taxing stockholders, undercutting the agent-principal relationship, and otherwise leading to ill consequences for society as a whole. This "shareholder-centric" rendering of the corporate objective function, relying on the largely unquestioned normative and empirical justifications of liberal economic theory, had long dominated dialogue concerning the nature and extent of corporate social responsibility. However, even Friedman recognized that businesspersons had an obligation to play by the rules of the game; that is, to obey their legal and contractual obligations and not to engage in blatantly unethical behavior. In this sense, even the shareholder model of management implicitly recognized, at least in theory if not always in practice, that there was a necessarily ethical component to business activity. The problem was that many proponents of the model failed to flesh out the implications of such a recognition, and these proponents tended to leave the impression that only the interests of shareholders were relevant to managerial decision making.

Going into the early 1980s, however, the business terrain showed signs of significant change and accordingly brought new and difficult managerial challenges. Most notably, this period witnessed the emerging influence of groups "external" to the managerial model on the achievement of a firm's objectives. The influence of external constituencies, such as governments, competitors, consumer advocates, activists, the media, and nongovernmental organizations, cut both ways. That is, doing business in a complex and increasingly global economy required new levels of extended outreach and cooperation, while, at the same time, it opened the firm up to unanticipated externalities and, often as a result, unpredictable yet tangible losses. In confronting these new challenges, the managerial model of the firm proved to be without the conceptual framework to predict, represent, and leverage external changes for the firm's advantage. In short, a new conceptual model of the firm, one that incorporated and that was sensitive to changes in the external environment, was needed.

At the same time, management theorists and practitioners began to recognize changes in attitudes and public expectations pertaining to the proper responsibilities of business. Sometimes attributed to the socially minded cultures of the 1960s, organizational theorists and management practitioners describe a general movement away from narrow and shareholder-centric conceptions of managerial responsibility and the corporate objective function to a wider sense of corporate social responsibility. Many well-known cases about the ethics of managerial decisions, such as the Ford Pinto case, and the growing concern over the costs of business externalities associated with pollution and environmental damage exacerbated the perceived need within society for a change in managerial outlook. Furthermore, both academics and working professionals began to respond to issues raised by various social trends, such as the emergence of the consumer rights movement, the demand for equal rights on the part of women and racial minorities, and a general growth in health consciousness among Americans as well.

Against this backdrop Freeman formulated the stakeholder model of the firm, essentially assimilating the external environment and extending constituencies, effectively redrawing the boundaries of strategic management. Trying to capture a broad range of individuals and groups, Freeman thus designated the term "stakeholder" to include any group or individual who can affect or is affected by the achievement of the organization's objectives. For the skeptics who questioned the legitimacy of new stakeholder groups, Freeman's response was clear and very pragmatic: if you want to be an effective manager in "turbulent times" you must take stakeholders into account. Regardless of whether or not managers personally or conventionally regarded stakeholders as legitimate organizational concerns, stakeholders ought to be considered legitimate at least in terms of their capacity for impacting organizational aims and goals. As such, it is in a manager's interest to identify stakeholders and their perceived stakes, establish processes for stakeholder valuation and assessment, and implement transactions or bargains sufficient for "balancing" stakeholder demands and surfacing discontent. As such, the corporate objective function shifts from maximizing shareholder profit to balancing the interests of all of an organization's stakeholders.

The establishment of stakeholder theory led to concerns of both a theoretical and a practical nature. On the theoretical side, two main issues have come to the fore in the literature about the normative foundations of stakeholder theory. On the one hand, Freeman's theory seemed to suppose, even if his own justification was largely pragmatic, that managers had distinct obligations toward stakeholders that ought to factor into their managerial decisions, above and beyond their obligations toward their shareholders. Critics of stakeholder theory have argued that allowing such factors to influence managerial decisions could potentially violate the fiduciary obligation that managers have toward their stockholders, an obligation that is based clearly in the ownership model of the corporation. In response to such criticisms, defenders of stakeholder theory have taken one of two tactics (though in practice these are often combined). On the one hand, many defenders of stakeholder theory have attempted to further delineate the nature of the managerial obligation toward stakeholders and demonstrate that such obligations are as well founded as the fiduciary obligation toward stockholders. Thus, defenders of stakeholder theory have attempted to use social contractarian, Kantian, or other ethical theories to ground the basic nature of stakeholder obligations. On the other hand, a number of defenders of stakeholder theory have argued that the nature of stakeholder obligations, when properly specified, does not actually conflict with stockholder obligations. According to such views, respecting stakeholder obligations does not violate the nature of the fiduciary obligation toward stockholders and thus, the putative conflict is merely illusory.

However, even if the existence of stakeholder obligations can be established, there is still a need to determine the nature and extent of such obligations.

Thus, a second theoretical concern that emerged within the literature of stakeholder theory focused on how to factor and weigh various competing stakeholders into managerial models. Here too, two main issues rose to the fore. For one, given the wide range of parties that might be affected by contemporary business activities in a variety of diverse ways, proponents of stakeholder theory need to specify which affected groups count as legitimate stakeholders in managerial decisions as well as what kinds of effects represent genuine infringements of stakeholder rights. In this regard, much of the literature following Freeman attempts to further delineate the nature and extent of stakeholder obligations. Second, since different stakeholders might make different claims upon managerial decisions and actions, the problem of coordinating and balancing competing stakeholder claims within a coherent managerial model became apparent. Taking this into consideration, proponents of stakeholder theory began an intense scrutiny of questions surrounding the proper harmonization of stakeholder interests.

Such theoretical interests naturally spilled over into a practical interest on the part of corporate managers wishing to institute stakeholder models of management within business institutions. For, on the practical side, if stakeholder theory is to represent a viable model of managerial decision making, managers need to be able to incorporate stakeholder concerns into their managerial considerations in a way that is both clear and efficient. Otherwise, stakeholder theory will remain a matter of purely academic interest. Not surprisingly then, a large number of persons interested in stakeholder theory soon turned their attention to developing concrete models of stakeholder management. Indeed, a good deal of the recent literature on stakeholder theory has been devoted to the application of the theory within specific managerial models and contexts. The literature that has developed out of these efforts contains a number of different approaches to this task. Some authors have attempted to develop general decision models for stakeholder management. Others have attempted to demonstrate the applicability of stakeholder models through the use of case studies or by relating stakeholder models to existing regulatory or legal standards. Still other authors have concentrated on developing industry-specific models of stakeholder management. Not surprisingly, as the literature on stakeholder theory has grown, the range of cases and industries to which stakeholder models of management have been applied has continued to grow as well.

Furthermore, as the range of applications of stakeholder theory within businesses has grown, another phenomenon in recent years has involved the extension of the stakeholder model into domains beyond the traditional business context in which stakeholder theory was first developed. Indeed, what is surprising is the extent to which the notion of stakeholder analysis has found its way into other contexts. In recent years, one is apt to hear considerations of stakeholders being appealed to in a diverse range of organizations and arenas. Administrators from educational, governmental, nonprofit, healthcare, and a host of other organizations have taken to analyzing their own decision-making and organizational obligations in terms of stakeholder analysis and integration. Here too, though, issues arise as to how the stakeholder theory can be properly applied to decision making in these diverse contexts. Questions such as "Who are the legitimate stakeholders in such arenas?" and "How should decision makers in these domains integrate stakeholder concerns into their decisions?" arise in these arenas in their own distinctive way. An additional important development of stakeholder theory has involved the attempt to answer such questions on the part of those working in the relevant disciplines as they strive to appropriate the theory in such disparate fields.

There is no doubt that stakeholder theory has come to occupy a prominent place within the landscape of both academia and society at large, and the theory's influence on discussions of business ethics continues unabated. Indeed, because of the widespread and interdisciplinary interest in stakeholder theory, the literature on the theory is immense. No single volume could include more than a sampling of this vast literature. As such, our choice of readings has been guided by a very specific set of criteria in order to most effectively provide readers with a solid introduction to stakeholder theory.

First, the readings that we have included in this volume are meant to capture both the depth and the breadth of the literature on stakeholder theory. We have tried to include readings on as many of the facets of stakeholder theory as was feasible in order to illustrate the breadth of the theory. The readings include contributions from diverse academic disciplines from management to philosophy. As an interdisciplinary area of inquiry, we believe it is important to illustrate the various disciplines that have contributed to stakeholder theory. Furthermore, we have tried to emphasize both the theoretical issues involved in the development of stakeholder theory as well as issues concerning the application of stakeholder management models within the corporate world. Such a balance underscores the dual appeal of stakeholder theory as both a theoretical and a practical model of management. On the side of depth, we have tried to choose those selections that most clearly and fully deal with the most important questions raised by the various aspects of stakeholder theory. In regard to the latter point, we would note that the selections include many of the most prominent and cited scholars in the field of stakeholder theory.

Second, we have tried to include selections representative of the development of stakeholder theory. From its initial emergence, the discourse about stakeholder theory has grown and progressed in response to both continuing academic debate and emerging social and practical concerns, and we believe it is important to give the reader a sense of how this historical development has occurred. The articles we have selected thus range from some of the first work on stakeholder theory to selections dealing with the most recent trends in stakeholder theory. Stakeholder theory represents an ongoing project as those working in the field respond to and incorporate previous work, and expand the boundaries of stakeholder theory. We believe that it is important to give readers a sense of the dynamic nature of stakeholder theory in this regard. Indeed, as the reader will note, many of the selections included here reference each other and give a sense of the on-going conversation that has channeled the historical evolution of stakeholder theory.

Finally, we have tried to choose a set of selections that will appeal to a wide audience of readers. By selecting and organizing the readings in terms of a number of different aspects of stakeholder theory, we have both provided a general introduction to stakeholder theory as a whole while also providing a resource that can be profitably used by persons of diverse backgrounds and interests. As such, we believe this book can be used as both a classroom tool and as a scholarly resource by students, teachers, and academic researchers from diverse disciplines, as well as by working professionals and interested laypersons. We have provided brief overviews of the articles contained in each section and suggestions for further reading to help the reader who is interested in some particular aspect of stakeholder theory. Given the prevalence of references to stakeholder theory within the contemporary literature, anyone who is seriously interested in either management theory or business ethics today must be familiar with at least some aspects and elements of the theory. We believe this volume offers just such a ready aid to those seeking to enhance their understanding in this regard.

PART 1.

THE ORIGINS OF STAKEHOLDER THEORY

Busieness management is a dynamic activity. When commercial environments experience significant change, managers must sufficiently alter their conceptual schemes to somehow capture, react to, and anticipate new challenges. For some time, managers could successfully drive organizational performance by addressing the interests of a small, core group of owners, suppliers, and customers. This, however, is no longer the case. Changes in technology, law, economics, markets, and social and political conditions have rendered many of the old ways of understanding and doing business inefficient and largely obsolete. It was from a wide variety of important environmental factors that the stakeholder concept arose and accordingly marked significant changes in prevailing attitudes toward the corporate objective function. In general, the emergence of the stakeholder theory represented a movement away from traditional, cloistered, and shareholder centric-driven conceptions of managerial responsibility to a more expanded understanding of the social responsibility of business. In this section we include readings that document some of the more prominent environmental changes that served to inform and shape the contours of stakeholder management theory, the influence of which is still present in many contemporary stakeholder management theory formulations and applications.

While the stakeholder theory itself is a relativity recent phenomennon, the issues it responds to can be traced much further back. In 1951 Frank W. Abrams addressed prominent changes in business attitudes and practices from the standpoint of an industry executive. While serving as chairman of the board for Standard Oil, Abrams authored "Management Responsibilities

23

in a Complex World" to focus on the impact of environmental changes on management professions. Expressing an early version of the now widely used notion of "balancing" vested interests, Abrams argued that core management responsiblities derive from the general obligation to maintain an equitable and workable balance among the claims of the various interested groups. Extending beyond maximizing profit for stockholders, Abrams claimed that managers are thus equally responsible for minding and advancing the interests of employees, customers, communities, and the general public at large. Likewise realizing the need to support such contentions on normative grounds, Abrams appealed to nonpedantic conceptions of justice, the common good, and human dignity for support.

The reading by Russell L. Ackoff analyzes changing conceptions of the corporation within the context of a "systems" approach. In his "Creating the Corporate Future," Ackoff traces the development of the modern corporation from the industrial and machine ages to contemporary and organizational descriptions of the firm, and he associates each view with a corresponding specification of the corporate objective function. While traditional approaches associate the purpose of the corporation with maximizing profit, an organization that is conceived as being composed of interrelated and mutually dependent systems of control, people, and environments leads to different conclusions. Ackoff accordingly draws out a systems-oriented and stakeholder-driven conception of the modern corporation and maintains that the proper function of such an organzation is to serve all stakeholders by increasing their ability to efficiently and effectively improve their quality of life.

William R. Dill's "Strategic Management in a Kibitzer's World" represents one of the first attempts to bring the stakeholder concept to the center of strategic management and planning concerns. Highlighting the growing demand by stakeholders for a more pronounced and direct role in strategic development and managerial decision making, Dill portrays the pressing challenge in contemporary business as one that requires managers to successfully forward organizational goals amid the adversarial and controlling interests of a number of powerful constituencies. Moving beyond traditional treatments of externality influence, which tend to focus on the end impacts of stakeholder pressure on the bottom line, Dill argues that managers must bring stakeholders into the decision-making fold by way of establishing active and participatory relationships. In terms of offering specific recommendations for practice, Dill lays out innovative suggestions for stakeholder mapping, intermediary communication, and contending with the reality of expanding management paradigms.

In the final article, "Stockholders and Stakeholders: A New Perspective on Corporate Governance," R. Edward Freeman and David L. Reed begin by tracing the historical evolution of the stakeholder concept and articulate some of the outstanding theoretical and analytical problems associated with previous work. In particular, the problem of stakeholder identity and legitimacy (discussed in chapter 5) is called to the fore as one of the more pressing issues. Addressing this concern and moving beyond Dill's narrow analysis of stakeholder power and influence, the authors advance a wide definition of stakeholders that includes any identifiable group or individual who can affect the achievement of an organization's objectives *or* who is affected by the achievement of an organization's objectives (our emphasis). Additionally, Freeman and Reed discuss two key processes for the application of stakeholder theory: the Stakeholder Strategy Process and the Stakeholder Audit Process. The Stakeholder Strategy Process provides a systematic account of which stakeholders matter most to corporate decision making; this approach then uses that systematic analysis of stakeholders to determine how best to meet stakeholder needs and concerns. Stakeholder audits then help a company determine the effectiveness of strategies developed by the Stakeholder Strategy Process.

1.

MANAGEMENT'S RESPONSIBILITY IN A COMPLEX WORLD

Frank W. Abrams

Like all vital, living things, the practice of business management is not static. It changes—sometimes at a relatively slow pace, sometimes more rapidly. I believe that a number of important changes have occurred in a comparatively brief recent period. These changes may not be widely and fully recognized. Yet they are important, not only to businessmen themselves but to all the other groups of our society who have a stake in the national economy, which means everyone.

Many businessmen, perhaps, have not been fully conscious of this evolution, simply because their day-to-day tasks keep their eyes so closely focused on their own particular part of the business picture. They do not have so much opportunity as they should to stand back and see it in its full dimensions.

MANAGEMENT NOW A PROFESSION

Briefly, it seems to me that business management in the United States is acquiring more and more the characteristics of a profession.

The hallmark of a profession is its sense of duty. None of the great, recognized professions are without a strong sense of responsibility to the community. Professional men do not work solely for themselves, but also for the good of mankind. The profession of medicine would not have the high

Excerpts from Frank W. Abrams, "Management's Responsibilities in a Complex World," *Harvard Business Review* 29, no. 3 (May 1951): 29–34. © *Harvard Business Review*. Reprinted by permission.

standing it now enjoys if physicians did not observe the Hippocratic Oath of service. The legal profession would not be so highly regarded if it had not behind it a history of public service. The respect which the world gives to the teaching profession is not solely due to a respect for learning. It is also a salute to the men and women who have devoted themselves to one of the most important activities in society—the instruction of youth.

It is my belief that business managers are gaining in professional status partly because they see in their work the basic responsibilities that other professional men have long recognized in theirs. Businessmen are learning that they have responsibilities not just to one group but to many.

Because a large and well-established enterprise is accustomed to looking far into the future and making long-term decisions, it particularly needs broad social and political understanding as well as economic understanding.

The job of professional management, as I see it, is to conduct the affairs of the enterprise in its charge in such a way as to maintain an equitable and workable balance among the claims of the various directly interested groups. Business firms are man-made instruments of society. They can be made to achieve their greatest social usefulness—and thus their future can be best assured—when management succeeds in finding a harmonious balance among the claims of the various interested groups: the stockholders, employees, customers, and the public at large. But management's responsibility, in the broadest sense, extends beyond the search for a balance among respective claims. Management, as a good citizen, and because it cannot properly function in an acrimonious and contentious atmosphere, has the positive duty to work for peaceful relations and understanding among men—for a restoration of faith of men in each other in all walks of life . . .

INTERESTS OF STOCKHOLDERS

First, let us consider the interests of stockholders. As the owners of the business, they have invested their money in it and expect it to be run in such a way that they will receive a fair return, security, and a reasonable gain in the value of their equity as the industry grows.

Those two words, "fair" and "reasonable," mark the asserted claims not only of a corporation's stockholders but of all other groups as well. Very few groups ever believe that they make unfair or unreasonable claims. But often what one group thinks fair is regarded as entirely unreasonable by another. It takes professional judgment, experience, and knowledge of the consequences of specific decisions to resolve all the claims and to keep all the groups in cooperative support of the joint enterprise.

This reconciliation of interests is not always as difficult as it may seem. It is in part a matter of recognizing true long-term interests, as distinguished from interests that may seem real because they are more immediate.

There was a time, not so very long ago, when management thought of itself as being exclusively preoccupied with the stockholders' *immediate* interest. The stockholder, who had invested his capital in the enterprise, naturally had an interest in maximizing profits and dividends. As a general rule, therefore, management, as the stockholders' representative, vigorously contested the claims of labor for higher wages, and of customers for lower prices and better quality unless competition decreed otherwise. In that way higher profits and dividends, it was believed, could best be realized.

Let us examine that notion more closely to see whether such an attitude was really in the interest of the stockholder. It might have been if the stockholder was an in-and-out speculator. But if he was an investor, and had committed his capital for the purpose of acquiring an equity in a continuing enterprise that might grow and prosper over the years, then his interest might have been very badly served by such an attitude on the part of his management representatives.

Public approval is no less essential to the continued existence of today's kind of business than adequate capital, or efficient management. A satisfied and loyal group of employees, for instance, is an asset to the enterprise and its owners, of far greater value for its long-term success than many other items which carry a dollar-and-cents valuation in the balance sheet.

THE NATURE OF PROFITS

Even profits . . . are not so much an immediate prerogative of stockholders as was once thought. True, in the accounting sense and in the legal sense, all profits accrue to the beneficial interest of shareholders, but that does not necessarily mean that shareholders receive in payment all of what is accounted as profits.

If management is to make good its responsibility to preserve the long-run interests of stockholders, it must produce job opportunities in which men can maximize their productivity. That takes money. The task is an impossible one without the availability of adequate profits, a large part of which are directly or indirectly reinvested.

It can thus be seen that profits are not simply a withdrawal from the business for the exclusive benefit of stockholders. Actually they are used in large part to make secure the competitive position of the enterprise by increasing the productivity of its workers and thus, as an all-important by-product, increasing the real income of the nation.

Only by thinking of profits in these larger terms can management feel assured that it is doing an effective job in the stockholders' overall interest. Fortunately, in the long run, the stockholders' interest and the other interests of the community tend to coincide, and enlightened stockholders are seeing this more clearly all the time.

MANAGEMENT AND EMPLOYEES

Just as stockholders have invested their money, so, too, the men and women who work for a corporation have invested their time, their energies, and many of their hopes for security and happiness in their jobs. The employee's satisfaction comes not only from fair wages but from good working conditions—and also from opportunities for promotion and recognition as the business grows. But this is not all.

"The dignity of man"—the deep-seated desire to be treated like a worthy human being—has long been a foundation stone of our way of life. The claim of all employees to respect and consideration as human beings, with ambition and the capacity for self-improvement, poses a major responsibility for the management of any modern business. In fact, modern business management might well measure its success or failure as a profession in large part by the satisfaction and opportunities it is able to produce for its employees. . . .

In stressing the modern corporation's responsibilities to its employees, I am not advocating a program of paternalism. Businesses are in business to make money and not to stand in the place of parents, school, or church. But what I am saying is that no corporation can prosper for any length of time today if its sole purpose is to make as much money as possible, as quickly as possible, and without concern for other values. A modern corporation management, which has developed good social sense as well as good business sense, will accept the major responsibility to contribute to a satisfactory way of life for the men and women who work for it.

MANAGEMENT AND THE CUSTOMERS

The customers make up a third group which has claims on business management. As any corporate manager knows, customers are in the driver's seat. They are very likely to demand and gain pretty much what they want. A large part of the skill and technique of management is devoted to the professional task of coordinating and synchronizing the capital of stockholders with the talents of workers in a manner that will most effectively give the customer what he wants—more and better products at reasonable prices. . . .

During the last half of the twentieth century, especially, there have been times when the pressure on prices to advance or to contract violently has been great. Although many of the forces that make for inflation or deflation are outside the control of businessmen, I firmly believe that management, in the exercise of true business statesmanship, should do all in its power to dampen disruptive swings in the behavior of prices. Great instability is not in the interest of the stockholders or the employees—and it is certainly not in the interest of the customers.

Business management *does* have a responsibility to provide a flow of supplies needed to meet the requirements of the economy. Therefore, I believe, we must always try to foresee the results of a particular price change in terms of its effect on probable future supplies. It would be hard to show that the public interest is served by price changes that do not assist in stimulating either supply or demand, as one or the other may be needed from time to time.

Now these three groups that I have considered are the people with whom corporation managements have a direct and working contact. They are all very important. Each of their interests must be served and related one to the other, to the best of management's ability.

THE GENERAL PUBLIC'S INTEREST

But that is not the end of the story—the general public has a vital interest as well. Modern management must look beyond those groups of people that are immediately interested in the affairs of the business. It must understand that the general public—men and women everywhere—have a very deep interest in, and are affected by, what is going on. Contemporary management realizes that the actions it takes have definite and often far-reaching effects—effects that go beyond stockholders, employees, and customers.

The duty of business management to the general public is of a twofold nature. First, there is the obligation to keep the policies and actions of a particular business constantly in tune with national policies and interests, because in many cases a company is a very large factor in a community.

The second phase of this obligation to attend to the public interest arises out of the fact that the thing we call public interest is crystallized in public policy, and public policy has a very positive ultimate bearing on the success of the businesses that are entrusted to our care. We must participate in the formation of public policy even though the specific issues may not have an immediate influence on our individual businesses. . . .

PARTICIPATION IN PUBLIC ATTITUDES

. . . The geographical pioneering of this country's development is pretty much accomplished. Population has increased and shifted to the point where congestion occurs in many locations. The problems incident to increased population are accentuated by more rapid transportation and improved means of communication. People have been brought into closer association. Their opportunities for personal differences have multiplied.

It has become more important for us to learn how to live in harmony in a new kind of world. People now are more concerned with each other, and much less with the mastery of their physical environment. . . . Yet suspicion and acrimony exist among people and seem to be growing stronger.

Well, then, what can be done about it? In my opinion . . . management must apply to its relationships with the rest of the community the same type of searching analysis that it would make of its more usual business problems. It must do this in terms of what it knows, and can learn, about the basic wants and needs of men. After all, when you stop to think about it, it is absurd that business and the public, of which business is a part, should be regarded as being in conflict; or, again, that management should be opposed to labor's basic interest, and labor to management's. . . .

2.

OUR CHANGING CONCEPT
OF THE CORPORATION

Russell L. Ackoff

Corporations and the way we conceptualize them have evolved a great deal in the last hundred years. The modern corporation is a product of the Industrial Revolution, which, in turn, was a product of the Machine Age. Recall that in this age Western man conceptualized the universe as a machine created by God to do his work. Furthermore, man took himself to be a part of this machine and to have been created in the image of God. The Industrial Revolution was a consequence of man's efforts to imitate God by creating machines to do his work.

THE CORPORATION AS A MACHINE

The industrial organizations produced by the Industrial Revolution were taken to be related to their creators, their owners, much as the universe was to God. They were thought of as machines whose function was to serve their creators by providing them with an adequate return on their investment of time and money. Therefore, the principal, if not the only, function of such organizations was to make a profit.

In corporations so conceived, employees were treated as replaceable machines or machine parts even though they were known to be human beings. Their personal objectives, however, were considered irrelevant by employers. Employment involved an implicit acceptance by employees of the employer's right to treat them as though they were machines. Furthermore, the very simple repetitive tasks they were given to do were designed as though they were to be performed by machines. . . .

This conception of corporation as machine was tenable only as long as the following conditions held:

1. The owner had and could exercise virtually unlimited power over his employees—he could hire, fire, and otherwise reward or punish them as much as he saw fit.
2. The threat to employees of economic destitution resulting from unemployment was large and real.
3. The skills required of workers were generally low, hence easily obtainable.
4. The levels of education and aspiration of ordinary workers were relatively low.

. . . After the turn of the century the conditions necessary to support the mechanistic concept of the corporation began to change. First, opportunities for company growth generally exceeded what could be internally financed. Therefore, many privately owned companies "went public," or incorporated. Their ownership was dispersed among a large group of anonymous stockholders who seldom came into direct contact with workers. In effect, God disappeared. He became an abstract spirit rather than a concrete presence. Management emerged as a clergy that interpreted their God's desires and administered its will on the workers.

Second, the emergence of a management distinct from ownership was accompanied by the growth of unionization, social welfare, and the economy, each of which reduced the threat of economic destitution that faced the labor force.

Third, increasing mechanization required greater skills of workers. The more skills they acquired, the more difficult and costly it became to replace them.

Finally, the increase of compulsory education and the passage of laws restricting use of child labor raised the levels of education and aspiration of those entering the work force. They became less willing to accept a machine-like work life.

The mechanistic concept of the corporation could not stand up to this barrage of change.

THE CORPORATION AS AN ORGANISM

After World War I a new concept of the corporation gradually emerged: the corporation as an *organism*. So conceptualized, the corporation was taken to have a life and purposes of its own. Its principal purposes, like those of any organism, were believed to be *survival and growth*. Corporate profit came to be viewed in much the same way as oxygen is to an organism—necessary, but not the reason for its existence.

Because of the continued dispersion of corporate ownership and its increasingly transitory nature due to speculation on the stock exchange, the claims made by management of access to God by revelation became less believable. Managers had to accept full responsibility for their decisions.

Management was characterized as the brain or head of the firm and employees as its organs. Because organs are less easily replaced than machines or machine parts, their health and safety became corporate concerns. Working conditions became the focus of union-management negotiations. However, the concept and the nature of work itself were not called into question except when they affected health and safety.

Workers, their work places, and the society that contained them continued to change. Such change was greatly accelerated by World War II, when exceptional demands were made on both managers and workers. It became apparent that how workers felt about their work had a large effect on how much work they did and how well they did it. When work became less satisfying, output decreased. . . .

As automation was introduced and spread, the technical content of many jobs increased significantly; hence learning became an essential part of these jobs. The investment in the education and training of workers became a major one, making their replacement even more costly. Furthermore, the greater the skills required of a worker, the more difficult it became for his boss to tell him how to do his work. Few managers, for example, could instruct computer programmers or airline pilots. Managers could specify the kind of output or performance they wanted but not how it was to be obtained. In this way the increase in the technological content of work brought about increased freedom of, and dependence on, nonmanagerial employees.

As the skills of workers increased, the less inclined they were to give blind loyalty to their employing organizations. They began to think of themselves as professionals. Therefore, their personal aspirations and work-related requirements became increasing concerns to employers seeking their skills. . . .

The immense flood of talented young executives that poured into business would alone have disposed of the idea of the corporation as a machine, even without worker dissatisfaction. The major role of this new group of managers, as Jennings observed, was *innovation*—the exact antithesis of machinelike behavior. The idea of a corporation as an organism was harder to discredit. To be regarded as the brain of a corporation had a seductive appeal. But the brain merely proposes; the body, other human beings, and the environment taken together dispose. In the turbulent environment of post–World War II, managers quickly perceived that their major problem was managing people. Those who had returned from the service were no longer willing to be treated in the mechanistic way that the military had treated them. They insisted on consideration of their individual aspirations and hopes. Therefore, their treatment as purposeful individuals of intrinsic as well as extrinsic value could hardly be avoided.

The new entrants into the workforce were raised in families and educated in schools that were increasingly permissive. The products of permissiveness did not submit easily to authority. Furthermore, the continued development of the welfare state made economic destitution even less real. For these reasons and others the work ethic was significantly undermined.

Finally, in the post–World War II period the accumulated effects of the behavior of industrial organizations on their social and physical environments were increasingly seen as bad. The social responsibility of the corporation became a major public issue. Consumerism and environmentalism were launched, and the energy crisis added considerable fuel to these fires. Such movements pushed government toward more intervention in the conduct of business.

THE CORPORATION AS AN ORGANIZATION

For all the foregoing reasons and others, the concept of a corporation as an organism has become less tenable. A new concept has begun to emerge: the corporation as an *organization*. The corporation, of course, has always been thought of as an organization, but the implications of this have only in the last decades of the twentieth century come into collective consciousness.

An organization is (1) a purposeful system that is (2) part of one or more purposeful systems, and (3) parts of which, people, have purposes of their own. The first of these properties disposes of the concept of a corporation as a machine. The second denies that it is environment free. The third renders inapplicable the analogy of a corporation as an organism. These negative inferences from the properties of an organization simply clear the way to what these properties imply in an affirmative sense. This is a longer story.

We have become increasingly aware of the interactions of these three levels of purpose: societal, organizational, and individual; and that how well a corporation performs depends on how it is affected by both the people who are part of it and the systems of which it is part. Additionally, we are beginning to see more clearly that how an organization's parts affect it depends on how it affects them; and, similarly, the way in which the containing system affects it depends on how it affects that system. To put it another way, management is seen as having three major interdependent types of responsibility: first, to the purposes of the system they manage (*control*); second, to the purposes of the people who are part of the managed system (*humanization*); and third, to the purposes of the containing system and other systems that it contains (*environmentalization*).

Humanization problems have become pervasive and critical in contemporary society. Problems between races, the women's liberation movement, the generation gap, the third world problem, and alienation from work are examples. In each, purposeful individuals who are part of the same system organize to protest the way they are treated by their containing system.

Environmentalization problems such as ecological consideration and consumerism are also pervasive and critical. Such problems are created when purposeful individuals or organizations in the environment of a system organize to protest the way they are affected by that system. The environmentalization problem arises outside an organization; the humanization problem within it.

The task of management is seen increasingly as that of directing the corporation to satisfy the three types of demand that are placed on it. To a large extent the difficulty of this task derives from the fact that the three sets of demands, and even the demands within each set, are often incompatible. Effective management in the face of this sort of conflict requires a clear concept of an organization's functions relative to its parts and the system of which it is part, as well as its own purposes. We now turn to the development of such a concept.

THE STAKEHOLDER VIEW OF THE FIRM

The way we conceptualize a corporation affects the way we look at and describe its activities. To conceptualize a corporation as an organization is to see it as its *stakeholders* do. Stakeholders are all those inside or outside an organization who are directly affected by what it does. Therefore, they include all those whom managers should take into account, including managers themselves. From their perspectives a corporation engages in six types of exchanges:

1. An exchange of money for work with *employees*.
2. An exchange of money for goods and services with *suppliers*.
3. An exchange of goods and services for money with *customers*.
4. An exchange of money paid later for money received now with *investors* and *lenders*.
5. An exchange of money paid now for money received later with *debtors*.
6. An exchange of money for goods, services, and regulation with *government* (e.g., water, waste collection and disposal, and fire and police protection).

An examination of the flow between a corporation and its stakeholders reveals that, in a very general sense, a corporation does two things: it consumes, and it makes consumption possible. It makes consumption possible by making goods and services available, and by providing others with money with which they can purchase goods and services. The wealth produced by a corporation is the difference between the consumption it makes possible and its own consumption. Clearly, one societal function of industrial and commercial corporations is the production of wealth. Not so clear is the fact that it has another equally important societal function: the distribution of income through which consumption is made possible.

Employment is the principal means by which income is distributed in industrialized societies, whatever their politics. If corporations fail to provide enough employment to perform this function satisfactorily (as has been the case, for example, in many less developed countries) their governments have no alternative but to take over all or part of it. Increased social welfare and government employment (through nationalization of corporations, for instance) are two of the more common ways by which such a takeover is achieved.

There are not many examples of governments that run wealth-producing organizations efficiently. Furthermore, because welfare institutions are not wealth producing, the cost to society of having its government distribute income is generally larger than that of having it done by private corporations. Nevertheless, some feel that doing so is worth the additional cost because it can yield a more equitable distribution of wealth than a private distribution system. As yet, no exclusively private system for distributing wealth in a society has been able to eliminate poverty, but some public and some combined public-private systems have.

Some governments are reluctant to control or take over the task of creating and maintaining employment but feel obliged to do so because private corporations fail to do the job adequately. Increased governmental regulation of corporate behavior is a consequence. For example, the governments of many European countries have made it very difficult for employers to fire anyone. Unions have joined governments in forcing corporations to treat wages as virtually a fixed cost. This can, but need not, be disastrous to corporations. Whether it is depends on how management reacts to it.

Most private corporations attempt to maximize the return on the investment in their fixed assets, facilities, and equipment. Profit enables them to provide a return to their investors. This way of looking at a corporation, although commonplace, is arbitrary. It derives from earlier conditions that have changed or are changing: shortage of capital and a commodity-like labor market. Relevant social values are also changing; for example, as societies develop, their tolerance for poverty decreases.

Legislation, regulation, and labor contracts are making it increasingly difficult to treat the cost of labor as a variable and, therefore, as an expense. Social pressure is forcing managers to attempt to maximize the return on a relatively fixed cost of labor. In a sense, the cost of labor is changing from an expense to an investment. This does not mean, however, that the need to increase the productivity of labor or of facilities and equipment is less pressing, but it does require a higher level of management skill to determine how to use a relatively fixed workforce productively. This implies that when workers are replaced by machines, new productive work must be found for them. Since growth is also an objective of most corporations, this need not place much of an additional burden on management. However, it requires coordination of growth and increases of productivity. (One can argue moralistically that an organization that cannot increase its productivity does not deserve to grow.) It is not at all unlikely that efforts to maximize the return on labor would yield larger corporate profits than efforts to maximize return on fixed assets. In any event, pressure for this changeover in management perspective is more likely to grow than to diminish in the foreseeable future.

Corporations have a social responsibility not merely for distributing wealth, but for doing so equitably. *Equity* in this context does not necessarily mean *equally*, not even in communist societies. Its most widely accepted meaning implies the elimination of poverty. Poverty refers to a level of income that reduces opportunities for self-realization and life expectancy.

When management and labor disagree on what is a fair distribution of the wealth created by a corporation, at least one of these parties feels that it is being exploited by the other. It is this feeling that leads one or both parties to seek a larger portion of the pie. The consequence is inflation. Inflation, of course, has many other sources, but this is a major one. For this reason the rate of inflation is an indicator of social dissatisfaction with the distribution of wealth. This is as true between nations as it is within them, which is apparent from the behavior of the OPEC countries in the past.

To return to the question of the appropriate objective of a corporation conceptualized as an organization: it is *not* to serve any one of its stakeholder groups to the exclusion of any of the others. *It is to serve all of them by increasing their ability to pursue their objectives more efficiently and effectively.* . . .

3.

STRATEGIC MANAGEMENT IN A KIBITZER'S WORLD

William R. Dill

For a company that wants to be known for strategic prowess and entrepreneurial style, there are three main challenges. First, and best explored, is the need to get management thinking in strategic, entrepreneurial ways. . . . Once management has adopted a strategic perspective and built its plans, the second challenge is to assure organizational response. . . .

The next required advance in the state of the art, the third challenge, is not yet well understood. It is the challenge of coping with an active, intrusive environment that not only presents enterprises with challenges and opportunities, but that is made up of individuals and organizations kibitzing and seeking direct influence on enterprises' strategic decisions. Each enterprise has a broad aggregation of people outside—call them *stakeholders* . . . —who have ideas about what the economic and social performance of the enterprise should include. These external constituencies—sometimes other organizations, sometimes diffuse collections of individuals, rarely a single powerful voice—are increasingly moving from such short-term concerns as product price and quality to initiatives on questions like environmental protection, overseas investment policies, and employment practices which have long-range strategic implications. They can be quite specific in advice and demands about how companies set goals and how critical design and resource-allocation decisions are made.

For a long time, we have assumed that the views and initiatives of stake-

William R. Dill, "Strategic Management in a Kibitzer's World," in *From Strategic Planning to Strategic Management*, ed. H. Igor Ansoff, Roger P. Declerck, and Robert L. Hayes (London: John Wiley & Sons, 1976). Copyright © 1976 by John Wiley & Sons. Reprinted by permission.

holders could be dealt with as externalities to the strategic planning and management process: as data to help management shape decisions, or as legal and social constraints to limit them. We have been reluctant, though, to admit the idea that some of these outside stakeholders might seek and earn active roles with management to make decisions. The move today is from *stakeholder influence* toward *stakeholder participation*.

THE PRESSURE FOR STRATEGIC INTERVENTION

A growing demand by stakeholders for strategic intervention should not be regarded as surprising. It is a corollary to the developing interest in strategic management within firms. Inside, managers have recognized that slow, steady refinement of existing policy and practice is not enough to keep pace with rapid changes in markets, technology, politics, and social values. Such changes have forced probing questions about goals and difficult choices about what to emphasize as the distinctive focus or mission of the enterprise. Such questions and choices have been forced even more by the realization that no enterprise, whatever its size or rate of growth, commands unlimited resources. Strategic management, in short, has taken hold because it has seemed crucial to managers in a changing world for corporate survival.

Now consider the view from outside. There, too, people have found it inadequate to rely on a slow, steady refinement of existing patterns of influence, market response, and regulation to protect themselves or improve society against the impact of corporate initiatives. They have questions about societal goals and corporate missions that they do not trust corporate managers to answer alone, and they see for themselves and society significant side effects of what previously might have been allowed to pass as autonomous corporate decisions.

There is a new consciousness among stakeholders of the fragility of world social systems, of global resource limits, and of unanticipated outcomes of both private and public action. From this awareness come ideas and convictions about directions and limits for corporate action. Strategic intervention appeals increasingly to stakeholders because as people heretofore excluded from the management of economic enterprises they find participation in corporate decisions important for societal survival.

Much as corporations today may be dismayed by the trend, they have helped encourage it. Firms have worked hard in recent years through public relations and marketing efforts to picture themselves as sensitive, open, and responsive organizations. They have invited newsmen, researchers, and case writers in to look around when what they were doing seemed sure to win societal approval. They have, within employee ranks, encouraged men and women at many levels to participate in internal planning efforts.

Organizations which describe themselves as "open" invite stakeholders to take them at their word. Organizations which like to "rap" about what they are doing when things are going well can hardly close the door when their decisions get controversial. Organizations which train their personnel to be active and confident participants in decisions within have unwittingly helped prepare the same people to be active and confident kibitzers from outside for other organizations.

Thus, the requests from outside stakeholders for roles in making strategic decisions are not a passing fad. The requests are likely to grow in strength and variety, and planners and managers will have to adjust to a kibitzer's[1] world.

The kinds of intervention by stakeholders that firms can anticipate, it must be emphasized, are not necessarily predecessors to higher degrees of formal social regulation and control. In fact, one of the hopeful possibilities is that active and decentralized kibitzing on strategic issues, like active and decentralized responses in the markets to current products and prices, will lessen our reliance on restraining rules and laws. Regulation, even when wisely devised and sensitively administered, tends to be tied more to yesterday's problems than to tomorrow's needs. We need a behavioral theory for balancing the kibitzing process to serve societal goals that matches the economists' theory which justifies preservation of competitive markets, in a way which achieves long-run social performance and, at the same time preserves a kind of flexible decentralized control, provides for narrower dimensions of economic performance.

MAPPING THE WORLD OF STAKEHOLDERS

The domain of stakeholders for a corporation is difficult to map. It includes individuals, groups, and organizations. It is usually described by labels such as "customer," which imply a specific relationship to the firm. It keeps changing in composition and membership, and to the extent that events make corporations and society more interdependent, keeps growing in size and complexity.

Questions of inclusion and questions of role are difficult to answer in purely objective terms because for some stakeholders, like parties concerned with the ecological impact of corporate actions, the "stake" perceived by the external claimants may not be acknowledged by the enterprise. In reverse, "stakes" recognized by the enterprise, such as a customer's role, may not be acknowledged by supposed customers. Instead of a single, simple mapping, any effort to define the external constituencies of an enterprise is likely to produce multiple mappings from different perspectives. . . .

While we usually build maps in terms of role labels like *customer*, or *competitor*, we ought to be looking first at dimensions of the whole citizen. Few people or organizations can be confined to just one of these "relational" roles, and it is hard for a firm to decide which of the relational roles is most important. This is not the age of the stockholder, for example, but an era when shareowners, individual or institutional, are little more than another kind of customer, buying and selling on the basis of expectations of capital gains and dividends. Neither, as some have proposed, is it the age of the consumer, a concept too specifically tied to the products and services an enterprise currently offers. It is more truly an age of the concerned citizen, of consumers and investors together in many cases looking out for themselves and their immediate selfish needs in part, but also trying in other ways to speak for broader community interests and for the well-being of future generations.

Looking at stakeholders in holistic fashion, one looks at dimensions such as sex, age, ethnic background, and community ties sociologists have long demonstrated are important. These dimensions do not tie immediately to relations with the enterprise. They do establish, though, the basic sense of identity; a lifestyle; values, goals, and aspirations; and patterns of affiliation and association that will determine specific roles and actions *vis-à-vis* business firms and other organizations.

The relational roles which develop from the more holistic dimensions of people and from contacts and experience with firms include more categories than we normally consider. Some of these categories, like supplier and employee, may be almost too comfortable and familiar, and may in fact be ambiguous categories for serious research on problems of stakeholder relations and intervention. Others, though, like involuntary consumers of by-products, express relationships of which we are newly conscious in an age when pollution has become one of the main topics for strategic challenges from outside the firm.

Stakeholders often relate to organizations in multiple ways: the owner-conserver, such as stockholders who start proxy battles to force greater investment in pollution control; the customer-regulator, such as the federal government which has tried to shape competition in the computer industry both by purchasing decisions and by antitrust suits; and so forth. Of stakeholders holding multiple relational roles, some are fairly stable in terms of predicting which will dominate; others are less stable and much harder to predict.

It makes a difference whether individuals or organizations control their involvement in certain roles. Being an analyst or critic is clearly at the stakeholder's option. Being a customer, investor, or employee usually is, but sometimes has involuntary aspects. Being a consumer of pollution by-products, however, or being a supplier in many situations often has a large involuntary component. Dissatisfaction with voluntary roles can lead to disengagement and withdrawal; the alternative in the case of involuntary roles has to include reaction and confrontation.

Relational roles have different time orientations, too. One problem inherent in most of the roles is that the occupants, like operating management within the firm, are constrained to think in terms of present relationships rather than future possibilities and needs. Thus, those within the enterprise concerned with strategic questions may have especially high interest in conservers, analysts, competitors, and others who share a forward-looking orientation. Strategic thinkers inside must also keep an eye on potential stakeholders—new customers, new critics, and so forth—as well as on those currently involved with the firm.

Out of their characteristics as persons and groups, out of the single and hybrid roles that they play, come the stances that stakeholders take *vis-à-vis* strategic decision making in the firm. Since strategic awareness is probably lower in the populace at large than within many of the firms, many stakeholders simply continue as nonparticipants. Others may be content to express views on surveys and proxies, or through various ways to provide direct substantive inputs of ideas and opinions to the planning and decision-making process. There are some interveners whose challenge is not to specific plans or decisions, but to the autonomy and direction of the business system itself. These challengers, probably less numerous and less influential than many businessmen currently believe, might be labeled "antipreneurs" as one businessman has done.[2] Still others may be able by assertion or by position in government and other regulatory groups to achieve power as referees, evaluating and ratifying or restricting strategic decisions. . . .

CHALLENGES TO OUR STRATEGIC
MANAGEMENT PARADIGMS

... What has to be done to build a greater awareness within management and stakeholders of the true dimensions of strategic issues in which they and the firm share interests? What is necessary to establish a higher level of knowledge and expertise about the problems that both enterprises and society face in making strategic decisions? How can one establish the levels of trust and credibility between firm and stakeholders that firms now understand they have to build between management and employees? How, against the realities of opportunistic action by many of the intermediaries with which the firms must deal, can channels of communication and influence be established with stakeholders to minimize the distortions and dangers that unchecked opportunism threatens?

Answering these questions poses challenges to traditional ways of managing. One element in designing better paradigms is to find ways to broaden and diversify the daily person-to-person interactions that strategic managers have. Much of the disenchantment with business that threatens controversial strategic intervention comes not from people who are remote from involvement with business, but from employees, associates, neighbors, and even members of their families who see options and consequences of decisions in different ways than the manager does. Other questioning coming from remote sources can be understood only if our basic premise about stakeholders—getting to know them first as whole persons rather than in terms of their visible relational roles to the enterprise—is right. The tradeoff in broadening these contacts is greater understanding in return for the diversion of scarce managerial time; the risk is that the approach to learn and to seek understanding will be interpreted as an invitation to kibitz, so that the pressures for outside participation will increase. Nevertheless, the record of the retail industry versus the securities industry in keeping pace with changes in consumer views suggests that the investment is worth making.

A second element is the need to make stakeholders understand better how and why strategic decisions are being made, so that if they are satisfied that their interests are being considered they will not make or back spurious demands for interventions, and so that if they are motivated to intervene they will intervene in relevant and responsible ways. Greater stakeholder understanding, though, means "opening the kimono" more: more willingness to have what the enterprise is doing and what it is planning to do reviewed and reported by journalists, students, historians, collectors of teaching cases for business schools, and researchers. The gains in understanding and agreement by many stakeholders, especially to the degree that their views are now distorted by "antipreneurs" as many businessmen fear, can be very great. Openness in any area of life is one of the key ingredients toward establishing stable attitudes of confidence and trust. Anticipatory reporting can also provide better protection against inevitable false or misleading charges that may be made than after-the-fact attempts at rebuttal. . . .

A third element in improving the preparatory climate for dealing with strategic intervention from outside the firm is the issue of repersonalizing the image that corporations present to the outside world. Again, as a matter of tradition and, to a degree, as a matter of law, corporations tend to choose low profiles on public issues. Even on disputes involving the conduct of a firm within an industry where stakeholders and opportunists may be mounting a major campaign for intervention, companies which have not been part of causing the problem will stay out of the debate and will not publicly take sides against the firm or firms which need to be forced into corrective action. Neutrality easily becomes interpreted as indifference or opposition; silence as insensitivity or incompetence. . . .

A final problem which is real, but as yet badly defined, concerns the processes by which a firm uses media to keep direct relations with stakeholders and how, among both media and kibitzers, it defends itself against opportunists who will take advantage of the firm and stakeholders as well. The reality is that most media have to be opportunistic, as firms themselves are, to stay in business; for most are businesses, and with traditions of a free press which are important to maintain for other reasons, most are freer of public control than the enterprises they report about. . . .

CONCLUSION

This chapter represents a preliminary statement of problems, rather than a finished report of answers. It grew from a concern that we have only halfway developed the definition of what strategic management is all about. Strategic management has gained currency as a way to give enterprises greater leverage for progress or survival in a competitive, changing, and unstable world. But managers in enterprises today must also respond to the concerns of all those outside the enterprise who have present or future stakes in the decisions it makes. Executives who understand what these stakeholders want can no more decide without consulting them and inviting their participation than they can plan on purely internal matters without consulting and inviting participation from many of their employees. Strategic management, then, must wrestle with the desire of outside stakeholders for consideration and participation. It must be prepared, as well, to deal with more active outside challenges: initiatives by stakeholders on particularly important issues for strategic intervention. Responding to this broader view of strategic management means new efforts to map the domain of stakeholders in the enterprise and of the intermediary groups that provide linking channels of communication and influence. It means expanding the paradigms we have for strategic management and probably some fundamental changes, particularly toward openness about what heretofore have been private and internal operations, in the way that companies behave. Planners must get used to living in a kibitzer's world.

NOTES

1. From Yiddish, a word well used by American card-game players to describe people who look on and offer unwanted advice or comments.

2. C. Howard Hardesty Jr., in a speech to the American Mining Congress, where he was concerned with "single minded, persistent, and totally myopic critics" of business.

4.

STOCKHOLDERS AND STAKEHOLDERS

A New Perspective on Corporate Governance

R. Edward Freeman and David L. Reed

M anagement thought has changed dramatically in the past years. There have been, and are now under way, both conceptual and practical revolutions in the ways that management theorists and managers think about organizational life.[1] The purpose of this article is to understand the implications of one of these shifts in worldview; namely, the shift from "stockholder" to "stakeholder."

THE STAKEHOLDER CONCEPT

It has long been gospel that corporations have obligations to stockholders, holders of the firm's equity, that are sacrosanct and inviolable. Corporate action or inaction is to be driven by attention to the needs of its stockholders, usually thought to be measured by stock price, earnings per share, or some other financial measure. It has been argued that the proper relationship of management to its stockholders is similar to that of the fiduciary to the *cestui que trustent*, whereby the interests of the stockholders should be dutifully cared for by management.[2] Thus, any action taken by management must ultimately be justified by whether or not it furthers the interests of the corporation and its stockholders.

There is also a long tradition of departure from the view that stock-

R. Edward Freeman and David L. Reed, "Stockholders and Stakeholders: A New Perspective on Corporate Governance," *California Management Review* 25, no. 3 (Spring 1983): 88–105. Copyright © 1983 the Regents of University of California. Reprinted by permission of the Regents.

holders have a privileged place in the business enterprise. Berle and Means were worried about the "degree of prominence entitling (the corporation) to be dealt with as a major social institution."[3] Chester Barnard argued that the purpose of the corporation was to serve society, and that the function of the executive was to instill this sense of moral purpose in the corporation's employees.[4] Public relations and corporate social action have a history too long to be cataloged here.[5] However, a recent development calls for a more far-reaching change in the way that we look at corporate life, and that is the good currency of the idea of "stakeholders."

The stakeholder notion is indeed a deceptively simple one. It says that there are other groups to whom the corporation is responsible in addition to stockholders: those groups who have a *stake* in the actions of the corporation.[6] The word *stakeholder*, coined in an internal memorandum at the Stanford Research Institute in 1963,[7] refers to "those groups without whose support the organization would cease to exist." The list of stakeholders originally included shareowners, employees, customers, suppliers, lenders, and society. Stemming from the work of Igor Ansoff and Robert Stewart (in the planning department at Lockheed) and, later, Marion Doscher and Stewart (at SRI), stakeholder analysis served and continues to serve an important function in the SRI corporate planning process.

From the original work at SRI, the historical trail diverges in a number of directions. One recent author was forced to claim, "The precise origins of stakeholder theory are impossible to determine."[8] In his now classic *Corporate Strategy: An Analytic Approach to Business Policy for Growth and Expansion*, Igor Ansoff makes limited use of the theory.

> While as we shall see later, "responsibilities" and "objectives" are not synonymous, they have been made one in a "stakeholder theory" of objectives. This theory maintains that the objectives of the firm should be derived by balancing the conflicting claims of the various "stakeholders" in the firm: managers, workers, stockholders, suppliers, vendors.[9]

Ansoff credits Abrams and Cyert and March with a similar view,[10] but goes on to reject the stakeholder theory in favor of a view which separates objectives into "economic" and "social" with the latter being a "secondary modifying and constraining influence" on the former.

For the most part the development of the stakeholder concept was slow during the late 1960s and early 1970s, except for the continued work at SRI by a number of researchers and consultants. A notable exception is the work of Eric Rhenman in Sweden, who applied the concept to industrial democracy.[11]

In the mid-1970s, researchers in systems theory, led by Russell Ackoff, "rediscovered" stakeholder analysis, or at least took Ansoff's admonition more seriously.[12] Propounding essentially an open systems view of organizations, Ackoff argues that many social problems can be solved by the redesign of fundamental institutions with the support and interaction of stakeholders in the system.

A second trail from Ansoff's original reference is the work of William Dill, who in concert with Ackoff sought to move the stakeholder concept from the periphery of corporate planning to a central place. . . .

A related development is primarily responsible for giving the stakeholder concept a boost; namely, the increase in concern with the social involvement of business. The corporate social responsibility movement is too diverse and has spawned too many ideas, concepts, and techniques to explain here.[13] Suffice it to say that the social movements of the 1960s and 1970s—civil rights, the antiwar movement, consumerism, environmentalism, and women's rights—served as a catalyst for rethinking the role of the business enterprise in society. From Milton Friedman to John Kenneth Galbraith, there are a diversity of arguments. However, one aspect of the corporate social responsibility debate is particularly relevant to understanding the good currency of the stakeholder concept.

In the early 1970s the Harvard Business School undertook a project on corporate social responsibility. The output of the project was voluminous, and of particular importance was the development of a pragmatic model of social responsibility called "the corporate social responsiveness model."[14] . . .

By the late 1970s the need for strategic management processes to take account of nontraditional business problems in terms of government, special interest groups, trade associations, foreign competitors, dissident shareholders, and complex issues such as employee rights, equal opportunity, environmental pollution, consumer rights, tariffs, government regulation, and reindustrialization had become obvious. To begin to develop these processes, the Wharton School began, in 1977 in its Applied Research Center, a "stakeholder project." The objectives of the project were to put together a number of strands of thought and to develop a theory of management which enabled executives to formulate and implement corporate strategy in turbulent environments. Thus, an action research model was used whereby stakeholder theory was generated by actual cases.

The project has explored the implications of the stakeholder concept on three levels: as a management theory; as a process for practitioners to use in strategic management; and as an analytical framework.

At the theoretical level the implications of substituting *stakeholder* for *stockholder* needs to be explicated. The first problem at this level is the actual definition of *stakeholder*. SRI's original definition is too general and too exclusive to serve as a means of identifying those external groups that are strategically important. The concentration on generic stakeholders, such as society and customers, rather than specific social interest groups and specific customer segments produces an analysis which can only be used as a background for the planning process. Strategically useful information about the actions, objectives, and motivations of specific groups, which is needed if management is to be responsive to stakeholder concerns, requires a more specific and inclusive definition.

We propose two definitions of *stakeholder*: a wide sense, which includes groups that are friendly or hostile, and a narrow sense, which captures the essence of the SRI definition, but is more specific.[15]

- *The Wide Sense of Stakeholder*: Any identifiable group or individual who can affect the achievement of an organization's objectives or who is affected by the achievement of an organization's objectives. (Public interest groups, protest groups, government agencies, trade associations, competitors, unions, as well as employees, customer segments, shareowners, and others are stakeholders, in this sense.)
- *The Narrow Sense of Stakeholder*: Any identifiable group or individual on which the organization is dependent for its continued survival. (Employees, customer segments, certain suppliers, key government agencies, shareowners, certain financial institutions, as well as others are all stakeholders in the narrow sense of the term.)

While executives are willing to recognize that employees, suppliers, and customers have a stake in the corporation, many resist the inclusion of adversary groups. But from the standpoint of corporate strategy, *stakeholder* must be understood in the wide sense: strategies need to account for those groups who can affect the achievement of the firm's objectives. Some may feel happier with other words, such as *influencers*, *claimants*, *publics*, or *constituencies*. Semantics aside, if corporations are to formulate and implement strategies in turbulent environments, theories of strategy must have concepts, such as the wide sense of *stakeholder*, which allow the analysis of all external forces and pressures whether they are friendly or hostile.[16] In what follows we will use *stakeholder* in the wide sense. . . .

A second issue at the theoretical level is the generation of prescriptive propositions which explain actual cases and articulate regulative principles for future use. Thus, a *post hoc* analysis of the brewing industry and the problem of beverage container legislation, combined with a similar analysis of the regulatory environments of public utilities have led to some simple propositions which serve as a philosophical guideline for strategy formulation.[17] For example:

- Generalize the marketing approach
- Establish negotiation processes . . .
- Establish a decision philosophy that is oriented toward seizing the initiative . . .
- Allocate organizational resources based on the degree of importance of . . . the stakeholders' claims.

Other prescriptive propositions can be put forth, especially with respect to issues of corporate governance. One proposition that has been discussed is to "involve stakeholder groups in strategic decisions," or "invite stakeholders to participate in governance decisions." While propositions like this may have substantial merit, we have not examined enough cases nor marshaled enough evidence to support them in an unqualified manner. There are cases where participation is appropriate. Some public utilities have been quite successful in the use of stakeholder advisory groups in matters of rate setting.[18] However, given the breadth of our concept of stakeholder we believe that cooptation through participation is not always the correct strategic decision.

The second level of analysis is the use of stakeholder concepts in strategy formulation processes. Two processes have been used so far: the Stakeholder Strategy Process and the Stakeholder Audit Process. The Stakeholder Strategy Process is a systematic method for analyzing the relative importance of stakeholders and their cooperative potential (how they can help the corporation achieve its objectives) and their competitive threat (how they can prevent the corporation from achieving its objectives). The process is one which relies on a behavioral analysis (both actual and potential) for input, and an explanatory model of stakeholder objectives and resultant strategic shifts for output. The Stakeholder Audit Process is a systematic method for identifying stakeholders and assessing the effectiveness of current organizational strategies.[19] By itself, each process has a use in the strategic management of an organization. Each analyzes the stakeholder environment from the standpoint of organizational mission and objectives and seeks to formulate strategies for meeting stakeholder needs and concerns.

The use of the stakeholder concept at the analytical level means thinking in terms which are broader than current strategic and operational problems. It implies looking at public policy questions in stakeholder terms and trying to understand how the relationships between an organization and its stakeholders would change given the implementation of certain policies.

One analytical device depicts an organization's stakeholders on a two-dimensional grid map. The first dimension is one of "interest" or "stake" and ranges from an equity interest to an economic interest or marketplace stake to an interest or stake as a "kibitzer" or influencer.[20] Shareowners have an equity stake; customers and suppliers have an economic stake; and single-issue groups have an influencer stake. The second dimension of a stakeholder is its power, which ranges from the formalistic or voting power of stockholders to the economic power of customers to the political power of special interest groups. By *economic power* we mean "the ability to influence due to marketplace decisions" and by *political power* we mean "the ability to influence due to use of the political process."[21]

. . . Finally, there is a need to develop new and innovative management processes to deal with the current and future complexities of management issues. At the theoretical level, stakeholder analysis has been developed to enrich the economic approach to corporate strategy by arguing that kibitzers with political power must be included in the strategy process. At the strategic level, stakeholder analysis takes a number of groups into account and analyzes their strategic impact on the corporation.

NOTES

1. One problem which plagues management theorists is the tendency for the field to become compartmentalized and fragmented. Thus, we have no confidence that any two people who read this article will agree that there is a discipline of management or what that discipline contains. Thomas Kuhn's *The Structure of Scientific Revolutions*, 2nd ed. (Chicago: University of Chicago Press, 1970) and the resulting literature in philosophy of science—see I. Lakatos and A. Musgrave, eds., *Criticism and the Growth of Knowledge* (Cambridge: Cambridge University Press, 1970) and G. Gutting, ed., *Paradigms and Revolutions* (Notre Dame, IN: University of Notre Dame Press, 1980)—are of some help . . .

2. A. Berle and G. Means, *The Modern Corporation and Private Property* (New York: Commerce Clearing House, 1932), pp. 220–21. For a discussion of the implications for corporate governance, see W. Evan, *Organization Theory* (New York: John Wiley and Sons, 1976), pp. 89–107.

3. Berle and Means, *The Modern Corporation and Private Property*, p. 3.

4. C. Barnard, *The Function of the Executive* (Cambridge, MA: Harvard University Press, 1938).

5. For an excellent history, see F. Sturdivant, *Business and Society* (Itomewood, IL: R. D. Irwin, 1977), pp. 1–125.

6. See R. Clark, "Does the Nonprofit Form Fit the Hospital Industry?" *Harvard Law Review* 93, no. 7 (May 1980): 1417–89; and H. Hansmann, "The Role of Nonprofit Enterprise," *Yale Law Journal* 89, no. 5 (April 1980): 835–901.

7. *Stakeholder* appears in Webster's as "one who holds the stakes in a gamble." It does not appear in the Oxford English Dictionary.

8. F. Sturdivant, "Executives and Activists: A Test of Stakeholder Management," *California Management Review* 22, no. 1 (Fall 1979): 53–59. For a complete history of the concept, see R. E. Freeman, *Strategic Management: A Stakeholder Approach* (Marshfield, MA: Pitman, 1983), see especially chap. 2.

9. Igor Ansoff, *Corporate Strategy* (New York: McGraw-Hill, 1965), pp. 33–35.

10. F. Abrams, "Management Responsibilities in a Complex World," in *Business Education for Competence and Responsibility*, ed. T. H. Carroll (Chapel Hill, NC: University of North Carolina Press, 1954); R. M. Cyert and J. G. March, *A Behavioral Theory of the Firm* (Englewood Cliffs, NJ: Prentice Hall, 1963).

11. E. Rhenman, *Industrial Democracy and Industrial Management* (London: Tavistock Publications Limited, 1968).

12. R. L. Ackoff, *Redesigning the Future* (New York: John Wiley and Sons, 1974).

13. See F. Sturdivant, *Business and Society: A Managerial Approach* (Homewood, IL: R. D. Irwin, 1977); and T. A. Klein, *Social Costs and Benefits of Business* (Englewood Cliffs, NJ: Prentice Hall, 1977).

14. See R. W. Ackerman, "How Companies Respond to Social Demands," *Harvard Business Review* 51, no. 4 (1973); R. W. Ackerman, *The Social Challenge to Business* (Cambridge, MA: Harvard University Press, 1975); and R. W. Ackerman and R. A. Bauer, *Corporate Social Responsiveness: The Modern Dilemma* (Reston, VA: Reston, 1976), as well as other books and articles.

15. While we offer two definitions in order to ease the linguistic change, we are ultimately wedded to the wide inclusive sense of stakeholder. The authors wish to thank Dr. Marvin Olassky of DuPont for the suggestion of different levels of definitions.

16. The importance of external forces for business strategy is explored in R. Charan and R. E. Freeman, "Planning for the Business Environment of the 1980s," *Journal of Business Strategy* 1, no. 2 (Fall 1980): 9–19.

17. The initial results of the Wharton Stakeholder Project have been published as "Who's Butting into Your Business," *Wharton Magazine* (Fall 1979), and "Stakeholder Management: A Case Study of the U.S. Brewers Association and the Con-

tainer Issue," in *Applications of Management Science,* ed. R. Schultz (Greenwich: JAI Press, 1981).

18. J. A. Baude et al., *Perspectives on Local Measured Service* (Kansas City: Telecommunications Industry Workshop Organizing Committee, 1979).

19. For another stakeholder technique, see H. L. Lee and R. L. Banker, "Stakeholder Decision Analysis," working paper 20880 (Wharton Applied Research Center); and R. E. Freeman, R. L. Banker, and H. L. Lee, "A Stakeholder Approach to Health Care Planning," in *Systems Science in Health Care*, ed. C. Tilquin (Toronto: Pergamon Press, 1981).

20. William Dill first used "kibitzer" to refer to external groups that try to use the political process to influence the affairs of the corporation. Its use is not meant pejoratively.

21. Some have argued that markets and politics are inherently connected. We agree. Our distinctions are useful, however, in order to understand how and why they are connected. The analyses of C. E. Lindbloom, *Politics and Markets* (New York: Basic Books, 1977), and A. O. Hirschman, *Exit, Voice and Loyalty* (Cambridge, MA: Harvard University Press, 1970), do not pay adequate attention to the positions of shareholders and directors and hence, to questions of corporate governance.

SUGGESTIONS FOR FURTHER READING

Ackerman, R. *The Social Challenge to Business*. Cambridge, MA: Harvard University Press, 1975.

Ackerman, R., and R. Bauer. *Corporate Social Responsiveness: The Modern Dilemma*. Reston: Reston Publishing Company, 1976.

Ansoff, I. *Corporate Strategy*. New York: McGraw-Hill, 1965.

Berle, A., and G. Means. *The Modern Corporation and Private Property*. New York: Commerce Clearing House, 1932.

Brenner, S., and E. Molander. "Is the Ethics of Business Changing?" *Harvard Business Review* 58 no. 1 (1977): 54–65.

Charan, R., and R. E. Freeman. "Planning for the Business Environment of the 1980s." *Journal of Business Strategy* 1, no. 2 (1980): 9–19.

Clark, M. "The Changing Basis of Economic Responsibility." *Journal of Political Economy* 24, no. 3 (1916): 209–29.

Coase, R. "The Nature of the Firm." *Economica* 4, no. 16 (1937): 386–405.

———. "The Problem of Social Cost." *Journal of Law and Economics* 3, no. 1 (1960): 1–44.

Cyert, R., and J. March. *A Behavioral Theory of the Firm*. Englewood Cliffs, NJ: Prentice Hall, 1963.

Dodd, E. "For Whom Are Corporate Managers Trustees?" *Harvard Law Review* 45, no. 1 (1932): 1145–63.

Freeman, R. E. *Strategic Management: A Stakeholder Approach*. Boston: Pitman Publishing, 1984.

Friedman, M. "The Social Responsibility of Business Is to Create Profits." *New York Times Magazine*, September 13, 1970, pp. 32–33, 122, 126.

Hargreaves, J., and J. Dauman. *Business Survival and Social Change*. New York: John Wiley and Sons, 1975.

Jensen, M., and W. Mechling. "Theory of the Firm: Managerial Behavior, Agency

Costs, and Capital Structure." *Journal of Financial Economics* 3, no. 10 (1976): 305–60.

Rhenman, E. *Industrial Democracy and Industrial Action*. London: Tavistock Publishing, 1968.

Taylor, B. "The Future Development of Corporate Strategy." *Journal of Business Policy* 2, no. 2 (1971): 22–38.

———. "Managing the Process of Corporate Development." In B. Taylor and J. Sparkes, eds., *Corporate Strategy and Planning*. New York: John Wiley and Sons, 1977.

Thompson, J. *Organizations in Action*. New York: McGraw-Hill, 1967.

Part 2.
NORMATIVE FOUNDATIONS

T raditional theories of the firm assert that the proper focus of managerial attention and corporate decision making is to maximize profit for shareholders. As the previous section indicated, this view has been readily challenged on the very practical ground that, due in large part to a changing business environment, prudent and effective management requires a redrawing of the corporate landscape to include all groups that have a "stake" in organizational activities and their outputs. For this reason, stakeholder claims receive a degree of "managerial" or "instrumental" legitimacy, at least in the sense that it is recognized that stakeholders decidedly impact the ultimate success of corporate endeavors and the realization of corporate aims and goals. Moving beyond strategic arguments for stakeholder legitimacy, the past few decades have witnessed considerable attention paid to elucidating the normative foundations of stakeholder theory and, as such, to laying out the various normative obligations prompting and stemming from adopting a stakeholder point of view. As evidenced in the business ethics literature itself, this attention has engendered a rich and complex debate over the normative grounds of stakeholder theory, the implications of which are profound for managerial decision making, leadership, and organizational management. Within the debate itself, we find a wide variety of scholarly work that draws upon the rich history of normative ethics from Aristotle, through Kant and Mill, and to contemporary and even "postmodern" accounts.

In "The Stakeholder Theory of the Corporation: Concepts, Evidence, and Implications," Thomas Donaldson and Lee E. Preston sort through the body of stakeholder literature and contend that arguments advanced in favor of the stakeholder concept generally fall into three essential categories: descriptive, instrumental, and normative. That is, stakeholder theory simultaneously serves to describe what the corporation is, relates how stakeholder management influences organizational performance, and articulates the moral basis for attending to stakeholder interests. In their final analysis, Donaldson and Preston, while recognizing the mutually supportive role of each of the three realms, argue that the ultimate justification for stakeholder theory must be based on normative reasons. More specifically, they contend that in examining the requisite conditions through which a stakeholder is said to have a "stake" in corporate activities, we readily find that the stakeholder model is normatively justified vis-à-vis an appeal to a contemporary and pluralistic theory of property rights.

R. Edward Freeman has been one of the foremost champions of a stakeholder approach to management, diligently trying to elucidate the strategic implications and normative dimensions of stakeholder engagement. Moving beyond earlier attempts to draw out the Kantian foundations of stakeholder management theory, this second reading represents Freeman's current and more-developed normative considerations. In "Managing for Stakeholders," Freeman sets forth the following arguments. First, Freeman maintains that the dominant, shareholder-centric theory of the firm represents a morally suspect and no longer workable model for strategic and organizational management. Second, the stakeholder model, which ultimately dictates that executive management ought to create as much value as possible for stakeholders, without resorting to "trade-offs," solves the various problems endemic to the dominant model. Lastly, and speaking directly to the theme of this chapter, Freeman demonstrates how various consequentialist, deontological, and virtue-based arguments, which speak in favor of stakeholder management, more meaningfully and effectively coalesce in a form of ethical pragmatism. In the end, the overt normative charge to management and stakeholders alike amounts to collectively working to create better selves and communities by engendering and institutionalizing collaborative stakeholder relationships.

Robert A. Phillips in his "Stakeholder Theory and a Principle of Fairness" seeks to develop a justificatory framework for stakeholder theory along contractarian lines. Relying heavily on Rawlsian political theory, Phillips explains that the same state of affairs that gives rise to "fairness"-based obligations in cooperative associations is likewise present in stakeholder models of the firm. That is, stakeholder relationships, understood as forms of economic exchange, reflect the following: they are designed to be mutually beneficial and relatively just, and they should require mutual sacrifices from participants and involve the voluntary acceptance of cooperative benefits. As a result, the tacit or explicit acceptance of such conditions creates obligations of "fair play" on the part of participants, most notably, to cooperate in proportion to the benefits accepted. While Phillips recognizes that this formulation says more about the source of normative obligations and less about their specific content, it does suggest that, as opposed to merely predicating stakeholder relationships along adversarial and competitive lines, business practices ought to be structured to reflect a cooperative model of stakeholder interaction and managerial decision making. Phillips goes on to suggest an ethics-based discourse procedure, as reflected in the work of Jürgen Habermas, for determining the acceptability of operative norms.

In the last selection, Brian K. Burton and Craig P. Dunn advance a version of stakeholder management theory that is grounded in a theory of feminist ethics. In their "Feminist Ethics as a Moral Grounding for Stakeholder Theory," the authors argue that traditional approaches to ethics, which are in large part based upon "abstract," "masculine," and "individualistic" moral principles, fail to capture the vital and emotive characteristics of moral behavior and, as a result, reduce them to legalistic, indifferent, and ultimately deficient decision-making models. Summarizing the work of Carol Gilligan, Nel Noddings, and Andrew Wicks, Burton and Dunn chart the development of ethics of care within moral and stakeholder theory and apply theoretical conclusions to situations in which stakeholder interests conflict, notably, the case of Taiwainese workers in the "Global Dumping Ground." For the authors, this case demonstrates the moral inadequacy of previously articulated principles of care, in that the application of these principles would lead to the morally unacceptable position where caring for a closely related group actually causes harm to a group with fewer advantages. In light of the need to complement a principle of care with an acceptable theory of justice, the authors propose a hybrid principle for decision making: care enough for the least advantaged stakeholders so that they not be harmed, and insofar as they are not harmed, privilege those stakeholders with whom you have a close relationship. The principle is subsequently used to resolve difficulties in the "Global Dumping Ground" case and other, more common managerial dealings with shareholders, communities, and employees.

5.

THE STAKEHOLDER THEORY OF THE CORPORATION

Concepts, Evidence, and Implications

Thomas Donaldson and Lee E. Preston

T he idea that corporations have *stakeholders* has now become common-place in the management literature, both academic and professional. . . . Unfortunately, anyone looking into this large and evolving literature with a critical eye will observe that the concepts *stakeholder, stakeholder model, stakeholder management,* and *stakeholder theory* are explained and used by various authors in very different ways and supported (or critiqued) with diverse and often contradictory evidence and arguments. The purpose of this article is to point out some of the more important distinctions, problems, and implications associated with the stakeholder concept, as well as to clarify and justify its essential content and significance. . . .

THE PROBLEM OF JUSTIFICATION

The underlying epistemological issue in the stakeholder literature is the problem of justification: Why should the stakeholder theory be accepted or preferred over alternative conceptions? . . . The stakeholder theory is justi-fied in the literature, explicitly or implicitly, in ways that correspond directly to the three approaches to the theory set out in the previous section: descrip-tive, instrumental, and normative. . . . In our view, the three aspects of the stakeholder theory are nested within each other. The external shell of the theory is its descriptive aspect; the theory presents and explains relationships that are observed in the external world. The theory's descriptive accuracy is supported, at the second level, by its instrumental and predictive value; *if* certain practices are carried out, *then* certain results will be obtained. The central core of the theory is, however, normative. The descriptive accuracy of the theory presumes the truth of the core normative conception, insofar as it presumes that managers and other agents act *as if* all stakeholders' interests have intrinsic value. In turn, recognition of these ultimate moral values and obligations gives stakeholder management its fundamental normative base. . . .

DESCRIPTIVE JUSTIFICATIONS

There is ample descriptive evidence . . . that many managers believe themselves, or are believed by others, to be practicing stakeholder management. . . . Managers may not make explicit reference to "stakeholder theory," but the vast majority of them apparently adhere in practice to one of the central tenets of the stakeholder theory, namely, that their role is to satisfy a wider set of stakeholders, not simply the shareowners. . . . Another kind of descriptive justification for the stakeholder theory stems from the role it plays as the implicit basis for existing practices and institutions, including legal opinion and statutory law. . . .

But neither the legal developments nor the management survey results provide definitive epistemological justification for the stakeholder theory. Managers adopting the stakeholder approach may be relieved to learn that they are not alone, and indeed that they are conforming to the latest management or legal trends, but both the survey results and the legal developments are, at bottom, simply facts. They do not constitute the basis for the stakeholder (or any other) theory of management. Indeed, even if the stakeholder concept is implicit in current legal trends (a proposition that is not universally accepted), one cannot derive a stakeholder theory of management from a stakeholder theory of law any more than one can derive a "tort" theory of management from the tort theory of law.

. . . This suggests that the descriptive support for the stakeholder theory, as well as the critiques of this support to be found in the literature, are of limited significance and that the most important issues for stakeholder theory lie elsewhere.

INSTRUMENTAL JUSTIFICATIONS

Because the descriptive approach to grounding a stakeholder theory is inadequate, justifications based on a connection between stakeholder strategies and organizational performance should be examined. . . . Unfortunately, the large body of literature dealing with the connections, if any, between various aspects of corporate social performance or ethics, on one hand, and conventional financial and market performance indicators, on the other, does not translate easily into a stakeholder theory context. Whatever value the social/financial performance studies may have on their own merits, most of them do not include reliable indicators of the stakeholder management (i.e., the independent variable) side of the relationship. . . .

ANALYTICAL ARGUMENTS

Even without empirical verification, however, stakeholder management can be linked to conventional concepts of organizational success through analytical argument. The main focus of this effort in the recent literature builds on established concepts of principal-agent relations[1] and the firm as a nexus of contracts.[2] Agency theory and firm-as-contract theory, although arising from different sources, are closely related and share a common emphasis: efficiency. (They also share the terminology and methodology of the new transaction cost literature.)[3]

Hill and Jones are responsible for the most ambitious attempt to integrate the stakeholder concept with agency theory.[4] These authors enlarged the standard principal-agent paradigm of financial economics, which emphasizes the relationship between shareowners and managers, to create "stakeholder-agency theory," which constitutes, in their view, "a generalized theory of agency." According to this conception, managers "can be seen as the agents of [all] other stakeholders."[5] . . . This brief summary cannot do justice to their rich conception, but the key point for current purposes is that the stakeholders are drawn into relationships with the managers to accomplish organizational tasks as efficiently as possible; hence, the stakeholder model is linked instrumetally to organizational performance.

A similar theme emerges from the firm-as-contract analysis of Freeman and Evan.[6] They recommended integrating the stakeholder concept with the Coasian view of the firm-as-contract and a Williamson-style analysis of transaction costs to "conceptualize the firm as a set of multilateral contracts over time." According to Freeman and Evan,

Managers administer contracts among employees, owners, suppliers, customers, and the community. Since each of these groups can invest in asset specific transactions which affect the other groups, methods of conflict resolution, or safeguards must be found.[7] . . .

Once again, the stakeholder model (and its implementation through a set of acceptable implicit contracts) is seen as essential to successful organizational performance.

WEAKNESSES OF INSTRUMENTAL JUSTIFICATIONS

Perhaps the most important similarity between these two independent attempts to justify the stakeholder model lies in the fact that although they draw initially on the conceptual apparatus of instrumental or efficiency-based theories (i.e., principal-agent relations and "firm-as-contract" theory), they ultimately rely upon noninstrumental or normative arguments. This shift is less conspicuous in the case of Hill and Jones, who implied that monitoring and enforcement mechanisms will be sufficient to curb opportunistic behavior by managers at the expense of other stakeholders. The authors would no doubt agree, however, that the ultimate success of stakeholder-agency theory would require a fundamental shift in managerial objectives away from shareowners and toward the interests of all stakeholders; such a shift would necessarily involve normative, rather than purely instrumental, considerations. Freeman and Evan's recourse to a Rawlsian concept of "fairness" as the ultimate criterion for stakeholder bargains is an overt elevation of normative criteria over instrumental ones. No theorist, including Rawls, has ever maintained that bargains reached on the basis of a "veil of ignorance" would maximize efficiency. By elevating the fairness principle to a central role, Freeman and Evan shifted their attention from ordinary economic contracts of the sort envisaged by Coase, Williamson, and the mainstream agency theorists, which are governed by individual efficiency considerations. Instead, they emphasized what have been called "heuristic" or "social" contracts that rest upon broad normative principles governing human conduct.[8]

It should come as no surprise that stakeholder theory cannot be fully justified by instrumental considerations. The empirical evidence is inadequate, and the analytical arguments, although of considerable substance, ultimately rest on more than purely instrumental grounds. This conclusion carries an important implication: Although those who use the stakeholder concept often cite its consistency with the pursuit of conventional corporate performance objectives (and there is no notable evidence of its inconsistency), few of them would abandon the concept if it turned out to be only as *equally* efficacious as other conceptions.

NORMATIVE JUSTIFICATIONS

The normative basis for stakeholder theory involves its connection with more fundamental and better accepted philosophical concepts. The normative assumptions of traditional economic theory are too feeble to support stakeholder theory, and the concept of a free market populated with free and rational preference seekers, however correct and important, is compatible with both stakeholder and nonstakeholder perspectives. Of course, the two normative propositions stated at the beginning of this article—that stakeholders are identified by *their* interest in the affairs of the corporation and that the interests of all stakeholders have intrinsic value—can be viewed as axiomatic principles that require no further justification. Unfortunately, this approach provides no basis for responding to critics who reject these propositions out of hand. . . .

FORMAL ANALYSIS: THEORY OF PROPERTY

. . . There is a subtle irony in proposing that the stakeholder model can be justified on the basis of the theory of property, because the traditional view has been that a focus on property rights justifies the dominance of shareowners' interests. Indeed, the fact that property rights are the critical base for conventional shareowner-dominance views makes it all the more significant that the current trend of thinking with respect to the philosophy of property runs in the opposite direction. In fact, this trend—as presented in the now-classic contributions of Coase and Honore and in more recent works by Becker and Munzer—runs strongly counter to the conception that private property exclusively enshrines the interests of owners.

Considerable agreement now exists as to the theoretical definition of property as a "bundle" of many rights, some of which may be limited. Coase chided economists for adhering to a simplistic concept of ownership:

We may speak of a person owning land . . . but what the land-owner in fact possesses is the right to carry out a circumscribed list of actions. The rights of a land-owner are not unlimited. . . . [This] would be true under any system of law. A system in which the rights of individuals were unlimited would be one in which there were no rights to acquire.[9]

Honore specifically included the notion of restrictions against harmful uses within the definition of property itself. Pejovich, probably the most conservative economic theorist working in this area, emphasized that "property rights are relations between individuals" and thus "it is wrong to separate human rights from property rights"; he further noted that "the right of ownership is not an unrestricted right."[10]

The notion that property rights are embedded in human rights and that restrictions against harmful uses are intrinsic to the property rights concept clearly brings the interests of others (i.e., of nonowner stakeholders) into the picture. Of course, *which* uses of property should be restricted and *which* persons should count as stakeholders remain unspecified. Simply bringing nonowner stakeholders into the conception of property does not provide by itself justification for stakeholder arguments assigning managerial responsibilities toward specific groups, such as employees and customers. The important point, however, is that the contemporary theoretical concept of private property clearly does not ascribe unlimited rights to owners and hence does not support the popular claim that the responsibility of managers is to act solely as agents for the shareowners. (The necessary compromise between individual property rights and other considerations is highlighted in the "takings" issue— i.e., modified to protect the interests of others or society in general.)[11]

These comments examine the *scope* of property rights, but it is also relevant to examine their *source* (i.e., What basic principles determine *who* should get [and be allowed to keep] *what* in society?). Unless property rights are regarded as simple, self-evident moral conceptions, they must be based on more fundamental ideas of distributive justice. The main contending theories of distributive justice include Utilitarianism, Libertarianism, and social contract theory.[12] The battle among competing theories of distributive justice is most often a battle over which characteristics highlighted by the theories—such as need, ability, effort, and mutual agreement—are most relevant for determining fair distributions of wealth, income, and so on. (The role of theories of justice within organizations is attracting considerable current attention.)[13]

For example, when the characteristic of *need* (a feature highlighted by Utilitarianism) is the criterion, the resulting theory of property places formidable demands upon property owners to mitigate their self-interest in favor of enhancing the interests (i.e., meeting the needs) of others. When *ability* or *effort* (features highlighted by Libertarianism) is the criterion, the resulting theory leaves property owners freer to use their resources (acquired, it is assumed, as a result of ability and effort) as they see fit. Social contract theory places primary emphasis on expressed or implied understandings among individuals and groups as to appropriate distributions and uses of property.

Many of the most respected contemporary analysts of property rights reject the notion that any *single* theory of distributive justice is universally applicable. Indeed, it seems counterintuitive that any one principle could account for all aspects of the complex bundle of rights and responsibilities that constitutes "property." Beginning with Becker's 1978 analysis, the trend is toward theories that are pluralistic, allowing more than one fundamental principle to play a role.[14] But if a pluralistic theory of property rights is accepted, then the connection between the theory of property and the stakeholder theory becomes explicit. All critical characteristics underlying the classic theories of distributive justice are present among the stakeholders of a corporation, as they are conventionally conceived and presented in contemporary stakeholder theory. For example, the "stake" of long-term employees who have worked to build and maintain a successful business operation is essentially based on effort. The stake of people living in the surrounding community may be based on their need, say, for clean air or the maintenance of their civic infrastructure. Customer stakes are based on the satisfactions and protections implicitly promised in the market offer, and so on. One need not make the more radical assertion that such stakes constitute formal or legal property rights, although some forceful critics of current corporate governance arrangements appear to hold this view.[15] All that is necessary is to show that such characteristics, which are the same as those giving rise to fundamental concepts of property rights, give various groups a moral interest, commonly referred to as a "stake," in the affairs of the corporation. Thus, the normative principles that underlie the contemporary pluralistic theory of property rights also provide the foundation for the stakeholder theory as well. . . .

CONCLUSION

We have argued that the stakeholder theory is "managerial" and recommends the attitudes, structures, and practices that, taken together, constitute a *stakeholder* management philosophy. The theory goes beyond the purely descriptive observation that "organizations have stakeholders," which, although true, carries no direct managerial implications. Furthermore, the notion that stakeholder management contributes to successful economic performance, although widely believed (and not patently inaccurate), is insufficient to stand alone as a basis for the stakeholder theory. Indeed, the most thoughtful analyses of why stakeholder management might be casually related to corporate performance ultimately resort to normative arguments in support of their views. For these reasons, we believe that the ultimate justification for the stakeholder theory is to be found in its normative base. The plain truth is that the most prominent alternative to the stakeholder theory (i.e., the "management serving the shareowners" theory) is morally untenable. The theory of property rights, which is commonly supposed to support the conventional view, in fact—in its modern and pluralistic form—supports the stakeholder theory instead.

NOTES

1. M. C. Jensen and W. Meckling, "Theory of the Firm: Managerial Behavior Agency Costs, and Capital Structure," *Journal of Financial Economics* 3 (October 1976): 305–60.

2. O. E. Williamson and S. G. Winter, eds., *The Nature of the Firm: Origins, Evolution, and Development* (New York: Oxford University Press, 1991).

3. See, by way of comparison, O. E. Williamson, *The Economic Institutions of Capitalism* (New York: Free Press, 1985).

4. See also A. Sharplin and L. D. Phelps, "A Stakeholder Apologetic for Management," *Business and Professional Ethics Journal* 8, no. 2 (1989): 41–53.

5. C. W. L. Hill and T. M. Jones, "Stakeholder Agency Theory," *Journal of Management Studies* 28 no. 2 (1992): 131–54.

6. W. M. Evan and R. E. Freeman, "Corporate Governance: A Stakeholder Interpretation," *Journal of Behavioral Economics* 19, no. 4 (1990): 337–59; see also W. M. Evan and R. E. Freeman, "A Stakeholder Theory of the Modern Corporation: Kantian Capitalism," in *Ethical Theory and Business*, ed. T. Beauchamp and N. Bowie (Englewood Cliffs, NJ: Prentice Hall, 1988), pp. 75–93.

7. Evan and Freeman, "Corporate Governance," pp. 337–59.

8. T. Donaldson and T. W. Dunfee, "Towards a Unified Conception of Business Ethics: Integrative Social Contracts Theory," *Academy of Management Review* 19 (1994): 252–84.

9. R. H. Coase, "The Problem of Social Cost," *Journal of Law and Economics* 3 (1960): 1–44.

10. S. Pejovich, *The Economics of Property Rights: Towards a Theory of Comparative Systems* (Dordrecht, The Netherlands: Kluwer Academic Publishers, 1990), pp. 27–28.

11. For a survey of current views on this complex matter, see N. Mercuro, ed., *Taking Property and Just Compensation* (Boston: Kluwer, 1992).

12. L. C. Becker, "Property," in *Encyclopedia of Ethics*, vol. 2, ed. L. D. Becker and C. B. Becker (New York: Garland, 1992), pp. 1023–27.

13. See, by way of comparison, J. Greenberg, "A Taxonomy of Organizational Justice Theories," *Academy of Management Review* 12 (1987): 9–22.

14. Becker, "Property," pp. 1023–27; see also S. R. Munzer, *A Theory of Property* (New York: Cambridge University Press, 1992).

15. R. Nader and M. Green, eds., *Corporate Power in America* (New York: Grossman, 1973).

6.

MANAGING FOR STAKEHOLDERS[1]

R. Edward Freeman

I. INTRODUCTION

The purpose of this essay is to outline an emerging view of business that we shall call "managing for stakeholders."[2] This view has emerged over the past thirty years from a group of scholars in a diverse set of disciplines, from finance to philosophy.[3] The basic idea is that businesses, and the executives who manage them, actually do and should create value for customers, suppliers, employees, communities, and financiers (or shareholders). And that we need to pay careful attention to how these relationships are managed and how value gets created for these stakeholders. We contrast this idea with the dominant model of business activity; namely, that businesses are to be managed solely for the benefit of shareholders. Any other benefits (or harms) that are created are incidental.[4]

Simple ideas create complex questions, and we proceed as follows. In the next section we examine why the dominant story or model of business that is deeply embedded in our culture is no longer workable. It is resistant to change, not consistent with the law, and for the most part, simply ignores matters of ethics. Each of these flaws is fatal in the business world of the twenty-first century.

We then proceed to define the basic ideas of "managing for stakeholders" and why it solves some of the problems of the dominant model. In particular

R. Edward Freeman, "Managing for Stakeholders," in *Ethical Theory and Business*, 8th ed., ed. Tom L. Beauchamp, Norman E. Bowie, and Dennis G. Arnold, 1–27 (Englewood Cliffs, NJ: Prentice Hall, 2008). Reprinted by permission of the author.

we pay attention to how using "stakeholder" as a basic unit of analysis makes it more difficult to ignore matters of ethics. We argue that the primary responsibility of the executive is to create as much value for stakeholders as possible, and that no stakeholder interest is viable in isolation of the other stakeholders. We sketch three primary arguments from ethical theory for adopting "managing for stakeholders." We conclude by outlining a fourth "pragmatist argument" that suggests we see managing for stakeholders as a new narrative about business that lets us improve the way we currently create value for each other. Capitalism is on this view a system of social cooperation and collaboration, rather than primarily a system of competition.

II. THE DOMINANT STORY: MANAGERIAL CAPITALISM WITH SHAREHOLDERS AT THE CENTER

The modern business corporation has emerged during the twentieth century as one of the most important innovations in human history. Yet the changes that we are now experiencing call for its reinvention. Before we suggest what this revision, "managing for stakeholders" or "stakeholder capitalism," is, first we need to understand how the dominant story came to be told.

Somewhere in the past, organizations were quite simple and "doing business" consisted of buying raw material from suppliers, converting it to products, and selling it to customers. For the most part owner-entrepreneurs founded such simple businesses and worked at the business along with members of their families. The development of new production processes, such as the assembly line, meant that jobs could be specialized and more work could be accomplished. New technologies and sources of power became readily available. These and other social and political forces combined to require larger amounts of capital, well beyond the scope of most individual owner-manager-employees. Additionally, "workers," or nonfamily members, began to dominate the firm and were the rule rather than the exception.

Ownership of the business became more dispersed, as capital was raised from banks, stockholders, and other institutions. Indeed, the management of the firm became separated from the ownership of the firm. And, in order to be successful, the top managers of the business had to simultaneously satisfy the owners, the employees and their unions, suppliers, and customers. This system of organization of businesses along the lines set forth here was known as managerial capitalism, laissez faire capitalism, or more recently, shareholder capitalism.[5]

As businesses grew, managers developed a means of control via the divisionalized firm. Led by Alfred Sloan at General Motors, the divisionalized firm with a central headquarters staff was widely adapted.[6] The dominant model for managerial authority was the military and civil service bureaucracy. By creating rational structures and processes, the orderly progress of business growth could be well managed.

Thus, managerialism, hierarchy, stability, and predictability all evolved together, in the United States and Europe, to form the most powerful economic system in the history of humanity. The rise of bureaucracy and managerialism was so strong, that the economist Joseph Schumpeter predicted that it would wipe out the creative force of capitalism, stifling innovation in its drive for predictability and stability.

During the last fifty years this "Managerial Model" has put "shareholders" at the center of the firm as the most important group for managers to worry about. This mind-set has dealt with the increasing complexity of the business world by focusing more intensely on "shareholders" and "creating value for shareholders." It has become common wisdom to "increase shareholder value," and many companies have instituted complex incentive compensation plans aimed at aligning the interests of executives with the interests of shareholders. These incentive plans are often tied to the price of a company's stock which is affected by many factors not the least of which is the expectations of Wall Street analysts about earnings per share each quarter. Meeting Wall Street targets, and forming a stable and predictable base of quarter-over-quarter increases in earnings per share has become the standard for measuring company performance. Indeed, all of the recent scandals at Enron, WorldCom, Tyco, and others are in part due to executives trying to increase shareholder value, sometimes in opposition to accounting rules and law. Unfortunately, the world has changed so that the stability and predictability required by the shareholder approach can no longer be assured.

The Dominant Model Is Resistant to Change

The Managerial View of business with shareholders at the center is inherently resistant to change. It puts shareholders' interests over and above the interests of customers, suppliers, employees, and others, as if these interests must conflict with each other. It understands a business as an essentially hierarchical organization fastened together with authority to act in the shareholders' interests. Executives often speak in the language of hierarchy as "working for shareholders," "shareholders are the boss," and "you have to do what the shareholders want." On this interpretation, change should occur only when the shareholders are unhappy; and as long as executives can produce a series of incrementally better financial results, there is no problem. According to this view the only change that counts is change oriented toward shareholder value. If customers are unhappy, if accounting rules have been compromised, if product quality is bad, if environmental disaster looms, even if competitive forces threaten, the only interesting questions are whether and how these forces for change affect shareholder value, measured by the price of the stock every day. Unfortunately in today's world there is just too much uncertainty and complexity to rely on such a single criterion. Business in the twenty-first century is global and multifaceted, and shareholder value may not capture that dynamism. Or, if it does, as the theory suggests it must eventually, it will be too late for executives to do anything about it. The dominant story may work for how things turn out in the long run on Wall Street, but managers have to act with an eye to Main Street as well, to anticipate change to try and take advantage of the dynamism of business.[7]

The Dominant Model Is Not Consistent with the Law

In actual fact the clarity of putting shareholders' interests first, above that of customers, suppliers, employees, and communities, flies in the face of the reality of the law. The law has evolved to put constraints on the kinds of trade-offs that can be made. In fact the law of corporations gives a less clear answer to the question of in whose interest and for whose benefit the corporation should be governed. The law has evolved over the years to give *de facto* standing to the claims of groups other than stockholders. It has in effect required that the claims of customers, suppliers, local communities, and employees be taken into consideration.

For instance, the doctrine of "privity of contract," as articulated in *Winterbottom v. Wright* in 1842, has been eroded by recent developments in products liability law. *Greenman v. Yuba Power* gives the manufacturer strict liability for damage caused by its products, even though the seller has exercised all possible care in the preparation and sale of the product and the consumer has not bought the product from nor entered into any contractual arrangement with the manufacturer. *Caveat emptor* has been replaced in large part with *caveat venditor*. The Consumer Product Safety Commission has the power to enact product recalls, essentially leading to an increase in the number of voluntary product recalls by companies seeking to mitigate legal damage awards. Some industries are required to provide information to customers about a product's ingredients, whether or not the customers want and are willing to pay for this information. Thus, companies must take the interests of customers into account, by law.

A similar story can be told about the evolution of the law forcing management to take the interests of employees into account. The National Labor Relations Act gave employees the right to unionize and to bargain in good faith. It set up the National Labor Relations Board to enforce these rights with management. The Equal Pay Act of 1963 and Title VII of the Civil Rights Act of 1964 constrain management from discrimination in hiring practices; these have been followed with the Age Discrimination in Employment Act of 1967, and recent extensions affecting people with disabilities. The emergence of a body of administrative case law arising from labor-management disputes and the historic settling of discrimination claims with large employers have caused the emergence of a body of management practice that is consistent with the legal guarantee of the rights of employees.

The law has also evolved to try and protect the interests of local communities. The Clean Water Act of 1977 and the Clean Air Act of 1990, and various amendments to these classic pieces of legislation, have constrained management from "spoiling the commons." In a historic case, *Marsh v. Alabama*, the Supreme Court ruled that a company-owned town was subject to the provisions of the US Constitution, thereby guaranteeing the rights of local citizens and negating the "property rights" of the firm. Current issues center around protecting local businesses, forcing companies to pay the healthcare costs of their employees, increases in minimum wages, environmental standards, and the effects of business development on the lives of local community members. These issues fill the local political landscapes, and executives and their companies must take account of them.

Some may argue that the constraints of the law, at least in the United States, have become increasingly irrelevant in a world where business is global in nature. However, globalization simply makes this argument stronger. The laws that are relevant to business have evolved differently around the world, but they have evolved nonetheless to take into account the interests of groups other than just shareholders. Each state in India has a different set of regulations that affect how a company can do business. In China the law has evolved to give business some property rights but it is far from exclusive. And, in most of the European Union, laws around "civil society" and the role of "employees" are much more complex than even US law.

"Laissez faire capitalism" is simply a myth. The idea that business is about "maximizing value for stockholders regardless of the consequences to others" is one that has outlived its usefulness. The dominant model simply does not describe how business operates. Another way to see this is that if executives always have to qualify "maximize shareholder value" with exceptions of law, or even good practice, then the dominant story isn't very useful anymore. There are just too many exceptions. The dominant story could be saved by arguing that it describes a normative view about how business should operate, despite how actual businesses have evolved.[8] So, we need to look more closely at some of the conceptual and normative problems that the dominant model raises.

The Dominant Model Is Not Consistent with Basic Ethics

Previously we have argued that most theories of business rely on separating "business" decisions from "ethical" decisions.[9] This is seen most clearly in the popular joke about "business ethics as an oxymoron." More formally we might suggest that we define:

> *The Separation Fallacy*—It is useful to believe that sentences like "x is a business decision" have no ethical content or any implicit ethical point of view. And, it is useful to believe that sentences like "x is an ethical decision, the best thing to do all things considered" have no content or implicit view about value creation and trade (business).

This fallacy underlies much of the dominant story about business, as well as in other areas in society. There are two implications of rejecting the Separation Fallacy. The first is that almost any business decision has some ethical content. To see that this is true one need only ask whether the following questions make sense for virtually any business decision:

> *The Open Question Argument*
> (1) If this decision is made, for whom is value created and destroyed?
> (2) Who is harmed and/or benefited by this decision?
> (3) Whose rights are enabled and whose values are realized by this decision (and whose are not)?
> (4) What kind of person will I (we) become if we make this decision?

Since these questions are always open for most business decisions, it is reasonable to give up the Separation Fallacy, which would have us believe that these questions aren't relevant for making business decisions, or that they could never be answered. We need a theory about business that builds in answers to the "Open Question Argument." One such answer would be "Only value to shareholders counts," but such an answer would have to be enmeshed in the language of ethics as well as business. Milton Friedman, unlike most of his expositors, may actually give such a morally rich answer. He claims that the responsibility of the executive is to make profits subject to law and ethical custom. Depending on how "law and ethical custom" is interpreted, the key difference with the stakeholder approach may well be that we disagree about how the world works. In order to create value we believe that it is better to focus on integrating business and ethics within a complex set of stakeholder relationships rather than treating ethics as a side constraint on making profits. In short we need a theory that has as its basis what we might call:

> The Integration Thesis—Most business decisions, or sentences about business have some ethical content, or implicit ethical view. Most ethical decisions, or sentences about ethics have some business content or implicit view about business.[10]

One of the most pressing challenges facing business scholars is to tell compelling narratives that have the Integration Thesis at its heart. This is essentially the task that a group of scholars, "business ethicists," and "stakeholder theorists" have begun over the last thirty years. We need to go back to the very basics of ethics. Ethics is about the rules, principles, consequences, matters of character, and so forth, that we use to live together. These ideas give us a set of open questions that we are constantly searching for better ways to answer in reasonable complete ways.[11] One might define "ethics" as a conversation about how we can reason together and solve our differences, recognize where our interests are joined and need development, so that we can all flourish without resorting to coercion and violence. Some may disagree with such a definition, and we do not intend to privilege definitions, but such a pragmatist approach to ethics entails that we reason and talk together to try and create a better world for all of us.

If our critiques of the dominant model are correct then we need to start over by reconceptualizing the very language that we use to understand how business operates. We want to suggest that something like the following principle is implicit in most reasonably comprehensive views about ethics.

> *The Responsibility Principle*—Most people, most of the time, want to, actually do, and should accept responsibility for the effects of their actions on others.[12]

Clearly the Responsibility Principle is incompatible with the Separation Fallacy. If business is separated from ethics, there is no question of moral responsibility for business decisions. More clearly still, without something like the Responsibility Principle it is difficult to see how ethics gets off the ground. "Responsibility" may well be a difficult and multifaceted idea. There are surely many different ways to understand it. But, if we are not willing to accept the responsibility for our own actions (as limited as that may be, due to complicated issues of causality and the like), then ethics, understood as how we reason together so we can all flourish, is likely an exercise in bad faith.

If we want to give up the Separation Fallacy and adopt the Integration Thesis, if the open question argument makes sense, and if something like the Responsibility Thesis is necessary, then we need a new model for business. This new story must be able to explain how value creation at once deals with economics and ethics, and how it takes account of all of the effects of business action on others. Such a model exists, and has been developing over the years by management researchers and ethics scholars, and there are many businesses who have adopted this "stakeholder framework" for their businesses.

III. MANAGING FOR STAKEHOLDERS

The basic idea of "managing for stakeholders" is quite simple. Business can be understood as a set of relationships among groups which have a stake in the activities that make up the business. Business is about how customers, suppliers, employees, financiers (stockholders, bondholders, banks, and so on), communities, and managers interact and create value. To understand a business is to know how these relationships work. And the executive's or entrepreneur's job is to manage and shape these relationships, hence the title, "managing for stakeholders."

The idea of "managing for stakeholders" can be interpreted in a variation of the classic "wheel and spoke" diagram.[13] However, it is important to note that the stakeholder idea is perfectly general. Corporations are not the center of the universe, and there are many possible pictures. One might put customers in the center of such a diagram to signal that a company puts customers as the key priority. Another might put employees in the center and link them to customers and shareholders. We prefer the generic diagram because it suggests, pictorially, that "managing for stakeholders" is a theory about management and business; hence, managers and companies in the center. But, there is no larger metaphysical claim here.

Stakeholders and Stakes

Owners or financiers (a better term) clearly have a financial stake in the business in the form of stocks, bonds, and so on, and they expect some kind of financial return from them. Of course, the stakes of financiers will differ by type of owner, preferences for money, moral preferences, and so on, as well as by type of firm. The shareholders of Google may well want returns as well as to be supportive of Google's articulated purpose of "Do No Evil." To the extent that it makes sense to talk about the financiers "owning the firm," they have a concomitant responsibility for the uses of their property.

Employees have their jobs and usually their livelihood at stake; they often have specialized skills for which there is usually no perfectly elastic market. In return for their labor, they expect security, wages, benefits, and meaningful work. Often, employees are expected to participate in the decision making of the organization; and if the employees are management or senior executives, we see them as shouldering a great deal of responsibility for the conduct of the organization as a whole. Employees are sometimes financiers as well, since many companies have stock ownership plans, and loyal employees who believe in the future of their companies often voluntarily invest. One way to think about the employee relationship is in terms of contracts.

Customers and suppliers exchange resources for the products and services of the firm and in return receive the benefits of the products and services. As with financiers and employees, the customer and supplier relationships are enmeshed in ethics. Companies make promises to customers via their advertising, and when products or services don't deliver on these promises, then management has a responsibility to rectify the situation. It is also important to have suppliers who are committed to making a company better. If suppliers find a better, faster, and cheaper way of making critical parts or services, then both supplier and company can win. Of course, some suppliers simply compete on price, but even so, there is a moral element of fairness and transparency to the supplier relationship.

Finally, the local community grants the firm the right to build facilities, and in turn, it benefits from the tax base and economic and social contributions of the firm. Companies have a real impact on communities, and being located in a welcoming community helps a company create value for its other stakeholders. In return for the provision of local services, companies are expected to be good citizens, as is any individual person. It should not expose the community to unreasonable hazards in the form of pollution, toxic waste, and the like. It should keep whatever commitments it makes to the community, and operate in a transparent manner as far as possible. Of course, companies don't have perfect knowledge, but when management discovers some danger or runs afoul of new competition, it is expected to inform and work with local communities to mitigate any negative effects as far as possible.

While any business must consist of financiers, customers, suppliers, employees, and communities, it is possible to think about other stakeholders as well. We can define "stakeholder" in a number of ways. First of all we could define the term fairly narrowly to capture the idea that any business, large or small, is about creating value for "those groups without whose support, the business would cease to be viable." The inner circle of our diagram would depict this view. Almost every business is concerned at some level with relationships among financiers, customers, suppliers, employees, and communities. We might call these groups "primary" or "definitional." However, it should be noted that as a business starts up, sometimes one particular stakeholder is more important than another. In a new business start-up, sometimes there are no suppliers, and paying lots of attention to one or two key customers, as well as to the venture capitalist (financier), is the right approach.

There is also a somewhat broader definition that captures the idea that if a group or individual can affect a business, then the executives must take that group into consideration in thinking about how to create value. Or, a stakeholder is any group or individual that can affect or be affected by the realization of an organization's purpose. At a minimum some groups affect primary stakeholders and we might see these as stakeholders in the outer ring of our diagram and call them "secondary" or "instrumental."

There are other definitions that have emerged over the years, some based on risks and rewards, some based on mutuality of interests. The debate over finding the one "true definition" of "stakeholder" is not likely to end. We prefer a more pragmatic approach of being clear of the purpose of using any of the proposed definitions. Business is a fascinating field of study. There are very few principles and definitions that apply to all businesses all over the world. Furthermore, there are many different ways to run a successful business, or if you like, many different flavors of "managing for stakeholders." We see limited usefulness in trying to define one model of business, either based on the shareholder or stakeholder view, that works for all businesses everywhere. We see much value to be gained in examining how the stakes work in the value-creation process and in the role of the executive.

Primary   Secondary

IV. THE RESPONSIBILITY OF THE EXECUTIVE IN MANAGING FOR STAKEHOLDERS

Executives play a special role in the activity of the business enterprise. On the one hand, they have a stake like every other employee, in terms of an actual or implied employment contract. And that stake is linked to the stakes of financiers, customers, suppliers, communities, and other employees. In addition, executives are expected to look after the health of the overall enterprise, to keep the varied stakes moving in roughly the same direction, and to keep them in balance.[14]

No stakeholder stands alone in the process of value creation. The stakes of each stakeholder group are multifaceted and inherently connected to each other. How could a bondholder recognize any returns without management paying attention to the stakes of customers or employees? How could customers get the products and services they need without employees and suppliers? How could employees have a decent place to live without communities? Many thinkers see the dominant problem of "managing for stakeholders" as how to solve the priority problem, or "which stakeholders are more important," or "how do we make trade-offs among stakeholders." We see this as a secondary issue.

First and foremost, we need to see stakeholder interests as joint, as inherently tied together. Seeing stakeholder interests as "joint" rather than opposed is difficult. It is not always easy to find a way to accommodate all stakeholder interests. It is easier to trade off one versus another. Why not delay spending on new products for customers in order to keep earnings a bit higher? Why not cut employee medical benefits in order to invest in a new inventory control system?

Managing for stakeholders suggests that executives try to reframe the questions. How can we invest in new products and create higher earnings? How can we be sure our employees are healthy and happy and are able to work creatively so that we can capture the benefits of new information technology such as inventory control systems? In a recent book reflecting on his experience as CEO of Medtronic, Bill George summarized the managing for stakeholders mind-set:

> Serving all your stakeholders is the best way to produce long term results and create a growing, prosperous company. . . . Let me be very clear about this: there is no conflict between serving all your stakeholders and providing excellent returns for shareholders. In the long term it is impossible to have one without the other. However, serving all these stakeholder groups requires discipline, vision, and committed leadership.[15]

The primary responsibility of the executive is to create as much value as possible for stakeholders.[16] Where stakeholder interests conflict, the executive must find a way to rethink the problems so that these interests can go together, so that even more value can be created for each. If trade-offs have to be made, as often happens in the real world, then the executive must figure out how to make the trade-offs, and immediately begin improving the trade-offs for all sides. Managing for stakeholders is about creating as much value as possible for stakeholders, without resorting to trade-offs.

We believe that this task is more easily accomplished when a business has a sense of purpose. Furthermore, there are few limits on the kinds of purpose that can drive a business. Wal-Mart may stand for "everyday low price." Merck can stand for "alleviating human suffering." The point is that, if an entrepreneur or an executive can find a purpose that speaks to the hearts and minds of key stakeholders, it is more likely that there will be sustained success.

Purpose is complex and inspirational. The Grameen Bank wants to eliminate poverty. Fannie Mae wants to make housing affordable to every income level in society. Tastings (a local restaurant) wants to bring the taste of really good food and wine to lots of people in the community. And all of these organizations have to generate profits, or else they cannot pursue their purposes. Capitalism works because we can pursue our purpose with others. When we coalesce around a big idea, or a joint purpose evolves from our day-to-day activities with each other, then great things can happen.

To create value for stakeholders, executives must understand that business is fully situated in the realm of humanity. Businesses are human institutions populated by real live complex human beings. Stakeholders have names and faces and children. They are not mere placeholders for social roles. As such, matters of ethics are routine when one takes a managing-for-stakeholders approach. Of course this should go without saying, but a part of the dominant story about business is that businesspeople are only in it for their own narrowly defined self-interest. One main assumption of the managerial view with shareholders at the center is that shareholders only care about returns, and therefore their agents, managers, should only care about returns. However, this does not fit either our experiences or our aspirations. In the words of one CEO, "The only assets I manage go up and down the elevators every day."

Most human beings are complicated. Most of us do what we do because we are self-interested and interested in others. Business works in part because of our urge to create things with others and for others. Working on a team, or creating a new product or delivery mechanism that makes customers' lives better, or happier, or more pleasurable, all can be contributing factors to why we go to work each day. This is not to deny the economic incentive of getting a paycheck. The assumption of narrow self-interest is extremely limiting, and can be self-reinforcing—people can begin to act in a narrow self-interested way if they believe that is what is expected of them, as some of the scandals such as Enron have shown. We need to be open to a more complex psychology—one that any parent finds familiar as he or she has shepherded the growth and development of children.

V. SOME ARGUMENTS FOR MANAGING FOR STAKEHOLDERS

Once you say stakeholders are persons, then the ideas of ethics are automatically applicable. However you interpret the idea of "stakeholders," you must pay attention to the effects of your actions on others. And something like the Responsibility Principle suggests that this way of thinking is a cornerstone of any adequate ethical theory. There are at least three main arguments for adopting a managing-for-stakeholders approach. Philosophers will see these as connected to the three main approaches to ethical theory that have developed historically. We shall briefly set forth sketches of these arguments, and then suggest that there is a more powerful fourth argument.[17]

The Argument from Consequences

A number of theorists have argued that the main reason that the dominant model of managing for shareholders is a good idea is that it leads to the best consequences for all. Typically these arguments invoke Adam Smith's idea of the invisible hand, whereby each business actor pursues her own self-interest and the greatest good of all actually emerges. The problem with this argument is that we now know with modern general equilibrium economics that the argument only works under very specialized conditions that seldom describe the real world. Furthermore, we know that if the economic conditions get very close to those needed to produce the greatest good, there is no guarantee that the greatest good will actually result.

Managing for stakeholders may actually produce better consequences for all stakeholders because it recognizes that stakeholder interests are joint. If one stakeholder pursues its interests at the expense of all the others, then the others will either withdraw their support, or look to create another network of stakeholder value creation. This is not to say that there are not times when one stakeholder will benefit at the expense of others, but if this happens continuously over time, then in a relatively free society, stakeholders will either: (1) exit to form a new stakeholder network that satisfies their needs; (2) use the political process to constrain the offending stakeholder; or, (3) invent some other form of activity to satisfy their particular needs.[18]

Alternatively, if we think about stakeholders engaged in a series of bargains among themselves, then we would expect that as individual stakeholders recognized their joint interests, and made good decisions based on these interests, better consequences would result, than if they each narrowly pursued their individual self-interests.[19]

Now it may be objected that such an approach ignores "social consequences" or "consequences to society," and hence, that we need a concept of "corporate social responsibility" to mitigate these effects. This objection is a vestigial limb of the dominant model. Since the only effects on that view were economic effects, then we need to think about "social consequences" or "corporate social responsibility." However, if stakeholder relationships are understood to be fully embedded in morality, then there is no need for an idea like corporate social responsibility. We can replace it with "corporate stakeholder responsibility," which is a dominant feature of managing for stakeholders.

The Argument from Rights

The dominant story gives property rights in the corporation exclusively to shareholders, and the natural question arises about the rights of other stakeholders who are affected. One way to understand managing for stakeholders is that it takes this question of rights seriously. If you believe that rights make sense, and further that if one person has a right to X then all persons have a right to X, it is just much easier to think about these issues using a stakeholder approach. For instance, while shareholders may well have property rights, these rights are not absolute, and should not be seen as such. Shareholders may not use their property to abridge the rights of others. For instance, shareholders and their agents, managers, may not use corporate property to violate the right to life of others. One way to understand managing for stakeholders is that it assumes that stakeholders have some rights. Now it is notoriously difficult to parse the idea of "rights." But if executives take managing for stakeholders seriously, they will automatically think about what is owed to customers, suppliers, employees, financiers, and communities, in virtue of their stake and in virtue of their basic humanity.

The Argument from Character

One of the strongest arguments for managing for stakeholders is that it asks executives and entrepreneurs to consider the question of what kind of company they want to create and build. The answer to this question will be in large part an issue of character. Aspiration matters. The business virtues of efficiency, fairness, respect, integrity, keeping commitments, and others are all critical in being successful at creating value for stakeholders. These virtues are simply absent when we think only about the dominant model and its sole reliance on a narrow economic logic.

If we frame the central question of management as "how do we create value for shareholders," then the only virtue that emerges is one of loyalty to the interests of shareholders. However, if we frame the central question more broadly as "how do we create and sustain the creation of value for stakeholders" or "how do we get stakeholder interests all going in the same direction," then it is easy to see how many of the other virtues are relevant. Taking a stakeholder approach helps people decide how companies can contribute to their well-being and the kinds of lives they want to lead. By making ethics explicit and building it into the basic way we think about business, we avoid a situation of bad faith and self-deception.

The Pragmatist's Argument

The previous three arguments point out important reasons for adopting a new story about business. Pragmatists want to know how we can live better, how we can create both ourselves and our communities in a way where values such as freedom and solidarity are present in our everyday lives to the maximal extent. While it is sometimes useful to think about consequences, rights, and character in isolation, in reality our lives are richer if we can have a conversation about how to live together better. There is a long tradition of pragmatist ethics dating to philosophers such as William James and John Dewey. More recently philosopher Richard Rorty has expressed the pragmatist ideal:

> . . . [P]ragmatists . . . hope instead that human beings will come to enjoy more money, more free time, and greater social equality, and also that they will develop more empathy, more ability to put themselves in the shoes of others. We hope that human beings will behave more decently toward one another as their standard of living improves.[20]

By building into the very conceptual framework we use to think about business a concern with freedom, equality, consequences, decency, shared purpose, and paying attention to all of the effects of how we create value for each other, we can make business a human institution, and perhaps remake it in a way that sustains us.

For the pragmatist, business (and capitalism) has evolved as a social practice; an important one that we use to create value and trade with each other. On this view, first and foremost, business is about collaboration. Of course, in a free society, stakeholders are free to form competing networks. But the fuel for capitalism is our desire to create something of value, and to create it for ourselves and others. The spirit of capitalism is the spirit of individual achievement together with the spirit of accomplishing great tasks in collaboration with others. Managing for stakeholders makes this plain so that we can get about the business of creating better selves and better communities.

NOTES

1. The ideas in this paper have had a long development time. The ideas here have been reworked from: R. Edward Freeman, *Strategic Management: A Stakeholder Approach* (Boston: Pitman, 1984); R. Edward Freeman, "A Stakeholder Theory of the Modern Corporation," in *Ethical Theory and Business*, 7th ed., ed. T. Beauchamp and N. Bowie (Englewood Cliffs, NJ: Prentice Hall, 2005), also in earlier editions coauthored with William Evan; Andrew Wicks, R. Edward Freeman, Patricia Werhane, and Kirsten Martin, *Business Ethics: A Managerial Approach* (Englewood Cliffs, NJ: Prentice Hall, forthcoming in 2008); and R. Edward Freeman, Jeffrey Harrison, and Andrew Wicks, *Managing for Stakeholders* (New Haven, CT: Yale University Press, 2007). I am grateful to editors and coauthors for permission to rework these ideas here.

2. It has been called a variety of things from "stakeholder management," "stakeholder capitalism," "a stakeholder theory of the modern corporation," and so forth. Our reasons for choosing "managing for stakeholders" will become clearer as we proceed. Many others have worked on these ideas, and should not be held accountable for the rather idiosyncratic view outlined here.

3. For a stylized history of the idea, see R. Edward Freeman, "The Development of Stakeholder Theory: An Idiosyncratic Approach," in *Great Minds in Management*, ed. K. Smith and M. Hitt (Oxford: Oxford University Press, 2005).

4. One doesn't manage "for" these benefits (and harms).

5. The difference between managerial and shareholder capitalism is large. However, the existence of agency theory lets us treat the two identically for our purposes here. Both agree on the view that the modern firm is characterized by the separation

of decision making and residual risk bearing. The resulting agency problem is the subject of a vast literature.

6. Alfred Chandler's brilliant book, *Strategy and Structure* (Boston: MIT Press, 1970), chronicles the rise of the divisionalized corporation. For a not-so-flattering account of General Motors during the same time period, see Peter Drucker's classic work, *The Concept of the Corporation*, rep. ed. (New York: Transaction Publishers, 1993).

7. Executives can take little comfort in the nostrum that in the long run things work out and the most efficient companies survive. Some market theorists suggest that finance theory acts like "universal acid" cutting through every possible management decision, whether or not actual managers are aware of it. Perhaps the real difference between the dominant model and the "managing for stakeholders" model proposed here is that they are simply "about" different things. The dominant model is about the strict and narrow economic logic of markets, and the "managing for stakeholders" model is about how human beings create value for each other.

8. Often the flavor of the response of finance theorists sounds like this. The world would be better off if, despite all of the imperfections, executives tried to maximize shareholder value. It is difficult to see how any rational being could accept such a view in the face of the recent scandals, where it could be argued that the worst offenders were the most ideologically pure, and the result was the actual destruction of shareholder value. (See *Breaking the Short Term Cycle* [Charlottesville, VA: Business Roundtable Institute for Corporate Ethics/CFA Center for Financial Market Integrity, 2006].) Perhaps we have a version of Aristotle's idea that happiness is not a result of trying to be happy, or Mill's idea that it does not maximize utility to try and maximize utility. Collins and Porras have suggested that even if executives want to maximize shareholder value, they should focus on purpose instead; that trying to maximize shareholder value does not lead to maximum value. (See J. Collins and J. Porras, *Built to Last* [New York: HarperCollins, 2002].)

9. See R. Edward Freeman, "The Politics of Stakeholder Theory: Some Future Directions," *Business Ethics Quarterly* 4 (1994): 409–22.

10. The second part of the integration thesis is left for another occasion. Philosophers who read this essay may note the radical departure from standard accounts of political philosophy. Suppose we began the inquiry into political philosophy with the question of "how is value creation and trade sustainable over time" and suppose that the traditional beginning question, "how is the state justified" was a subsidiary one. We might discover or create some very different answers from the standard accounts of most political theory. See R. Edward Freeman and Robert Phillips, "Stakeholder Theory: A Libertarian Defense," *Business Ethics Quarterly* 12, no. 3 (2002): 331–ff.

11. Here we roughly follow the logic of John Rawls in *Political Liberalism* (New York: Columbia University Press, 1995).

12. There are many statements of this principle. Our argument is that whatever the particular conception of responsibility there is some underlying concept that is captured like our willingness or our need, to justify our lives to others. Note the

answer that the dominant view of business must give to questions about responsibility: "Executives are responsible only for the effects of their actions on shareholders, or only in so far as their actions create or destroy shareholder value."

13. The spirit of this diagram is from R. Phillips, *Stakeholder Theory and Organizational Ethics* (San Francisco: Berret-Koehler Publishers, 2003).

14. In earlier versions of this essay . . . we suggested that the notion of a fiduciary duty to stockholders be extended to "fiduciary duty to stakeholders." We believe that such a move cannot be defended without doing damage to the notion of "fiduciary." The idea of having a special duty to either one or a few stakeholders is not helpful.

15. Bill George, *Authentic Leadership* (San Francisco: Jossey Bass, 2004.)

16. This is at least as clear as the directive given by the dominant model: Create as much value as possible for shareholders.

17. Some philosophers have argued that the stakeholder approach is in need of a "normative justification." To the extent that this phrase has any meaning, we take it as a call to connect the logic of managing for stakeholders with more traditional ethical theory. As pragmatists we eschew the "descriptive vs. normative vs. instrumental" distinction that so many business thinkers (and stakeholder theorists) have adopted. Managing for stakeholders is inherently a narrative or story that is at once: *descriptive* of how some businesses do act; *aspirational* and *normative* about how they could and should act; *instrumental* in terms of what means lead to what ends; and *managerial* in that it must be coherent on all of these dimensions and actually guide executive action.

18. See S. Venkataraman, "Stakeholder Value Equilibration and the Entrepreneurial Process," *Ethics and Entrepreneurship*, Ruffin Series 3 (2002): 45–57; S. R. Velamuri, "Entrepreneurship, Altruism, and the Good Society," *Ethics and Entrepreneurship*, Ruffin Series 3 (2002): 125–43; and, T. Harting, S. Harmeling, and S. Venkataraman, "Innovative Stakeholder Relations: When 'Ethics Pays' (and When It Doesn't)," *Business Ethics Quarterly* 16 (2006): 43–68.

19. Sometimes there are trade-offs and situations that economists would call "prisoner's dilemmas," but these are not the paradigmatic cases, or if they are, we seem to solve them routinely, as Russell Hardin has suggested in *Morality within the Limits of Reason* (Chicago: University of Chicago Press, 1998).

20. E. Mendieta, ed., *Take Care of Freedom and Truth Will Take Care of Itself: Interviews with Richard Rorty* (Stanford, CA: Stanford University Press, 2006), p.68.

7.

STAKEHOLDER THEORY AND A PRINCIPLE OF FAIRNESS

Robert A. Phillips

INTRODUCTION

Obligations of fairness arise when individuals and groups of individuals interact for mutual benefit. Such persons and groups engage in voluntary activities that require mutual contribution and restriction of liberty. These voluntary activities provide a normative justification (on par with consent) for the idea of stakeholder management; or so I will argue. I will also argue that obligations of fairness hold some interesting theoretical and practical advantages over consent-based obligations including the more frequent occurrence of requisite obligation creating activity and the existence of such obligations irrespective of the intent to become obligated or the awareness of the obligations created on the part of the actor. . . .

A PRINCIPLE OF FAIRNESS

While H. L. A. Hart is most often credited with the first explicit contemporary discussion of the idea in 1955,[1] obligations and duties similar to those based on fair play were discussed by John Stuart Mill in 1859:

> When a person, either by express promise or by conduct, has encouraged another to rely upon his continuing to act in a certain way—to build expec-

tations and calculations, and stake any part of his plan of life upon that sup-position—a new series of moral obligations arises on his part towards that person, which may possibly be overruled, but cannot be ignored. . . . A person is bound to take all these circumstances into account, before resolving on a step which may affect such important interests of theirs; and if he does not allow proper weight to those interests, he is morally respon-sible for the wrong.[2]

This idea finds further elaboration in the works of John Rawls, A. John Sim-mons, Kent Greenawalt, and George Klosko, among many others.[3] Rawls describes the principle as follows:

The principle of fair play may be defined as follows. Suppose there is a mutually beneficial and just scheme of cooperation, and that the advantages it yields can only be obtained if everyone, or nearly everyone, cooperates. Suppose further that cooperation requires a certain sacrifice from each person, or at least involves a certain restriction of his liberty. Suppose finally that the benefits produced by cooperation are, up to a certain point, free: that is, the scheme of cooperation is unstable in the sense that if any one person knows that all (or nearly all) of the others will continue to do their part, he will still be able to share a gain from the scheme even if he does not do his part. Under these conditions a person who has accepted the benefits of the scheme is bound by a duty of fair play to do his part and not to take advantage of the free benefit by not cooperating.[4]

Taking this definition as a good starting point, I would now like to ana-lyze the conception of obligations of fairness and alter the definition as nec-essary.[5] From the above passage we can isolate six qualifications for consid-eration as a cooperative scheme in which the duty of fair play is operative:

    a. mutual benefit
    b. justice
    c. benefits accrue only under conditions of near unanimity of cooperation
    d. cooperation requires sacrifice or restriction of liberty on the part of participants
    e. the possibility of free riders exists
    f. voluntary acceptance of benefits of cooperative scheme.

    a. *Mutual benefit*—The idea of commerce as being to the mutual benefit of the participants is as old as economics. Indeed, it is the very foundation of the oft-quoted passage in Adam Smith's *Wealth of Nations* concerning the butcher, brewer, and baker.[6] I would add merely that "benefit" need not be a direct personal benefit to the cooperator. Benefit may include other directed desires in addition to purely egoistic ones. For instance, if a person is engaged in a cooperative scheme in order to obtain a benefit for her child or friend, the scheme may still be considered mutually beneficial for the purposes of this essay.

b. *Justice*—The second requisite feature of an appropriate cooperative scheme is that it be relatively just. As my focus is on the economic cooperative scheme and there are many who seriously question the justness of such a scheme (or at least the capitalist version of it practiced in the United States and much of the world), this condition, if indeed necessary, could have a serious impact upon my arguments.

> Rawls defends the justness condition by claiming it is generally agreed that extorted promises are void *ab initio*. But similarly, unjust social arrangements are themselves a kind of extortion, even violence, and consent to them does not bind.[7]

The problem with this line of argument lies in the meaning of extortion. While it may be quite correct that an extorted promise is no promise at all, it does not follow that consent to an unjust institution is necessarily coerced. The analogy of a promise to an unjust person is instructive here. It would be absurd to suggest that a promise to an evil or unjust person results in no obligation to fulfill the promise. Rather, it is the strength of the obligation that can be mitigated or overridden by other (possibly) higher-order moral considerations such as a duty to fight injustice. Thus, if I voluntarily (i.e., uncoercedly) make a promise I always incur an obligation to fulfill this promise. Whether such an obligation dictates action depends upon the existence of other possibly mitigating circumstances. Hence, I see no convincing reason to view such justness as a necessary precondition for the existence of fairness-based obligations. Therefore I amend the concept to reflect this conclusion.

c. *Benefits accrue only under conditions of near unanimity of cooperation*—There are also strong reasons for doubting the necessity of this precondition for obligations of fairness. If all of the other necessary conditions obtain, it would still be unfair to take the benefits of a cooperative scheme without contribution even if the benefits could be obtained under conditions of substantially less than unanimity of cooperation (i.e., the benefits could be obtained with only one-half or two-thirds of the people cooperating). Indeed, when the possibility of a great many free riders exists, obligations of fairness take on an even greater significance.

Rawls includes the unanimity condition because the principle was originally suggested as a grounding for political obligations. In the current context, it is argued that the principle serves to create obligations in economic interactions. That is, it is being used here to determine between which persons and groups obligations of fairness obtain. As such, the unanimity condition may be a logical impossibility in this usage as the principle is designed to determine just who should or should not be included in the operative group. Therefore, the question, "unanimity among whom?" would be begged by the necessity of this condition. If the particular group is unknown or undelimited, it is impossible to know how close the group is to unanimity. Hence, this condition is discarded for economic uses.

d. *Cooperation requires sacrifice or restriction of liberty on the part of participants*—In the case of the previous two conditions, I did not seek to determine whether or not commercial transactions qualified because the two conditions were found unnecessary. Returning now to conditions of central importance to the idea of fairness, I also return to the effort of ascertaining the extent to which such conditions obtain in the sphere of economic dealings. When a person engages in a trade there arise several restrictions on liberty. The most obvious example is that of the worker. When she agrees to sell the product of her labor to a company, she generally must arrive at work on time, stay for a set period, and in general obey the rules of the company. This clearly constitutes a restriction on the person's liberty. So too is the case with the exchange of property. A property right is nothing more than a right to more or less exclusive use and thus in exchanging property, one actually sacrifices one's liberty to use that property.[8] Similarly, when a community allows a company to build a plant in its vicinity, it sacrifices its land and many other resources to the cooperative venture with the company and the company sacrifices some of its capital assets as well. Clearly, then, commercial transactions involve sacrifice and restriction of liberty and thus meet this qualification as a cooperative scheme in which obligations of fairness may arise.

e. *The possibility of free riders exists*—Given the breathtaking amount of research and literature on the problems of free riders in economic systems, it is difficult to conceive of what an argument against their existence would look like. I therefore take it as axiomatic that this condition is adequately met in the case of economic transaction and interaction.[9]

f. *Voluntary acceptance of benefits of cooperative scheme*—This condition is vital to the existence of obligations of fair play. It is the voluntary acceptance of the benefits of a scheme that actually creates the obligations of which I speak. The voluntarist condition, one may notice, is not mentioned explicitly in the passage from which I take my definition. It is, however, present in Rawls's definition in *Theory* and is vital to the relevance of the principle.

I take it to be axiomatic that uncoerced consent creates obligations on the part of the consentor and would thus provide adequate normative justification for such obligations. However, consent is not the only type of activity that may create such obligations. The voluntary engagement in, and acceptance of the benefits of, a cooperative scheme can similarly serve to create obligations of equal strength to the obligations created by consent. Such voluntary actions, then, also provide strong normative justification for such obligations. In addition, such obligations based on fairness may be more useful than consent-based obligations due to the more frequent occurrence of the requisite obligation-creating activity. Further, obligations of fairness exist even if the obligation creating implications of such activities are unknown to the benefitee. This is in contrast to consent-based theories wherein knowledge of the content of the obligation is imperative. Even express dissent cannot diminish the existence of obligations of fairness if the dissenter has undertaken the requisite acceptance of benefits from a cooperative scheme. The idea of voluntary acceptance will become more clear as I proceed.

I conclude on the basis of the above discussion that commercial transactions do indeed qualify as cooperative schemes and further that these schemes admit of obligations of fairness. My working definition of fairness is as follows:

> *Whenever persons or groups of persons voluntarily accept the benefits of a mutually beneficial scheme of cooperation requiring sacrifice or contribution on the parts of the participants and there exists the possibility of free riding, obligations of fairness are created among the participants in the cooperative scheme in proportion to the benefits accepted. . . .*

FAIRNESS AND CONSENT

Normative Justification in Stakeholder Theory. . . . [O]ne of the criticisms of the stakeholder model was that it relied on no normative justificatory framework. This criticism has always been, strictly speaking, false. The stakeholder model as propounded by Freeman in 1984 relied on a prudential justification that has been used by philosophers for centuries (e.g., Hobbes and Gauthier). The actual problem is that the framework on which it relies is not explicitly made known and is furthermore inadequate in dealing properly with ethical issues. For instance, recall the problem of accounting for oblig-

ations owed to those who are affected by but do not affect the firm in any significant way. Freeman explains these obligations with the argument that such
people or groups may someday come to affect the firm and, indeed, this may
be the only recourse available within a purely prudential framework. This
then is the primary area in which the principle of fairness strengthens the
stakeholder model. To the extent that a person or group is involved in a cooperative scheme with others involving the voluntary receipt of benefits, an
obligation is owed to the scheme and those others based on the principle of
fairness. With this understanding, the stakeholder model is no longer vulnerable to either the criticism that it appeals to no adequate justificatory framework or that it inadequately accounts for the demands of those persons or
groups that are unable to affect the firm in any meaningful way. . . .

   Stakeholders as Cooperators—the fairness-based stakeholder model suggests a reconceptualization of many business interactions from that of cutthroat
competition—even with those on whom the corporation depends in various
ways—to that of a cooperative scheme. By viewing economic dealings of all
kinds as cooperative schemes rather than competitive battles, many apparent
stakeholder conflicts may be avoided altogether. Stakeholders become more
partners for the achievement of mutual advantage and less persons and institutions that need to be managed and their impacts minimized. . . .

   Stakeholder Procedures and Discourse Ethics—Of the currently available
models of organizational ethics, stakeholder theory is best able to account for
an ethical procedure of managerial decision making. How and with whom in
mind a manager goes about making decisions that may affect stakeholders is
the main strength of stakeholder theory. Habermas provides convincing arguments concerning the morally appropriate procedures for deriving appropriate
norms. Habermas argues for a principle of discourse ethics:

> (D) Only those norms can claim to be valid that meet (or could meet) with
> the approval of all affected in their capacity as *participants in a practical
> discourse.*[10]

. . . A final point of importance should be made. The principle of stakeholder
fairness only derives the obligations to stakeholders. It says little about the
content of these obligations. That is, the principle provides only the most
general guidelines for managerial decision making (e.g., that the effects of a
decision on stakeholders must ethically be considered in the decisions). It is
the norms themselves, derived through stakeholder discourse, that more
specifically direct managerial decision making. The principle of stakeholder
fairness indicates that obligations do, in fact, exist, as well as which parties

are to be included in the discourse on the legitimacy of norms. The principle is not used to derive the norms themselves. In short, the principle of stakeholder fairness provides for the generation of the obligations, not the content of the obligations. The actual norms are derived and tested by the methodology of stakeholder discourse.

NOTES

1. H. L. A. Hart, "Are There Any Natural Rights?" *Philosophical Review* 64 (April 1955).

2. John Stuart Mill, *On Liberty* (1859; Cambridge: Cambridge University Press, 1989), pp. 103f.

3. John Rawls, *A Theory of Justice* (Cambridge, MA: Belknap Press of Harvard University Press, 1971), pp. 108–17, 333–55, and "Legal Obligation and the Duty of Fair Play," in *Law and Philosophy*, ed. S. Hook (New York: New York University Press, 1964); A. John Simmons, *Moral Principles and Political Obligations* (Princeton, NJ: Princeton University Press, 1979), pp. 101–42; Kent Greenawalt, *Conflicts of Law and Morality* (New York: Oxford University Press, 1987), pp. 121–58; George Klosko, *The Principle of Fairness and Political Obligation* (Lanham, MD: Rowman & Littlefield Publishers, 1992) and "Presumptive Benefit, Fairness, and Political Obligation," *Philosophy and Public Affairs* 16 (1987): 241–59; Garrett Cullity, "Moral Free Riding," *Philosophy and Public Affairs* 24, no. 1 (Winter 1995): 3–34.

4. Rawls, "Legal Obligation," pp. 9–10.

5. This first passage will rely heavily on Simmons's critique of the same work.

6. Adam Smith, *The Wealth of Nations*, D. D. Raphael and A. L. Macfie, ed. (1776; Oxford: Oxford University Press, 1976). Repr. ed. (Indianapolis, IN: Liberty Classics, 1982).

7. Rawls, *Theory of Justice*, p. 343.

8. For a discussion of the implications of property rights for the stakeholder model, see Thomas Donaldson and L. E. Preston, "The Stakeholder Theory of the Corporation: Concepts, Evidence, and Implications," *Academy of Management Review* 20, no. 1 (1995): 65–91.

9. See Cullity, "Moral Free Riding," for an excellent summary treatment on free riding.

10. Jürgen Habermas, "Discourse Ethics: Notes on a Program of Philosophical Justification," in *Moral Consciousness and Communicative Action*, trans. Christian Lenhardt and Shienry Weber Nicholsen (Cambridge, MA: MIT Press, 1990), p. 66, Habermas's emphasis. See also Habermas, *The Theory of Communicative Action* (Boston: Beacon Press, 1984, 1987); and Seyla Benhabib and Fred Dalimayr, eds., *The Communicative Ethics Controversy*, trans. Thomas McCarthy (Cambridge, MA: MIT Press, 1990).

8.

FEMINIST ETHICS AS A MORAL GROUNDING FOR STAKEHOLDER THEORY

Brian K. Burton and Craig P. Dunn

F eminist theory has been suggested by Freeman and Gilbert (1992) as a possible fruitful source for new views of business. Wicks, Gilbert, and Freeman (1994) have followed that suggestion by discussing the contributions feminist theory can make to conversations regarding the stakeholder concept. The current paper continues that conversation by arguing that a feminine view of morality can ground decision making in a stakeholder model, thereby making that model a viable option for those managers interested in operating according to moral principles.

FEMINIST THEORY

Before examining feminist ethics, we must understand the fundamental differences between a feminist approach to philosophy and the more traditional approach—what Wicks et al. call the masculinist approach—that underlies traditional ethics. These differences are shown most clearly in ontology and epistemology. Traditional ethics is founded on an ontology of the individual self. "Others" are seen as threats, so rights become of prime importance. The resulting moral theories tend to be legalistic or contractual in nature. . . .

Traditional ethics is also based on a view of knowledge as abstract, universal, impartial, and rational. Rawls's (1971) initial position, Kant's practical reason, and Bentham's (1988) utilitarian calculus all are based on impartiality and reasoned thought. They are meant to be applied universally. Within such constructions, persons are easily substitutable one for another, with no impact on the ethical outcome of the action under consideration. These moral frameworks are also meant to be applied through reasoned calculation. . . .

As Wicks et al. imply, feminist theory is founded on totally different assumptions regarding the state of the world and the definition of knowledge. Feminist philosophers view the person as essentially relational, not individualistic. . . . According to feminist philosophers, this emphasis on relationships in turn emphasizes their moral worth—and by extension the responsibilities inherent in the relationship, rather than rights as in traditional ethics. While traditional ethics can be viewed as being built on responsibilities, particularly the Kantian conception of duties, traditional moral theories turn much more quickly to a discussion of rights, whereas feminist philosophers continue to discuss responsibilities through the notion of caring.

Feminists' ontology of humans as essentially relational beings is tied to their epistemology. They believe that humans only know through relationship. If relationships are identifying characteristics of humans, then the abstract, universal, impartial, and rational standard of what is knowledge is inadequate in decision making. That standard does not acknowledge the fact people have relationships and will be affected by those relationships, producing knowledge. It is wrong to ask that we do not take our relationships into account when making decisions regarding right action. We know particular things about particular humans, and because of this knowledge we are partial toward some of those humans. These facts not only will affect, more to the point they should affect, our decisions—through emotions, which feminists[1] count as knowledge.

ETHICS OF CARING

These differences in ontology and epistemology lead to an emphasis on caring as opposed to justice in feminist moral theory. Two discussions of caring in particular have gained notice, those of Carol Gilligan and Nel Noddings. Gilligan's concepts are the background of the work of Wicks et al., but there are sufficient differences between her work and that of Noddings that both should be explicated in any discussion of theories of caring.

GILLIGAN AND A DIFFERENT VOICE

Gilligan's ideas concerning caring form not so much a theory as a critique of a theory, in this case that of Lawrence Kohlberg (1981). Gilligan takes issue with Kohlberg's findings that women are less morally developed than men. She believes those findings are biased because men and women speak different moral languages. Men tend to speak and act in the language of justice and rights. As this is the language of traditional moral theories and is what Kohlberg attempts to measure, it is not surprising that men show relatively high levels of moral development. Women, on the other hand, are less likely to speak in this language, so they do not perform well responding to Kohlberg's moral dilemmas. Instead, women speak and act in the language of caring and responsibilities, the differences between the genders being based on infantile experiences.

Women move in and out of three moral levels according to Gilligan. One is where the self is the sole object of concern. The second is where the chief desire is to establish connections and participate in social life—in other words, maintain relationships or direct one's thoughts toward others. This is the level Gilligan says forms the conventional notion of women. The third level is where the woman recognizes both her own needs and the needs of those with whom she has relationships. While women never settle completely at any level, as they attain moral maturity more of their decisions will be made using the third level. This level gives all parties in a relationship responsibilities, as it requires that they consider both their own good (responsibilities to oneself) and the other's good (responsibilities to others) when deciding what is right action. It requires care for others as well as for oneself. In other words, it moves morality away from the legalistic, self-centered approach feminists view as characterizing traditional ethics.

NODDINGS AND CARING

Noddings, unlike Gilligan, attempts to formulate a general moral theory of care. Her position is that traditional theories that place justice as the foundation of morality are wrong. Instead, care should be the foundation, with justice as the superstructure. For Noddings, ethics is about the desire to be a good person, not about what "good" is. And ethics is concerned with relationships, not with atomistic individuals.

According to Noddings, people naturally privilege their family members and friends in making decisions, and this is as it should be. She wants us to move beyond that immediate circle, however, to care for others who are related to us either through our intimates or through some role we play—for example, at work. Even though our caring for these people may be less than our caring for those in our immediate circle, Noddings believes it is imperative that we exhibit some care for them. Noddings sees relationships, and thus caring, as not stopping even with everyone we know. Instead, we are even to care for those with whom we have no present relationship, merely an anticipated hypothetical relationship.

Noddings defends herself against the charge of ethical relativism by arguing that a caring attitude is universal, indeed that it is fundamental to all humans. However, she rejects universal laws, saying that ethics is about concrete, particular relationships, not abstract concepts like the good of society.

Noddings does not deny that humans are at some level self-interested. Instead, she claims that we affirm our own interests by affirming another's needs. This is because one fundamental desire of all humans is to be related to other humans. Noddings further believes that our persons are defined by the set of relationships we have as physical selves. Therefore, by affirming another's need we are remaining related, fulfilling our desire and continuing to define ourselves as persons.

Moral dilemmas for Noddings are not individual but relational, not a monologue but a dialogue, because each moral dilemma will involve a relationship and thus affect all people involved in that relationship. Consensus is the goal of all those engaged in dialogue regarding moral dilemmas. Noddings does not want conflict or competition to be involved in moral decision making. Morality is not about being the best, it is about reducing evil. The dichotomous thinking that traditional ethics espouses—me versus you—is replaced by thinking about us. Above all, we are not to cause anyone pain or separation. No good is worth that.

THE PROBLEMS WITH FEMINIST ETHICS

There are caveats that we feel must be noted regarding feminist ethics, caveats not considered by Wicks et al. First, there is the question of how to model the ideal relationship. Feminist scholars often look to the mother-child relationship, although (as previously noted) some do not like to use that particular relationship. Indeed, there are problems with the metaphor of the mother-child relationship. It is not voluntary, while most relationships in the real world are voluntary. It is permanent, while most relationships are not. It is an unequal relationship; the mother has great power but also great responsibility to care for the child, who is dependent on the mother for at least part of the relationship. While unequal relationships certainly exist in the real world, we should question whether we want our ideal relationship to be inherently unequal.

These attributes have led other feminists to consider friendship as the ideal relationship.[2] This relationship is voluntary, not permanent, and can be equal—although it often is not. It seems to be a better model for real-world relationships, particularly among stakeholders, but other relationships also exist in the real world—relationships of convenience or necessity that may not be modeled well by friendship.

Another problem with feminist ethics is that it often seems to place caring and justice in opposition to each other. Tong (1993) argues that caring and justice are not opposed but complementary attributes of the good society: both are necessary but not sufficient. Wicks et al. take pains to point out that adopting a feminist perspective does not mean that the masculinist perspective is irrelevant. We agree with them; however, we feel it is possible to be both just and caring in a feminist conception of morality, which we will discuss in a later section of this paper.

A third caution regarding feminist ethics is that it is easy to represent the relational self as really no self at all. Noddings does this to an extent when she says persons are defined by the set of relations into which their physical selves are thrown. But this view of the self leads naturally to the view that others are all important in the definition of the self, that the self does not exist without others. Gilligan's third level of moral development argues against this in that at this highest stage caring for oneself as well as others becomes important. However, it is still an important point to make.

Wicks et al. walk the fine line between Noddings's conception of the self and that implied by Gilligan. Their proposed definition of the corporation as *"constituted by the network of relationships which it is involved in"*[3] sounds very similar to Noddings's definition of the self—and to neoclassical economics, if one were to substitute "contracts" for "relationships." Yet Wicks et al. also note that they do not want to rid the firm of an individual identity, which is consistent with Gilligan's views. Their definition could be better written as "the corporation is constituted by both itself as an entity *and* the network of relationships in which it is involved." This definition would both give clarity to their intent and be true to Gilligan's idea of the self, which seems to us better than that of Noddings.

But this definition leads to the idea of a firm as a caring entity, as it must be under a feminist interpretation of stakeholder theory. It seems intuitively apparent that some firms "care" more than others. For example, Levi Strauss seems to be a more "caring" firm than Union Carbide. But what do we mean when we say that a firm "cares"?

If one follows the argument of French (1977), one could say that a firm would care if, as an intentional system, it exhibits caring behavior consistent with firm policy. One does not have to argue that a firm itself can care, however. Following and drawing analogy to Werhane's (1985) discussion of corporate actions, what seem to be a firm's caring actions are more appropriately characterized as a corporation's secondary actions derived from the primary caring of corporate agents for stakeholders who are privileged by the corporation's decision makers. For example, a supplier of long standing has earned a place of privilege among the organization's stakeholders through quality work, timely performance, and low prices. In that sense, the people inside the organization with whom the supplier has worked have cared for the supplier. A purchasing agent who has formed a close working relationship with the supplier eliminates the system of bidding for contracts for the parts the supplier makes. The actions within the organization seem to be an example of caring by the organization; in reality they are the caring of the purchasing agent. Thus, the firm can exhibit caring behavior, even if we do not want to say that a firm "cares." This view is consistent with feminist theory. Thus, whichever side of the argument regarding the moral status of organizations one takes, we can talk about caring in an organizational context and be understood.

A final caveat that must be mentioned is that caring can be taken too far. For example, Noddings wants us to extend our chains of caring to all those with whom we have even the possibility of forming a relationship. But if we follow her words literally we shall end up actively caring for hundreds, even thousands of people, wearing ourselves out and possibly having no energy left for those we should care about most, those in our immediate circles. This must be avoided, and the solution is to limit those for whom we care—not to our immediate circle, but to those for whom we can reasonably care while at the same time caring for ourselves.

FEMINIST THOUGHT AND STAKEHOLDER THEORY

It is evident that stakeholder theory and the ethics of caring put forward by Gilligan and Noddings have many points of contact. In fact, in one sense it might be said that traditional, economics-based approaches to management have concentrated on the legalistic, contractual, masculine side of human existence. As Wicks et al. imply, stakeholder theory might then be said to be the feminine counterpart to traditional management, as the ethics of care are the feminine counterpart to traditional moral theory.

Stakeholder theory posits the firm as contractually related to any number of stakeholders. This is inherent in Freeman's definition of a stakeholder as any entity that can affect or be affected by the firm's actions.[4] Only a firm that does not act will not have stakeholders under this definition, so part of being a going concern is that one must have stakeholders.

Wicks et al. point out that this view forces us to see the firm in a different way. Traditional management views the firm as being in competition with other firms, protecting and seeking to further its own interests—almost always at another's expense. Legal, contractual relationships are formed to prevent the worst forms of exploitation from occurring. Williamson notes that such contractual relationships are a surrogate for "trust" in the relationship, thereby reducing the possibility of "opportunism," defined by Williamson as "self-interest seeking with guile."[5]

Stakeholder theory, on the other hand—particularly considering Freeman's plea for voluntarism in dealing with stakeholders—seems to promote a more cooperative, caring type of relationship. Firms should seek to make decisions that satisfy stakeholders, leading to situations where all parties involved in a relationship gain. The inherent relatedness of the firm under stakeholder theory forces firms to examine the effect of their decisions on others, just as the inherent relatedness of humans in feminist theory forces us to examine the effect of our decisions on others. Feminists may call humans "second persons"; stakeholder theorists could call firms "second enterprises."

Stakeholder theory also deals with concrete relationships. Traditional management theory discusses "competitors," "suppliers," "buyers," and other firms in abstract terms. Universal rules for dealing with other organizations may be set. Rationality is also a key part of traditional theory. Even those who turn from "optimizing" to "satisficing,"[6] or discuss "cognitive limits" on rational decision making,[7] do so in an implicit climate of rational thinking. Stakeholder theory has the potential to make stakeholders concrete. It is not a matter of dealing with "suppliers" but of this supplier of that product, raw material, or service. The question is the type of effect your decision has on that particular supplier, not "suppliers" in general.

And one of the problems with research into stakeholder theory may not be a shortcoming of the theory at all, but rather that researchers have been attempting to apply it in a rational fashion. Stakeholder theory implicitly appeals to the emotions, to our intuitions regarding the worth of certain relationships. We consider the effect of our decision on a supplier. We have an emotional response to that consideration. We feel that the relationship is important. Either we see that the effect on the stakeholder is positive, in which case we are happy and proceed to act on our decision; or we see that the effect is negative, in which case we are unhappy and pause to reconsider our decision. Emotions therefore become part of knowledge in stakeholder theory, just as they do in feminist theory.

Stakeholder theory also stresses our responsibilities to others more than our rights, as might be expected from a theory that emphasizes relationships. This is a fundamental tenet of feminist moral theory as well. . . . Traditional management, in contrast, focuses on rights, as does traditional moral theory. Even the duties enjoined by traditional moral theory are based on rights we have and so must grant to others, not responsibilities we have irrespective of others' responsibilities. Traditional moral theory would require only that we consider others' situations, feelings, and outcomes and rationally decide what is best for all concerned, perhaps taking into account principles of justice, autonomy, and universalizability. This is not the same as involving those affected by our decisions in the decision process itself, as would be required by a feminist perspective.

A TRANSLATION TO BUSINESS DECISION MAKING

One of the basic problems with the application of stakeholder theory to practical business decisions is that it gives no moral rules for decision making. . . .

Wicks et al. propose a rule of consensus and understanding following feminist, caring ethics. First, the attempt is made to find win-win solutions to the issue confronting the firm and its stakeholders. If this seems impossible, communication is urged to encourage understanding of others' positions and eventual acceptance of a "second best" result.[8] However, this approach will only work if all the involved stakeholders adopt a caring approach to their interactions. Those firms that still operate under a masculinist approach to interactions among stakeholders will insist on their "rights" as stakeholders; they will not accept "second best status." If the firm, in the interests of consensus (or elimination of conflict), moves to satisfy the "squeaky wheel" stakeholder, it may be making a decision that is not consistent with its own or society's best interests. It may take a long time for the principles Wicks et al. advocate to be adopted by all stakeholders—if indeed they ever all adopt those principles—so we need to find another decision rule for the firm that wants to apply the stakeholder concept to its interactions with stakeholders today.

The other possible rule is another that invokes caring. This rule would, following Noddings, be one such as, "I will privilege those with whom I have a close relationship." As Noddings argues, this is not a relativistic rule. Relativism concerns a rule that is adopted by a particular individual or society as applicable only to that individual or society. A relational rule such as Noddings proposes would be applicable universally.

Such a principle would not entail the disregard of others. An ethic of caring requires that we care for all with whom we have a relationship. In the case of stakeholder theory, this would mean that we try to satisfy all reasonable stakeholder demands, as we care about and for all stakeholders. However, remembering the caveat that we cannot care for everyone equally, this principle would recognize that trade-offs must be made in dealing with stakeholders and give us guidance for making those trade-offs.

However, feminine ethics such as that of Noddings and the principles derived from them cannot be applied in isolation. Not only do we have the word of Tong that a society—or a person, or a firm—cannot be caring unless it is also just. And not only do we have the words of Wicks et al. that favoring one side of the debate does not mean that we must exclude the other side. We can cite many situations where the caring principle enunciated above, applied to stakeholder theory, will result in harm—something Noddings says cannot be countenanced.

One of the best examples of the problems a principle such as "Privilege those with whom you have a close relationship" causes comes from the documentary "Global Dumping Ground." This film tells the story of a firm that must dispose of scrap metal, including lead acid batteries. The firm wants to be a good corporate citizen and recycle the batteries. However, it is concerned about the cost of such a move, and it must be careful in such a project because of regulations in the United States pertaining to employee safety. The firm therefore sends the batteries to Taiwan for recycling. In Taiwan the regulations regarding employee safety are less stringent, and the employees there are subject to many hazards in dealing with the old batteries.

The firm in the film is following a principle similar to "Privilege those with whom you have a close relationship." The people with whom the firm is close in this case are the firm's employees—certainly a close (in distance, if not always in emotion) relationship. By privileging these employees, however—by keeping them safe from the harmful effects of dealing with old batteries—the firm is harming another group. This group consists of the employees in Taiwan who must, under worse conditions, work with the old batteries. By privileging the closer group, the firm causes harm to a group with fewer advantages.

A PRINCIPLE FOR BUSINESS DECISIONS

A caring principle must take situations like this into account. What is necessary from Noddings's point of view is that harm not be caused—but this seems impossible to fulfill in real life. What we propose instead is a hybrid approach, recommending that special attention be given to the least advantaged members of the moral community—which in this case includes groups as well as individuals.[9] The principle would then read, "Care enough for the least advantaged stakeholders that they not be harmed; insofar as they are not harmed, privilege those stakeholders with whom you have a close relationship."

This principle may not eliminate harm, but it at least limits harm among those who are most vulnerable and who will suffer more from harms than the more advantaged in society. The least advantaged stakeholders thus enjoy a special relationship with the firm. In the case discussed above, the firm would form a special relationship with workers in places such as Taiwan. It could do this in a number of ways, such as ensuring safe working conditions for them or performing the work in the United States or somewhere else where such conditions are mandated. . . .

More generally, a firm following this principle must perform a stakeholder analysis not merely to understand which stakeholders have power and which have a stake in the decision, but also to understand which stakeholders are most vulnerable to the action. In any situation where trade-offs are required, the firm thus gains a special, very close relationship with those disadvantaged stakeholders and must care for them to the extent possible, even if that caring requires a withholding of benefits that would normally come to other stakeholders. The firms must attempt to avoid causing actual harm in all decisions.

It is important to understand the various applications of this principle. . . . Let us consider another . . . common business decision—that of which supplier to use in a purchasing situation. Suppliers typically would not be considered disadvantaged stakeholders. Presumably they are business firms in an attempt to make money. Although benefits will be withheld from those suppliers who are not chosen, this is no harm. . . . Much more important in this situation are the relationships the firm has with various suppliers. Remember that we cannot reasonably care for everyone. We must accept the trade-offs involved and give our business to the supplier with whom we have a close relationship—a relationship built upon trust, experience, and mutual accommodation over the years. A supplier in such a relationship would not raise prices to take advantage of the purchasing firm; instead, the supplier will give good prices to such a loyal customer, one with whom the supplier has an understanding.

Another situation may concern moving a factory. The principal stakeholders involved in this decision are the shareholders, the employees, and the local community. In a case where the factory has been in operation for a long time, relationships will have developed between the firm's managers and the employees and community. The managers will feel a greater need to care for these stakeholders than they might if the factory had been in operation only a few months. Of course, the factory may not be easily sold. Closing a factory that cannot be easily sold might then cause great harm to the employees and community, and caring managers could not cause such harm. On the other hand, if the factory is easily sold, or the firm has already lined up a buyer, much less harm is caused, and caring managers might feel the trade-off needs to be made.

This brings us to the case of stockholders. Much debate has occurred regarding the status of stockholders under stakeholder theory.[10] Under our principle, large stockholders will have a special relationship with some managers, specifically top management, through personal contacts as well as the board of directors. However, small stockholders, say the individual who owns 100 shares of a firm with 10,000,000 outstanding shares, will not have a close relationship with any manager, and few lower-level managers will have a close relationship with any stockholder. Does this mean that stockholders would not be privileged under our principle? In many situations, this may indeed be the case. However, stockholders should indirectly benefit from, not be harmed by, decisions made under this principle. For example, if the firm continues a long relationship with a supplier, it is assured of competitive prices and continued supply. This allows more efficient production, benefiting shareholders. . . . .

But what about the case of moving the factory? In such a situation, if it is imperative to the firm's survival that lower production costs be achieved, caring managers must consider small stockholders—and, perhaps, those people who have invested their savings in the mutual fund that controls a large percentage of the firm's stock—as stakeholders that could be greatly harmed if the firm kept the factory open. The firm's managers will need to consider the closeness of the relationship with employees and community, and the harms inflicted on each group, before making a final decision. It thus is not inconceivable that stockholders would be privileged under this principle, but it is not a given, either, as neoclassical economists have suggested. As with any relationship under this principle, harm must be minimized. . . .

NOTES

1. For example, A. M. Jagger, "Love and Knowledge: Emotion in Feminist Epistemology," in *Women, Knowledge and Reality*, ed. A. Garry and M. Pearsall (Boston: Unwin Hyman, 1989).

2. See, for example, Baier, *Postures of the Mind: Essays on Mind and Morals* (Minneapolis: University of Minnesota Press, 1985); L. Code, "Second Persons," in *Science Morality and Feminist Theory*, ed. M. Hanen and K. Nielsen (Calgary: University of Calgary Press, 1987).

3. A. C. Wicks, D. R. Gilbert Jr., and R. E. Freeman, "A Feminist Reinterpretation of the Stakeholder Concept," *Business Ethics Quarterly* 4 (1994): 483.

4. R. E. Freeman, *Strategic Management: A Stakeholder Approach* (Boston: Pitman, 1984), p. 46.

5. O. Williamson, *Markets and Hierarchies: Analysis and Antitrust Implications* (New York: Free Press, 1975), p. 225.

6. For example, see H. A. Simon, *Administrative Behavior* (New York: Macmillan, 1958).

7. See, for example, C. R. Schwenk, "Cognitive Simplification Processes in Strategic Decision-Making," *Strategic Management Journal* 5 (1984): 111–28.

8. Wicks et al., "A Feminist Reinterpretation," p. 488.

9. John Rawls, *A Theory of Justice* (Cambridge, MA: Belknap Press of Harvard University Press, 1971).

10. For example, see K. E. Goodpaster, "Business Ethics and Stakeholder Analysis," *Business Ethics Quarterly* 1 (1991): 53–73; and J. R. Boatright, "What's So Special about Shareholders?" *Business Ethics Quarterly* 4 (1994): 393–407.

SUGGESTIONS FOR FURTHER READING

Argandona, A. "The Stakeholder Theory and the Common Good." *Journal of Business Ethics* 17, no. 9/10 (1988): 1093.

Asher, C., and J. Mahoney. "Towards a Property Rights Foundation for a Stakeholder Theory of the Firm." *Journal of Management and Governance* 9, no. 1 (2005): 5.

Boatright, J. "Business Ethics and the Theory of the Firm." *American Business Law Journal* 34, no. 2 (1996): 217–38.

Carroll, A. *Business and Society: Ethics and Stakeholder Management.* Cincinnati, OH: South-Westers, 1989.

Donaldson, T., and T. Dunfee. "Contractarian Business Ethics: Current Status and Next Steps." *Business Ethics Quarterly* 5, no. 2 (1995): 173–86.

———. "Towards a Unified Conception of Business Ethics: Integrative Social Contracts Theory." *Academy of Management Review* 18, no. 2 (1994): 252–84.

Etzioni, A. "A Communitarian Note on Stakeholder Theory." *Business Ethics Quarterly* 8, no. 4 (1998): 679.

Evan, W., and R. E. Freeman. "A Stakeholder Theory of the Modern Corporation: Kantian Capitalism." In *Ethical Theory and Business*, ed. T. Beauchamp and N. Bowie. Englewood Cliffs, NJ: Prentice Hall, 1993, pp. 75–84.

Freeman, R. E., and R. Phillips. "Stakeholder Theory: A Libertarian Defense." *Business Ethics Quarterly* 12, no. 3 (2002): 331–54.

Gibson, K. "The Moral Basis of Stakeholder Theory." *Journal of Business Ethics* 26, no. 3 (2000): 245–57.

Hill, C., and T. Jones. "Stakeholder Agency Theory," *Journal of Management Studies* 29, no. 2 (1992): 131–54.

Jensen, M. "Value Maximization, Stakeholder Theory, and the Corporate Objective Function." *Business Ethics Quarterly* 12, no. 2 (2002): 235.

Jones, T. "Instrumental Stakeholder Theory: A Synthesis of Ethics and Economics." *Academy of Management Review* 20 (1995): 404–37.

Lea, D. "The Imperfect Nature of Corporate Responsibilities to Stakeholders." *Business Ethics Quarterly* 14, no. 2 (2004): 201.

Reed, D. "Stakeholder Management: A Critical Theory Perspective." *Business Ethics Quarterly* 9, no. 3 (1999): 453–83.

Rowley, T. "A Normative Justification for Stakeholder Theory." *Business and Society* 37, no. 1 (1998): 105.

Van de Ven, B. "Human Rights as a Normative Basis for Stakeholder Legitimacy." *Corporate Governance* 5, no. 2 (2005): 48–59.

Wicks, A., D. Gilbert, and R. E. Freeman. "A Feminist Reinterpretation of the Stakeholder Concept." *Business Ethics Quarterly* 4, no. 4 (1984): 475–97.

Wijnberg, N. "Normative Stakeholder Theory and Aristotle: The Link between Ethics and Politics." *Journal of Business Ethics* 25, no. 4 (2000): 329–42.

PART 3.
NORMATIVE CONTROVERSIES

Despite the widespread appeal to stakeholder theory within the contemporary literature on business ethics, debates remain about the acceptability of the normative implications of stakeholder theory. In this regard, although stakeholder theory is intended to represent a model of ethical management practice, some critics have suggested that the theory itself fails on moral grounds. Probably the most prominent version of this argument rests on claims about the moral and legal duties that managers have to corporate stockholders. Simply put, defenders of the stockholder theory of management have argued that corporate managers have an *ethical* duty to act solely in the interests of the company shareholders, given that the shareholders are the owners of the corporation. In being entrusted to act as agents for stockholders, management is taken to have a special fiduciary obligation toward shareholders. Since acting in the interests of other stakeholders could potentially cause managers to act contrary to the best interests of their stockholders, defenders of the stockholder theory of management have thus argued that the adoption of stakeholder theory results in a violation of the fiduciary obligation that grounds the relation between corporate management and stockholders. What is most interesting about this critique of the stakeholder theory of management is that it attempts to dispute the very morality of corporate management taking into account interests other than those of stockholders. In responding to this criticism, defenders of stakeholder theory have attempted to further clarify and defend the nature and extent of corporate obligations to stakeholders, including those to stockholders. In this chapter, we include several articles that deal with this and related criticisms involving the normative acceptability of the stakeholder theory of the firm.

111

We begin this section with selections from two articles that raise criticisms of stakeholder theory of the kind discussed above. In the first selection John Hasnas argues against stakeholder theory on the grounds that it entails a violation of the fundamental obligation of business managers. He begins with the assumption that the ordinary responsibility of a business manager is to manage business resources in pursuit of the specific purposes for which that business is constituted. This obligation, he maintains, has an ethical basis since this is what the manager is hired to do for the company. To expand company resources for purposes other than to meet this aim, Hasnas argues, is to use resources in a manner that is contrary to the underlying purpose for which the business was formed. Since the stockholders of the company can normally be presumed to have the increase of wealth as their purpose in investing in the company, the manager would be misusing resources entrusted to her if she used company resources for purposes distinct from increasing shareholder wealth. Hasnas's defense of the stockholder theory is interesting in part because he makes it clear that it rests on deontological grounds and not, as is often the case, purely utilitarian considerations concerning overall market efficiency. Indeed, he goes on to argue that stakeholder theory is not ethically justifiable precisely because it violates this basic deontological obligation in entailing that managers should act contrary to the wishes of stockholders. As Hasnas summarizes his position, he thus claims that only stockholder theory properly recognizes this deontological obligation founded in the voluntary acceptance by managers to act in their position as stewards for the resources entrusted to them by stockholders.

Alexei M. Marcoux picks up and expands upon Hasnas's claims about the deontological obligation in question in "A Fiduciary Argument against Stakeholder Theory." Marcoux examines the underlying notion of a fiduciary duty through an examination of fiduciary relations in nonbusiness contexts, as found in the legal and healthcare fields. In doing so, Marcoux argues that the moral obligations that attach to such relations are of a particularly morally important kind. Marcoux maintains that the business relation of managers to shareholders also has the same features as those other relations. As such, Marcoux claims that the fiduciary obligation is a morally essential component of a manager's duties toward her company's shareholders. Furthermore, Marcoux argues that stakeholder theory denies the fundamental moral significance of the fiduciary relationship. Indeed, Marcoux maintains that stakeholder theory fails to recognize the legitimate moral claims of fiduciaries in treating all stakeholders' interests as equal. As such, Marcoux concludes that stakeholder theory is deficient in failing to properly account for the moral significance and legitimacy of the fiduciary obligation of managers to shareholders.

Since the fiduciary obligation to stockholders plays such a central role in the most prominent criticisms of stakeholder theory, defenders of stakeholder theory have also devoted considerable attention to further explicating the nature of this obligation. In "Upping the Stakes: A Response to John Hasnas on the Normative Viability of the Stockholder and Stakeholder Theories," Daniel E. Palmer reacts directly to the kind of criticisms raised by Hasnas and Marcoux against stakeholder theory based upon the fiduciary obligation of management toward stockholders. In effect, Palmer agrees with Hasnas and Marcoux that management does have a responsibility of trust to use company money and resources to promote the interests of stockholders. However, Palmer argues that Hasnas and other defenders of the stockholder theory misconstrue this obligation as being absolute, when in fact the fiduciary duty in question can only plausibly be seen as a prima facie duty. Here, Palmer uses W. D. Ross's influential account of moral obligation and prima facie duties to clarify the nature of the moral duty in question. As a prima facie duty, the fiduciary obligation has relevance for managerial decision making, but not one that is inconsistent with the recognition of other prima facie duties on the part of management. As such, he argues that there is nothing conceptually incoherent with allowing that managers can have obligations to stakeholders other than stockholders, even if such duties sometimes come into conflict. Nor, he concludes, should we think that the fiduciary obligation is so stringent that it should always outweigh any other stakeholder obligations that management might have.

While the fiduciary obligation is often discussed as a moral obligation, it can also be treated as a legal obligation on the part of management as well. In this respect, the normativity of the fiduciary obligation is twofold, a point often stressed by defenders of the stockholder theory. Indeed, critics of stakeholder theory have often appealed to legal cases such as *Dodge Bros. v. Ford* in arguing that management has a clear legal obligation to put stockholder interests above the interests of other potential stakeholders. In their article "Getting Real: Stakeholder Theory, Managerial Practice, and the General Irrelevance of Fiduciary Duties Owed to Shareholders," Richard Marens and Andrew Wicks argue that criticisms of stakeholder theory that appeal to this putative legal obligation on the part of management have misconstrued the legal nature of the fiduciary obligation. In particular, Marens and Wicks argue that the legal nature of the fiduciary obligation is not as stringent as is often suggested by critics of stakeholder theory, and that it is one that is quite compatible with stakeholder accounts of managerial obligation. They also argue that the recognition of the existence of a fiduciary obligation on the part of management toward stockholders would not make the implementation of stakeholder theory by management pragmatically problematic. In closely examining the actual facts of *Dodge Bros. v. Ford* and other relevant case law, Marens and Wicks forcefully seek to illustrate these points concerning the legal nature of the fiduciary obligation and its relation to the debate over stakeholder theory.

The final selection in this chapter represents the most comprehensive treatment of contemporary criticisms of stakeholder theory to date by some of its most prominent proponents. In "What Stakeholder Theory Is Not," Robert Phillips, R. Edward Freeman, and Andrew Wicks argue that much of the debate concerning the normative adequacy of stakeholder theory stems from misinterpretation of the fundamentals of stakeholder theory, on the part of both hostile critics and friendly defenders alike. As such, Phillips, Freeman, and Wicks first suggest that stakeholder theory has often been either distorted in ways that make the theory obviously prone to criticism or held to standards that are unreasonable for any theory of a similar nature. Having provided a general account of the two ways in which the evaluation of stakeholder theory has tended to be misconstrued, the authors go on to catalog a number of specific criticisms of the theory, including several that rest on claims about the relation between management and stockholders discussed above. In each case, the authors try to show that the criticisms rest on critical distortions of the theory or of the relevant standards of evaluation. Like the selections from Palmer and Marens and Wicks, this article explicitly addresses the concerns about obligations to shareholders raised by critics of stakeholder theory, and argues that such concerns are either misconceived or rest on a misrepresentation of stakeholder theory. Along the way, they clarify their own account of the precise character of stakeholder theory. While Phillips, Freeman, and Wicks believe that there is still work to be done in fleshing out the details of stakeholder theory, particularly at the level of managerial implementation, they conclude that the theory is immune to the major theoretical criticisms that have been leveled at it since its inception.

9.

THE NORMATIVE THEORIES OF BUSINESS ETHICS

A Guide for the Perplexed[1]

John Hasnas

THE STOCKHOLDER THEORY

The first normative theory of business ethics to be examined is the stockholder theory.[2] According to this theory, businesses are merely arrangements by which one group of people, the stockholders, advance capital to another group, the managers, to be used to realize specified ends and for which stockholders receive an ownership interest in the venture.[3] Under this view, managers act as agents for the stockholders. They are empowered to manage the money advanced by the stockholders, but are bound by their agency relationship to do so exclusively for the purposes delineated by their stockholder principals.[4] The existence of this fiduciary relationship implies that managers cannot have an obligation to expend business resources in ways that have not been authorized by the stockholders regardless of any societal benefits that could be accrued by doing so. . . .

Strictly speaking, the stockholder theory holds that managers are obligated to follow the (legal) directions of the stockholders, whatever these may be. Thus, if the stockholders vote that the business should not close a plant without giving its employees ninety days notice, should have no dealings with a country with a racist regime, or should endow a local public library, the management would be obligated to carry out such a directive regardless of its effect on the business's bottom line . . . the stockholder theory is often imprecisely expressed as requiring managers to maximize the financial returns of the stockholders. . . .

It is important to note that even in this imprecise form, the stockholder theory does not instruct managers to do anything at all to increase the profitability of the business. It does not assert that managers have a moral blank check that allows them to ignore all ethical constraints in the pursuit of profits. Rather, it states that managers are obligated to pursue profit *by all legal, nondeceptive means*.[5] Far from asserting that there are no ethical constraints on a manager's obligation to increase profits, the stockholder theory contends that the ethical constraints society has embodied in its laws plus the general ethical tenet in favor of honest dealing constitute the ethical boundaries within which managers must pursue increased profitability.[6]

For whatever reason, the stockholder theory has come to be associated with the type of utilitarian argument frequently advanced by free market economists.[7] Thus, supporting arguments often begin with the claim that when individual actors pursue private profit in a free market, they are led by Adam Smith's "invisible hand" to promote the general interest as well. It is then claimed that since, for each individual, "[b]y pursuing his own interest he frequently promotes that of the society more effectually than when he really intends to promote it,"[8] it is both unnecessary and counterproductive to exhort businesses or businesspersons to act directly to promote the common good. From this it is concluded that there is no justification for claiming that businesses or businesspersons have any social responsibilities other than to legally and honestly maximize the profits of the firm.

Although this consequentialist argument is the one most frequently cited in support of the stockholder theory, it must be noted that there is another, quite simple deontological argument for it as well. This argument is based on the observation that stockholders advance their money to business managers on the condition that it be used in accordance with their wishes. If the managers accept the money on this condition and then proceed to spend it to accomplish social goals not authorized by the stockholders, they would be violating their agreement and spending other people's money without their consent, which is wrong.[9]

. . . It is important to note that the fact that the utilitarian argument for the stockholder theory may be seriously flawed does not mean that the theory is untenable. This is because the deontological argument for the theory, which has frequently been overlooked, is, in fact, the superior argument. To the extent that it has received serious consideration, the primary objection against it seems to consist in the contention that it is not wrong to spend other people's money without their consent *as long as it is being done to promote the public interest.*[10] This contention is usually bolstered by the observation that this is precisely what democratic governments do all the time (at least, in theory). Since such action is presumably justified in the political realm, so the objection goes, there is no reason to think that it is not equally justified in the business realm.

There are two serious problems with this objection, however. The first is that it misses the essential point of the argument. As stated above, this argument is deontological in character. It is based on an underlying assumption that there are certain principles of conduct that must be observed regardless of the generalized benefits that must be foregone by doing so. One of the most fundamental of these principles states that individuals must honor the commitments they voluntarily and knowingly undertake. Hence, the essence of the argument is the claim that it is morally wrong to violate one's freely assumed agreement to use the stockholders' resources only as specified even though society could be made a somewhat better place by doing so. To assert that a manager may violate his or her agreement with the stockholders whenever doing so would promote the public interest is simply to deny this claim. It is to declare that one's duty to advance the common good overrides one's duty to honor one's agreements, and that the moral quality of one's actions must ultimately be judged according to a utilitarian standard. While some ethicists argue that the principle of utility is indeed the supreme ethical principle, this is far from obviously true, and any contention that merely assumes that it is cannot serve as a compelling objection to a deontological argument.

The second problem is that the objection is based on a false analogy. The assumption that democratic governments are morally justified in spending *taxpayers'* money without their consent to promote the general interest does not imply that businesses or businesspersons are justified in spending *stockholders'* money without their consent for the same reason. Consider that once the citizens have made their required contribution to governmental efforts to benefit society, all should be equally entitled to the control of their remaining assets. Should a citizen elect to invest them in a savings account to provide for his or her children's education or his or her old age, a banker who diverted some of these assets to other purposes, no matter how worthy, would clearly be guilty of embezzlement. For that matter, should the citizen elect to use his or her assets to purchase a new car, go on an extravagant vacation, or even take a course in business ethics, a car dealer, travel agent, or university that failed to deliver the bargained-for product in order to provide benefits to others would be equally guilty. Why should it be any different if the citizen elects to invest in a business? At least superficially, it would appear that citizens have a right to control their after-tax assets that is not abrogated merely because they elect to purchase stock and that would be violated were business managers to use these assets in unauthorized ways. If this is not the case, some showing is required to demonstrate why not.

Of course, these comments in no way establish that the stockholder theory is correct. The most that they can demonstrate is that some of the objections that are frequently raised against it are ill-founded. Other more serious objections remain to be considered.[11] However, they do suggest that the cavalier dismissal the stockholder theory sometimes receives is unjustified, and that, at least at present, it should continue to be considered a serious candidate for the proper normative theory of business ethics.[12]

THE STAKEHOLDER THEORY

... When viewed as a normative theory, the stakeholder theory asserts that, regardless of whether stakeholder management leads to improved financial performance, managers *should* manage the business for the benefit of all stakeholders. It views the firm not as a mechanism for increasing the stockholders' financial returns, but as a vehicle for coordinating stakeholder interests and sees management as having a fiduciary relationship not only to the stockholders, but to all stakeholders. According to the normative stakeholder theory, management must give equal consideration to the interests of all stakeholders[13] and, when these interests conflict, manage the business so as to attain the optimal balance among them. This, of course, implies that there will be times when management is obligated to at least partially sacrifice the interests of the stockholders to those of other stakeholders. Hence, in its normative form, the stakeholder theory does imply that businesses have true social responsibilities.

The stakeholder theory holds that management's fundamental obligation is not to maximize the firm's financial success, but to ensure its survival by balancing the conflicting claims of multiple stakeholders. This obligation is to be met by acting in accordance with two principles of stakeholder management. The first, called the principle of corporate legitimacy, states that "the corporation should be managed for the benefit of its stakeholders: its customers, suppliers, owners, employees, and the local communities. The rights of these groups must be ensured and, further, the groups must participate, in some sense, in decisions that substantially affect their welfare."[14]

The second, called the stakeholder fiduciary principle, states that "management bears a fiduciary relationship to stakeholders and to the corporation as an abstract entity. It must act in the interests of the stakeholders as their agent, and it must act in the interests of the corporation to ensure the survival of the firm, safeguarding the long-term stakes of each group.[15]

The stakeholder theory enjoys a considerable degree of approbation from both theorists and practitioners. In fact, it is probably fair to say that the stakeholder theory currently enjoys a breadth of acceptance equal to what the stockholder theory was said to have enjoyed in the past. To some extent, this may result from the fact that the theory seems to accord well with many people's moral intuitions, and, to some extent, it may simply be a spillover effect of the high regard in which the empirical version of the stakeholder theory is held as a theory of management. It is clear, however, that the normative theory's widespread acceptance does not derive from a careful examination of the arguments that have been offered in support of it. In fact, it is often remarked that the theory seems to lack a clear normative foundation.[16]

An argument that is frequently cited in support of the stakeholder theory is the one offered by Ed Freeman and William Evan in their article.[17] That argument asserts that management's obligation to the stakeholders can be derived from Immanuel Kant's principle of respect for persons. This fundamental ethical principle holds that every human being is entitled to be treated not merely as a means to the achievement of the ends of others, but as a being valuable in his or her own right; that each person is entitled to be respected as an end in himself or herself. Since to respect someone as an end is to recognize that he or she is an autonomous moral agent, i.e., a being with desires of his or her own and the free will to act upon those desires, the principle of respect for persons requires respect for others' autonomy.

Freeman and Evan apply this principle to the world of business by claiming that businesses are bound to respect it as much as anyone else. Thus, businesses may not treat their stakeholders merely as means to the business's ends, but must recognize that as moral agents, all stakeholders are entitled "to agree to and hence participate (or choose not to participate) in the decisions to be used as such."[18] They then claim that it follows from this that all stakeholders are entitled to "participate in determining the future direction of the firm in which they have a stake."[19] However, because it is impossible to consult with all of a firm's stakeholders on every decision, this participation must be indirect. Therefore, the firm's management has an obligation to "represent" the interests of all stakeholders in the business's decision-making process. Accordingly, management is obligated to give equal consideration to the interests of all stakeholders in developing business policy and to manage the business so as to optimize the balance among these interests.

The main problem with this argument is that there is a gap in the reasoning that leads from the principle of respect for persons to the prescriptions of the stakeholder theory. It may readily be admitted that businesses are ethically bound to treat all persons, and hence all stakeholders, as entities worthy of respect as ends in themselves. It may further be admitted that this requires businesses to treat their stakeholders as autonomous moral agents, and hence, that stakeholders are indeed entitled "to agree to and hence participate (or choose not to participate) in the decisions to be used"[20] as means to business ends. The problem is that this implies only that no stakeholder may be forced to deal with the business without his or her consent, not that all stakeholders are entitled to a say in the business's decision-making process or that the business must be managed for their benefit.

It is certainly true that respect for the autonomy of others requires that one keep one's word. To deceive someone into doing something he or she would not otherwise agree to do would be to use him or her merely as a means to one's own ends. For this reason, the principle of respect for persons requires businesses to deal honestly with all of their stakeholders. This means that businesses must honor the contracts they enter into with their customers, employees, suppliers, managers, and stockholders and live up to any representations they freely make to the local community. However, it is simply incorrect to say that respect for another's autonomy requires that the other have a say in any decision that affects his or her interests. A student's interests may be crucially affected by what grade he or she receives in a course as may a Republican's by the decision of whom the Democrats nominate for president. But the autonomy of neither the student nor the Republican is violated when he or she is denied a say in these decisions.

An adherent of the stockholder theory could point out that employees (including managers), suppliers, and customers negotiate for and autonomously accept wage and benefit packages, purchasing arrangements, and sales contracts, respectively. It does not violate their autonomy or treat them with a lack of the respect they are due as persons to fail to provide them with benefits in excess of those they freely accept. However, if managers were to break their agreement with the stockholders to use business resources only as authorized in order to provide other stakeholders with such benefits, the managers would be violating the autonomy of the stockholders. Therefore, the stockholder theorist could contend that not only is the stakeholder theory not entailed by the principle of respect for persons, but to the extent that it instructs managers to use the stockholders' money in ways they have not approved, it is, in fact, violative of it.

NOTES

1. Apologies to Maimonides.

2. In this article, I intentionally speak in terms of "the stockholder theory" rather than "agency theory" to emphasize that I am discussing a normative theory. "Agency theory" seems to be used ambiguously to refer to both the attempt to produce an empirical description of the relationship between managers and stockholders and the normative implications that would flow from such a relationship. See Norman E. Bowie and R. Edward Freeman, "Ethics and Agency Theory: An Introduction," in *Ethics and Agency Theory* 3, ed. Norman E. Bowie and R. Edward Freeman (New York: Oxford University Press, 1992), pp. 3–4. In order to avoid this ambiguity in the present context, I employ the label "stockholder theory" to indicate that I am referring strictly to a theory of how businesses or businesspeople should behave.

3. Historically, the normative theories of business ethics grew out of the litera-ture on corporate social responsibility. As a result, they are often expressed as though they apply only to corporations rather than to businesses generally. This is certainly the case with regard to the stockholder theory. To be adequate, however, a normative theory of business ethics should apply to businesses of all types. For ease of expres-sion, I intend to follow the convention and employ the terminology of the corporate form in my representation of the theories. However, I will attempt to show how each of the theories may be generalized to apply to other forms of business as well.

4. I wish to emphasize again that the stockholder theory is a normative and not a descriptive theory. As such, it asserts not that managers are, in fact, the agents of the stockholders, but that they are ethically obligated to act as though they were.

5. Milton Friedman, "The Social Responsibility of Business Is to Increase Its Profits," *New York Times Magazine*, September 13, 1970, pp. 32–33. The additional restriction of Friedman's formulation that requires managers to engage solely in open and free competition is usually ignored. In today's regulatory environment, it is not regarded as unethical to lobby the government for favor. In many cases, such activi-ties are necessary as a matter of corporate self-defense.

6. It may be accurate to characterize the stockholder theory as proposing an "ethical division of labor." According to the stockholder theory, the nature of the busi-ness environment itself imposes a basic duty of honest dealing on businesspeople. However, the theory also claims that for there to be any more extensive restrictions on managers, it is the job of society as a whole to impose them through the legislative process. It is, of course, true that this approach defines managers' ethical obligations partially in terms of their legal obligations and implies that their ethical obligations will change as the legislation that defines and regulates the business environment

changes. This, in turn, implies that the stockholder theory is not self-sufficient, but is dependent upon the political theory (which delimits the scope of the state's power to legislate) within which it is embedded. This dependence does not render the theory unintelligible, however. At any particular point in time, the theory can be understood as asserting that a business or businessperson must refrain from engaging in deceptive practices and violating the laws of the land as they exist at that time.

7. See, e.g., Dennis P. Quinn and Thomas M. Jones, "An Agent Morality View of Business Policy," *Academy of Management Review* 20 (1995): 22, 24; William M. Evan and R. Edward Freeman, "A Stakeholder Theory of the Modern Corporation: Kantian Capitalism," in *Ethical Theory and Business*, 4th ed., ed. Tom L. Beauchamp and Norman E. Bowie (Englewood Cliffs, NJ: Prentice Hall, 1993), pp. 75, 77.

8. Adam Smith, *The Wealth of Nations*, bk. IV, ch. 2, para. 9.

9. See Friedman, "The Social Responsibility of Business Is to Increase its Profits," note 5. See also Friedman, *Capitalism and Freedom* (Chicago: University of Chicago Press, 1962), p. 135.

10. This highly telescoped formulation of what is, in truth, a considerably more sophisticated consequentialist argument is employed strictly in the interest of conciseness.

11. For two examples, see below.

12. Because of its historical association with debate over corporate social responsibility, the stockholder theory is expressed in language that suggests the corporate form, e.g., stock, stockholders. Despite this, the stockholder theory can be applied to all forms of business. In its generalized form, the theory would simply state that managers are ethically obligated to use business resources that have been advanced to them under the condition that they be used for specified purposes to accomplish only those purposes.

13. See, e.g., Max B. E. Clarkson, "A Stakeholder Framework for Analyzing and Evaluating Corporate Social Performance," *Academy of Management Review* 20 (1995): 92, 105–108.

14. Evan and Freeman, *Business Ethics Quarterly* 167 (1995): 82.

15. Ibid. Clearly, this is Goodpaster's multifiduciary stakeholder synthesis. See K. E. Goodpaster, "Business Ethics and Stakeholder Analysis," *Business Ethics Quarterly* 1, no. 1 (1991): 53–73. This feature of the normative stakeholder theory immediately gives rise to the objection that it is based on an oxymoron. Given the meaning of the word "fiduciary," it is impossible to have a fiduciary relationship to several parties who, like the stakeholders of a corporation, have potentially conflicting interests. Further, even if this did make sense, placing oneself in such a position would appear to be unethical. For example, an attorney who represented two parties with conflicting interests would clearly be guilty of a violation of the canon of ethics.

16. See, e.g., Donaldson and Preston; Evan and Freeman, *Business Ethics Quarterly* 167 (1995): 76–77; Thomas Donaldson and Lee E. Preston, "The Stakeholder Theory of the Corporation: Concepts, Evidence, and Implications," *Academic Management Review* 20, no. 1 (1995): 81–82, esp. 72, who point out that in most of the

stakeholder literature "the fundamental normative principles involved are often unexamined."

17. Evan and Freeman, *Business Ethics Quarterly*. This was not the earliest attempt to provide a normative grounding for the stakeholder theory. See, e.g., Thomas M. Jones and Leonard D. Goldberg, "Governing the Large Corporation: More Arguments for Public Directors," *Academy of Management Review* 7 (1982): 603. However, it does appear to be the first effort to derive the stakeholder theory directly from a widely accepted principle of philosophical ethics. This apparently accounts for the widespread attention it has commanded among the commentators.

18. Evan and Freeman, *Business Ethics Quarterly*.

19. Ibid. at 76.

20. Ibid. at 78.

10.

A FIDUCIARY ARGUMENT AGAINST STAKEHOLDER THEORY

Alexei M. Marcoux

1. NONFIDUCIARY STAKEHOLDER THEORY

Offered in contrast and opposition to *shareholder theory*, which holds that managers are fiduciaries for and ought to manage firms in the interests of shareholders, stakeholder theory holds that firms ought to be managed so as to coordinate the interests of their various stakeholders, usually shareholders, employees, customers, suppliers, and communities.[1] Each stakeholder's interest is to be treated equally in the formulation of business policy. Interests are to be "coordinated" or "balanced" by "trading off" competing interests (although in terms of what interests are to be coordinated, balanced, and/or traded off is not clear).[2]

A. Multifiduciary Stakeholder Theory

Some stakeholder theorists (e.g., Freeman) contend that theirs is a *multifiduciary* stakeholder theory. Multifiduciary stakeholder theory holds that managers are fiduciaries for, and ought to manage in, the interests of all of a firm's stakeholders.[3] In their landmark article, "A Stakeholder Theory of the Modern Corporation: Kantian Capitalism," Evan and Freeman argue for a "stakeholder fiduciary principle," the substance of which is that the interests of all of a firm's stakeholders are to be the object of the fiduciary duties of management.[4] . . .

I will argue, however, that in fact the stakeholder theory demands that

Alexei M. Marcoux, "A Fiduciary Argument against Stakeholder Theory," *Business Ethics Quarterly* 13, no. 1 (January 2003): 1–24. Copyright © 2003 by *Business Ethics Quarterly*. Reprinted by permission.

manager-stakeholder relations be *non*fiduciary in character. Rather than *extending* the fiduciary duties historically owed to shareholders alone to non-shareholding stakeholders as well, the stakeholder theory instead *eliminates* fiduciary duties from all manager-stakeholder relations. Whatever moral duties managers have to stakeholders according to the stakeholder theory, they are not—and indeed, *cannot* be—fiduciary duties.

B. Fiduciary Relations

In order to recognize this point, one must be clear about the nature of the fiduciary relation. The fiduciary relation is a triadic relation existing among and between two parties and some asset or project.

> The term [fiduciary] is derived from the Roman law, and means (as a noun) a person holding the character of a trustee, in respect to the trust and confidence involved in it and the scrupulous good faith and candor which it requires. A person having duty, created by his undertaking, to act primarily for another's benefit in matters connected with such undertaking.[5]

... To act as a fiduciary means to place the interests of the beneficiary ahead of one's own interests and, obviously, those of third parties, with respect to the administration of some asset(s) or project(s).[6] ...

C. Stakeholder Theory and Fiduciary Relations

If the multifiduciary stakeholder theory prescribes manager-stakeholder relations that are fiduciary in character, it must insist that managers are fiduciaries for the shareholders, employees, customers, suppliers, and communities of the firm—in short, for *all* the firm's stakeholders. But of course, managers cannot be fiduciaries for all of these groups. This is so for two reasons.

(1) It is conceptually impossible to simultaneously place the interests of the shareholders ahead of all the others, the interests of employees ahead of all the others (including shareholders), the interests of customers ahead of all the others (including shareholders and employees), the interests of suppliers ahead of all the others (including shareholders, employees, and customers), and so on.

(2) It is practically impossible to serve the interests of each of these groups simultaneously. As most everyone recognizes, the interests of shareholders, customers, suppliers, employees, and communities in the management of a firm's assets are conflicting.[7]

. . . As stakeholder theory demands that the interests of all stakeholders be counted, and presumably served equally (i.e., nonpartially) in the governance of the firm, and as fiduciary duties require partiality toward the interests of some (the beneficiaries) over others, it follows that stakeholder theory is non-fiduciary in character. . . .

2. MORALLY SUBSTANTIAL FIDUCIARY RELATIONS

A. Fiduciary Relations at Law

. . . The legal definition and treatment of the fiduciary relation gives some clue as to why it might be morally significant. The fiduciary relation arises "whenever confidence is reposed on one side, and domination and influence result on the other."[8] It exists "when there is a reposing of faith, confidence and trust, and the placing of reliance by one upon the judgment and advice of the other."[9] Indeed, the

> [f]iduciary relation is not limited to cases of trustee and cestui que trust, guardian and ward, attorney and client, or other recognized legal relations, but exists in all cases where confidence is reposed on one side and resulting superiority and influence on the other side arises.[10] . . .

B. Vulnerability

The common thread running through the myriad relations listed in the above-quoted passages is that each relation entails trust and confidence on one side of the relation and a corresponding influence and potential for domination on the other. The influencing and potentially dominating party bears fiduciary duties to the trusting and confiding party. In other words, the focus of the legal justification for fiduciary relations appears to be the *vulnerability* of one party (the beneficiary) to the other party (the fiduciary) in the relation.

Robert Goodin adverts to the explanatory power of vulnerability for widely held intuitions about many morally considerable relations in his book, *Protecting the Vulnerable*.[11] Goodin's principal objective is to show how vulnerability explains our moral intuitions about the obligations we have in a variety of contexts, as well as to justify still other obligations that may or may not accord with our intuitions because of the vulnerabilities that some people have. . . .

1. *Doctor-Patient.* Patients find themselves at a special disadvantage both before and upon entering the doctor-patient relationship. The doctor is

possessed of all the relevant knowledge about the patient's health and about the treatment strategies that would serve the patient best. The patient lacks an effective means of protecting himself in a world of disease and injury generally, let alone against a doctor who chooses to serve her own interests or those of others in formulating a treatment strategy. As such, the law demands of the doctor that she act as a fiduciary for her patient. In formulating a treatment strategy, the doctor has a duty to subordinate her (and all other) interests to those of the patient, because otherwise the patient's interests are wholly at the mercy of the doctor.

2. *Attorney-Client.* Similarly, clients find themselves at a special disadvantage both before and upon entering the attorney-client relationship. The attorney is expert in assessing the client's legal status and the client lacks an effective means of availing himself of legal remedies and defenses, let alone to check an attorney serving her own interests or those of others at the expense of the client. Here, too, the law demands of the attorney that she act as a fiduciary for her client. In advising the client, the attorney has a duty to subordinate her (and all other) interests to those of her client because otherwise the client's interests are wholly at the mercy of the attorney. Moreover, because of the special vulnerability of the client, the attorney is morally obligated not to withdraw from representing the client until a suitable replacement can be found.[12]

C. Vulnerability Reconsidered

. . . Clearly, if the fiduciary duties owed to those who are, as in the above examples, legally trained, medically trained, or of significant mental agility have a moral basis, it cannot be in virtue of garden-variety concerns about their vulnerability. For these examples suggest that if anyone is lacking in vulnerability to their fiduciaries, it is those who possess the capacities that permit them to evaluate the conduct of their fiduciaries. Indeed, perhaps only the computer whiz is unable to evaluate the conduct of the administrator of his trust. Nonetheless, I will argue that these beneficiaries *are* vulnerable to their fiduciaries in significant, though perhaps not readily apparent, ways.

1. *Control Vulnerability.* First, note that fiduciaries exercise a considerable degree of *control* over the affairs of their beneficiaries. . . . Call this type of vulnerability *control vulnerability.* Even if I am not vulnerable to my fiduciary in the way Goodin stresses, I almost invariably find myself control vulnerable in a relationship to which fiduciary duties attach.

2. *Information Vulnerability.* Second, fiduciaries typically have privi-

leged access to *information* about the affairs of the beneficiary. . . . Although I may be *initially* more knowledgeable about my circumstances, the fiduciary occupies a position of informational superiority, at least with respect to information about the transactions or projects over which the fiduciary relationship exists. As new information is acquired, the fiduciary has it and the beneficiary does not. Call this type of vulnerability *information vulnerability*. . . .

3. *Implications*. Note that the very viability of the relationships to which fiduciary duties attach depends critically upon the existence of control vulnerability and information vulnerability. The doctor-patient relation is a prime example. . . . If I could protect myself from both classes of vulnerability with respect to my doctor, I would have no use of her services. It is only the existence of both classes of vulnerability, coupled with fiduciary obligations on the part of the stronger party, that make it worthwhile and sensible to enter into relationships of this kind. . . .

D. The Moral Core of Fiduciary Relations

The beneficiaries of fiduciary duties at law exhibit morally salient features that appear to make fiduciary duties morally obligatory. If I transact with another in a situation in which she has all of the relevant knowledge and virtually all control over my assets, both the law and the moral intuitions supporting it suggest that she exercise a special duty of care for my interests. The fact that we have contracted gives rise to ordinary, contractual obligations on both our parts. The fact that I am vulnerable to her gives rise to special, fiduciary obligations on her part. I am vulnerable to her as she carries out the project for which we have transacted. Lacking both knowledge and control, I am without ready recourse if my interests are subordinated. Indeed, it is because of the harm that I may all-too-readily suffer at the hands of a doctor, attorney, or guardian—harm that I am ill-equipped to anticipate and counteract, and that is entirely within the control of the doctor, attorney, or guardian—that fiduciary duties are owed to me. . . .

3. THE MANAGER-SHAREHOLDER RELATION

One may agree that the argument of part 2 is substantially correct and that the fiduciary aspect of the doctor-patient, attorney-client, and guardian-ward relations is morally substantial, and yet still deny that managers are morally required to have fiduciary duties to shareholders. That is, one may deny that the manager-shareholder relation possesses the features of the doctor-patient, attorney-client, and guardian-ward relations that make the fiduciary duties that attend them morally substantial.[13] In part 3, I will argue that the manager-shareholder relation *does* possess those features.

A. Control and Information Vulnerabilities Revisited

... Shareholders suffer the special disadvantage of having their assets in the hands of a management team in possession of all of the relevant knowledge, in control of all aspects of their investment, and in control of the flow of information to the shareholders.

Shareholders exhibit control vulnerability because managers are entirely in control of shareholders' investments in the firm. Shareholders may regain control of their investments only if they can find another willing to assume their relationship with the firm (i.e., buy their shares) at or above the price at which shareholders initially acquired them.

Shareholders exhibit information vulnerability because managers have access to information about the day-to-day operations, the successes and failures, and the financial inflows and outflows of the firm. Shareholders generally lack and cannot easily acquire this sort of information. Shareholders are further information vulnerable because managers both have access to the information that shareholders generally lack and control the flow of information to shareholders. That is, managers may control who comes to acquire that important information and when or whether they acquire it.

Shareholder interests are protected only to the extent that managers take it upon themselves to advance the interests of shareholders and to apprise shareholders of their success or failure in that project. As such, shareholders generally lack the ability to monitor effectively their investment and the orientation of the firm's business policies toward their interests. ...

... [S]hareholders are the object of the fiduciary duties of managers because their contracts with the firm are fundamentally *incomplete.* ... Shareholders have no contractual guarantees that they will receive a return and, having once invested, may recoup their investment only if they can find another who will take their place (by purchasing their shares)—and do so at or above the price of their original investment. ... Moreover, shareholders generally lack the ability to insulate themselves against adverse policy once they have invested.

4. THE MANAGER (NONSHAREHOLDING) STAKEHOLDER RELATION

A. Employees and Suppliers

. . . Stated in terms of control and information vulnerability, employees and suppliers exhibit only limited control vulnerability. They turn control of their labor and goods over to the firm, but that control is limited by the relative ease with which employees can withdraw their labor from the firm and suppliers may interrupt the flow of their goods to the firm.

Employees and suppliers generally lack information vulnerability because their contracts with the firm require periodic specific performances by management. . . . The same analysis applies to suppliers. If the firm fails to pay the supplier in a timely manner or terminates a supply contract without the agreed-upon notice, then the supplier is apprised of the firm's performance on the contract and may then take steps to secure its interests.

By the same token, employees and suppliers generally lack that variant of information vulnerability that concerns the flow of information. This is because both action *and* inaction on the part of management conveys information about the course of performance on the contract. . . . Compare the shareholder, who may not conclude from the fact that the firm declares no dividend or that share prices fall that managers are not acting in his interests.

It would be truly strange, therefore, to extend the benefits of fiduciary duties to employees and suppliers.

B. Customers

Although, like shareholders, customers may invest money in the products of the firm up front, they are otherwise unlike shareholders. Like employees and suppliers, customers may, with relative ease, discover failures of the firm to live up to its contract (by failing to deliver what was bargained for). Moreover, they can easily terminate their relationship with the firm (by refusing to purchase more) and sue for damages if the firm has failed to live up to the bargain.

Like employees and suppliers, customers exhibit only limited control vulnerability, but generally lack information vulnerability. Therefore, it would be strange to extend fiduciary duties to customers.

C. Communities

Although, like shareholders, communities cannot readily sever their relationship with the firm, they are otherwise unlike shareholders. Communities may, by way of the law, seek to insulate themselves against losses due to their dealings with the firm through taxation, regulation, and, in extreme cases, exercise of eminent domain or outright proscription of entire industries and industrial activities within their borders. That is, communities possess significant powers via political and legal mechanisms to determine the nature and extent of their relationship with the firm. Moreover, they often have contractual agreements with firms not to relocate for a period of years in return, e.g., for tax rebates, charges for schools, sewage, and road costs. In these circumstances, communities are like other nonshareholding stakeholders: they are creditors of the firm who may easily discover breaches of their contracts and seek legal recourse for failure to perform.

In short, like employees, suppliers, and customers, communities generally exhibit at most limited control vulnerability. They do not, however, generally exhibit information vulnerability. Therefore, it would be strange to extend fiduciary duties to communities. . . .

5. THE MORAL INADEQUACY OF THE STAKEHOLDER THEORY

. . . The first conclusion is that shareholders have a legitimate moral claim to fiduciary duties from managers. . . . The second conclusion is that nonshareholding stakeholders do not have a legitimate moral claim to fiduciary duties from managers. . . . The third, and most important, conclusion is that stakeholder theory cannot account for the moral duties of managers toward their shareholders. This follows from the nonfiduciary character of the manager-stakeholder relations contemplated by stakeholder theorists argued for in part 1 and the legitimacy of shareholders' claims to fiduciary duties that falls out of the arguments of parts 2 and 3.

If shareholders have a legitimate moral claim on managers to act as fiduciaries for them, and stakeholder theory demands that managers not act as fiduciaries for anyone (including shareholders), then stakeholder theory fails to account for the legitimate moral claims of shareholders. Moreover, as stakeholder theory demands that managers be impartial among and between competing stakeholder interests, and as the very nature of a fiduciary duty requires that the one owing it practice partiality, the legitimacy of shareholders' claims to fiduciary duties from managers (and the lack of legitimacy of similar claims on the part of nonshareholding stakeholders) demonstrates that managers *cannot* be obligated to be impartial. Hence, stakeholder theory stands as a profoundly mistaken account of the moral obligations of managers generally.

NOTES

1. Some accounts of narrowly interpreted stakeholder theory include managers in this list, as well. Whether they may be subsumed by the "employees" heading, or must be regarded as a separate constituency of the firm, is a matter that need not detain us here.

2. The "coordinating" characterization is found in William M. Evan and R. Edward Freeman, "A Stakeholder Theory of the Modern Corporation: Kantian Capitalism," in *Ethical Theory and Business*, 3rd ed., ed. Tom L. Beauchamp and Norman Bowie (Englewood Cliffs, NJ: Prentice Hall, 1988), p. 103; and Freeman, "The Politics of Stakeholder Theory," in *Ethical Theory and Business*, p. 413. The "balancing" characterization is found in Thomas Donaldson and Lee E. Preston, "The Stakeholder Theory of the Corporation: Concepts, Evidence, and Implications," *Academy of Management Review* 20 (1995): 65–91, 79. The "trading-off characterization" is found in Goodpaster, "Business Ethics and Stakeholder Analysis," *Ethical Theory and Business*, p. 61.

3. Some refer to the stakeholder theory as "multifiduciary" in scare quotes, as I have done here (see, e.g., Goodpaster, "Business Ethics and Stakeholder Analysis"), suggesting the view that the stakeholder theory is not fiduciary in character. Others employ the term without scare quotes (see, e.g., Freeman, "The Politics of Stakeholder Theory"), suggesting that the stakeholder theory extends truly fiduciary duties to nonshareholding stakeholders.

4. They write: "Management bears a fiduciary relationship to stakeholders and to the corporation as an abstract entity. It must act in the interests of the stakeholders as their agent, and it must act in the interests of the corporation to ensure the survival of the firm, safeguarding the long-term stakes of each group. . . . [This] we might call The Stakeholder Fiduciary Principle . . ." (Evan and Freeman, "A Stakeholder Theory of the Modern Corporation," pp. 103–104).

5. "Fiduciary," in *Black's Law Dictionary*, 5th ed. (St. Paul, MN: West, 1979), p. 563.

6. That the fiduciary must also place the beneficiary's interests ahead of those of third parties is obvious because were the fiduciary to subordinate only his own interests to those of the beneficiary, but not those of third parties, then there would be no sense in which the beneficiary (or class of beneficiaries) is treated any differently

than third parties. The fiduciary would not have entered into any special relationship with the supposed beneficiary, but rather would merely have made an altruistic commitment to the world at large not to pursue his own interests over the project or asset he manages.

7. Evan and Freeman are perfectly aware of this point. They write: "Management, especially top management, must look after the health of the corporation, and this involves balancing the multiple claims of conflicting stakeholders. Owners want more financial returns, while customers want more money spent on research and development. Employees want higher wages and better benefits, while the local community wants better parks and daycare facilities." "A Stakeholder Theory of the Modern Corporation," p. 103, emphasis added. I say most everyone recognizes this because there exist at least some adherents of the stakeholder theory who regard conflicts among the interests of the various stakeholders in a firm as rare. See, e.g., Lee E. Preston and Harry J. Sapienza, "Stakeholder Management and Corporate Performance," *Journal of Behavioral Economics* 19 (1990): 361–75, cited approvingly in Thomas W. Dunfee and Thomas Donaldson, "Contractarian Business Ethics: Current Status and Next Steps," *Business Ethics Quarterly* 5 (1995): 173–86, 183.

8. *Matter of Heilman's Estate*, 37 Ill.App.3d 390, 345 N.E.2d 536, 540.

9. *Williams v. Griffin*, 35 Mich.App. 179, 192 N.W.2d 283, 285.

10. *Schweikhardt v. Chessen*, 161 N.E. 118, 123, 329 111, 637.

11. Robert Goodin, *Protecting the Vulnerable* (Chicago: University of Chicago Press, 1985).

12. Charles Fried, "The Lawyer as Friend: The Moral Foundations of the Lawyer-Client Relation," *Yale Law Journal* 85 (1976): 1060–89, 1077.

13. This is one way to read Boatright's argument in "Fiduciary Duties and the Shareholder-Management Relation."

11.

UPPING THE STAKES

A Response to John Hasnas on the Normative Viability of the Stockholder and Stakeholder Theories

Daniel E. Palmer

In "The Normative Theories of Business Ethics: A Guide for the Perplexed" John Hasnas provides an admirable critical survey of the three most prominent normative frameworks discussed in the current literature on business ethics: the stockholder theory, the stakeholder theory, and the social contract theory.[1] In doing so, Hasnas argues that the stockholder theory, though currently out of favor among business ethicists, is more plausible than commonly supposed and that the stakeholder theory, though the prevailing view, is prone to significant difficulties. While Hasnas's analysis of these theories is informative and often illuminating, I wish to argue here that Hasnas's reasons for favoring the stockholder theory over the stakeholder theory are not as strong as he suggests. Although Hasnas's analysis of the social contract theory also raises many interesting points, I will leave aside considerations of that theory in order to concentrate upon the claims specifically at issue between the stockholder and the stakeholder theories.

Before turning directly to Hasnas's arguments concerning the conceptual foundations of the stockholder and stakeholder theories, I first wish to briefly touch upon Hasnas's general methodological approach to theories of business ethics, as it will later become important in evaluating the strength of his claims about the viability of the theories. Hasnas, quite rightly, points out that the theories of business ethics in question occupy a sort of normative "middle ground." As Hasnas puts it, they "attempt to derive what might be called

'intermediate level' principles to mediate between the highly abstract principles of philosophical ethics and the concrete ethical dilemmas that arise in
the business environment."[2] These theories are then aimed at representing
those general ethical principles that normative ethics is concerned with establishing in a way that best exhibits their relevance and applicability to those
involved in the world of business. I wish to accent two parts of this account
that are of particular importance. First, since these theories are "mid-level,"
theories they presuppose or are dependent upon the more general theoretical
considerations discussed in normative ethics. So, in deciding between competing theories of business ethics, one needs to consider the more general
normative concerns that could count in their favor: utilitarian, deontological,
rights-based, and so forth. Second, the theories are designed to represent how
the above normative considerations are to factor into the ordinary decisions
of those involved in business in a clear and accurate fashion. Thus, the appropriate theory of business ethics will allow the businessperson to access most
clearly those considerations that our more general normative theory tells
them ought to factor into their decisions.

Bearing the above points in mind, we can now turn to Hasnas's claims
concerning the viability of the stockholder and stakeholder theories. Hasnas
first discusses the stockholder theory, for which he borrows the classic formulation by Milton Friedman that states "there is one and only one social
responsibility of business—to use its resources and engage in activities
designed to increase its profits so long as it stays within the rules of the game,
which is to say, engages in open and free competition, without deception or
fraud."[3] As Hasnas accents, this theory does not say that managers are not to
be constrained at all in their pursuit of profits, but rather that they are to pursue
profit by all legal and nondeceptive means.[4] Attention to these restrictions, as
Hasnas correctly points out, puts to rest some of the more common and exag-
gerated criticisms of the stockholder theory. Further, Hasnas again notes that
as the manager is carrying out her duty as an agent for the stockholders on this
view, if the stockholders express a desire to pursue nonprofitable activities for
the sake of social goods, then managers are not only permitted to do so but are
actually required to do so by the theory. However, since in most cases the
stockholders will express no such interest in nonprofit-generating pursuits, the
manager is to assume that their sole interest is to increase their profits and she
should act to fulfill this interest to the greatest extent.

In favor of the stockholder theory Hasnas considers two sorts of general
normative considerations: utilitarian and deontological. On the one hand, traditional proponents of the stockholder theory often made use of utilitarian

arguments by appealing to "the invisible hand" of the free market that guar-antees that the unrestrained pursuit of profit results in the greatest net benefit for all. However, Hasnas is well aware that such arguments are rather dubious and difficult to establish since: a) there is little actual empirical evi-dence that such free markets do best promote the welfare of all, and b) busi-nesses do not, in any case, presently operate under anything like the ideal free market these theories presuppose. However, Hasnas claims that the weakness of the traditional utilitarian arguments for the stockholder theory is not par-ticularly bothersome, since he thinks that a much better case can be made for the stockholder theory on deontological grounds. In this regard Hasnas states that "this argument is based on the observation that stockholders advance their money to business managers on the condition that it be used according to their wishes. If the managers accept the money on this condition and then proceed to spend it to accomplish social goals not authorized by the stock-holders, they would be violating their agreement and spending other people's money without their consent, which is wrong."[5] Thus for Hasnas, and as he remarks in a footnote for Friedman as well, the better foundation for the stockholder approach is a deontological one, based in the requirement not to spend the resources of others in ways to which they have not consented.

If the stockholder theory, in Hasnas's opinion, finds its real strength in a basic deontological obligation, the stakeholder theory, he argues, falters on that same deontological rock. The stakeholder theory, as a normative theory of ethics, and not an empirical theory of management, requires that a man-ager ought to form her managerial decisions by "balancing the conflicting claims of multiple stakeholders."[6] Though widely accepted, Hasnas claims that this theory "seems to lack clear normative foundation."[7] Hasnas does review one Kantian-type theory based upon the notion of respect for persons that has been offered in support of the stakeholder theory. However, Hasnas claims that any such theory is bound to turn against itself since, considering the interests of other parties in making their decisions, managers would "break their agreement with the stockholders to use business resources only as authorized . . . [and thus] would be violating the autonomy of the stock-holders."[8] As such, Hasnas claims that deontological considerations must favor the stockholder theory over the stakeholder theory.

Here I will argue that the case that Hasnas offers against the stakeholder theory is not as strong as he portrays it, at least given a certain interpretation of that theory.

Let us now consider the issue from the deontological perspective, the perspective from which Hasnas believes the stockholder theory derives its real strength over the stakeholder theory. Hasnas thinks that deontological considerations favor the stockholder approach, we have seen, because of the basic deontological constraint placed upon a manager due to her commitment to act as an agent for the interests of the stockholders. Hasnas is right to think that any plausible deontological theory will recognize such an obligation. However, does this alone show that a deontological theory will necessarily favor the stockholder approach? This will be so only if there are no other deontological obligations present that might mitigate a manager's obligations toward the stockholders. . . . It is just this possibility that I wish to argue for, suggesting that a certain kind of deontological theory might be understood to plausibly support a stakeholder approach to business ethics.

First, consider the following, admittedly fanciful, scenario. Kim is an executive manager in charge of purchasing for a retail clothing company. Available to Kim are two sources of a certain type of shirt that is carried in her stores, call them Company A and Company B. Both operate in developing third world countries. Company A can produce the shirts at a slightly cheaper rate, but makes use of child labor, pollutes the environment, and is financially connected with an oppressive government regime. All of these activities are, however, perfectly legal in the country in which Company A operates. Company B, on the other hand, charges a bit more for their product than Company A, but is extremely progressive, relative to other developing nations, in regard to employment and environmental practices and in its general commitment to sustainable economic and social development. Ruling out all other side effects for the sake of the argument, if the only consideration, other than legality and nondeception, that is to guide Kim's decision as a manager is the promotion of profit, then it seems clear that she ought to contract with Company A and not Company B. But to most of us it seems wrong, if not morally preposterous, not to have Kim consider these other facts about Company A in making her decision. Of course, I do not want the case to rest on our intuitions about a particular example alone, but I do want to suggest that if we take this kind of scenario seriously, we might begin to see how deontological constraints operate in our moral thinking.

What the above example is designed to illustrate is that one can acknowledge a basic obligation on the part of Kim toward her stockholders to produce a profit and also recognize other general obligations that she has as a result of her business position as well. And, many sorts of deontological theories are sensitive to just this fact in accounting for the nature of our obligations. In particular, W. D. Ross's notion of *prima facie* obligations was designed to capture precisely this idea of us having certain types of general obligations; obligations to keep our commitments, to not harm others, and so on.[9] However, Ross also recognized that simply because we have a *prima facie* obligation to do something, that does not entail that our actual obligation is to do that in a given situation. This is because, as pointed out above, we have many *prima facie* obligations and in some situations we may be unable to act in such a way as to fulfill all of these *prima facie* obligations. For instance, I may only be able to help a hurt bystander if I break my promise to meet a friend for lunch. Thus, in order to determine our actual obligation in any given situation we need to survey all of our *prima facie* obligations and determine which of these carries the most moral weight in the particular circumstances at hand. Simply having a *prima facie* obligation toward a particular person or group, such as stockholders, does not entail that this will always be our actual obligation, since we may well have other *prima facie* obligations that are more significant in some contexts. Hasnas is therefore wrong to think that simply showing that business managers have some obligation toward their stockholders entails that they cannot also have other sorts of obligations or that those obligations could never outweigh or mitigate their obligation toward the stockholders.

What I am suggesting is that at least one type of deontological theory, a Ross-style pluralism, actually favors a stakeholder theory over a stockholder theory. On this view, although the stockholder theory rightly accents a manager's central contractual obligation toward the stock owners, it wrongly supposes either that no other ethical obligations are ever relevant to business situations, or that such obligations could never outweigh the obligation a manager has toward the stockholders. Indeed, the stockholder position seems to rely upon a rather rigorous view of deontological principles that results in well-known problems: illustrated, for instance, by the oft-referred-to picture of the Kantian who tells the psychotic murderer where her friend is hiding because she refuses to tell a lie.[10] Ross-style pluralism could underwrite a stakeholder theory that is sensitive to the fact that in our business engagements many of our general obligations might become relevant, and that while the ethical manager will always have a *prima facie* obligation toward those who have invested their money in her trust, she must be sensitive to her other general obligations that may, at times, be of more moral importance. A businessperson thus must consider all of the possible *prima facie* obligations that could be relevant to any one of their decisions, that is to all of those who might have a moral stake upon their action.[11] Discharging one's obligations on this view is a matter of best weighing and balancing the various obligations that one incurs in one's relations with others in whatever activities one engages in, a view that is well suited to at least a certain version of the stakeholder theory.[12] Ironically, the stockholder theory seems itself to nod toward an acknowledgment of this point, for why else does the theory include the restrictions concerning honesty and legality, which otherwise seem ad hoc, that it does?

Further support for this view of how the business manager ought to think about the nature of her obligations can be given by considering the very nature of the obligation that Hasnas thinks serves as the basis of the stockholder theory, the obligation toward the stock owners. There are at least two difficulties with understanding this obligation as an absolute obligation to do whatever possible, again barring dishonest or illegal means, to increase the profits of the stock owners. First, it seems clear that we can easily imagine possible situations in which the best way to increase the absolute profits of the present stockholders would also involve doing things that would severely damage the long-term stability of the company. But if our only obligation is to the present stockholders, it seems as if the stockholder theory commits the manager to acting in those ways. The kind of stakeholder theory underpinned by a Ross-style pluralism, however, recognizes that while a manager has an obligation to procure profits for the present stockholders, she may also have other obligations, toward employees, the company, and perhaps even future stockholders and herself as well, that mitigate the absolute pursuit of that obligation. Second, if the only obligation that the manager has is to increase profits for the stockholder, then it seems clear that there will be possible scenarios in which they must do something, though legal and honest, that clearly seems unethical as well; say making use of slave labor in a country where it is legal. But clearly we cannot have an *ethical* obligation to do things that are unethical. And thus if one is even willing to acknowledge, as most of us are, a plurality of general deontological constraints or principles, it cannot make sense to say that a manager's obligation to the stockholders is so absolute as to *a priori* outweigh any other moral concerns. Such an obligation could hardly be an ethical obligation at all. Again, the stockholder theory appears insensitive to the plurality of obligations that one can have and to the different strengths that these obligations can have upon us in varying situations. The stakeholder theory better represents the plurality and degrees of the various obligations applicable to our actual choices, and gives the businessperson a more plausible framework in which to think about the nature and extent of those obligations. . . .

NOTES

1. John Hasnas, "The Normative Theories of Business Ethics: A Guide for the Perplexed," *Business Ethics Quarterly* 8 (1998): 19–42.

2. Ibid., p. 20.

3. Ibid., p. 22.

4. Like Hasnas, I will limit my discussion in this response to the decisions of business managers in for-profit corporations, assuming that the conclusions generated could be expanded to apply to persons involved at all levels and in all forms of businesses.

5. Hasnas, "Normative Theories of Business Ethics," p. 23.

6. Ibid., p. 26.

7. Ibid.

8. Ibid., p. 28.

9. For Ross's discussion of prima facie obligations see W. D. Ross, *The Right and the Good* (Oxford: Oxford University Press, 1930), particularly chapter 2.

10. Of course, I do not mean to imply that this sort of caricature correctly represents the Kantian viewpoint, only that it does bring to the fore a problem with any sort of view that takes too stringent a view of the nature of our individual deontological obligations.

11. Notice that this sort of theory would not entail, as Hasnas thinks stakeholder theories do, that anyone who can have a stake in the decision of a manager should get equal consideration in their decision. The kind of consideration the manager should give any party is dependent upon the kind of relation they have to that party and the kind of prima facie obligations that are relevant to that kind of relationship. For instance, the kind of obligation that a parent has toward his or her own children is stronger than the kind of obligation he or she has toward other people's children, though they still have some obligations toward those children, i.e., an obligation not to harm them or to deceive them.

12. Again, the stakeholder theory defended here will not be exactly the same as that which Hasnas's discussion presupposes. Its basis in the notion of prima facie duties requires a manager to consider only the various types of obligations that may be relevant to her decisions. As some of these prima facie obligations may not coincide with her actual obligation, it does not necessarily require that she always act to fulfill the interests of anyone who has a stake in her decision. Likewise the theory is perfectly compatible with Hasnas's claim that "individuals do not become burdened with unagreed-upon obligations by going into or joining a business," as the prima facie obligations in question are just general obligations that persons always have. The theory merely requires the manager to consider which of her prima facie obligations are relevant to her business engagements and to consider all of them in determining what her actual obligation is.

12.

GETTING REAL

Stakeholder Theory, Managerial Practice, and the General Irrelevance of Fiduciary Duties Owed to Shareholders

Richard Marens and Andrew Wicks

INTRODUCTION

O ver the last several years, business ethicists (Goodpaster, 1991; Boatright, 1994; Freeman, 1994; Goodpaster and Holloran, 1994; Donaldson and Preston, 1995) have disputed the implications for stakeholder theory of the fiduciary obligations owed by corporate management to shareholders. They have argued extensively as to whether this duty privileges shareholders and whether public policy could or should recalibrate the balance *vis-à-vis* other groups. The actual impact of these fiduciary responsibilities upon real-world business practice has received comparatively little attention. This paper attempts to address this neglect through a thorough examination of the relevant case law. In doing so, the authors have arrived at two conclusions. The first is that the existence of a fiduciary duty owed to stockholders presents few practical problems for a management team that wishes to implement a stakeholder-oriented approach to business. Second, the specific responsibilities generated by this fiduciary duty are in no way "over and above" the kind of treatment shareholders could reasonably expect to receive under a stakeholder regime. . . .

THE "STAKEHOLDER PARADOX"

Since Freeman's (1984) seminal book on stakeholder theory appeared in print, scholars of business ethics have increasingly used stakeholder theory as a conceptual framework to discuss the ethical dimensions and implications of corporate activity. Freeman began the discussion by arguing that successful managers must systematically attend to the interests of various stakeholder groups. . . .

Since each class of stakeholder has a different legal, economic, and social relationship to a particular business, a general stakeholder approach does not explain how managers should balance different kinds of dependencies. Particularly troublesome is the legal reality that managers owe shareholders a "fiduciary" duty not generally granted to any other group. While Donaldson and Preston (1995) are correct in pointing to contractual obligations and regulatory responsibilities designed to protect other groups from specific malefeasances such as discrimination or pollution, we argue below that Goodpaster (1991, 1994) was also accurate in characterizing the duty to stockholders as more general and proactive than what other constituencies can claim.

Goodpaster, however, goes further than this by insisting on a potential conflict arising out of this legal asymmetry, arguing for the existence of a "stakeholder paradox," where corporate management would find themselves (under all but the most ideal circumstances) having to choose between fulfilling this fiduciary duty and serving the interests of other stakeholders. Boatright (1994) argued that this paradox could be overcome by extending the fiduciary duty to cover other stakeholders, a suggestion criticized by Goodpaster and Holloran (1994) as both impractical and potentially unwise.

Freeman (1994) took a different approach, suggesting that the stakeholder paradox was fundamentally linked to the separation thesis—a conceptual artifact that both presupposes and reinforces the divisions between ethics and business. He also claimed that the mere existence of fiduciary duties owed to shareholders are theoretically irrelevant to the normative justification of stakeholder theory since such duties themselves must be morally defended and do not give managers license to violate normative ethics in their interactions with nonstockholders.[1] Donaldson and Preston (1995) go even further by suggesting that the legislation of protections to other groups implies that the broader norms of ethical behavior are consistent with stakeholder philosophy.

Not all behavior, however, that might be defensible as consistent with normative ethics will always prevail in a court of law, the arena in which legal rights are established and applied. Consequently, directors and managers might rightly concern themselves with their legal as well as their ethical position in relating to various stakeholder groups. As this paper will make clear, however, they have little to fear. An examination of the origin and meaning of fiduciary responsibility shows that this duty does little to threaten managers who set out to implement stakeholder-oriented policies.

THE ASYMMETRY OF LEGAL RELATIONSHIPS WITHIN THE CORPORATE "WEB"

Courts did not historically encumber corporate management with a fiduciary duty toward company stockholders in order to privilege shareholders vis-à-vis other stakeholder groups. Rather, it was designed to prevent self-dealing on the part of directors and top management that fell short of criminal behavior such as embezzlement.[2] . . .

When conflict of interest is not at issue, no case law or corporate statute argues that management's fiduciary duty should be equated with a right of stockholders to oversee managerial decision making.[3] If business ethicists seem to implicitly assume otherwise, the source of this misconception is not hard to deduce. Stakeholder theory is, at least in part, a response to neoclassical theories of the firm that impose an empirically false symmetry of legal relationships among corporate constituencies. By assuming that there might be some truth to such legal chimeras as "nexus of contracts" and "agency theory," stakeholder theorists would reasonably counter that these legal relationships are inadequate to support a stakeholder approach to business management. If stakeholder theorists erred, it was in assuming that these hypothesized relationships had some basis in law.

Corporations are not, in any meaningful legal sense, nexus of contracts, nor are directors agents of stockholders. To take the second point first, "agency"[4] is a highly specific two-way relationship in which the principal can direct or override the agent and the agent can, under highly restricted circumstances, legally bind or create liabilities for the principal. Neither directional arrow holds, in any meaningful way, between stockholder and director. Not only do individual stockholders lack legal standing to specify details of how a business should be managed, directors and top managers can neither bind individual shareholders to contracts with third parties or generate personal liabilities for them through debt or tort. On the other hand, directors (and their agents, high-level managers) can legally bind the corporate entity as a whole to either contractual obligations or financial liability.

This distinction is not merely semantic. The duties required of a fiduciary are not to obey a person, as an agent might, but to make every effort to protect their property, in this case the funds or other assets the stockholder has exchanged for corporate shares. As a fiduciary, a corporate director's relationship is not with the shareholder personally but with her investment.

Not only is this relationship not that of agency, it is also not contractual in any legally meaningful way. The general fiduciary obligation is one of fulfilling a normatively defined level of responsibility toward beneficiaries with little connection to contract law and its underlying presumption of voluntary bargaining between informed parties.[5] By contrast, the fiduciary principle evolved from the far older law of property, which directs trustees to manage property in the interest of those judged incompetent to do so themselves, historically because of age, gender, or infirmity.[6] . . .

The beneficiary/fiduciary relationship is considerably more straightforward than those derived from contracts in which parties negotiate some terms and explicitly or implicitly adopt others from extant regulations or currently accepted practices.[7] The typical penalty for breach of contract involves monetary damages, making all but the most egregious breaches a business decision as to whether cost of the penalty (and, possibly, damage to reputation) exceeds the gain from repudiation. By contrast, the fiduciary duties required of trustees—honesty, adequate care for the entrusted property, providing the owner with any relevant information, avoiding any unauthorized personal gain even when such gain does not hurt the beneficiary[8]— are not typically subject to negotiation, and a judge would carefully scrutinize the circumstances of any claim that a beneficiary freed the fiduciary from any of these duties.[9]

As a result, contractual duties and fiduciary duties are measured differently. Contractees are expected to complete certain acts while fiduciaries are required to act under certain motives. In the corporate setting, fiduciary duties do not impose a requirement that a business be run in a certain manner. No court equates this duty with "maximizing shareholder value," even assuming such an indeterminate concept could be estimated. What the duty does require is honesty and candor in the relationship with the stockholder and a general avoidance of using one's office for illegitimate personal gain. Traditionally such illegitimate self-dealing might have meant dealing with another company because a director has some financial interest in the other concern. A more modern application might mean keeping stockholders from voting on a tender offer because the inside directors fear for their jobs. There is nothing in the relationship that absolutely bars acts of generosity on the part of fiduciaries who are not themselves the beneficiary of the act, unless such generosity can be shown to harm the beneficiary.

Given the modest nature of this duty list, there are at least three reasons to doubt that they provide any serious obstacle to the implementation of stakeholder principles. First, it is not obvious that the right of shareholders to expect honesty, candor, and care on the part of management gives them a higher level of protection than the legal rights available to other stakeholders. Creditor interests, for example, are protected by bankruptcy law. Suppliers and customers can seek redress under the Uniform Commercial Code or more recent statutes such as "lemon laws" that cover used car sales. Tort victims are the beneficiaries of insurance requirements for various kinds of businesses. And employees can enlist government assistance in collecting unpaid wages or compensation for income-diminishing injuries and can demand fiduciary protection for pension assets and other benefits.[10]

Second, courts are starting to impose on corporate management fiduciary duties with regard to other groups under certain circumstances. . . . [T]he Supreme Court ruled in *Varity v. Howe* (1996) that a corporation that reorganized all of its money-losing ventures into a single subsidiary that eventually went bankrupt (leaving a healthy surviving parent) had breached its fiduciary duty to the employees of the subsidiary. The company had not only urged employees to transfer to the subsidiary without disclosing its precarious condition, it even transferred the benefit administration of several retirees to the subsidiary without their knowledge. As a result the parent corporation and several of its executives were found to have violated duties created under the Employee Retirement Income Security Act (ERISA) and assumed by corporations that administer their own benefit plans.[11] The Court . . . extended this reasoning to the protection of nonretirement benefits when it found for employees dismissed after refusing to accept employment with another company, but a company with whom their original employer had arranged for them to do exactly the same work but with reduced benefits (*Intermodal v. Sante Fe Railroad*, 1997).

And finally, as we will demonstrate in detail below, when stockholders have attempted to challenge managerial behavior as being overly generous toward another constituency, they have almost always lost.

BUT WHAT ABOUT *DODGE BROS. V. FORD?*

Stakeholder theorists who argue that shareholder interests are (fortunately or unfortunately) paramount typically cite the famous dictum from the Michigan case *Dodge Bros. v. Ford* that "the corporation exists for the benefit of the shareholders"[12] as evidence of a restraint on the discretion of management. Leaving aside the question as to whether dicta from a state court decision remains influential after more than seventy-five years, an examination of the context of the statement and the circumstances of the lawsuit makes it clear that this perspective was not meant to empower the shareholder at the expense of managerial discretion.

The lawsuit was aimed at Henry Ford's tightfisted dividend policy. Ford Motors had become one of the world's most profitable companies and was literally piling up unspent cash that it could not invest fast enough, yet was recently refusing to pay out much more than 1 percent of its net income in dividends. Because it was the company's principal shareholder, Henry Ford, who managed the company, this was a classic case of upholding the rights of minority shareholders against the tyranny of a majority investor. Ford Motors was, at the time, a privately held corporation and courts have been particularly sensitive to protect minority interests in such firms,[13] such as the Dodge Brothers plaintiffs'. Unlike holders of publicly traded shares, minority shareholders in a private corporation are not usually in a position to readily sell out and thereby exit from an unsatisfactory relationship and by definition minority holders possess little or no power to replace an unsatisfactory board of directors with one more amenable to their perspective. . . .

The court rejected Henry Ford's defense that "my ambition is to employ still more men, to spread the benefits of this industrial system to the greatest possible number, to help them build up their lives and their homes."[14] While his assertion is usually taken at face value to violate accepted norms of proper business purpose, the court may well have been aware that he was speaking with dubious sincerity.[15] . . . But whatever Ford's true motives were, it would be difficult to imagine that any normative stakeholder theory would deny shareholders the right to share in some of the prosperity generated by a successful business.

It should also be noted that the court did not hold that investors could interfere with managerial business planning or insist that their immediate financial gain become the only consideration of the board of directors. The judge actually dismissed most of the complaints filed by the Dodge Brothers, holding, for example, that Ford and his fellow directors had the right to plan the business as they judged best, free from second guessing on such business decisions as expanding production and smelting his own iron, and certainly under no obligation to forego these in favor of distributing further dividends.

Moreover, there is no evidence that the decision in any way affected Henry Ford's peculiar brand of paternalism in relations toward his employees. The court did not prevent Ford from continuing to pay higher-than-market wages or prevent him from subjecting them to speed-ups, invasions of privacy, and expectations of social conformity that went far beyond what was attempted by other employers. Working for Ford remained a trade-off of high wages and tight behavioral restriction.[16]

Reading the case, one might reasonably conclude that it strongly confirmed the principle that shareholders cannot interfere with managerial decisions that can be plausibly justified as enhancing business performance. The court acknowledged that Ford could build new plants, vertically integrate, or otherwise run the business as he saw fit. What they forbade was the company's decision to sit on a mountain of cash for allegedly philanthropic, not business, purposes, particularly when the court had reasons to doubt Ford's candor regarding his actual motive.

In fact, since *Dodge Bros. v. Ford*, courts have proven very reluctant to force corporations to pay out additional dividends or otherwise examine the economic wisdom of business decisions.[17] In *Grobow v. GM* (1988), the board of directors was permitted to exercise its collective judgment that paying H. Ross Perot seven hundred million dollars in order to remove him from the board of directors was in the best interest of the corporation. In finding a legitimate business purpose in spending these funds to eliminate Perot's unflagging dissension (as opposed to larger dividends or new investments), the highly influential Delaware Supreme Court implied that there would be few decisions not involving outright self-dealing that stockholders could enjoin boards from making.

DOING WELL BY DOING GOOD

An examination of a century of case law under circumstances less dramatic than what faced the Michigan Court in 1919 demonstrates that corporate managers have successfully defended generosity and consideration toward nonshareholding constituents. In the process, courts have often accepted arguments that anticipated instrumental stakeholder theory.[18] Whatever skepticism the court expressed in *Dodge Bros. v. Ford* toward charitable giving has largely disappeared in American jurisprudence since *A. F. Smith v. Barlow* recognized in 1953 an enlightened self-interest rationale for spending profits in this manner.[19] Similarly, courts established long ago that corporations can voluntarily agree to pay a tax bill that is higher than the law might strictly require as part of a political compromise with local communities (*Kelly v. Bell*, 1969). General Motors . . . applied this principle when, having won the right in court to disregard its own promises made in return for a property tax reduction, it agreed to a new investment program with the offended community.[20]

Historically, generosity toward employees has almost always won when, unlike in *Dodge Bros.*, the generous treatment is justified as a means of improving efficiency or productivity. In *Steinway v. Steinway and Sons* (1909), a family shareholder lost his court challenge to the building of a company town for manufacturing employees on the grounds that such an act of communitarianism would improve labor relations, and, as the court noted, help keep out unions. Later, corporations routinely defeated challenges by stockholders to various bonus and profit-sharing plans when justified by creating incentives for better corporate performance (*Diamond v. Davis*, 1935; *Gallin v. National City Bank*, 1945) until they too became legally unassailable.

ESOPs, or Employee Stock Ownership Plans, might appear to be theoretically more vulnerable to challenge since they often require the assumption of debt or the dilution of current stock holdings to implement. Yet, except in very rare cases in which the ESOP was thrown together at the last minute to prevent a takeover . . . ESOPs have been consistently upheld by courts as consistent with management's right to set personnel policy and select means of raising productivity (see *Herald v. Seawall*, 1972). One court, (In re *Dunkin Donuts*, 1990) even accepted management's argument that an ESOP would help heal the effects of a corporate downsizing on surviving employees.

One might argue that the need to justify acts of generosity through a finding of a rational business purpose such as higher productivity, long-term earning horizons, or beneficial public relations limits a stakeholder approach to a very timid instrumental use of the concept. However, it is also important for stakeholder theorists to understand that courtrooms are not forums for the expression of deeply held moral philosophy. Lawyers are trained to make the most conservative, precedent-supported argument that can plausibly defend a particular act or policy.

No competent attorney would allow her client to argue in court that their corporation made a decision because it "was the right thing to do" in the face of evidence that management knew of legal alternatives whose impact on the bottom line, short term and long term, were indisputably superior. It may smack of moral cowardice, but given the uncertainty of what sustains and makes a business profitable over a period of years, virtually any act that does not financially threaten the survival of the business could be construed as in the long-term best interest of shareholders. . . .

NOTES

1. See also Tom Jones, "Instrumental Stakeholder Theory: A Synthesis of Ethics and Economics," *Academy of Management Review* 20, no. 2 (1995): 404–24.

2. Victor Brudney, "Corporate Governance, Agency Costs, and the Rhetoric of Contract," *Colombia Law Review* 85, no. 7 (1985): 1403–44; Robert C. Clark, "Agency Costs versus Fiduciary Duties," in *Principals and Agents*, ed. John Pratt and Richard Zeckhauser (Boston: Harvard University Press, 1985).

3. Brudney, "Corporate Governance"; Lawrence E. Mitchell, review of "The Economic Structure of Corporate Law," *Texas Law Review* 71, no. 1 (1992): 217–42.

4. Clark, "Agency Costs."

5. Mitchell, "The Economic Structure."

6. Robert L. Mennell, *Wills and Trusts in a Nutshell* (St. Paul: West, 1994); Mitchell, "The Economic Structure."

7. Mitchell, "The Economic Structure."

8. Dennis J. Block et al., *The Business Judgment Rule: Fiduciary Duties of Corporate Directors* (Englewood Cliffs, NJ: Prentice Hall Law and Business, 1989).

9. Mitchell, "The Economic Structure."

10. Thomas Donaldson and L. E. Preston, "The Stakeholder Theory of the Corporation: Concepts, Evidence, and Implications," *Academy of Management Review* 20 (1995): 65–91.

11. James B. Shein, "A Limit on Downsizing: *Varity Corp. v. Howe*," *Pepperdine Law Review* 24, no. 1 (1996): 1–35.

12. Kenneth Goodpaster, "Business Ethics and Stakeholder Analysis," *Business Ethics Quarterly* 1 (1991): 69; John Boatright, "What's So Special about Shareholders?" *Business Ethics Quarterly* 4 (1994): 393–408.

13. Lawrence E. Mitchell et al., *Corporate Finance and Governance: Cases, Materials, and Problems* (Durham, NC: Carolina Academic Press, 1996).

14. *Dodge Bros. v. Ford* 170 N.W. 668 (Mich 1919), p. 505.

15. Anne Jardim, *The First Henry Ford: A Study in Personality and Business Leadership* (Cambridge, MA: MIT Press, 1970).

16. Stephen Meyer, *The Five Dollar Day: Labor Management and Social Control in the Ford Motor Company* (Albany: SUNY Press, 1981).

17. Victor Brudney, "Dividends, Discretion, and Disclosure," *Virginia Law Review* 66, no. 1 (1980): 85–129.

18. See Jones, "Instrumental Stakeholder Theory."

19. Gary von Stange, "Corporate Social Responsibility through Constituency Statutes: Legend or Lie?" *Hofstra Labor Law Journal* 11, no. 2 (1995): 461–97.

20. April Hattori, "General Motors Agrees to Seek New Use for Shuttered Plant," *Bond Buyer* (1994).

13.

WHAT STAKEHOLDER THEORY IS NOT

Robert Phillips, R. Edward Freeman, and Andrew Wicks

At its current stage of theoretical development, stakeholder theory may be undermined from at least two directions: distortions and friendly misinterpretations.[1] Some have sought to critique the theory based upon their own stylized conception of the theory and its implications. Though not always without some textual evidence for such characterizations, we argue that many of these distortions represent straw-person versions of the theory. At the least, the critical (mis)interpretations do not represent the strongest, most defensible variation of stakeholder theory. . . .

CRITICAL DISTORTIONS

Stakeholder Theory Is an Excuse for Managerial Opportunism

The shareholder wealth maximization imperative is frequently motivated by so-called agency problems: hazards arising from the separation of risk bearing and decision making (also known as ownership and control, respectively). The concern is that without this moral imperative, managers would enrich themselves at the expense of the organization and the recipients of its residual cash flows, the shareholders. . . .

Rather than morally superior, therefore, stakeholder theory is actually immoral inasmuch as it ignores this agency relationship—or so goes the argument.[2] This criticism is, however, the result of the over-extended metaphor of agency theory in economics. If managers are agents or fiduciaries at all, it is to the *organization* and not to the shareowners. Clark (1985) writes:

> To an experienced corporate lawyer who has studied primary legal materials, the assertion that corporate managers are agents of investors, whether debtholders or stockholders, will seem odd or loose. The lawyer would make the following points: (1) corporate officers like the president and treasurer are agents of the corporation itself; (2) the board of directors is the ultimate decision-making body of the corporation (and in a sense is the group most appropriately identified with 'the corporation'); (3) directors are not agents of the corporation but are *sui generis*; (4) neither officers nor directors are agents of the stockholders; but (5) both officers and directors are 'fiduciaries' with respect to the corporation and its stockholders.[3]

The corporation is not coextensive with the shareholders. It is an entity unto itself. It may enter into contracts and own property (including its own stock[4] or that of other corporations). It has standing in a court of law. Limited liability assures that shareowners are not, in general, personally liable for the debts of the organization.[5] Top managers are agents for the corporation and this is not merely a shorthand way of saying that they are agents for the shareholders. The corporation is meaningfully distinct.[6] The same goes for other limited liability . . . partnerships to the extent that it is the partnership that has legal standing separate from that of the partners themselves and the partners enjoy immunity from personal responsibility for the actions and debts of the organization.

Some have suggested that stakeholder theory provides unscrupulous managers with a ready excuse to act in their own self-interest thus resurrecting the agency problem that the shareholder wealth maximization imperative was designed to overcome. Opportunistic managers can more easily act in their own self-interest by claiming that the action actually benefits some stakeholder group or other.[7] "All but the most egregious self-serving managerial behavior will doubtless serve the interests of *some* stakeholder constituencies and work against the interests of others"[8] and by appealing to the interests of those who benefit, the manager is able to justify the self-serving behavior. Hence, stakeholder theory, "effectively destroys business accountability . . . because a business that is accountable to all, is actually accountable to none."[9]

The first response to this criticism is to point out that no small measure of managerial opportunism has occurred in the name of shareholder wealth maximization. In addition to the debacles at Enron and WorldCom, one need only consider the now-dethroned king of shareholder wealth Al Dunlap for an illustration.[10] Dunlap grossly mismanaged at least two companies to his own significant financial gain. And every move he made was in the name of shareholder wealth. Dunlap agreed to pay $15 million to settle a lawsuit brought by the shareholders of Sunbeam Corporation.[11] There is little reason to believe that stakeholder theory will provide any more or less justification for the opportunistic manager.

This criticism of stakeholder theory is a version of the evil genie argument. Managerial opportunism is a problem, but it is no more a problem for stakeholder theory than the alternatives. Indeed, there may be some reason to believe stakeholder theory is more resistant to managerial self-dealing. In their discussion of "stakeholder-agency" theory, Hill and Jones (1992) argue that managers' interest in organizational growth (citing remuneration, power, job security, and status as motivating this interest) runs contrary not only to the interests of stockholders, but also contrary to the interests of stakeholders. They write, "[o]bviously, the claims of different groups may conflict. . . . However, on a more general level, each group can be seen as having a stake in the continued existence of the firm."[12] Stakeholder theory, therefore, does not advocate the service of two masters. Rather, managers serve the interest of one master: the organization.

Stakeholder Theory Cannot Provide a Specific Objective Function for the Corporation

Another common critique concerns the "radical underdeterminism" of stakeholder theory. That is, "In rejecting the maximization of long-term owner value as the purpose of business, and requiring business instead simply to 'balance' the interests of all stakeholders, stakeholder theory discards the objective basis for evaluating business action,"[13] and the theory fails to be "illuminatingly action-guiding."[14]

In one sense, this critique is accurate. Stakeholder theory does fail to provide an algorithm for day-to-day managerial decision making. This is due to the level of abstraction at which the discussion is taking place. Stakeholder theory provides a method by which stakeholder obligations are derived and an admonition that managers must account for the interests of these stakeholders when making decisions. It is impossible to say *a priori* what these interests will be and how they may be accounted for due to the myriad ways that an organization might be arranged. Hence, it is impossible for such a theory to dictate specific action in the abstract.

However, this is another example of an evil genie criticism. The same critique may be leveled at the conventional shareholder-centered view. That is, the managerial dictate to maximize shareholder wealth stands mute when queried. How? This is because there are innumerable ways to do so.[15] Indeed, this indeterminacy and the impossibility of a one right way to manage is the reason for the business judgment rule discussed above and the courts' hesitance to pierce the corporate veil.

Ostensible critics of stakeholder theory, including Jensen and Sternberg, eagerly embrace an instrumental variation of stakeholder management as a means to "maximize the total market value of the firm" or "maximize long-term owner value," respectively. In his critique of stakeholder theory, Jensen concedes that, "value maximizing says nothing about how to create a superior vision or strategy,"[16] though "Maximizing the total market value of the firm—that is the sum of the market values of the equity, debt and any other contingent claims outstanding on the firm—is one objective function that will resolve the tradeoff problem among multiple constituencies."[17]

Perhaps taking the organization's objective function to be the maximization of total market value (or profits or wealth) does make *ex post* measurement of success more determinate than optimizing the well-being of multiple stakeholders.[18] Distributing the value thus created is a simpler matter for "shareholder theory" than for stakeholder theory as well. Shareholder theory could, thus, be considered superior in light of the fact of bounded rationality and the limits on human cognitive capacity. There is no reason to believe, however, that stakeholder management would be any easier or the theory more determinate *ex ante* when undertaken for instrumental rather than normative reasons. Moreover, every *ex post* decision provides the *ex ante* circumstances for the next set of decisions. Even considering value maximization as a scorekeeping device[19] is problematic when the score for the current game determines how subsequent games are played and coached.

As for the argument from simplicity, Albert Einstein is quoted as advising, "Make things as simple as possible—but no simpler." The theory and practice of management certainly can be simplified—consider bookstore shelves packed with books on how to manage in a minute. Simplicity, however, is not the lone criterion of usefulness. There is no reason to believe that stakeholder management would be any easier or the theory more determinate when undertaken for instrumental rather than normative reasons.

The belief that maximizing "the total market value of the firm" or "long-term owner value" is more determinate than the balancing of stakeholder interests may itself prove dangerous due to what we may term the delusion of determinacy. That is, under conditions of uncertainty and bounded rationality, managers may be led to believe that the standard objective function dictates action in a way that is more specific than stakeholder theory. It does not—and the belief that it does gives managers an unfounded sense of confidence in their decisions. Managerial wisdom and judgment are replaced with a false sense of mathematical precision. . . .

Stakeholder Management Means That All Stakeholders Must Be Treated Equally

It is commonly asserted that stakeholder theory implies that all stakeholders must be treated equally irrespective of the fact that some obviously contribute more than others to the organization.[20] Prescriptions of equality have been inferred from discussions of "balancing" stakeholder interests and are in direct conflict with the advice of some experts on organizational design and reward systems.[21]

Marcoux is among those who make this criticism in his analysis of the concept of balance in stakeholder theory. He begins by outlining three potential interpretations of balance (or equity) on a stakeholder account:

Egalitarianism—Distribution based on something like Rawls's
    difference principle.[22]
Equalitarianism—Equal shares for all stakeholders.
Pareto-Consequentialism—Making at least one better without
    diminishing anyone.

Marcoux's arguments against these three candidates are largely sound. However, he misses one of the more obvious—and indeed strongest—interpretations of balance among organizational stakeholders: meritocracy.[23] On the most defensible conception of stakeholder theory, benefits are distributed based on relative contribution to the organization. This interpretation is suggested in a quotation from the Sloan Colloquy. They write, "Corporations should attempt to distribute the benefits of their activities as equitably as possible among stakeholders, *in light of their respective contributions, costs, and risks.*"[24] Inasmuch as this quote was used early in the paper to exemplify the centrality of balance to stakeholder theory, it is surprising that Marcoux fails to appeal to it in his own interpretations of balance.

Similarly, Sternberg argues that "in maintaining that all stakeholders are of equal importance to a business, and that business ought to be answerable equally to them all, stakeholder theory confounds business with government."[25] She cites no author, however, who argues for such equality of importance or managerial answerability. This is, again, suggestive of a straw-person argument. A meritocratic interpretation of stakeholder balance overcomes the objection that a stakeholder-based firm using either the egalitarian or equalitarian interpretation would be unable to obtain equity or any other manner of financing. Certainly equity financing is centrally important to organizations and, as such, providers of this capital would garner a substantial portion of the economic benefits of the firm as well as receive a great deal of managerial attention in organizational decision making. On the conception of stakeholder theory proffered here, shareholders would get a fair return on their investment without managerial concern that is exclusive of other groups to whom an obligation is due.[26] Still less does the stakeholder theory confuse an organization with the state. As discussed below, stakeholder theory is a theory of organizational strategy and ethics and NOT a theory of the whole political economy.

This meritocratic hierarchy isn't the only criterion by which stakeholders may be arranged. Phillips (2003) has suggested that stakeholders may usefully be separated into normative and derivative stakeholders. Normative stakeholders are those to whom the organization has a direct moral obligation to attend to their well-being. They provide the answer to seminal stakeholder query, "For whose benefit ought the firm be managed?" Typically normative stakeholders are those most frequently cited in stakeholder discussions such as financiers, employees, customers, suppliers, and local communities.

Alternatively, derivative stakeholders are those groups or individuals who can either harm or benefit the organization, but to whom the organization has no direct moral obligation as stakeholders.[27] This latter group might include such groups as competitors, activists, terrorists, and the media.[28] The organization is not managed for the benefit of derivative stakeholders, but to the extent that they may influence the organization or its normative stakeholders, managers are obliged to account for them in their decision making. Far from strict equality, therefore, there are a number of more convincing ways that stakeholder theory may distinguish between and among constituency groups. . . .

FRIENDLY MISINTERPRETATIONS

Stakeholder Theory Is a Comprehensive Moral Doctrine

In his discussion of the idea of an overlapping consensus, Rawls (1993) distinguishes between his own theory and what he terms comprehensive moral doctrines. A comprehensive moral doctrine is one that is able to cover the entirety of the moral universe without reference to any other theory. All moral questions can be answered from within a comprehensive moral doctrine. Rawls claims that not only does his conception not depend on a single religious, national, cultural, or moral theory for its foundation, but that it is consistent with a "reasonable pluralism" of such doctrines. One need not convert from her preferred doctrine in order to accept justice as fairness. All reasonable moral doctrines already accept it from within their own conception.

Moreover, not only is stakeholder theory not a comprehensive moral doctrine, but it is yet another step removed even from Rawls's own theory. Stakeholder theory is a theory of organizational ethics. As described by Phillips and Margolis (1999), theories of organizational ethics are distinct from moral and political theories due to the difference in the subject matter of the various disciplines.[29] Contrary to the assumptions of political theory, organizations are, to use Rawls's (1993) terms, voluntary associations rather than a part of the basic structure of society. Further, interaction within and among organizations creates moral obligations over and above those duties that arise due simply to one's status as a human being or citizen of a nation.

Stakeholder theory is not intended to provide an answer to all moral questions. Stakeholder-based obligations do not even take precedence in all moral questions in an organizational context. Violations of the human rights of a constituency group by commercial organizations and the gratuitous destruction of the natural environment are morally wrong, but such judgments rely on concepts outside of stakeholder theory as herein delimited.[30] Stakeholder theory shares this delimitation with its supposed rival theory of shareholder wealth maximization—at least as elaborated by Friedman (1971). Friedman's defense of shareholder wealth maximization is a moral one based on the property rights of shareholders. Noteworthy for our purposes, Friedman's admonition includes the condition that shareholder wealth maximization must take place within the constraints of law and morality. This suggests that there is another level of analysis operative in Friedman's system. So too is the case with stakeholder theory. . . .

CONCLUSION

This paper attempts to add clarity to stakeholder theory by addressing a number of straw-person objections posed by critics of the theory as well as a few friendly overextensions and distortions averred by stakeholder theory advocates. We do not presume to dictate the research agenda of other scholars. However, we believe that it is important to avoid talking past the many intelligent and thoughtful opponents of stakeholder theory as well as avoid "preaching to choir" by offering extensions that will only convince one who already advocates some version of the theory. By clearing away some of the most common misconceptions of stakeholder theory, we suggest that we are in a better position to see both the power and the limitations of this approach.

NOTES

1. This categorization emerged during correspondence with Joshua Margolis.

2. Even should our arguments about agency and stakeholder theory prove unconvincing, we are not the first to address the issue. Previous accounts include Quinn and Jones (1995), Jones (1995), and the articles in Bowie and Freeman (1992).

3. Robert C. Clark, "Agency Costs versus Fiduciary Duties," in *Principals and Agents: The Structure of Business* (1985), pp. 55–79.

4. We might test the proposition that shareholders own the corporation through a thought experiment: who would own the corporation if it bought back all of its own stock?

5. See by comparison G. G. Sollars, "An Appraisal of Shareholder Proportional Liability," *Journal of Business Ethics* 32, no. 4 (2001): 329–45.

6. See also Orts (1997).

7. M. C. Jensen, "Value Maximization and the Corporate Objective Function," in *Breaking the Code of Change* (Boston: Harvard Business School Press, 2000), pp. 37–58; Marcoux, "Balancing Act," in *Contemporary Issues in Business Ethics*, 4th ed. (2000), pp. 92–100; E. Sternberg, *Just Business* (New York: Oxford University Press, 2000).

8. Marcoux, "Balancing Act," p. 97.

9. Sternberg, *Just Business*, p. 510.

10. Albert J. Dunlap. *Mean Business* (New York: Simon & Schuster); John A. Byrne, *Chainsaw* (New York: Harper Business).

11. "Former Sunbeam Chief Exec Settles Hldr Lawsuit for $15M," *Dow Jones Newswire*, January 14, 2002.

12. C. W. L. Hill and T. M. Jones, "Stakeholder-Agency Theory," *Journal of Managerial Studies* 29 (1992): 145.

13. Sternberg, *Just Business*, p. 51.

14. Marcoux, "Balancing Act."

15. There are also multiple means of measurement (e.g., accounting profits, firm value, dividends, long- and short-term market value for shares). Thanks to an anonymous reviewer for pointing this out.

16. Jensen, "Value Maximization," p. 49.

17. Ibid., p. 42.

18. Jensen refers to value maximization as a "scorekeeping device."

19. Jensen, "Value Maximization."

20. D. A. Gioia, "Practicability, Paradigms, and Problems in Stakeholder Theorizing," *Academy of Management Review* 24, no. 2 (1999): 228–32; Marcoux, "Balancing Act"; Sternberg, *Just Business*. See by comparison T. M. Jones and A. C. Wicks, "Letter to AMR Regarding 'Convergent Stakeholder Theory,'" *Academy of Management Review* 24, no. 4 (1999): 621–23.

21. David A. Nadler and Michael L. Tushman, *Competing by Design: The Power of Organizational Architecture* (New York: Oxford University Press, 1997).

22. Rawls's "difference principle" says that social institutions should be arranged such that any inequalities in the distribution of social goods must rebound to the benefit of the least well off.

23. Paul Glezen has also suggested "balance" may be insightfully interpreted in the sense meant when discussing balance in wine. We do not pursue this interpretation, but merely point it out as an interesting variation.

24. Sloan Stakeholder Colloquy, 1999, "Clarkson Principles." The Sloan Stakeholder Colloquy was a broad and important effort to promote and organize research on issues surrounding stakeholder theory.

25. Sternberg, *Just Business*, p. 50.

26. Notably, when profits are discussed among the visionary companies of Collins and Porra's (1994), it is not in terms of maximization, but "reasonable" (Cord), "fair" (Johnson vs. Johnson), "adequate" (Motorola), and "attractive" (Marriott).

27. The organization may have other duties or obligations to nonstakeholders, such as the duty to not cause harm to, lie to, or steal from them. These duties exist prior to and separate from stakeholder obligations and are not considered when establishing stakeholder status. See Phillips 1997.

28. These lists of typical stakeholders are only for the purpose of generic example. Which specific groups are what sort of stakeholder, or indeed which are stakeholders at all, cannot be determined in the abstract. This can only be determined by reference to actual organizations in actual relationships with other groups.

29. Orts (1997) traces scholarly interest in "intermediate associations" back to German sociologist Johannes Althusius, 1614/1964, *The Politics of Johannes Althusius*, Frederick S. Carney (trans.).

30. Eric W. Orts and Alan Strudler, "The Ethical and Environmental Limits of Stakeholder Theory," *Business Ethics Quarterly* 12, no. 2 (2002): 215–34; R. A. Phillips and J. Reichart, "The Environment as a Stakeholder? A Fairness-Based Approach," *Journal of Business Ethics* 23, no. 2 (2000): 183–97.

SUGGESTIONS FOR FURTHER READING

Boatright, J. "Fiduciary Duties and the Shareholder-Management Relation: Or, What's So Special about Shareholders?" *Business Ethics Quarterly* 4 (1994): 393–407.

Child, J., and A. Marcoux. "Freeman and Evan: Stakeholder Theory in the Original Position." *Business Ethics Quarterly* 9, no. 2 (1999): 207.

Cragg, W. "Business Ethics and Stakeholder Theory." *Business Ethics Quarterly* 12, no. 2 (2002): 113–41.

Donaldson, T. "Making Stakeholder Theory Whole." *Academy of Management Review* 24, no. 2 (1999): 237–41.

Dunfee, T. "Business Ethics and Extant Social Contracts." *Business Ethics Quarterly* 1 (1991): 23–51.

Dunfee, T., and T. Donaldson. "Contractarian Business Ethics: Current Status and Next Steps." *Business Ethics Quarterly* 5, no. 2 (1995): 173–86.

Freeman, R. E. "Divergent Stakeholder Theory." *Academy of Management Review* 24, no. 2 (1999): 233–36.

———. "The Politics of Stakeholder Theory: Some Future Directions." *Business Ethics Quarterly* 4, no. 4 (1994): 409–21.

Friedman, A., and S. Miles. "Developing Stakeholder Theory." *Journal of Management Studies* 39, no. 1 (2002): 1–21.

Goodpaster, K. "Business Ethics and Stakeholder Analysis." *Business Ethics Quarterly* 1 (1991): 53–73.

Goodpaster, K., and T. Holloran. "In Defense of a Paradox." *Business Ethics Quarterly* 4, no. 4 (1994): 423–29.

Heath, J. "Business Ethics without Stakeholders." *Business Ethics Quarterly* 16, no. 4 (2006): 533–57.

Jones, T., and A. Wicks. "Convergent Stakeholder Theory." *Academy of Management Review* 24, no. 2 (1999): 206–21.

Kaler, J. "Evaluating Stakeholder Theory." *Journal of Business Ethics* 69, no. 3 (2006): 249–68.

Kaufman, A. "Managers' Double Fiduciary Duty: To Stakeholders and to Freedom." *Business Ethics Quarterly* 12, no. 2 (2002): 189.

Kelsey, D., and F. Milne. "Externalities, Monopoly and the Objective Function of the Firm." *Economic Theory* 29, no. 3 (2006): 565–589.

Key, S. "Toward a New Theory of the Firm: A Critique of Stakeholder Theory." *Management Decision* 27, no. 4 (1999): 31–32 (2).

Langtry, B. "Stakeholder and the Moral Responsibility of Business." *Business Ethics Quarterly* 4, no. 4 (1994): 431–43.

Shankman, N. "Reframing the Debate between Agency and Stakeholder Theories of the Firm." *Journal of Business Ethics* 19, no. 4 (1999): 319–34.

Spurgin, E. "Do Shareholders Have Obligations to Stakeholders?" *Journal of Business Ethics* 1, no. 4 (2001): 287.

Sternberg, E. "The Defects of Stakeholder Theory." *Corporate Governance: An International Review* 5, no. 1 (1995): 3–10.

Van Buren, H. "If Fairness Is the Problem, Is Consent the Solution? Integrating ISCT and Stakeholder Theory." *Business Ethics Quarterly* 11, no. 3 (2001): 481.

Waxenberger, B., and L. Spence. "Reinterpretation of a Metaphor: From Stakes to Claims." *Strategic Change* 12, no. 5 (2003): 239–49.

Windsor, Duane. "Corporate Social Responsibility: Three Key Approaches." *Journal of Management Studies* 43, no. 1 (2006): 93–114.

PART 4.

STAKEHOLDER IDENTITY

As noted in the article by Phillips, Freeman, and Wicks in the previous section, even if the normative implications of stakeholder theory are defensible in the abstract, a much more practical concern with stakeholder theory involves its applicability to management practice. In this section, we thus bridge from articles whose concerns with stakeholder theory are primarily theoretical to those that involve discussions of a more practical orientation. In this section, we examine these issues in terms of the two most basic issues involved in implementing stakeholder theory. One issue concerns the determination of stakeholders. Given the wide range of persons or other entities that might be effected in one way or another by a firm's activities, who or what should count as a legitimate stakeholder in managerial decision making? It is particularly important for proponents of stakeholder theory to address this issue if the theory is to represent a useful alternative to stockholder theory within management. After all, managers are well cognizant of who their primary shareholders are and what demands they make upon corporate policy. Unless stakeholder theory can provide managers with a means of identifying other relevant stakeholders that makes them and their interests as readily apparent as those of stockholders, managers are unlikely to take the interests of other such stakeholders into account even when they should. However, even if stakeholder interests can be identified, there is still another issue related to the identification problem that managers will face. For stakeholder interests can come into conflict, and to be workable stakeholder theory also needs to provide some account of how stakeholder interests are to be factored into managerial decisions. In this regard, as a viable tool for management, stakeholder theory needs to provide guidance as how to both properly rank the different stakeholders identified and to weigh their competing interests.

In the seminal article "Toward a Theory of Stakeholder Identification and Salience: Defining the Principle of Who and What Really Counts," Ronald K. Mitchell, Bradley R. Agle, and Donna J. Wood attempt to delineate principles for the determination of stakeholder identity and relevance and indicate how they can be integrated into managerial practice. The authors maintain the stakeholders can be identified on the basis of their possession of one or more of the following characteristics: 1) their power to influence the firm, 2) the legitimacy of their relationship to the firm, and 3) the urgency of their claim on the firm. Using these three categories, the authors go on to argue for both an account of stakeholder identification and one of stakeholder salience. While identification concerns determining who counts as a legitimate stakeholder, stakeholder salience involves how managers give priority to competing claims from diverse stakeholder theories in their decision making. The theory of stakeholder salience put forth by Mitchell, Agle, and Wood is based upon an empirical account of the way in which managers do respond to different stakeholder claims. In this respect, the authors' account is meant to be descriptive and not normative. In this paper, their concern is with how managers do prioritize stakeholder claims, not with how they should do so. Nonetheless, they believe that by providing an account of the actual way in which stakeholder salience is determined in practice, they set the stage for future considerations of a more normative nature.

Explicitly following up on the issues dealt with by Mitchell, Agle, and Wood, Janita F. J. Vos examines the issue of stakeholder identification in light of a strategy of corporate social responsibility (CSR) in the article "Corporate Social Responsibility and the Identification of Stakeholders." The primary concern of this article is what Vos terms the "modeling issue," or the issue as to how organizations can determine who their stakeholders are. In order to provide a framework for such modeling, Vos makes use of the critical systems heuristics (CSH) developed by Werner Ulrich. As part of the systems tradition, CSH provides a means of making boundary decisions about the elements within a system. When applied to stakeholder theory, this means that CSH is meant to provide both a descriptive and a normative account of who is affected by organizational behavior. One important element of this modeling developed by Vos is that it includes the notion of a witness as a representative of those affected. Vos both develops the theoretical underpinnings of this notion of a witness as well as illustrates its application in light of a specific case study exemplifying the role of witnesses. Vos maintains that witnesses can provide an important role in bringing stakeholder claims to bear upon an organization.

In "Morality and Strategy in Stakeholder Identification," John Kaler further elaborates upon the different strategies for determining stakeholders that have been proposed. Having surveyed the extent literature on stakeholder theory, Kaler argues that in general there are three different means that have been offered for determining stakeholder interests, and that these different ways of defining stakeholder groups represent a deep divide in the application of stakeholder theory. Influencer definitions of stakeholders define stakeholders in terms of those who have the ability to influence an organization. Claimant definitions, on the other hand, define stakeholders in terms of those who have legitimate claims upon the activities of the firm. Combinatory definitions identify stakeholders as being those who belong in either or both of the influencer or claimant groups. Having illustrated the different ways of identifying stakeholders, Kaler goes on to argue that as a normative theory of business ethics, stakeholder theory ought to adopt claimant definitions of stakeholders. As influencer definitions are merely instrumental, and combinatory definitions are conceptually confusing, Kaler maintains that only claimant definitions are both normatively viable and practically applicable. Kaler goes on to use the notions of the perfect and imperfect duties of businesses to develop the definition of claimants for the purpose of stakeholder identification.

Finally, in "The Primordial Stakeholder: Advancing the Conceptual Consideration of Stakeholder Status for the Natural Environment," Cathy Driscoll and Mark Starik put forth the case in favor of integrating the natural environment as a stakeholder into managerial decision making. What is particularly interesting about the selection from Driscoll and Starik is that they make use of the model of stakeholder identification and salience put forth by Mitchell, Agle, and Wood in arguing their case. In doing so, they make use of the three criteria of influence, legitimacy, and urgency proposed by Mitchell, Agle, and Wood, but add a forth criterion to the list as well: that of proximity. The authors maintain that when these four features are properly characterized, a forceful case can be made for considering the natural environment as a legitimate stakeholder for all business firms, and that as such these organizations need to take their obligations to environmental sustainability seriously. Whether or not one agrees with Driscoll and Starik's conclusion will partly depend upon whether one accepts the legitimacy of the model of stakeholder identification and relevance that they adopt. In this sense, this article nicely illustrates how the adoption of different stakeholder models of identification and salience will influence the way in which the implications of stakeholder theory for managerial practice is played out.

14.

TOWARD A THEORY OF STAKEHOLDER IDENTIFICATION AND SALIENCE

Defining the Principle of Who and What Really Counts

Ronald K. Mitchell, Bradley R. Agle, and Donna J. Wood

STAKEHOLDER THEORY—STATE OF THE ART

Who Is a Stakeholder and What Is a Stake?

There is not much disagreement on *what kind of entity* can be a stakeholder. Persons, groups, neighborhoods, organizations, institutions, societies, and even the natural environment are generally thought to qualify as actual or potential stakeholders. We find that it is the view taken about the existence and nature of the *stake* that presents an area of argument, because it is upon the basis of "stake" that "what counts" is ultimately decided. . . .

Freeman's now-classic definition is this: "A stakeholder in an organization is (by definition) any group or individual who can affect or is affected by the achievement of the organization's objectives."[1] This is certainly one of the broadest definitions in the literature, for it leaves the notion of stake and the field of possible stakeholders unambiguously open to include virtually anyone. In this definition the basis of the stake can be unidirectional or bidirectional—"can affect or is affected by"—and there is no implication or necessity of reciprocal impact, as definitions involving relationships, transactions, or contracts require. Excluded from having a stake are only those

Ronald K. Mitchell, Bradley R. Agle, and Donna J. Wood, "Toward a Theory of Stakeholder Identification and Salience: Defining the Principle of Who and What Really Counts," *Academy of Management Review* 22, no. 4 (1997): 853–86. Copyright © 1997 *Academy of Management Review*. Reprinted by permission.

who cannot affect the firm (have no power) *and* are not affected by it (have no claim or relationship).

In contrast, Clarkson offers one of the narrower definitions of stakeholders as voluntary or involuntary risk-bearers: "Voluntary stakeholders bear some form of risk as a result of having invested some form of capital, human or financial, something of value, in a firm. Involuntary stakeholders are placed at risk as a result of a firm's activities. But without the element of risk there is no stake."[2] A stake, in this sense, is only something that can be lost. The use of risk to denote stake appears to be a way to narrow the stakeholder field to those with *legitimate claims*, regardless of their power to influence the firm or the legitimacy of their relationship to the firm. This search for legitimacy, we argue later, is necessary to understand fully a firm's stakeholder environment, but it also can be a powerful blinder to the real impact of stakeholder power and claim urgency. We argue, in contrast to the position of all those who appear to focus primarily on legitimacy, that this narrower view captures only one key attribute of stakeholder salience to managers.

Major differences between broad and narrow views. Narrow views of stakeholders are based on the practical reality of limited resources, limited time and attention, and limited patience of managers for dealing with external constraints. In general, narrow views of stakeholders attempt to define relevant groups in terms of their *direct relevance to the firm's core economic interests*. For example, several scholars define stakeholders in terms of their necessity for the firm's survival;[3] as noted, Clarkson (1995) defines stakeholders as those who have placed something at risk in relationship with the firm, whereas Freeman and Evan (1990), Hill and Jones (1992), and Cornell and Shapiro (1987) speak of stakeholders as contractors or participants in exchange relationships. . . .

The broad view of stakeholders, in contrast, is based on the empirical reality that companies can indeed be vitally affected by, or they can vitally affect, almost anyone. But it is bewilderingly complex for managers to apply. The idea of comprehensively identifying stakeholder types, then, is to equip managers with the ability to recognize and respond effectively to a disparate, yet systematically comprehensible set of entities who may or may not have legitimate claims, but who may be able to affect or are affected by the firm nonetheless, and thus affect the interests of those who do have legitimate claims. . . .

Claimants versus influencers. In order to clarify the term "stake," we need to differentiate between groups that have a legal, moral, or presumed claim on the firm and groups that have an ability to influence the firm's behavior, direction, process, or outcomes. Savage, Nix, Whitehead, and Blair (1991) consider two attributes to be necessary to identify a stakeholder: (1) a claim and (2) the ability to influence a firm. Brenner (1993) and Starik (1994), however, pose these attributes as either/or components of the definition of those with a stake.

In our view this is a muddled set, confusing and contrasting two of the three criteria we see as important. Influencers have power over the firm, whether or not they have valid claims or any claims at all and whether or not they wish to press their claims. Claimants may have legitimate claims or illegitimate ones, and they may or may not have any power to influence the firm. Power and legitimacy are different, sometimes overlapping dimensions, and each can exist without the other. A theory of stakeholder identification must accommodate these differences.

Actual versus potential relationship. Another crucial question leading to the comprehensibility of the term "stake" is whether an entity can be a stakeholder without being in actual relationship with the firm. Some scholars (e.g., Ring 1994) emphatically answer, "No." We argue that, on the contrary, the *potential* relationship can be as relevant as the actual one. Clarkson's (1994) idea of involuntary stakeholders as those with something not willfully placed at risk addresses the potentiality issue somewhat. Starik quite clearly includes potential when he refers to stakeholders as those who "are or might be influenced by, or are or potentially are influencers of, some organization."[4] We suggest that a theory of stakeholder identification and salience must somehow account for *latent* stakeholders if it is to be both comprehensive and useful, because such identification can, at a minimum, help organizations avoid problems and perhaps even enhance effectiveness.

Power, dependence, and reciprocity in relationships. If the firm and a stakeholder have a relationship, what is the nature of that relationship? The literature offers a confusing jumble of answers to this question, but most answers use a power-dependence frame of some sort. . . .

Overall . . . scholars who attempt to narrow the definition of stakeholder emphasize the *claim's legitimacy* based upon contract, exchange, legal title, legal right, moral right, at-risk status, or moral interest in the harms and benefits generated by company actions and that, in contrast, scholars who favor a broad definition emphasize the *stakeholder's power* to influence the firm's behavior, whether or not there are legitimate claims. As a bridging concept, we argue that the broad concept of stakeholder management must be better defined in order to serve the narrower interests of legitimate stakeholders. Otherwise, influencing groups with power over the firm can disrupt operations so severely that legitimate claims cannot be met and the firm may not survive. Yet, at the same time, it is important to recognize the legitimacy of some claims over others. Power and legitimacy, then, are necessarily core attributes of a comprehensive stakeholder identification model. We argue that when these attributes are evaluated in light of the compelling demands of urgency, a systematic, comprehensible, and dynamic model is the result.

WHAT ADDED VALUE DOES A THEORY OF STAKEHOLDER IDENTIFICATION OFFER?

. . . Agency, resource dependence, and transaction cost theories are particularly helpful in explaining why power plays such an important role in the attention managers give to stakeholders. The central problem agency theory addresses is how principals can control the behavior of their agents to achieve their, rather than the agent's, interests. The power of agents to act in ways divergent from the interests of principals may be limited by use of incentives or monitoring,[5] so that managers are expected to attend to those stakeholders having the power to reward and/or punish them. Resource dependence theory suggests that power accrues to those who control resources needed by the organization, creating power differentials among parties,[6] and it confirms that the possession of resource power makes a stakeholder important to managers. Transaction cost theory proposes that the power accruing to economic actors with small-numbers bargaining advantages will affect the nature of firm governance and structure.[7] That is, stakeholders outside the firm boundary who participate in a very small competitive set can increase transaction costs to levels that justify their absorption into the firm, where the costs of hierarchy are lower than the transaction costs of market failure—a clear indication of their significance to managers.[8]

These three organizational theories teach us why power is a crucial variable in a theory of stakeholder-manager relations. But, as previously noted, power alone does not help us to fully understand salience in the stakeholder-manager relationship. There remain stakeholders who do not have power, but who nevertheless matter to firms and managers. Other means to identify "Who or What Really Counts" are needed.

Organizational theories with an open system orientation,[9] including institutional and population ecology theories, help us to understand the crucial effects of the environment upon organizations, but they are less helpful when it comes to understanding power in stakeholder-manager relationships. In both theories organizational legitimacy is linked closely with survival.[10] In the socially constructed world within which managers engage stakeholders, these two theories suggest that "legitimate" stakeholders are the ones who "really count." Under institutional theory, "illegitimacy" results in isomorphic pressures on organizations that operate outside of accepted norms.[11] Under population ecology theory, lack of legitimacy results in organizational mortality.[12] According to these two theories, legitimacy figures heavily in helping us to identify stakeholders that merit managerial attention. However, emphasizing legitimacy and ignoring power leave major gaps in a stakeholder identification scheme, because some legitimate stakeholders have no influence....

... [W]e suggest that to better understand "The Principle of Who and What Really Counts," we need to evaluate stakeholder-manager relationships systematically, both actual and potential, in terms of the relative absence or presence of all or some of the attributes: power, legitimacy, and/or urgency.

DEFINING STAKEHOLDER ATTRIBUTES

Power. Most current definitions of power derive, at least in part, from the early Weberian idea that power is "the probability that one actor within a social relationship would be in a position to carry out his own will despite resistance."[13] Pfeffer rephrases Dahl's (1957) definition of power as "a relationship among social actors in which one social actor, A, can get another social actor, B, to do something that B would not otherwise have done."[14] Like Pfeffer and Weber, we concur that "power may be tricky to define, but it is not that difficult to recognize: '[it is] the ability of those who possess power to bring about the outcomes they desire.'"[15] This leads to the following question: How is power exercised, or, alternatively, what are the bases of power?

... [A] party to a relationship has power, to the extent it has or can gain access to coercive, utilitarian, or normative means, to impose its will in the relationship. We note, however, that this access to means is a variable, not a steady state, which is one reason why power is transitory: it can be acquired as well as lost.

Legitimacy. It is apparent from our analysis ... that narrow definition scholars, particularly those seeking a "normative core" for stakeholder theory, are focused almost exclusively on defining the basis of stakeholder legitimacy. Whether or not that core of legitimacy is to be found in something "at risk," or in property rights, in moral claims, or in some other construct, articulations of "The Principle of Who or What Really Counts" generally are legitimacy based.

However, the notion of "legitimacy," loosely referring to socially accepted and expected structures or behaviors, often is coupled implicitly with that of power when people attempt to evaluate the nature of relationships in society. Davis, for example, distinguishes legitimate from illegitimate use of power by declaring, "In the long run, those who do not use power in a manner which society considers responsible will tend to lose it."[16] Many scholars seeking to define a firm's stakeholders narrowly also make an implicit assumption that legitimate stakeholders are necessarily powerful, when this is not always the case (e.g., minority stockholders in a closely held company), and that powerful stakeholders are necessarily legitimate (e.g., corporate raiders in the eyes of current managers).

Despite this common linkage, we accept Weber's (1947) proposal that legitimacy and power are distinct attributes that can combine to create *authority* (defined by Weber as the legitimate use of power) but that can exist independently as well. An entity may have legitimate standing in society, or it may have a legitimate claim on the firm, but unless it has either power to enforce its will in the relationship or a perception that its claim is urgent, it will not achieve salience for the firm's managers. For this reason we argue that a comprehensive theory of stakeholder salience requires that separate attention be paid to legitimacy as an attribute of stakeholder-manager relations. . . .

Urgency. Viewing power and legitimacy as independent variables in stakeholder-manager relationships takes us some distance toward a theory of stakeholder identification and salience, but it does not capture the dynamics of stakeholder-manager interactions. We propose that adding the stakeholder attribute of urgency helps move the model from static to dynamic. "Urgency" is defined by the *Merriam-Webster Dictionary* as "calling for immediate attention" or "pressing." We believe that urgency, with synonyms including "compelling," "driving," and "imperative," exists only when two conditions are met: (1) when a relationship or claim is of a time-sensitive nature and (2) when that relationship or claim is important or critical to the stakeholder. Thus, similar to Jones's (1993) description of moral intensity as a multidimensional construct, we argue that urgency is based on the following two attributes: (1) time sensitivity—the degree to which managerial delay in attending to the claim or relationship is unacceptable to the stakeholder, and (2) criticality—the importance of the claim or the relationship to the stakeholder. We define urgency as the degree to which stakeholder claims call for immediate attention. . . .

ADDITIONAL FEATURES OF STAKEHOLDER ATTRIBUTES

. . . To support a dynamic theory of stakeholder identification and salience, however, we need to consider several additional implications of power, legitimacy, and urgency. First, each attribute is a variable, not a steady state, and can change for any particular entity or stakeholder-manager relationship. Second, the existence (or degree present) of each attribute is a matter of multiple perceptions and is a constructed reality rather than an "objective" one. Third, an individual or entity may not be "conscious" of possessing the attribute or, if conscious of possession, may not choose to enact any implied behaviors. These features of stakeholder attributes, summarized below, are important to the theory's dynamism; that is, they provide a preliminary framework for understanding how stakeholders can gain or lose salience to a firm's managers:

1. Stakeholder attributes are variable, not steady state.
2. Stakeholder attributes are socially constructed, not objective, reality.
3. Consciousness and willful exercise may or may not be present.

Thus, with respect to power, for example, access to the means of influencing another entity's behavior is a variable, with both discrete and continuous features. As we argued earlier, power may be coercive, utilitarian, or normative—qualitatively different types that may exist independently or in combination. Each type of power may range from nonexistent to complete. Power is transitory—it can be acquired as well as lost. Further, possession of power does not necessarily imply its actual or intended use, nor does possession of power imply consciousness of such possession by the possessor or "correct" perception of objective reality by the perceivers. An entity may possess power to impose its will upon a firm, but unless it is aware of its power and is willing to exercise it on the firm, it is not a stakeholder with high salience for managers. Rather, latent power exists in stakeholder relationships, and the exercise of stakeholder power is triggered by conditions that are manifest in the other two attributes of the relationship: legitimacy and urgency. That is, power by itself does not guarantee high salience in a stakeholder-manager relationship. Power gains authority through legitimacy, and it gains exercise through urgency.

Legitimacy, like power, is a variable rather than a steady state—a dynamic attribute of the stakeholder-manager relationship. It may be present or absent. If it is present, it is based upon a generalized virtue that is perceived for or attributed to a stakeholder at one or more social levels of analysis. Claimants may or may not correctly perceive the legitimacy of their claims; likewise, managers may have perceptions of stakeholder legitimacy that are at variance with the stakeholder's own perception. Also, like the power attribute, legitimacy's contribution to stakeholder salience depends upon interaction with the other two attributes: power and urgency. Legitimacy gains rights through power and voice through urgency.

Finally, urgency is not a steady-state attribute but can vary across stakeholder-manager relationships or within a single relationship across time. As is true of power and legitimacy, urgency is a socially constructed perceptual phenomenon and may be perceived correctly or falsely by the stakeholder, the managers, or others in the firm's environment. . . . Urgency by itself is not sufficient to guarantee high salience in the stakeholder-manager relationship. However, when it is combined with at least one of the other attributes, urgency will change the relationship and cause it to increase in salience to the firm's managers. Specifically, in combination with legitimacy, urgency promotes access to decision-making channels, and in combination with power, it encourages one-sided stakeholder action. In combination with both, urgency triggers reciprocal acknowledgment and action between stakeholders and managers.

STAKEHOLDER CLASSES

. . . In conjunction with the analysis of stakeholder types, and based on the assumption that managers' perceptions of stakeholders form the crucial variable in determining organizational resource allocation in response to stakeholder claims, we also present several propositions leading to a theory of stakeholder salience.

Therefore:

Proposition 1: Stakeholder salience will be positively related to the cumulative number of stakeholder attributes—power, legitimacy, and urgency—perceived by managers to be present.

LATENT STAKEHOLDERS

With limited time, energy, and other resources to track stakeholder behavior and to manage relationships, managers may well do nothing about stakeholders they believe possess only one of the identifying attributes, and managers may not even go so far as to recognize those stakeholders' existence. Similarly, latent stakeholders are not likely to give any attention or acknowledgment to the firm. Hence:

> *Proposition 1a: Stakeholder salience will be low where only one of the stakeholder attributes—power, legitimacy, and urgency—is perceived by managers to be present.*

In the next few paragraphs we discuss the reasoning behind this expectation as it applies to each class of latent stakeholder, and we also discuss the implications for managers.

Dormant stakeholders. The relevant attribute of a dormant stakeholder is power. Dormant stakeholders possess power to impose their will on a firm, but by not having a legitimate relationship or an urgent claim, their power remains unused. Examples of dormant stakeholders are plentiful. For instance, power is held by those who have a loaded gun (coercive), those who can spend a lot of money (utilitarian), or those who can command the attention of the news media (symbolic). Dormant stakeholders have little or no interaction with the firm. However, because of their potential to acquire a second attribute, management should remain cognizant of such stakeholders, for the dynamic nature of the stakeholder-manager relationship suggests that dormant stakeholders will become more salient to managers if they acquire either urgency or legitimacy. . . .

Discretionary stakeholders. Discretionary stakeholders possess the attribute of legitimacy, but they have no power to influence the firm and no urgent claims. Discretionary stakeholders are a particularly interesting group for scholars of corporate social responsibility and performance,[17] for they are most likely to be recipients of what Carroll (1979) calls discretionary corporate social responsibility, which he later redefined as corporate philanthropy (Carroll 1991). The key point regarding discretionary stakeholders is that, absent power and urgent claims, there is absolutely no pressure on managers to engage in an active relationship with such a stakeholder, although managers can choose to do so. . . .

Demanding stakeholders. Where the sole relevant attribute of the stake-holder-manager relationship is urgency, the stakeholder is described as "demanding." Demanding stakeholders, those with urgent claims but having neither power nor legitimacy, are the "mosquitoes buzzing in the ears" of managers: irksome but not dangerous, bothersome but not warranting more than passing management attention, if any at all. Where stakeholders are unable or unwilling to acquire either the power or the legitimacy necessary to move their claim into a more salient status, the "noise" of urgency is insufficient to project a stakeholder claim beyond latency. For example, a lone millenarian picketer who marches outside the headquarters with a sign that says, "The end of the world is coming! Acme chemical is the cause!" might be extremely irritating to Acme's managers, but the claims of the picketer remain largely unconsidered.

EXPECTANT STAKEHOLDERS

As we consider the potential relationship between managers and the group of stakeholders with two of the three identifying stakeholder attributes, we observe a qualitatively different zone of salience. In analyzing the situations in which any two of the three attributes—power, legitimacy, and urgency—are present, we cannot help but notice the change in momentum that characterizes this condition. Whereas one-attribute low-salience stakeholders are anticipated to have a latent relationship with managers, two-attribute moderate-salience stakeholders are seen as "expecting something," because the combination of two attributes leads the stakeholder to an active versus a passive stance, with a corresponding increase in firm responsiveness to the stakeholder's interests. Thus, the level of engagement between managers and these expectant stakeholders is likely to be higher. Accordingly:

> *Proposition 1b: Stakeholder salience will be moderate where two of the stakeholder attributes—power, legitimacy, and urgency—are perceived by managers to be present.*

. . . Dominant stakeholders. In the situation where stakeholders are both powerful and legitimate, their influence in the firm is assured, since by possessing power with legitimacy, they form the "dominant coalition" in the enterprise.[18] We characterize these stakeholders as "dominant," in deference to the legitimate claims they have upon the firm and their ability to act on these claims (rather than as a forecast of their intentions with respect to the firm—they may or may not ever choose to act on their claims). It seems clear to us, at least, that the expectations of any stakeholders perceived by managers to have power and legitimacy will "matter" to managers. . . .

Dependent stakeholders. We characterize stakeholders who lack power but who have urgent legitimate claims as "dependent," because these stakeholders depend upon others (other stakeholders or the firm's managers) for the power necessary to carry out their will. Because power in this relationship is not reciprocal, its exercise is governed either through the advocacy or guardianship of other stakeholders, or through the guidance of internal management values. . . .

Dangerous stakeholders. We suggest that where urgency and power characterize a stakeholder who lacks legitimacy, that stakeholder will be coercive and possibly violent, making the stakeholder "dangerous," literally, to the firm. "Coercion" is suggested as a descriptor because the use of coercive power often accompanies illegitimate status.

DEFINITIVE STAKEHOLDERS

Previously, we defined "salience" as the degree to which managers give priority to competing stakeholder claims. Thus:

> *Proposition 1c: Stakeholder salience will be high where all three of the stakeholder attributes—power, legitimacy, and urgency—are perceived by managers to be present.*

By definition, a stakeholder exhibiting both power and legitimacy already will be a member of a firm's dominant coalition. When such a stakeholder's claim is urgent, managers have a clear and immediate mandate to attend to and give priority to that stakeholder's claim. The most common occurrence is likely to be the movement of a dominant stakeholder into the "definitive" category. . . .

IMPLICATIONS FOR MANAGEMENT, RESEARCH, AND FUTURE DIRECTIONS

On the basis of the model we develop in this article, we can envision refinements in long-standing management techniques designed to assist managers in dealing with multiple stakeholders' interests. Presently, management techniques based on the stakeholder heuristic are being utilized to help managers deal effectively with multiple stakeholder relationships. Current methods include identification of stakeholder roles (e.g., employees, owners, communities, suppliers, and customers), analysis of stakeholder interests, and evaluation of the type and level of stakeholder power.[19] . . .

NOTES

1. R. E. Freeman, *Strategic Management: A Stakeholder Approach* (Boston: Pitman, 1984), p. 46.

2. M. Clarkson, "A Risk Based Model of Stakeholder Theory," in *Proceedings of the Second Toronto Conference on Stakeholder Theory* (Toronto: Centre for Corporate Social Performance & Ethics, University of Toronto, 1994), p. 5.

3. N. Bowie, "The Moral Obligations of Multinational Corporations," in *Problems of International Justice*, ed. S. Luper-Foy (Boulder, CO: Westview Press, 1988); R. E. Freeman and D. L. Reed, "Stockholders and Stakeholders: A New Perspective on Corporate Governance," *California Management Review* 25, no. 3 (1983): 93–94; J. Nasi, "What Is Stakeholder Thinking? A Snapshot of a Social Theory of the Firm," in *Understanding Stakeholder Thinking*, ed. J. Nasi (Helsinki: LSR-Julkaisut Oy, 1995), pp. 19–32.

4. M. Starik, "Essay by Mark Starik," of *The Toronto Conference: Reflections on Stakeholder Theory, Business & Society* 33 (1994): 90.

5. M. C. Jensen and W. F. Meckling, "Theory of the Firm: Managerial Behavior, Agency Costs, and Ownership Structure," *Journal of Financial Economics* 3 (1976): 305–60.

6. J. Pfeffer, *Power in Organizations* (Marshfield, MA: Pitman, 1981).

7. O. E. Williamson, *Markets and Hierarchies* (New York: Free Press, 1975); Ibid., *The Economic Institutions of Capitalism* (New York: Free Press, 1985).

8. G. R. Jones, and C. W. L. Hill, "Transaction Cost Analysis of Strategy-Structure Choice," *Strategic Management Journal* 9 (1988): 159–72.

9. W. R. Scott, *Organizations: Rational, Natural, and Open Systems* (Englewood Cliffs, NJ: Prentice Hall, 1987).

10. See J. W. Meyer and B. Rowan, "Institutional Organizations: Formal Structires as Myth and Ceremony," *American Journal of Sociology* 80 (1977): 340–63; and

G. R. Carroll and M. T. Hannan, "Density Delay in the Evolution of Organizational Populations: A Model and Five Empirical Tests," *Administrative Science Quarterly* 34 (1989): 411–30, respectively.

11. P. J. DiMaggio and W. W. Powell, "The Iron Cage Revisited: Institutional Isomorphism and Collective Rationality in Organization Fields," *American Sociologist Review* 46 (1983): 147–60.

12. Carroll and Hannan, "Density Delay in the Evolution of Organizational Populations."

13. M. Weber, *The Theory of Social and Economic Organization* (New York: Free Press, 1947).

14. Pfeffer, *Power in Organizations*.

15. G. R. Salancik and J. Pfeffer, "The Bases and the Use of Power in Organizational Decision Making: The Case of Universities," *Administrative Science Quarterly* 19 (1974): 3.

16. K. Davis, "The Case for and against Business Assumption of Social Responsibility," *Academy of Management Journal* 16 (1973): 314.

17. See D. J. Wood, "Corporate Social Performance Revisited," *Academy of Management Review* 16, no. 4 (1991): 691–718.

18. R. M. Cyert and J. G. March, *A Behavioral Theory of the Firm* (Englewood Cliffs, NJ: Prentice Hall, 1963).

19. See, for example, textbooks by A. B. Carroll, *Business and Society: Ethics and Stakeholder Management*, 2nd ed. (Cincinnati: South-Western, 1993); W. C. Frederick, J. E. Post, A. Lawrence, and J. Weber, *Business and Society: Corporate Strategy, Public Policy, Ethics*, 8th ed. (New York: McGraw-Hill, 1996); and D. J. Wood, *Business and Society*, 2nd ed. (New York: HarperCollins, 1994).

15.

CORPORATE SOCIAL RESPONSIBILITY AND THE IDENTIFICATION OF STAKEHOLDERS

Janita F. J. Vos

INTRODUCTION

Organizations that consider a strategy of corporate social responsibility (CSR) have to address the question "to whom are we responsible?" "To stakeholders" is the common answer to this question, which means that, to manage a CSR strategy, the identification of stakeholders is crucial. To a certain extent, management of CSR has become stakeholder management.[1]

As a management problem the stakeholder identification is not easily solved: it comprises, at least, a modeling and a normative issue. The modeling issue refers to questions such as "Who are our stakeholders?" or "To what extent is it possible to draw the line between stakeholders and non-stakeholders?"

The normative issue refers to the managerial implications. Relevant questions are "What stakeholders do we take into account?" or "To what stakeholders are we willing to listen?" Presumably, this category of stakeholders has the capacity to influence managerial and/or organizational behavior. . . .

To identify stakeholders, in the end, the normative issue needs to be resolved. However, this cannot be done without addressing the modeling issue as well. Before further specifying the main question for this paper, some clarifying notes need to be made concerning the *context of CSR*.

Janita F. J. Vos, "Corporate Social Responsibility and the Identification of Stakeholders," *Corporate Social Responsibility and Environmental Management* 10 (2003): 141–52. Copyright © 2003 John Wiley & Sons, Ltd., and ERP Environment, 2003. Reprinted by permission.

CSR is defined as *the obligations or duties of an organization to a specific system of stakeholders.* In defining the CSR concept a number of considerations have played a role. These considerations further clarify the normative perspective in this paper as well.

First, responsibility is described as "having a duty, an obligation." . . .

Second, a stakeholder is commonly seen as an individual or a group.[2] However, it must be emphasized that there are relationships between stakeholders. For example, coalitions of stakeholders are likely to have more influence than a stakeholder alone. . . .

Third, the organization is treated here as an entity that is responsible for its activities. Although this is usual in the literature on CSR and business ethics,[3] it has to be acknowledged that this perspective is only possible when human activity is involved.[4] In this paper, CSR is dealt with from a managerial point of view, which means, for instance, that corporate responsibility leads to managerial responsibility.

Finally, stressing that a system of stakeholders has to be modeled already involves an element of choice. Asking the question "To what stakeholders are we willing to listen?" further underlines the element of managerial choice. It must be emphasized that, in the end, the implication of a stakeholder perspective is a normative one: managers should acknowledge the validity of diverse stakeholder interests and should attempt to respond.[5]

In this paper the problem of stakeholder identification will be handled from the perspective of critical systems heuristics (CSH), which has been developed by Werner Ulrich (1983, 1988). CSH is a system approach, which offers a variety of boundary judgments. Leaving a more detailed explanation for the following sections, the essence of these boundary judgments is that they need to be made in a normative way, which is considered important in the context of corporate social responsibility. This leads to the following question for this paper: *to what extent can critical systems heuristics help in resolving the managerial problem of identifying stakeholders?* . . .

THE STAKEHOLDER DEBATE IN CSR LITERATURE

. . . If we can speak of a "stakeholder debate" in CSR literature at all, it is revealed by means of two related questions. The first question is "What are the responsibilities of an organization?" and the second question is "To whom is the organization responsible?" . . .

This leads, directly, to the stakeholder perspective on organizations.

"The organization is responsible to its stakeholders" is the common answer to that question. . . .

Freeman gives a very broad definition: "a stakeholder in an organization is (by definition) any group or individual who can affect or is affected by the achievement of the organization's objectives."[6] This definition is widely acknowledged because of its "landmark" position in stakeholder theory.[7] It has been numerously cited, usually as a starting point to give a narrower view on stakeholders, in which categorizations, different from the distinction between "can affect" and "affected," are described.

These categorizations are thoroughly analyzed by Mitchell et al. (1997). They argue that the narrower views attempt to define groups of stakeholders in terms of their direct relevance to the organization's core interests or their necessity for its survival. Clarkson (1995), for instance, makes a distinction between primary and secondary stakeholders. A primary stakeholder group is essential for the survival of the organization, which is not the case for a secondary stakeholder group.

Elsewhere, Clarkson stresses the importance of risk.[8] Without the element of risk there is no stake. A stake is, in this sense, something that can be lost. Consequently, a stakeholder is a risk-bearer. From this viewpoint the distinction is made between voluntary and involuntary stakeholders. "Voluntary stakeholders bear some form of risk as a result of having invested some form of capital, human or financial, something of value, in the firm. Involuntary stakeholders are placed at risk as a result of a firm's activities."[9]

Although stockholder dominance is seen as untenable, to some extent the position of the stockholder is still a point of discussion. Does the stockholder or shareowner have a special status among stakeholders? In the so-called "Principles of stakeholder management,"[10] the notion of risk has been used to point out that, although shareowners may have a special status, it is *not* because of higher risks. On the contrary, the risks of, e.g., employees or customers may be higher. Shareowners deserve their special position, according to this statement, because of the fact that they have agreed "that their potential gain or loss from their involvement with the corporation is determined as a residual: it depends upon what is *left over* after all other stakeholder claimants have received their specified distributions."

Goodpaster (1998/1991) stresses the special status of the stockholder as well. He states that, because of the property rights, the stockholder has a "fiduciary" relationship with the corporation. Management fulfills a *fiduciary* duty to the stockholder, in which trust is crucial. This means that management has the duty to keep the profit-maximizing promise. In other words,

Goodpaster makes a distinction between fiduciary and nonfiduciary stake-holders. He poses the question of whether a multifiduciary stakeholder orientation would be desirable. In other words, could there be "fiduciary" or trustlike relationships with other stakeholders as well?

Goodpaster rejects this multifiduciary position because management will then be caught in what he sees as a *stakeholder paradox*: "Management must face resistance from those who believe that a strategic orientation (i.e., stock-holder dominance) is the only legitimate one for business to adopt." The paradox lies in the fact that "there is an ethical problem whichever approach management takes." Preferably, management should not bear additional fiduciary relationships to third parties (i.e., nonstockholder stakeholders), but acknowledge moral obligations directly. Of course there are obligations to other parties. These obligations are moral obligations owed by organizations to those whose freedom and well-being are affected by their activities. These obligations are not instrumental, contingent, or indirect, but direct or "categorical."[11] It can be concluded that, although Goodpaster is a representative of a narrower view on stakeholders, his analysis of the managerial consequences is consistent with a broader view. . . .

How do managers deal with this complex problem? In other words, how do they choose their stakeholders and prioritize between competing stakeholder claims? Mitchell et al. (1997) and, in a follow-up article, Agle et al. (1999) try to answer this question by developing the "stakeholder salience" model. Stakeholder salience is defined as "the degree to which managers give priority to competing stakeholder's claims."[12] Their claim is that stakeholder salience is positively related to three key stakeholder attributes, i.e., power, legitimacy, and urgency, which management believes to be present.

Without discussing the model and the three attributes in detail, their line of reasoning can be summarized as follows. Managers perceive a variety of stakeholder groups. They give a high priority to a stakeholder if they believe that this stakeholder has a legitimate claim, which calls for immediate action (i.e., urgent), and possesses the power to influence the organization's activities. . . .

At this point, two conclusions will be drawn. First, various categorizations of stakeholders can be found in the literature. In particular, the study of Mitchell et al. (1997) has contributed to the analysis of these categorizations. In the introduction to this paper it was stated that the problem of stakeholder identification comprises a modeling and a normative issue. The modeling activity, which will be further explained in the next sections, is about projecting categories on the real world. Therefore, this knowledge about categorizations could be used with regard to the problem of stakeholder modeling.

Leaving aside the question "To what extent are these categorizations adequate for modeling purposes?" it cannot resolve the normative issue. Once more referring to the salience model, this study may explain why managers give attention to what stakeholders. However, to what extent these management decisions are justifiable from a normative standpoint is another matter.

Second, although the distinction between "affected" and "can affect" may be widely seen as insufficient for stakeholder identification, it is an important one, especially in the context of corporate social responsibility. With respect to this, following Goodpaster (1998/1991), organizations owe obligations to those whose freedom and well-being are affected by their activities. In other words, from a normative perspective, this group possesses justified interests in aspects of organizational activity and its members are, for that reason, legitimate stakeholders. Acknowledging this, however, further complicates the stakeholder identification problem. This leads to questions such as "To what extent and in what way is it possible to identify the affected?" and "How far does the inclusion of—potentially—affected stakeholders have to go?" . . .

SOME PRINCIPLES OF CRITICAL SYSTEMS HEURISTICS

The ideas of critical systems heuristics[13] have been used here to explore to what extent CSH can help resolve the stakeholder identification problem, especially with regard to the category of the affected. For this purpose, this section and the following one explain some principles and concepts from CSH. Evidently, this will lead to a limited discussion of CSH. The discussion is confined to what is considered relevant for modeling and choosing stakeholders.

CSH belongs to the tradition of systems theory. However, as will be explained below, it occupies a special position in this tradition. There are many system approaches such as soft systems methodology, system dynamics, or the conceptual systems approach. . . . Basically, a system consists of a number of elements and the relationships between those elements. Whenever a systems perspective is applied, decisions must be made that define the system concerned. It is important to note that these decisions are determined by the standpoint or purposes of the researcher or designer.

The most fundamental modeling decision bounds the system from its environment. With regard to the stakeholder issue, this could be rephrased in bounding the system of stakeholders (note the definition of CSR given in the introduction) from the environment of nonstakeholders.

To a certain extent Ulrich's ideas can be viewed as a modeling methodology and as such they rightly belong to the systems tradition. Ulrich develops a number of so-called boundary judgments by critically reflecting on systems theory in general, and more specifically on modeling activity. He advocates a so-called critically normative systems approach (Ulrich 1988). What matters here is that the modeling activity is acknowledged as a normative activity, which is in need of critical reflection. A model of a system is adequate when it makes its normative content explicit. Before dealing with Ulrich's boundary judgments in more detail in the next section, some principles and general notions of CSH will be explained.

There are four closely intertwined principles that guide the practice of CSH,[14] i.e., the idea of "human intentionality," the "systems idea," the "moral idea," and the "guarantor idea." In making plans for social reality, the "planner" (i.e., the designer) has to deal with human intentions and purposes. Plans—or proposals for design—have a meaning for individuals. For that reason, social systems have to be designed to become purposeful. A purposeful system is able to produce knowledge that is relevant to purposes and is able to encourage debate about purposes. In general, according to Flood and Jackson (1991), CSH is about the design and assessment of purposeful systems. With regard to this, it is important that it is not only about "how to do things," but that it helps us to decide what we "ought to do" in order to improve reality. . . .

Through the moral idea Ulrich stresses that the planner should aim to improve human conditions by means of his/her plans. This means that the planner must be aware of the moral implications of the plan. As will be explained in the following section, referring to the so-called "involved" and "affected" of the social system reveals this awareness of the planner.

The meaning of the guarantor idea is that, although there is no guarantee that planning leads to improvement, the planner should seek to incorporate as many sources of guarantee as possible. This leads to seeking opinions by the planner from as many experts and stakeholder groups as possible.[15] . . .

MODELING A SYSTEM OF STAKEHOLDERS: THE INVOLVED AND THE AFFECTED

The main conclusion so far is that the planner, during his designing activities, must refer to a variety of groups. At this point it is relevant to return to stakeholder management in the CSR practice. After that, we will proceed with the modeling of the involved and affected as specifications of stakeholder groups.

In the previous section it is explained that the planner fulfills the role of a designer in order to improve social reality. This means that the notion of planning must be interpreted very broadly; planning is understood as social systems design. The concepts of "planning" and "planner," as used by Ulrich, are used here in terms of "stakeholder management" and "stakeholder manager."

According to Ulrich,[16] planning is, or should be, a public activity if the group of involved planners is not identical with the affected citizens. This position is very interesting within the context of stakeholder management. It means that stakeholder management should be a public activity if the group of involved beneficiaries of organizational activities is not identical with the affected nonbeneficiaries. . . .

The term social actor is interpreted here as a stakeholder. Actor refers to a social *role* rather than individuals. This means that these roles have to be specified in a concrete case in order to decide what individuals or groups of individuals are representatives of what roles. The "planner" must be seen as a social role as well. As said previously, in relation to stakeholder management he fulfills the role of stakeholder manager. Furthermore, in order to guarantee the normative content of the modeling practice, the various roles *and their concerns* in relation to the social system have to be specified.

Ulrich acknowledges two reasons anyone can claim belonging to the system: (i) because he is actually or potentially affected by the outcome of the system and (ii) because he has some kind of resource (expertise, political or financial, and so on) to contribute to the system, i.e., because he is involved.[17] This leads to the two basic boundary judgments. The first judgment bounds the total system of the involved and the affected from the environment, that is, from the environment of nonstakeholders. The second one makes the distinction between the involved and the affected. The term affected is restricted to the group that is affected, but not involved. This means that those individuals or groups who are involved and affected are considered as belonging to the group of the involved.

Let us consider the two basic groups in more detail and begin with the involved. On the basis of three sources of influence Ulrich divides the involved into three subgroups.

> Sources of motivation: whose purposes (values, interests) are being (ought to be) served? This leads to the group "client."
> Sources of control: who has (ought to have) the power to decide? This leads to the group "decision maker."
> Sources of expertise: who has (ought to have) the necessary expertise? This leads to the group "planner."

Three notes are relevant. First, concepts or categories such as "involved," "affected," or "planner" are projected on aspects of the real world. This is what modeling is about. We decide to call a certain group with certain characteristics "client" or "planner." What may be confusing here is that the application of CSH is not limited to the practice of organizational design or change and so forth, but can also be used for practices such as policy development or community planning. In organization theory the terms "client" or "planner" usually have a more restricted meaning.

Second, every group can be considered a prototypical role and comprises a specific case of a variety of individuals, who may belong to more than one group.

Third, every question of which the answer leads to a boundary judgment should not only be phrased in the *is* mode, but also in the *ought* mode. In this way, according to Flood and Jackson (1991), the normative content of the system design is best seen.

The second basic group, the affected, is more difficult to specify. This group does not have a well-defined contribution, but they endure the unwanted side effects or pay some costs that are not endured by those who benefit from the system. As noted before, especially concerning the affected, the problem of identifying stakeholders gets through. Potentially, this group is very large and it is not clear where the boundaries of this group lie.

According to Ulrich the affected groups can rarely be bounded, because knowledge about the potential side effects and long-term risks is usually insufficient.[18] Because of this identification problem Ulrich concludes that "the affected" can only be bounded by means of a representation. It is crucial that not the involved, i.e., the planner, but the affected themselves will determine who is to represent them.

At this point, the question rises of whether we have made any progress in resolving the problem of identifying this type of stakeholder. Indeed, as we look at the definition by Freeman (1984) of a stakeholder as "any group or individual who can affect or is affected by the achievement of the organization's objectives," there is a striking similarity with the definition of the involved (i.e., can affect) and the affected (i.e., is affected).

What makes Ulrich's distinction noteworthy is that he comes up with a role that will argue the case of the affected; the essence of this role is that of a witness.[19] Ulrich states, "Rather than pretending that we can adequately grasp such issues by means of a detailed list of heuristically necessary categories, I suggest that we limit the claim for heuristic necessity to the one essential category of the '*witness*' . . . the planner cannot adequately trace the normative content of alternative boundary judgments . . . without referring to some social actors playing the role of witness."[20]

So far we have four categories of social actors who comprise the system of stakeholders, and should have an input in the organization concerned. The client, the decision maker, and the planner are directly involved in the outcome of the organization. The witness represents the affected, which means that he becomes—indirectly—involved. . . .

THE WITNESS: A REPRESENTATIVE OF THE AFFECTED

While it is possible to describe the roles of the client, the decision maker, and the planner in functionalistic terms, that is not the case for the witness. Witnesses do not contribute resources or expertise, nor do their goals motivate organizational activity.

Ulrich reasons that the witnesses represent what he calls "the crucial source of legitimation."[21] By arguing the case of the affected towards the involved, they remind the involved of their moral responsibility for all the practical consequences of organizational activity. It is important that this responsibility goes beyond the effective functioning of the organization.

Basically, the different concerns of the involved and affected may be fundamentally conflicting. The essential point is, according to Ulrich, that the affected must be given the chance of emancipating themselves from being treated merely as means for purposes of others to "an end in themselves." This is why Ulrich designates "emancipation" as the major concern for the witness. Accordingly, this leads to the key problem . . . for the determination of this group. Conflicting concerns may be rooted in different worldviews (*weltanschauung*). In order to account for this fact, the different worldviews of the involved and the affected must be traced.

Who could be considered witnesses and in what way do they fulfill their role? In general, one could think of action groups, pressure groups, and the media when, and solely in this case, they argue the case of the affected with regard to a specific issue. . . .

CONCLUSION

This paper has focused on the question "To what extent can critical system heuristics (CSH) help in resolving the managerial problem of identifying stakeholders?" It has been argued that this identification problem comprises a modeling and a normative issue. The practice of corporate social responsibility means responding to a variety of stakeholders with different interests and needs. Consequently, there are always decisions to be made among conflicting interests and needs. Although CSH is by no means—in the terms of Ulrich—*a guarantor* for adequately dealing with those conflicting interests, it positively helps us to become aware of them. Furthermore, by answering the boundary questions the system of stakeholders can be modeled and this helps to reflect on the implications of decisions made. . . .

After these more general remarks, the following conclusions refer to the identification of the affected and to the witness as a representative of the affected. First, the distinction between the involved and the affected is considered crucial, not only because the involved have the possibility to influence organizational behavior and the affected do not have. The distinction is particularly important because of the modeling problems with regard to the affected. Acknowledging these problems along with the moral claim that an organization owes obligations to those whose freedom and well-being are affected, the notion of the witness possibly offers a way out. It reduces the modeling problems, not least because the initiative lies with those who consider themselves affected. The witness stands up for the interests of a specific group, as some medical experts did for the cancer patients in the "Petten case." As also shown in this case, the affected is not a homogeneous group for an organization. It is likely this category comprises different groups with varying interests, depending on the decision(s) on the agenda.

Second, the witness can be viewed as a channel for the affected to influence the organization, which means that, to some extent, they become involved. However, there is another side of the picture. As said before, there are always decisions to be made among conflicting interests and needs. Sometimes it comes down to finding a responsible balance between two evils. This is what Wempe (1998) calls the "dirty hands dilemma." Finding a responsible balance makes detailed investigation into the nature of the dilemma necessary. The notion of a witness may offer a means to investigate the nature of various stakeholder claims.

Third, it appears relevant to differentiate between witnesses depending on the amount and nature of their influence. There is a difference between a witness who stands up for the interests of a specific group and a witness who fulfills the role of a "mediator" between the organization and a group of affected. A witness mobilizes forces to influence the organization; a mediator tries to settle the differences.

Finally, an important question is "When can an individual rightfully be considered a witness?" An individual is solely a witness when he or she represents a group or individual that is affected by the organization's activities. It is the role of the witness to argue that the claim is justified. It must be emphasized that the reverse is not necessarily true. In other words, someone who *witnesses*, e.g., in the media, an organizational problem or failure is not necessarily *affected* by this event nor is a *representative* of the affected. This is why Ulrich stresses that it is only the affected themselves who can determine who is to represent them. Even so, a proactive attitude from the perspective of stakeholder management seems to be important. This leads to questions such as "In what way are witnesses determined?" "What kind of witness is available or adequate?" and "Whom are they representing?"

NOTES

1. T. Donaldson and L. Preston, "The Stakeholder Theory of the Corporation: Concepts, Evidence, and Implications," *Academy of Management Review* 20, no. 1 (1995): 65–91.

2. See, for example, R. E. Freeman, *Strategic Management: A Stakeholder Approach* (Boston: Pitman-Ballinger, 1984).

3. T. Takala and P. Pallab, "Individual, Collective, and Social Responsibility of the Firm," *Business Ethics: A European Review* 9, no. 2 (2000): 112.

4. J. Wempe, *Market and Morality: Business Ethics and the Dirty and Many Hands Dilemma* (Delft: Eburon, 1998).

5. See by means of comparison, Donaldson and Preston, "The Stakeholder Theory of the Corporation: Concepts, Evidence, and Implications," p. 87.

6. Freeman, *Strategic Management*, p. 46.

7. See by means of comparison, D. J. Wood, "Corporate Social Performance Revisited," *Academy of Management Review* 16, no. 4 (1991): 691–719; and M. Clarkson, "A Stakeholder Framework for Analyzing and Evaluating Corporate Social Performance," *Academy of Management Review* 20, no. 1 (1995): 92–117.

8. In R. K. Mitchell, B. R. Agle, and D. J. Wood, "Toward a Theory of Stakeholder Identification and Salience: Defining the Principle of Who and What Really Counts," *Academy of Management Review* 22, no. 4 (1997): 853–86.

9. Mitchell et al., "Toward a Theory of Stakeholder Identification and Salience."

10. "Redefining the Corporation" (2000), http://www.mgmt.utoronto.ca/~stake/Principles.htm (accessed January 31, 2002).

11. K. E. Goodpaster, "Business Ethics and Stakeholder Analysis," in *The Cor-

poration and Its Stakeholders: Classic and Contemporary Readings, ed. M. B. E. Clarkson (Toronto: University of Toronto Press, 1998), pp. 113, 117.

12. Mitchell et al., "Toward a Theory of Stakeholder Identification and Salience," p. 854.

13. W. Ulrich, *Critical Heuristics of Social Planning: A New Approach to Practical Philosophy* (Chichester: Wiley, 1983); Ibid., "Systems Thinking, Systems Practice, and Practical Philosophy: A Program of Research," *Systems Practice* 1, no. 2 (1988): 137–63; R. L. Flood and M. C. Jackson, *Creative Problem Solving: Total Systems Intervention* (Chichester: Wiley, 1991).

14. Flood and Jackson, *Creative Problem Solving*, p. 202.

15. Ibid., p. 204.

16. Ulrich, *Critical Heuristics of Social Planning*, p. 24.

17. Ibid., p. 248.

18. See, for example, the discussions about the unknown effects of changing the biological genes of our food.

19. Ulrich, *Critical Heuristics of Social Planning*, p. 252.

20. Ibid.

21. Ibid., p. 256.

16.
MORALITY AND STRATEGY IN STAKEHOLDER IDENTIFICATION

John Kaler

INTRODUCTION

Whatever the merits of a stakeholder approach to understanding how businesses could, should, or do operate (and this paper is neutral on all three issues), there can be no coherent assessment of those merits without a reasonably clear idea of what it is to be a stakeholder in a business; that is to say, a reasonably clear idea of what is meant by the term "stakeholder" in relation to businesses. This is not to expect a single, universally agreed definition. . . .

The dichotomy in question is amply demonstrated by a survey of twenty-eight definitions[1] covering a period from 1963 to 1995. What it shows is that apart from a few apparently neutral definitions where the connection of stakeholders to business is left unspecified, there is a more or less even split between definitions which see stakeholders as people for whom businesses have to take responsibility and definitions which see them as people who have to be taken account of but not necessarily because of any responsibility for them.[2] For definitions of the former sort, what matters, if only in a sometimes rather strained sense (a qualification to be returned to), is that stakeholders in a business have some kind of claim on the services of that organization. For definitions of the latter sort, what very unequivocally matters is that stakeholders can influence the workings of the business in some way. Appropriately enough then, definitions of the first sort have been described as seeing stakeholders as "claimants" and the second as seeing them as "influencers."[3]

Given that these are the status categories on offer for defining what it is to be a stakeholder, then the choice is between (a) an exclusively claimant definition, or (b) an exclusively influencer definition, or (c) allowing that a stakeholder can be either or both of these two things. With this third option we have what I shall call a "combinatory" definition. It is the option, or something like it, favored by the authors of the survey. They assume that what they call "a theory of stakeholder identification"[4] must not only accommodate the issues of "legitimacy" and "power" attendant upon a status as claimants and/or influencers respectively, but also a third dimension deriving from the "urgency" of a stakeholder's claims and/or influence.[5]

In contrast, this paper will favor the altogether simpler option of an exclusive rather than inclusive definition. It will argue that, at least for the purposes of business ethics, some form of claimant definition is required—if only in the strained sense hinted at earlier. . . .

DIVIDING DEFINITIONS[6]

The allowing of a strained sense as well as a specification of the claim as a moral one is needed because of the lack of any agreed way of attributing claimant status to stakeholders. Among our twenty-eight definitions, for instance, the talk does not merely fluctuate between "claims" and "rights," with the added complication that they can be "legal" or "moral" or simply "legitimate"; there are also what might only be claimantlike definitions which talk of stakeholders being people for whom an organization is "responsible," of them being "contract holders," of them being people with investments at "risk," or just people with "legitimate interests."

Despite differences in the kinds of claims being talked about and, it must be allowed, differing degrees of explicitness that claims *are* being talked about, it is noteworthy that these definitions seem to make no concessions to the fact that claimants can also be influencers.[7] What makes this noteworthy is that the same (or rather its converse) cannot be said to be true of at least some of the definitions on the influencer side of the divide. They talk of stakeholders giving "support" to organizations, of those organizations "depending" or being "dependent" on them, of stakeholders being able to "affect" an organization, of them being able to "influence" it or be "influencers" of it, or simply being capable of having an "impact" upon it.[8] But some of them also juxtapose this with talk of stakeholders "depending on" an organization, of them being "affected by" it, "influenced by" it, and "impacted by" it. With this juxtaposing they are recognizing that the causal connection between stakeholder and organization can be a two-way affair and not simply, as with nonjuxtaposing definitions of the influencer-type, the influencing of organizations *by* stakeholders. In so doing, the juxtaposing definitions are not, as might be supposed,[9] combining influencer and claimant definitions. All they are doing in recognizing that stakeholders can be "affected by" as well as "affect" organizations is including what might be, and probably is, a *necessary* condition for being a claimant.[10]

To see why it might be a necessary condition, one need merely reflect that there seems to be no point in having claims against anything which cannot affect us in any way. The whole point of claims, be they legal or moral, is the obtaining of benefits or protection from harm. (Otherwise, why have claims?) So as we can only be benefited or protected by something that *can* affect us (because being benefited or protected *is* being affected), it follows that a capacity to be affected by something is a necessary condition for having a claim against it. Equally obviously, to see why that capacity is not also a sufficient condition, one needs merely reflect on the fact that if it were then we would be subject to claims up to the limit of our capacity to affect other people and that the result would be lives almost entirely devoted to the services of others. That is to say, everything we *could* do by way of affording benefit and protection to others would be something we are *required* to do. What, in practice, law and morality actually require of us is, however, somewhat below the possible. In practice, what we are required to do falls short of what we could do. Consequently, the fact of being affected by someone is not enough for having a claim against them which would be required to be met.[11] Consequently, juxtaposing talk of stakeholders as people who can "affect" an organization with talk of them being "affected by" it is not enough for constituting what I have characterized as a combinatory definition of stakeholding.[12]

LIMITS TO CLAIMS

Before dealing with stakeholders as claimants it is necessary to discuss some of the ways in which limits to the meeting of claims are set. The most obvious limitation is law and morality not requiring too much of us by way of self-sacrifice in benefiting or protecting others. At a more theoretical level, it is by the recognition of different kinds of duties.[13] One such distinction is between "universal" or "general" duties incumbent on everyone and merely "special" or "role-specific" duties incumbent only on those fulfilling a particular social role in relation to particular individuals. Another relevant distinction is that between "perfect" duties for which there is a corresponding right and merely "imperfect" duties, typically duties of benevolence, for which there is not. Both, in their different ways, set limits to the claims that we are required to meet. The first does this by limiting claims in excess of those demanded by general duties to people with role-specific duties; the second by not recognizing rights in relation to certain kinds of duties.

STAKEHOLDING FOR THE
PURPOSES OF BUSINESS ETHICS

Whatever else can be said about the nature of business ethics as a subject, and there is clearly room for a variety of opinions here, that it is centrally concerned with the moral conduct of business is true almost by definition. Furthermore, unless it is to be relegated to the status of a purely descriptive subject free of that element of prescription common to subjects within the business studies curriculum, then its ultimate concern is with *improving* the moral conduct of business.[14] From this it follows that, for the purposes of business ethics, stakeholding has to be ultimately about improving the moral conduct of business.

Despite the absence of anything like a standard account of stakeholding, the way in which it could, in principle, lead to an improvement in the moral conduct of business is reasonably clear. The starting point is the assumption common to any and all definitions of what it is for a person to be a stakeholder, that it is someone with interests "at stake" in relation to the activities of a business. (There is, it can be suggested, nothing else for "stakeholder" to mean in this context.) Consequently, it has to be as a better way of serving interests that stakeholding would, in principle, lead to an improvement in the moral conduct of business; in short, by being an improvement in distributive justice.[15] . . .

ASSESSING DEFINITIONS

(a) *Claimant definitions.* On the basis of the above analysis, there is a clear presumption in favor of a claimant definition. If stakeholding for the purposes of business ethics is (in summary) requiring businesses to serve more than just the interests of owners, then there is a clear implication that stakeholders are people with some sort of claim on the services of a business (in addition to claims based on right of ownership). I would conclude, therefore, that unless it can be shown that there are clear advantages to favoring one or other of the other two options, or at least the avoidance of disadvantages, then the presumption has to be in favor of some sort of claimant definition or, at least, something related to it.

The qualification that the presumption might only need to be for something close to a claimant definition allows for definitions which talk only of business having "responsibility" for stakeholders . . . and, therefore, leave it open as to whether they are speaking of a perfect duty for which there is a corresponding right or a merely imperfect duty for which there is not. . . . If the latter, then we have something which although it can be aligned with definitions speaking of a perfect duty (what might be called claimant definitions "proper"), is saying something rather different about the nature of stakeholding. The contrast is that whereas the postulating of a perfect duty makes serving the interests of stakeholders something which they can demand as of right, a definition postulating only an imperfect duty does not. Consequently, although in requiring that those interests be served a definition based on an imperfect duty joins claimant definitions proper in doing what business ethics demands of stakeholding, it does so in a way which makes the serving voluntary. The serving of those interests is a mere duty of benevolence: an act of philanthropy. As such, it is something which businesses may or may not engage in, depending on how generous they choose to be. In contrast, given that the claim has to be legitimate (see below), with a claimant definition proper, what options there might be reside with the stakeholders in that it could be possible for them to choose not to exercise their right to have their interests served. So while the beneficiaries of an imperfect duty have a claim only in what might be called the "weak" sense of a claim on our conscience, the beneficiaries of a perfect duty are claimants in what might, in contrast, be called the "strong" sense of an appeal to a right recognized in morality and/or law. Thus, while definitions based on either kind of duty will, for convenience, be spoken of as "claimant" definitions, it must be borne in mind that it is only in terms of that somewhat strained sense spoken of as "weak" that definitions appealing to a merely imperfect duty toward stakeholders warrant that appellation; that in terms of the contrasting "strong" sense, what we have is two subcategories of duty-based definitions with only those appealing to a perfect duty toward stakeholders warranting the appellation "claimant" definition.[16]

Whether they be strong or weak, what is very obviously demanded of these claims by business ethics is that they should be, first, role-specific, second, moral, and third, legitimate. They have to be role-specific because, whatever else it is, the responsibility involved is something over and above a general duty incumbent upon everyone.[17] (There need be no acceptance of stakeholding to acknowledge the fact that businesses cannot go around killing and stealing, for example.) Even more obviously, given that business ethics requires stakeholding to be a vehicle for improving the moral conduct of business, it follows that the claim involved must be moral as it is only in being directed toward meeting moral claims that stakeholding can be such a vehicle.[18] So given the truism that legality is no guarantee of morality (apart from anything else, the laws themselves might be immoral), it also follows that, for the purposes of business ethics, these claims cannot only, or even also, be required to be legal. They are only required to be moral. . . .

(b) *Influencer definitions.* The standard complaint that stakeholding entails both an unfeasibly wide range of stakeholders and offers no way of discriminating between their often-competing claims[19] is made more plausible by a starting point in an influencer definition.[20] This is because if all that is demanded of stakeholders is that they can influence (or be influenced by) a business, then there is almost no limit to who might count as a stakeholder and, in terms of the definition, no basis for discriminating between the bewilderingly wide range of interests they represent. After all, just about anyone in any sort of causal interaction with a business is going to be capable of influencing (or being influenced by) its operations. In fact, as critics are keen to point out[21] and advocates have to acknowledge,[22] it will even follow that competitor firms and such thoroughly illegitimate groups as terrorists are counted as stakeholders.

In contrast, a claimant definition, at least in the characterization favored, is appreciably more selective. It will only admit those with morally legitimate claims against a business to stakeholder status (thereby excluding terrorists and the like) and also makes the serving of their interests specific to their role in relation to the business (thereby offering a basis for discriminating between competing interests). But however effectively claimant definitions might overcome these problems of range and discrimination (and being neutral on the merits of stakeholding, no opinion need be offered here), the crucial point to be made here is that these problems can be assumed to beset influencer definitions *only* on the assumption that they are required to serve that very same function of recognizing which interests must be served that claimant definition so obviously fulfill.[23] If, however, we look at what can be loosely described as the "logic" of influencer definitions then we see that regardless of the intention of their framers (which may be otherwise), such definitions do *not* characterize stakeholders in terms of interests to be served. Their characterization is entirely in terms of the influence which stakeholders can exert on a business (or the influence it can exert upon them). Consequently, their concern is not with *interests* but, as noted by Mitchell et al., *power*.[24] Thus, in so far as influencer definitions are equipped to serve any function at all (which I go on to doubt), it is in relation to the subject of strategy rather than that of business ethics.[25]

This follows from the fact that, whatever else it involves, the subject of strategy is centrally concerned with the process of setting and achieving objectives rather than determining what those objectives should be. It leaves that to those in control of businesses, offering prescriptions only with regard to means rather than ends.[26] Consequently, a definition of stakeholders in terms of a power to influence is perfectly compatible with the demands of strategy in that it entails no presuppositions about what the objectives of a business should be. . . .

(c) *Combinatory definitions*. It is here, in the marriage of two apparently very dissimilar subjects that the attractions of a combinatory definition lie. What attracts is the prospect of bringing business ethics into the mainstream of business subjects by integrating its concerns with those of businesses in general and, in particular, their pursuit of profit. A combinatory definition holds out this prospect because, as the combining of ethics and strategy, it presents itself as a vehicle for making ethical concerns compatible with whatever objectives businesses happen to have—including the pursuit of profit. We are presented with a vehicle for not only that combining of ethics and strategy which Freeman calls "an enterprise strategy"[27] but also, through that combining, a way of overcoming that claim for a dichotomy between "the discourse of business and the discourse of ethics" which he identifies as the "separation thesis." In fact, according to Freeman, "the whole point of the stakeholder approach is to deny the Separation Thesis."[28]

What Freeman means by the separation thesis seems obvious enough. What it basically amounts to is the rather commonplace contention that the pursuit of purely commercial objectives is different from, and perhaps even conflicts with, the pursuit of ethical objectives. What is less clear, at least to me, is whether Freeman is saying that a stockholder approach is predicated on the assumption that the separation thesis is false or suggesting that adoption of the approach brings about an integration of the discourses of business and ethics which makes it false. But in terms of a supposed role for a combinatory definition in bringing about such an integration, it has to be the latter because if the two discourses are already integrated then that role is redundant (along, perhaps, with any need to adopt a stakeholding approach).[29] However, to suppose that this or any other definition of stakeholding bas any sort of role in bringing about an integration of business and ethics is to accept that without that intervention the two things are separate; in other words, that the separation thesis is true.

There are at least two possible ways the adoption of stakeholding could overcome this presumed separation of business and ethics. The first and most obvious is that by adding ethical considerations to what would otherwise be decision making based entirely upon purely commercial considerations, stakeholding requires a balancing of the two sets of concerns. The second and less obvious way is that in requiring decision making based (wholly or partly) on ethical considerations, stakeholding leads to greater commercial success than would be the case if that decision making were based on purely commercial considerations alone: a specifically stakeholder version of the "ethics pays" contention that Donaldson and Preston (1995) have identified as the "instrumental" aspect to stakeholder theory.

Whichever of the two options is favored, there is no more or less of integration of ethics and business with a combinatory definition of stakeholding than there would be with an exclusively claimant definition. All that the influencer element within a combinatory definition can add to its claimant element is a consideration of strategic factors (subsection (b)). These are, however, factors that would still have to be taken into consideration with stakeholding based on an exclusively claimant definition. They would have to be because given that they are, by definition, the factors that have to be taken into consideration in setting and achieving objectives (subsection (b)), there is no way that there can be objectives of any kind without consideration of strategic factors. Thus, while the claimant element within a combinatory definition adds ethical considerations to an integration of business and ethics, the influencer element adds nothing to the business side of the integration that would not be there on the basis of an exclusively claimant definition.

It might be claimed that although not necessary for a consideration of strategic factors, conceiving of such factors in terms of stakeholders as influencers is a better way of taking them into consideration than could otherwise be the case. However, in the absence of any demonstration to the contrary (and I know of no way it could be demonstrated), there is no reason to suppose that a straightforward consideration of strategic factors is any less effective than their rather less straightforward consideration in terms of stakeholders as influencers. In fact, although conceiving of strategic factors in this way adds a superficial air of comprehensiveness to the term "stakeholder" in that it is used in a way which covers both ethics and strategy, that coverage is not just, as this subsection has shown, a needless extension of the term but also, as this entire paper has shown, a very confusing equivocation. . . .

NOTES

1. R. K. Mitchell et al., "Toward a Theory of Stakeholder Identification and Salience: Defining Who and What Really Counts," *Academy of Management Review* 22, no. 4 (1997): 853–86.

2. For convenience (reinforced by inclination), I will assume that only people are stakeholders and not also entities such as other businesses, public institutions, or the environment. I will also, though here strictly for reason of convenience, ignore stakeholders in nonbusiness organizations.

3. Mitchell et al., "Toward a Theory of Stakeholder Identification and Salience: Defining Who and What Really Counts," p. 859.

4. Ibid.

5. Ibid., pp. 865–68.

6. Unfortunately owing to space restrictions it is not possible to reproduce all twenty-eight definitions here. (For this the reader is referred to Mitchell et al., 1997, p. 858.) However, by my reckoning, thirteen are influencer, eleven claimant, three neutral, and one, B. Langtry 1994, p. 433, combinatory. (Though only the initial claimant half of the definition is cited by Mitchell et al.)

7. The fact that claimants can also be influencers is expanded on in J. Frooman 1999.

8. Definitions talking of "support" and "depending" constitute what Freeman and Reed (1983, cited Evan and Freeman, 1993, p. 259) call "narrow" as opposed to "wide" definitions in that only those essential to the workings of an organization count as stakeholders. In contrast, definitions that simply talk of "affect," "influence," "influencers," and "impact" are wide definitions in that almost anyone having any kind of causal influence on an organization can count among its stakeholders. Wide definitions are, therefore, particularly open to the frequently voiced criticism that an unmanageable number of different groups count as stakeholders; a criticism which, I will suggest, misses the point with regard to influencer definitions.

9. J. Frooman, "Stakeholder Influence Strategies," *Academy of Management Review* 24, no. 2 (1999): 192.

10. As, following Freeman (1984, p. 46), the "affect/ affected by" formulation is probably the single most cited definition of any kind, influencer or claimant, it is appropriate as well as convenient to use this form of words in demonstrating how such juxtaposing definitions are not fully combinatory in character. (It is also the form of words relied on in the example just cited of the juxtaposing being assumed

to constitute a combining definition—though Frooman's claim, p. 192—that the same assumption is made by Goodpaster [see 1991, p. 59] is questionable.)

11. Claims that are not required to be met are, of course, not subject to any conditions: being legally and/or morally illegitimate, they are simply made rather than possessed. However, as will be pointed out, illegitimate claims can only play a part in relation to influencer definitions: the claimant definitions which concern us here can, it will be noted, only deal in legitimate claims.

12. Given that in Freeman's formulation the full definition is "affect or affected by the achievement of the organization's objectives" [Kaler's emphasis], it seems reasonably clear that the fact of being affected is being required to be taken into account only insofar as it has strategic implications (presumably by way of an adverse or favorable reaction). As such, and despite also being a necessary condition for a claimant definition, the "affected by" part of the formulation is as influencer orientated as the "affect" part.

13. For a brief outline of these distinctions, see O'Neill 1992, p. 192; for a somewhat longer discussion (and the use of "general" and "role-specific" rather than "universal" and "special"), see Chyssides and Kaler 1993, pp. 104–106.

14. J. Kaler, "Positioning Business Ethics in Relation to Management and Political Philosophy," *Journal of Business Ethics* 24, no. 3 (2000): 264.

15. I. Maitland, "Distributive Justice in Firms: Do the Rules of Corporate Governance Matter?" *Business Ethics Quarterly* 11, no. 1 (2001): 129–43.

16. The weak sense of "claim" generates a correspondingly weak conception of stakeholding exemplified in the unenforceable duty to employees of section 309 of the present UK Companies Act (Parkinson 1994, pp. 18–19), in the US corporate constituency statutes (Orts 1992), and in the "nonfiduciary" approach to stakeholders other than shareholders advocated by Goodpaster (1991, p. 67).

17. Friedman recognizes this point when he acknowledges that even a business operating on the basis of his stockholding approach has to stay within the "basic rules" of law and "ethical custom." (Friedman 1993, p. 249).

18. This requirement does not deny that being a vehicle for improving the moral conduct of business may sometimes involve meeting immoral claims in order to secure a moral end, for even under those circumstances the directing is still toward meeting moral claims.

19. For citations see T. Ambler and A. Wilson, "Problems of Stakeholder Theory," *Business Ethics: A European Review* 4, no. 1 (1995): 33; and C. E. Metcalfe, "The Stakeholder Corporation," *Business Ethics: A European Review* 7, no. 1 (1998): 32.

20. For example, see Elaine Sternberg, "Stakeholder Theory: The Defective State It's In," in *Stakeholding and Its Critics* (London: Institute of Economics Affairs, 1997), pp. 71–72.

21. Sternberg, "Stakeholder Theory: The Defective State It's In," p. 71.

22. R. E. Freeman, *Strategic Management: A Stakeholder Approach* (Pitman, Marshfield, 1984), pp. 53–55.

23. Assuming that an influencer definition serves a claimant function conflates an influencer criterion for identifying stakeholders with a claimant criterion for the purpose of the identification: a conflation of "who?" with "why?" so to speak.

24. This is not, of course, to deny that just as stakeholders can be claimants as well as influencers, they can also have interests and well as power. It is simply that only the latter aspect figures within influencer definitions—despite what might be the intention of their framers to include both elements (e.g., Freeman 1984, pp. 60–61).

25. In being related to strategy, stakeholding goes back to what might be its academic roots (Freeman 1984, pp. 31–33); though its nonacademic roots may be earlier and less unequivocally strategic (Clarkson 1995, pp. 105–106).

26. Neutrality with regard to objectives is a feature of standard definitions of "strategy" and "strategic" in the context of business (as demonstrated by entries in Cooper and Argyris 1998, pp. 624–42). It is also why Goodpaster (1991, p. 60) describes stakeholding based on what I have identified as an influencer definition as "strategic."

27. Freeman, *Strategic Management: A Stakeholder Approach*, p. 90.

28. R. E. Freeman, "The Politics of Stakeholder Theory: Some Future Directions," *Business Ethics Quarterly* 4, no. 4 (1994): 412.

29. There is an integration of ethics and business making stakeholding apparently redundant if, as Friedman (1993) famously claimed the pursuit of anything except strictly commercial objectives would be an immoral transgression of property rights or, as Adam Smith even more famously claimed, the pursuit of strictly commercial objectives (unintentionally) maximizes benefits to society at large.

17.

THE PRIMORDIAL STAKEHOLDER

Advancing the Conceptual Consideration of Stakeholder Status for the Natural Environment

Cathy Driscoll and Mark Starik

THE STAKEHOLDER CONCEPT

Stakeholder theory concerns the nature of the relationships between organizations and their respective stakeholders and the processes and outcomes of these relationships for organizations and their stakeholders.[1] The manager is typically placed at the center of the contractual relationship between a business organization and its stakeholders.[2] Definitions of stakeholder in the literature range from the broad and inclusive to the narrow and exclusive. The inclusive definition is typically prescriptive, adopting a public relations or moral focus. For example, stakeholders have often been considered to include any groups or individuals who can significantly affect or be affected by an organization's activities,[3] but has been broadened to include nonhumans.[4] . . .

Normative stakeholder theory focuses on defining the basis of stakeholder legitimacy, whether it is risk, property rights, or moral claims.[5] For example, Donaldson and Preston (1995) contend that managers should enter into a mutually supportive relationship with their stakeholders because it is morally right. A "social contract" exists between business and society. According to these authors, "stakeholders are identified through the actual or potential harms and benefits that they experience or anticipate experiencing as a result of the firm's actions or inactions."[6] Normative stakeholder theory has been criticized, however, for the lack of a specific framework and for problems in identifying stakeholders.[7]

Mitchell et al. (1997) attempted to address this gap by specifying theoretically "who [or what] really counts" as a stakeholder in management thinking. According to these authors, stakeholders have one or more of the following attributes: *power* to influence the firm; *legitimacy* of a relationship; and/or *urgency* of a claim. They predict "the salience of a particular stakeholder to the firm's management is low if only one of these attributes is present, moderate if two attributes are present, and high if all three attributes are present."[8] "Definitive stakeholders" have not only power and legitimacy, but also an urgent claim on the firm, which gives these stakeholders managerial priority. According to their framework, the natural environment is a "dependent stakeholder" or one that depends on other dominant stakeholders "for the power necessary to carry out [its] will."[9] In their view, nature's claims are often seen as legitimate and urgent; however, the natural environment is not salient to managers unless other dominant stakeholders exercise their power to support the natural environment or unless managerial values lean in a "green" direction. . . .

POWER, LEGITIMACY, AND URGENCY

Power

Many conventional management theories emphasize the central role of power in decision making, focusing on utilitarian resource exchange and dependence-based relationships.[10] Similarly, most stakeholder models have emphasized managerial perceptions of power in identifying and prioritizing stakeholders.[11] An instrumental stakeholder perspective defines stakeholders as those groups or individuals who are in a mutually dependent or exchange relationship with the firm.[12] . . .

It is readily recognizable that the natural environment has a mutually dependent, exchange-based relationship with business organizations. The firm depends on local ecosystems, as well as the broader ecosphere, for raw materials, plant, animal, and microbial inputs, and energy.[13] In fact, business organizations exchange more with the natural environment than with any other stakeholder, interacting through "myriad ecosystem service transactions that ultimately keep organizations alive."[14] Other scholars have described the complex interdependencies among ecosystems, human systems, and business organizations.[15]

Mitchell et al. (1997) applied Etzioni's (1964) organizational bases of power to their stakeholder attribute of power. Their application implies that a stakeholder has power to the extent that it can use coercive (force/threat), utilitarian (material/ incentives), or normative (symbolic influence) power to "impose its will in the relationship."[16] While we may never identify nature's "will," the natural environment holds coercive and utilitarian power over business organizations as shown by countless examples of the natural environment's significant influence on industrial activity. . . . However, the influence of nature, especially the subtle influence over time, such as the effect bodies of water have on their shores and, consequently, on land-based human activities, such as residential developments, is overlooked in most conceptualizations of stakeholder power. . . .

Moreover, it has been suggested that the social power of the stakeholder in stakeholder theory is based on economic exchange and that conventional stakeholder theories overlook such topics as asymmetrical relations of power and systemic inequalities, which can lead to environmental injustice.[17] The natural environment supplies "critical resources" to the firm but usually not through economic exchange relationships. . . .

Legitimacy

. . . [T]he management literature comprises both strategic and moral bases for legitimacy. In stakeholder theory, these include contractual relationships (based on legal, moral, or ownership rights)[18] or exchange-based relationships in which those who own the resources supply "critical resources" to the firm.[19] According to Hybels (1995), however, resource flows provide the best evidence of organizational legitimacy.

Most literature suggests that stakeholder legitimacy is grounded in pragmatic evaluations of stakeholder relationships rather than in normative assessments of moral propriety.[20] For example, Barney asserts that "[t]o be a stakeholder, a party must make important resources (such as labor, money, and loyalty) available to a firm."[21] Pragmatic approaches to legitimacy assume an instrumental view of the concept, in which legitimacy is seen as a resource that can be manipulated.[22] This approach focuses on the "self-interested calculations of an organization's most immediate audiences" and has been referred to as "exchange legitimacy" or "influence legitimacy."[23] This instrumental view also parallels the power-dependence and resource-exchange approach to firm-stakeholder relationships discussed in the previous section. Moral legitimacy, on the other hand, is based on normative approval and the rightness or wrongness of organizational actions, down-playing managerial agency and instrumentality.[24] . . .

The natural environment has attained legitimacy from the world's scientific community, which has reached consensus on the deteriorating state of the environment and the links to human activity.[25] For example, global climate change has been associated with human carbon emissions, including business use of fossil fuels, and the loss of biodiversity, again linked to habitat-destroying human economic activities such as fishing, forestry, and residential and commercial construction.[26] Yet, while significant effort has been invested in attempting to slow or reverse global environmental damage and deterioration in the past several decades, a number of world environmental challenges have proved intractable, and several have worsened in that time.[27] . . .

Urgency

Mitchell et al. (1997) defined stakeholder urgency as the stakeholder's claim for immediate attention based on the ideas of time sensitivity or the "degree to which managerial delay in attending to the claim or relationship is unacceptable to the stakeholder" and criticality or the "importance of the claim or the relationship to the stakeholder."[28] However, a recent review of the strategy literature found that the subjective nature of "time," including how social processes affect perceptions of time, has been overlooked by researchers.[29] For example, society's attention is often focused on high-profile, large-scale crises, such as the human-made environmental catastrophes of oil and chemical spills, hazardous waste leaks, and industrial explosions. . . . However, salience is still lacking regarding "slowly evolving issues," where the impact on humans is not as obvious as environmental catastrophes (e.g., urban sprawl, coastal development, biodiversity loss, and endangerment of species extinction).

Like power and legitimacy, urgency has a *social* and an *economic* connotation. Although the focus in the Mitchell et al. model is on the stakeholder's perception of the urgency of the stakeholder's claim, managers' perceptions of urgency drive most stakeholder models and those perceptions are biased toward economic short-termism,[30] which is often precipitated by the use of cost-benefit analysis, rates of return, and changes in stock prices. Agle et al. (1999) have recently found evidence supporting the idea that shareholder urgency drives most corporate managerial strategies. Others have similarly suggested that managers are short-sighted in their planning horizons and focus on short-term profits.[31] The resurgence in the number of mergers, acquisitions, and downsizings in North America and Europe over the past decade, along with the recent cases of fraudulent accounting practices among major North American companies, provides further evidence of a short-term economic focus.

Although environmental management strategies have been developed to consider environmental impact related to waste and pollution, such as pollution-prevention-pays and the natural resource-based view, less attention is given to longer-term, less observable and incremental impacts, such as those affecting biodiversity and the overall ecosystem. Starik and Rands suggest that, "[g]iven the criticality of economic contingencies, we would not be surprised if most organizations gave insufficient attention to ecological contingencies until they became too dramatic to ignore."[32] . . .

What's Wrong with This Picture?

While the three criteria for "stakeholderness" that have been forwarded, in whole or part, by Freeman (1984), Carroll (1993), Mitchell et al. (1997), and others appear necessary in determining stakeholder identification and salience, the attributes of power, legitimacy, and urgency as currently conceptualized fail to give the natural environment primary stakeholder status. That is, definitions associated with these three constructs and their corresponding bases are inadequate for incorporating the near and the far, the short and the long term, and the actual and the potential. However, by reinterpreting these three attributes, we can make the natural environment–primary organizational stakeholder connection more obvious. We are assisted by previous scholars' work in the areas of eco-sustainability[33] and the moral standing of the natural environment.[34]

REVISITING POWER, LEGITIMACY, AND URGENCY

Mitchell et al. suggested that normative stakeholder theory's search for stakeholder legitimacy "can be a powerful blinder to the real impact of stakeholder power and claim urgency."[35] Alternatively, we suggest that the limited conceptions of power that continue to dominate stakeholder thought and practice are a powerful blinder to the importance of many legitimate stakeholders, including the natural environment. The context of the resource-dependent relationship between the firm and the natural environment is different from social theory perspectives under an *eco-sustainability paradigm*. Here, power is used equitably in accordance with *both social and ecological needs*. Instead of focusing on social domination and control, the relationships among nature, society, and economy are emphasized, such as those relationships among nature, equity, and development. In this alternate paradigm, power is "gained through the emergence of collaborative assemblies, interdependent domains, and cooperative networks."[36] The mutual dependence between the firm and the natural environment is seen as critical to firm survival, and human agency and ability to influence, directly and perceptibly, are not considered necessary attributes for determining stakeholder salience.[37] Moreover, it is nature, not the firm that holds the balance of power. Firms acknowledge their biophysical foundations and the interconnectedness of all life cycles.

To better identify and make salient the long-range threats and far-reaching material impacts related to the business organization–natural environment relationship, we suggest that the concept of pervasiveness (the degree to which stakeholder impact is spread over distance and time) be incorporated into both coercive power and utilitarian power. These are two of the bases for stakeholder power described in the Mitchell et al. model.

The nature of legitimacy also changes under an eco-sustainablity perspective, as ecological, economic, and social priorities change, as evidenced by the increased number of legal and moral claims made on behalf of the natural environment. Management theory and practice focus on moral depictions of legitimacy, which are grounded in broader cultural and ecological values. For example, Wood's (1991) bases for organizational legitimacy to stakeholder identification and salience could be broadened to include ecological as well as individual, organizational, and societal levels. . . . In this respect, stakeholder theory would focus on the mutual symbiosis between business organizations and their stakeholders. As human individuals develop ever numerous and complex relationships with the nonhuman natural environment, more human organizations will also begin to recognize explicitly the stakeholder status of nonhuman nature. . . .

We suggest that probability (potentiality or likelihood of interaction) be included as a basis for urgency in addition to Mitchell et al.'s bases of time sensitivity and criticality. While *actual* effects between any two entities can imply a stakeholder relationship, a probable or potential interaction can also imply a stakeholder relationship as in a firm's customer prospects, its possible suppliers undergoing firm qualification, and its job applicants. In each of these and similar cases, the stakeholder aspect of "affect or affected by" may already be occurring even before the more traditional stakeholder relationships have begun. We assert that the more likely these entities are of being converted from potential to actual customers, suppliers, and employees, respectively, the more likely they can be considered stakeholders. This suggestion follows a well-known concept in the issues management literature called the probability-impact matrix, in which issues with high probability and high impact are prescribed for the greatest amount of attention.[38] The issues management "impact" variable has already been included or at least implied in the "power" criterion for "stakeholderness." Therefore, at least those aspects of nonhuman nature that have high probabilities of affecting business organizations or being affected by them, such as projected shortages of fuel, fish, and forest stocks, might be considered to have firm stakeholder status since cognizant organizations will already factor likely-occurring environmental phenomena into their respective plans before such shortages occur. . . .

EXPANDING THE SET OF STAKEHOLDER CRITERIA

While much of the stakeholder literature identifies two or more possible stakeholder criteria, a recent work on stakeholder identity by Phillips and Reichart (2000) holds that only a fairness-based set of criteria is appropriate for ascription of stakeholder status. In our opinion, confining stakeholder determinations to one criterion, such as fairness, reduces the usefulness of the concept, in this case ostensibly applicable only to humans in justice-oriented relationships with one another. Such a limited perspective of "stakeholderness" may not even include those relationships most academics and practitioners have readily accepted, such as the inclusion of national environmental groups among the stakeholders of major multinational companies that have been responsible for major environmental problems.[39] Rather, we believe that stakeholder theory needs to reflect more rather than fewer stakeholder aspects to make the concept more comprehensive and realistic. In addition, other criteria might further help in developing a stakeholder identification and salience model that considers the nonhuman natural environment to be one or more key stakeholders of the firm. The concept of proximity seems especially applicable to both defining "stakeholderness" and including the rest of nature in the stakeholder considerations of organizations.

Proximity

Proximity is suggested here as a possible "stakeholderness" criterion because spatial distance can be as important in stakeholder interactions as is time, which is associated with the urgency criteria suggested by Mitchell et al.[40] Others, such as Gladwin et al., have suggested that stakeholder models need to be "more spatially and temporally inclusive."[41] Proximity, or "the state, quality, or fact of being near or next" in "space, time, or order,"[42] has been an important concept in a wide variety of scholarly fields, including healthcare,[43] the arts,[44] the social sciences,[45] and business.[46] When applied to spatial relationships, proximity allows for the common observation that entities, including organizations that share the same physical space or are adjacent to one another, often affect one another. From nation states that share borders through firms whose headquarters are located in the same towns to individuals and households who are residential neighbors, their respective proximity characteristics contribute significantly to their development of stakeholder relationships. As such, spatial nearness is one of many factors that can play a role in stakeholder recognition and interaction. We can, therefore, theorize that the greater the proximity, the greater the likelihood of the development of stakeholder relationships, ceteris paribus.

However, this connection between proximity and stakeholder status is highly nuanced, as are perhaps other stakeholder criteria. In addition to physical proximity, organizations can be said to be proximate if they share the same or similar ideas, approaches, and actions, that is, they are proximate to one another in concept or practice or that they occupy the same "field."[47] For example, firms in the same industry (defined here as a "product-market") are well-accepted stakeholders of one another, particularly if they are members of the same or of allied industry associations. In addition, firms that share stakeholders, say, retail customers, or firms that consider themselves buyers or suppliers of one another, are considered proximate stakeholders in their shared value chains. Thus, proximity may be associated with the well-researched business variable of relatedness,[48] as well as with the emerging idea of stakeholder networks,[49] in which the relevant context is a set or system of interconnected stakeholders (i.e., a business's stakeholders who also have stakeholders, and so forth).

Two relevant variables of networks that are related to the proximity concept are centrality and density,[50] in which entities such as organizations can be considered to be controlling hubs if they are located more centrally among a group of other network entities especially when these entities are positioned in networks "thick with" nodes, that is, the linkages among these entities are numerous and interactive.

A special case of the application of proximity is that in which an entity lies within, or is embedded in, the other entity, that is, they share a physical space. Organizational facilities located within the physical boundaries of an organization; companies located in specific neighborhoods, cities, and states; and firms that operate within national government jurisdictions are examples of stakeholder embeddedness. Such embeddedness sets the stage for stakeholder interaction since the embedded entity cannot help affecting, at least marginally, the larger entity it is within, since the former is a component of the latter larger entity.[51]

Similarly, the concept of ubiquity, in which an entity is not only surrounded by another, but one in which a stakeholder is so multifaceted as to be virtually omnipresent, also applies to the attribute of proximity. Here the mutuality of the coexistence between, say, an organization and its stakeholders, such as the organization's members, is the relevant stakeholder criterion. . . .

Since nonhuman nature surrounds all human business and is the ultimate context in which all human business is conducted, it would qualify as one or more firm critical stakeholders under the subcriterion of embeddedness. The case for considering nature as one or more organizational stakeholders includes each of the aspects of proximity discussed above. The most obvious connection between the proposed proximity stakeholder criterion and our assertion that organizations and the natural environment interactions can be considered stakeholder relationships (especially in eco-sustainability perspectives) is the immediate local impacts produced by organizations that pollute or deplete local ecosystems, and the local impacts the natural environment, such as weather patterns, can have on organizations in or nearby affected areas. For a combined example, coal-fired power plants in the US Ohio River valley often create smog over wide swaths of the national parks located just east of that region as prevailing winds transport various airborne pollutants from one region to the next, reducing the visibility of national park tourists and the financial health of tour operators.[52] Many similar locally proximate organization and natural environment interactions in which industrial facility emissions were found to affect significantly contiguous neighborhoods also support this argument.[53]

The proximity of organizations to various natural environments establishes a stakeholder connection between the two since these entities continually affect one another in the physical world. The network aspects of centrality and density, for example, play key roles in this argument, since most considerations of the natural environment are place based. Organizations that produce contaminants, such as small farms that allow their nitrogen wastes to run off into nearby streams, are not quite as central and are much less dense than larger, more urban feedlot operations with inadequate livestock waste control. In this case, both small and larger businesses may be stakeholders of the proximate water bodies, but the latter might be considered to have the stronger stakeholder "effect."[54] . . .

DISCUSSIONS AND IMPLICATIONS

Business organizations interact with both global ecological systems and specific local environments. . . . As a result, business organizations impact on, change, and/or interfere with the complexity and interconnectedness found in the natural environment. . . .

Theoretical development is needed to reconceptualize the salience of the business organization–natural environment relationship and to demonstrate how managers can integrate this relationship into managerial decision making. Some scholars have advanced stakeholder theory by recognizing the multilateral and dynamic nature of stakeholder-firm relations and by describing the socially constructed nature of stakeholder attributes.[55] However, these stakeholder models are still largely anchored in a social-only paradigm bounded by overly narrow economic rationality and traditional political influence. As the concepts of economy and society have broadened through globalization and an electronically interconnected world, the concept of stakeholder also needs to be broadened to acknowledge the interdependence between business organizations and ecological systems.

The lack of managerial salience attributed to the nonhuman natural environment can be partially explained by the way the stakeholder attributes of power, legitimacy, and urgency have been defined and operationalized. Scholars and practitioners need to acknowledge the limitations to current managerial conceptualizations of power, legitimacy, and urgency as the primary attributes used to determine stakeholder salience. It is not news that legitimacy and power are problematic concepts or that power and legitimacy are often coupled in organizational studies. However, we have pointed out some additional conceptual problems surrounding legitimacy, power, and urgency in relation to stakeholder identification and salience. First, these three stakeholder attributes are defined within a social system—only framework rather than an ecological one, which includes both human and nonhuman nature. . . . In addition, we have shown how legitimacy and urgency also appear to be coupled with power in much of current traditional stakeholder thinking. By reinterpreting legitimacy and urgency, therefore, we can, in turn, change managerial perceptions of stakeholder power.

Although Donaldson and Preston (1995) asserted that no a priori prioritization of stakeholders exists, we believe that the normative core of stakeholder theory must acknowledge the priority of the natural environment among the firm's stakeholders. . . .

So how do we integrate ecological impact, ecological interdependence, and longer-term planning into the stakeholder model? A stakeholder theory legitimated in an ecological exchange relationship would likely be based more frequently but not exclusively on a mutual and caring relationship than only on a contractual, power, and exchange-based relationship. It would incorporate both ecological and social sustainability criteria. The focus would be on a systems context and network-based and would complement current exploratory and manipulation approaches. An ecosystem-centered, network-based approach allows for the redefinition of power, legitimacy, and urgency and the inclusion of other stakeholder criteria, such as proximity. . . .

NOTES

1. T. M. Jones and A. C. Wicks, "Convergent Stakeholder Theory," *Academy of Management Review* 24, no. 2 (1999): 206–21.

2. C. W. L. Hill and T. M. Jones, "Stakeholder Agency Theory," *Journal of Management Studies* 29, no. 2 (1992): 131–54.

3. W. Evan and R. E. Freeman, "A Stakeholder Theory of the Modern Corporation: Kantian Capitalism," in *Ethical Theory and Business*, eds. T. Beauchamp and N. Bowie (Englewood Cliffs, NJ: Prentice Hall, 1988); R. E. Freeman, *Strategic Management: A Stakeholder Approach* (New York: Basic Books, 1984); T. Donaldson and L. Preston, "The Stakeholder Theory of the Corporation: Concepts, Evidence, and Implications," *Academy of Management Review* 20, no. 1 (1995): 65–91; G. E. Greenley and G. R. Foxall, "Multiple Stakeholder Orientation in UK Companies and the Implications for Company Performance," *Journal of Management Studies* 34, no. 2 (1997): 259–84.

4. R. A. Buchholz, *Principles of Environmental Management* (Englewood Cliffs, NJ: Prentice Hall, 1993); M. Starik, "Should Trees Have Managerial Standing? Toward Stakeholder Status for Nonhuman Nature," *Journal of Business Ethics* 14, no. 3 (1995): 207–17; J. G. Stead and W. E. Stead, "Ecoenterprise Strategy: Standing for Sustainability," *Journal of Business Ethics* 24, no. 4 (2000): 313–29.

5. R. K. Mitchell, B. R. Agle, and D. J. Wood, "Toward a Theory of Stakeholder

Identification and Salience: Defining the Principle of Who and What Really Counts," *Academy of Management Review* 22, no. 4 (1997): 853–86.

6. Donaldson and Preston, "The Stakeholder Theory of the Corporation," p. 86.

7. W. C. Frederick, "Moving to CSR4: What to Pack for the Trip," *Business & Society* 37, no. 1 (1998): 40–59; T. M. Jones, "Corporate Social Responsibility Revisited, Redefined," *California Management Review* 22, no. 2 (1980): 59–67; Mitchell et al., "Toward a Theory of Stakeholder Identification and Salience"; T. J. Rowley, "Moving beyond Dyadic Ties: A Network Theory of Stakeholder Influences," *Academy of Management Review* 22, no. 4 (1997): 887–910; J. K. Thompson, S. L. Wartick, and H. L. Smith, "Integrating Corporate Social Performance and Stakeholder Management: Implications for a Research Agenda in Small Business," *Research in Corporate Social Performance and Policy* 12 (1991): 207–30.

8. Mitchell et al., "Toward a Theory of Stakeholder Identification and Salience," p. 879.

9. Ibid., p. 877.

10. See, for example, P. Blau, *Exchange and Power in Social Life* (New York: Wiley, 1964); C. Oliver, "Strategic Responses to Institutional Processes," *Academy of Management Review* 16, no. 1 (1991): 145–79; J. Pfeffer, *Managing with Power: Politics and Influence in Organizations* (Boston, MA: Harvard Business School Press, 1992); and J. Pfeffer and G. R. Salancik, *The External Control of Organizations* (New York: Harper & Row, 1978).

11. M. Clarkson, "A Stakeholder Framework for Analyzing and Evaluating Corporate Social Performance," *Academy of Management Review* 27 (1995): 42–56; Greenley and Foxall, "Multiple Stakeholder Orientation in UK Companies"; J. S. Harrison and C. H. St. John, "Managing and Partnering with External Stakeholders," *Academy of Management Executive* 10, no. 2 (1996): 46–58; Mitchell et al., "Toward a Theory of Stakeholder Identification and Salience"; J. Nasi, S. Nasi, N. Philips, and S. Zyglidopoulos, "The Evolution of Corporate Social Responsiveness: An Exploratory Study of Finnish and Canadian Forestry Companies," *Business and Society* 3, no. 6 (1997): 296–321.

12. R. E. Freeman, *Strategic Management*; R. E. Freeman and W. Evan, "Corporate Governance: A Stakeholder Interpretation," *Journal of Behavioral Economics* 19 (1990): 337–59; Hill and Jones, "Stakeholder Agency Theory"; J. Nasi, "What Is Stakeholder Thinking? A Snapshot of a Social Theory of the Firm," in *Understanding Stakeholder Thinking*, ed. J. Nasi (Helsinki: LSR-Julkaisut Oy, 1995), pp. 19–32; Nasi et al., "The Evolution of Corporate Social Responsiveness."

13. G. Bateson, *Steps to an Ecology of Mind* (New York: Ballantine Books, 1972); T. N. Gladwin, J. K. Kennelly, and T. S. Krause, "Shifting Paradigms for Sustainable Development: Implications for Management Theory and Practice," *Academy of Management Review* 20, no. 4 (1995): 874–907; Starik, "Should Trees Have Managerial Standing?"

14. Gladwin et al., "Shifting Paradigms for Sustainable Development," p. 875.

15. See, for example, Bruntland Commission, *The World Commission on Envi-*

ronment and Development: Our Common Future (Oxford, UK: Oxford University Press, 1987); H. E. Daly and J. B. Cobb Jr., *For the Common Good: Redirecting the Economy toward Community, the Environment, and a Sustainable Future* (Boston: Beacon Press, 1994); D. Jennings and P. A. Zanderbergen, "Ecologically Sustainable Organizations: An Institutional Approach," *Academy of Management Review* 20, no. 4 (1995): 1015–52; R. E. Purser, C. Park, and A. Montuori, "Limits to Anthropocentrism: Towards an Ecocentric Organization Paradigm?" Special topic forum on ecologically sustainable organizations, *Academy of Management Review* 20 (1995): 1053–89; M. Starik and G. P. Rands, "Weaving and Integrated Web: Multilevel and Multisystem Perspectives of Ecologically Sustainable Organizations," *Academy of Management Review* 20, no. 4 (1995): 908–35.

16. Mitchell et al., "Toward a Theory of Stakeholder Identification and Salience," p. 865.

17. S. B. Banerjee, "Whose Land Is It Anyway? National Interest, Indigenous Stakeholders, and Colonial Discourses: The Case of the Jabiluka Uranium Mine," *Organization & Environment* 13, no. 1 (2000): 3–38.

18. See by way of comparison, Evan and Freeman, "A Stakeholder Theory of the Modern Corporation."

19. Hill and Jones, "Stakeholder Agency Theory," p. 133.

20. See by way of comparison, H. Aldrich and C. M. Fiol, "Fools Rush In? The Institutional Context of Industrial Creation," *Academy of Management Review* 19 (1994): 645–70.

21. J. B. Barney, *Gaining and Sustaining Competitive Advantage* (Reading, MA: Addison-Wesley, 1997).

22. For example, J. B. Dowling and J. Pfeffer, "Organizational Legitimacy: Social Values and Organizational Behavior," *Pacific Sociological Review* 18 (1975): 122–36; Pfeffer and Salancik, *The External Control of Organizations*; M. C. Suchman, "Managing Legitimacy: Strategic and Institutional Approaches," *Academy of Management Review* 20 (1995): 571–610; and M. A. Zimmerman and G. J. Zeitz, "Beyond Survival: Achieving New Venture Growth by Building Legitimacy," *Academy of Management Review* 27, no. 3 (2002): 414–31.

23. Suchman, "Managing Legitimacy," p. 578.

24. Aldrich and Fiol, "Fools Rush In?"; Suchman, "Managing Legitimacy," p. 576.

25. National Academy of Sciences Web site: www4.nationalacademies.org/news.nsf/isbn/0309075742?OpenDocument (2002) (accessed August 1, 2002).

26. Intergovernmental Panel on Climate Change, *Emissions Scenarios 2000: Special Report of the Intergovernmental Panel on Climate Change*, eds. N. Nakicenovic and R. Swart (Cambridge: Cambridge University Press, 2000), p. 570.

27. L. Brown, "Challenges of the New Century," in *State of the World 2000*, ed. L. Brown (New York: W. W. Norton & Co., 2000), pp. 3–21.

28. Mitchell et al., "Toward a Theory of Stakeholder Identification and Salience," p. 867.

29. E. Mosakowski and P. C. Earley, "A Selective Review of Time Assumptions in Strategy Research," *Academy of Management Review* 25, no. 4 (2000): 796–812.

30. K. J. Laverty, "Economic 'Short-Termism': The Debate, the Unresolved Issues, and the Implications for Management Practice," *Academy of Management Review* 21, no. 3 (1996): 825–60.

31. E. F. Schumacher, *Small Is Beautiful: Economics as If People Mattered* (New York: Harper & Row, 1973); P. Srikantia and D. Bilimoria, "Isomorphism in Organization and Management Theory," *Organization & Environment* 10, no. 4 (1997): 384–406; W. E. Stead and J. G. Stead, *Management for a Small Planet*, 2nd ed. (Thousand Oaks, CA: Sage, 1996).

32. Starik and Rands, "Weaving an Integrated Web," p. 920.

33. See, for example, Bruntland Commission, *The World Commission on Environment and Development*; Purser et al., "Limits to Anthropocentrism"; P. Shrivastava, "The Role of Corporations in Achieving Ecological Sustainability," *Academy of Management Review* 20, no. 4 (1995): 936–60.

34. See, for example, T. Berry, *The Dream of the Earth* (San Francisco: Sierra Club Books, 1988); A. Leopold, *A Sand County Almanac with Essays on Conservation from Round River* (New York: Ballantine, 1970); Purser et al., "Limits to Anthropocentrism"; and H. Rolston, *Conserving Natural Value* (New York: Columbia University Press, 1994).

35. Mitchell et al., "Toward a Theory of Stakeholder Identification and Salience," p. 857.

36. Purser et al., "Limits to Anthropocentrism," p. 1080.

37. See by means of comparison, S. N. Brenner, "The Stakeholder Theory of the Firm and Organizational Decision Making: Some Propositions and a Model," in *Proceedings of the Fourth Annual Meeting of the International Association for Business and Society*, eds. J. Pasquero and D. Collins (San Diego, 1993), pp. 205–10; and M. Starik, "What Is a Stakeholder?" pp. 89–95 of the Toronto Conference: Reflections on Stakeholder Theory, *Business & Society* 33 (1994): 82–131.

38. A. B. Carroll, *Business & Society: Ethics and Stakeholder Management*, 2nd ed. (Cincinnati: South-Western, 1993).

39. R. A. Phillips and J. Reichart, "The Environment as Stakeholder? A Fairness-based Approach," *Journal of Business Ethics* 23, no. 2 (2000): 185–97.

40. R. M. Lee and S. B. Robbins, "Understanding Social Connectedness in College Women and Men," *Journal of Counseling and Development* 78, no. 4 (2000): 484–91.

41. Gladwin et al., "Shifting Paradigms for Sustainable Development," p. 898.

42. *Webster's II New Riverside Dictionary*, ed. A. H. Soukhanov (Boston, MA: Houghton-Mifflin, 1984), p. 948.

43. M. Benedetti, "Cancer Risk Associated with Residential Proximity to Industrial Sites," *Archives of Environmental Health* 56, no. 4 (2001): 342–50.

44. T. Clark, *Distance & Proximity* (Edinburgh: Edinburgh University Press, 2000).

45. D. M. Smith, "Proximity: Locality and Community" in *Moral Geographies: Ethics in a World of Difference,* ed. D. M. Smith (Edinburgh: Edinburgh University Press, 2000).

46. S. Park, "Industry Clustering for Economic Development," *Economic Development Review* 12, no. 2 (1994): 26–38; *Industrial Networks and Proximity,* eds. M. B. Green and R. B. McNaughton (Burlington, VT: Ashgate, 2000).

47. P. Bansal and K. Roth, "Why Companies Go Green: A Model of Ecological Responsiveness," *Academy of Management Journal* 43, no. 4 (2000): 717–36.

48. W. Tsai, "Social Capital, Strategic Relatedness, and the Formation of Intraorganizational Linkages," *Strategic Management Journal* 21, no. 9 (2000): 925–39; J. P. H. Fan and H. P. Lang, "The Measurement of Relatedness: An Application to Corporate Diversification," *Journal of Business* 73, no. 4 (2000): 629–60.

49. M. A. Heuer and M. Starik, "Multidirectional Stakeholder Networks: Specifying Capability, Turbulence, and Reputation," presented at the Academy of Management Meetings, Denver, CO, August 2002.

50. T. J. Rowley, "Moving beyond Dyadic Ties: A Network Theory of Stakeholder Influences," *Academy of Management Review* 22, no. 4 (1997): 887–910.

51. B. Uzzi, "Social Structure and Competition in Interfirm Networks: The Paradox of Embeddedness," *Administrative Sciences Quarterly* 42, no. 1 (1997): 35–67.

52. National Parks and Conservation Association, *Our Endangered Parks* (San Francisco: Foghorn Press, 1994).

53. See, for example, B. Bolin, "Environmental Equity in a Sunbelt City: The Spatial Distribution of Toxic Hazards in Phoenix, Arizona," *Environmental Hazards* 2, no. 1 (2000): 11–24; and R. Morello-Frosch, M. Pastor, and J. Sadd, "Environmental Justice and Southern California's 'Riskscape': The Distribution of Air Toxics Exposures and Health Risks among Diverse Communities," *Urban Affairs Review* 36, no. 4 (2001): 551–78.

54. T. J. Centner, "Evolving Policies to Regulate Pollution from Animal Feeding Operations," *Environmental Manager* 28, no. 5 (2001): 599–609.

55. See, for example, J. Frooman, "Stakeholder Influence Strategies," *Academy of Management Review* 24 (1999): 191–205; Mitchell et al., "Toward a Theory of Stakeholder Identification and Salience"; and Rowley, "Moving beyond Dyadic Ties."

SUGGESTIONS FOR FURTHER READING

Crane, A., D. Matten, and J. Moon. "Stakeholders as Citizens? Rethinking Rights, Participation, and Democracy." *Journal of Business Ethics* 53, no. 1/2 (2004): 107.

Dunham, L., R. E., Freeman, and J. Liedtka. "Enhancing Stakeholder Practice: A Particularized Exploration of Community." *Business Ethics Quarterly* 16, no. 1 (2006): 23.

Fitchett, J. "Consumers as Stakeholders: Prospects for Democracy in Marketing Theory." *Business Ethics* 14, no. 1 (2005): 14.

Graafland, J., and B. van de Ven. "Strategic and Moral Motivation for Corporate Social Responsibility." *Journal of Corporate Citizenship* 22 (2006): 111–23.

Hall, J., and H. Vredenburg. "Managing Stakeholder Ambiguity." *MIT Sloan Management Review* 47, no. 1 (2005): 11–13.

Maury, M. "A Circle of Influence: Are All the Stakeholders Included?" *Journal of Business Ethics* 23, no. 1 (2000): 117–21.

Morsing, M., and M. Schultz. "Corporate Social Responsibility Communication: Stakeholder Information, Response, and Involvement Strategies." *Business Ethics: A European Review* 15, no. 4 (2006): 323–38.

Orts, E., and A. Strudler. "The Ethical and Environmental Limits of Stakeholder Theory." *Business Ethics Quarterly* 12, no. 2 (2002): 215–33.

Phillips, R. "The Environment as a Stakeholder? A Fairness-Based Approach." *Journal of Business Ethics* 23, no. 2 (2000): 185–97.

———. "Stakeholder Legitimacy." *Business Ethics Quarterly* 12, no. 1 (2003): 25–41.

Rasche, A., and D. Esser. "From Stakeholder Management to Stakeholder Accountability." *Journal of Business Ethics* 65, no. 3 (2006): 251–67.

Reynolds, S., F. Schultz, and D. Hekman. "Stakeholder Theory and Managerial Decision-Making: Constraints and Implications of Balancing Stakeholder Interests." *Journal of Business Ethics* 64, no. 3 (2006): 285–301.

Schwartz, M. "God as a Managerial Stakeholder?" *Journal of Business Ethics* 66 (2006): 291–306.

Spence, L., A. Coles, and L. Harris. "The Forgotten Stakeholder? Ethics and Social Responsibility in Relation to Competitors." *Business and Society Review* 106, no. 4 (2001): 331.

Starik, M. "Should Trees Have Managerial Standing? Toward Stakeholder Status for Nonhuman Nature." *Journal of Business Ethics* 14, no. 3 (1995): 207.

Wood, D., and T. Jones. "Stakeholder Mismatching: A Theoretical Problem in Empirical Research on Corporate Social Performance." *International Journal of Organizational Analysis* 3 (1995): 229–67.

Yamak, S., and O. Suer. "State as a Stakeholder." *Corporate Governance* 5, no. 2 (2005): 111.

Zinkin, J. "Strategic Marketing: Balancing Customer Value with Stakeholder Value." *Marketing Review* 6, no. 2 (2006): 163–81.

PART 5.

APPLICATIONS 1:
STAKEHOLDER THEORY AT WORK
IN THE CORPORATE DOMAIN

T his section examines the practical and empirical issues associated with the application of stakeholder theory to management practices. Stakeholder thinking often requires a paradigm shift in one's approach to management practices. These articles address concrete problems and issues faced by managers who make an effort to apply stakeholder theory on the job. In particular, this chapter explores how stakeholder theory affects management models and explores methods by which companies can determine and evaluate empirical measures for the application of stakeholder theory.

In the first article, David Wheeler and Rachel Davies examine the implications of stakeholder applications for corporate governance in their piece, "Gaining Goodwill: Developing Stakeholder Approaches to Corporate Governance." Wheeler and Davies argue that intangible assets are increasingly important to corporate value. Good will and the social capital it generates for companies enable companies to produce products and services with a value-added component. This added value is difficult to quantify, but cannot be ignored. On this view, enhanced social capital and/or an enhanced reputation for board leaders (premised either upon the board leaders' legitimacy as leaders or their prestige) can create good will on the part of stakeholders. Good stakeholder management is therefore crucial to increasing good will on the part of stakeholders. Since all relevant value indicators for companies are at least in part socially constructed, Wheeler and Davies argue that management can derive extra potential value from the application of stakeholder management theory as it is more inclusive of stakeholders in managerial decision making.

In the second article, Isabelle Maignan, O. C. Ferrell, and Linda Ferrell examine the application of stakeholder theory to marketing in their piece, "A Stakeholder Model for Implementing Social Responsibility in Marketing." They note that a stakeholder approach to marketing is important not just to integrated stakeholder management of the company as a whole, but specifically in terms of allowing marketers to meet their professional obligations. The American Marketing Association's 2004 definition of marketing actually includes specific reference to benefiting stakeholders. Maignan, Ferrell, and Ferrell see stakeholder management in marketing as crucial to developing a stakeholder-friendly corporate culture; this is especially important in corporate attempts to communicate corporate social responsibility measures to stakeholders outside of the corporation. To that end, Maignan, Ferrell, and Ferrell suggest concrete strategies for marketing management using stakeholder analysis.

In the third selection, Mette Morsing and Majken Schultz focus on how to drive and ultimately leverage stakeholder awareness. In their article, "Corporate Social Responsibility Communication: Stakeholder Information, Response, and Involvement Strategies," Morsing and Schultz stress the importance of paying careful attention to how management communicates with the company's stakeholders. In order to reap the potential benefits of creating the sort of good will among stakeholders discussed by Wheeler and Davies, Morsing and Schultz argue that companies must be very careful to disseminate information concerning corporate social responsibility policies in the right sort of way. While mere propaganda efforts may serve companies well in advertising sporting events, for example, they may actually do more harm than good when a company is trying to communicate its efforts to be more ethically responsive to a diverse array of stakeholders. They argue that the theory of sense-making, rather than merely sense-giving, is crucial to effective stakeholder management. Thus, rather than merely telling stakeholders what to think about corporate policy, namely, by trying to provide sense-giving to stakeholders, Morsing and Schultz insist that management should find ways to engage with stakeholders to create a dialogue in which sense-making for both management and other stakeholders can arise. Morsing and Schultz then discuss the importance of context in finding ways to involve stakeholders outside of management in making sense of corporate policy. If handled improperly, Morsing and Schultz argue that stakeholder management can sometimes lead a company to fall into a sort of self-promoter's paradox whereby excessively touting one's own success actually causes others to regard that success with suspicion. On the other hand, so long as managers cultivate what Morsing and Schultz refer to as an effective stakeholder information strategy, attempts to engage in and communicate corporate social responsibility initiatives can benefit both the company and its stakeholders.

For managers who wonder how they can analyze whether or not their company's attempts at stakeholder management and corporate social responsibility have been effective, Maria Sillanpää offers an account of her experience with The Body Shop in "The Body Shop Value Report—Towards Integrated Stakeholder Auditing." As the ethical audit team manager for The Body Shop International and as a council member of the United Kingdom government-sponsored Ethical Trading Initiative, Sillanpää has ample experience on which to draw. In this article, she outlines how The Body Shop conducted social audits on a wide array of issues of special interest to Body Shop stakeholders. She argues that by conducting these sorts of audits, which include outside verification of the social audit, The Body Shop is more competitive in the global marketplace where stakeholders increasingly expect companies to listen and respond to their moral concerns. Sillanpää discusses the sorts of questionnaires distributed, the levels at which reports were gathered, the goals for improvement identified by the stakeholder audits, and the measures taken to ensure that stakeholder feedback from participants about the effectiveness of the audit itself was collected.

18.

GAINING GOODWILL

Developing Stakeholder Approaches to Corporate Governance

David Wheeler and Rachel Davies

FROM GOODWILL TO GOOD GOVERNANCE

. . . **M**acMillan and Downing (1999) . . . advocated the concept of "goodwill" as a key driver of shareholder value: "Goodwill tends to constitute most of the value of successful businesses, especially today's service and hi-tech businesses. That is where Shareholder Value is really to be found." . . . MacMillan and Downing identified a potential fault line in corporate governance along which a number of once-celebrated corporations such as Enron, Tyco, and WorldCom were soon to be found floundering.

. . . We add some contemporary observations on Canadian corporations that we believe add weight to MacMillan's analysis and we explore some of the implications of this analysis for how we might approach the effective design and execution of corporate governance in service of value creation for all stakeholders and the long-term sustainability of the firm. . . .

GOOD GOVERNANCE AND THE EFFECTIVE STEWARDSHIP OF RESOURCES

. . . From a stewardship perspective, the governance challenge arises in being able to value both tangible and intangible resources and ensure that they are

Excerpts from David Wheeler and Rachel Davies, "Gaining Goodwill: Developing Stakeholder Approaches to Corporate Governance," *Journal of General Management* 30, no. 2 (Winter 2004): 51–74. Copyright © 2004 Braybrooke Press.

adequately protected from risk, consistent with their present and future value to the firm.

It is normally assumed that tangible resources comprise firm assets that are simple to measure and reflect on balance sheets. However, even tangible resources may be subject to novel risks that are very difficult to quantify. . . .

. . . Even if we could assess novel risks to tangible assets accurately enough . . . we know that the market valuation of firms is increasingly dependent on intangible, and largely nonmeasurable assets. . . .

Notwithstanding their value, a significant complicating feature of intangible resources is that such assets are rarely controlled entirely or directly by the firm. For example, the economic value of intellectual capital can be captured indirectly through measures of patents held and proprietary know-how, routines, or formulas controlled. However, as Nahapiet and Ghoshal (1998) have noted, . . . it is the firm's capabilities to leverage resources through its relationships with employees, suppliers, and business partners, i.e., by mobilizing its social capital that value is created. Similarly, the human capital that is represented by a well-trained, knowledgeable workforce is worthless or even of negative value if part of that workforce is motivated to frustrate managerial initiatives or decides to depart altogether, perhaps to join a competitor. Thus, facilitating the building of social capital across the firm and with outside stakeholders is now advocated as a key role for human resource managers.[1] We conclude that social capital seems to be central to the mobilization of both human and intellectual capital. . . .

In their wide-ranging review article on the concept of social capital, Adler and Kwon (2002) describe social capital as: "the goodwill available to individuals or groups. Its source lies in the structure and content of the actor's social relations. Its effects flow from the information, influence, and solidarity it makes available to the actor."[2] In an earlier and equally influential definition, Nahapiet and Ghoshal described social capital as "the sum of the actual and potential resources embedded within, available through, and derived from the network of relationships possessed by an individual or social unit."[3] . . .

How can a board of directors or a senior management team be held accountable for a resource or asset that is *de facto* co-owned by stakeholders who may or may not wish to value or manage the resource in the same way as the firm? If a company has been granted a legitimate mineral concession by a distant government and yet the local community decides to use civil disobedience to deny the firm access to the mineral resources,[4] what then *is* the concession worth? . . .

Herein lies both the challenge and the opportunity for boards, senior teams, and their corporate governance processes. A firm that can recognize novel liabilities to tangible resources and put some kind of risk-management envelope around them will be more likely to avoid shocks to the investment community and other stakeholders than one that simply does not bother to assess and manage such risks. . . .

But if the size and/or the likelihood of an environmental or social liability occurring cannot be accurately measured (e.g., . . . in the case of tobacco firms in the 1990s) does this mean that boards and managements should ignore it? If ownership of a brand is central to the market capitalization of a large corporation (as is the case for Coca-Cola, McDonald's, and Nike today), but it is impossible to calculate the precise dollar value of that brand, does the board of the company not discuss it? . . . Any answer other than a resounding "no" to all of the above propositions would be ludicrous. . . . The maxim "what cannot be measured cannot be managed," when applied in its economic, rational, and literal sense, exposes the complete inadequacy of the dominant Western theoretical framework for corporate governance.

Since the corporate scandals of the opening years of the twenty-first century, the accounting profession has been examining its role in society and its responsibilities to corporations and their stakeholders.[5] Some in the profession have also been active in exploring how its members might best add value to their clients' businesses in an era where intangible assets may represent the majority of the market valuation of the firm.[6]

. . . Mainstream financial institutions are also increasingly interested in measurements that may help pinpoint lapses in stewardship and elucidate novel risks to future performance and/or intangible resources.

. . . Presumably, financial institutions and individual investors would have been very pleased to have received earlier indications on asbestos risks (Lloyds), oil-tanker spill risks (Exxon), chemical explosion risks (Union Carbide), human health risks (various tobacco companies), human rights risks (Nike and Gap), community dissent risks (RTZ and Shell), customer safety risks (Ford), customer rejection risks (Monsanto), ethical lapse risks (Tyco and Hollinger), theft risks (Maxwell), and of course accounting lapse risks (Arthur Andersen).

. . . The experience of Enron and associated scandals has precipitated renewed focus on how board and senior team performance and corporate governance processes can be better aligned to steward and grow resources for the benefit of the firm and its stakeholders rather than simply enrich managements and their advisors.[7]

CORPORATE GOVERNANCE AND PERFORMANCE

Based on our observations so far, it would seem reasonable to posit that good corporate governance practices should lead to more effective stewardship of tangible and intangible resources, the minimization of risks to those resources (including stakeholder mediated risks), and the maximization of opportunities arising from them. This more effective stewardship of resources should then lead to enhanced future firm performance.

Given these observations, we undertook a pilot study to explore two questions:

(i) What are the ways in which corporate governance is assessed by analysts with a particular interest in and/or knowledge of risks to tangible and intangible resources; and

(ii) is there evidence that such in-depth rankings provide insights on future firm performance?

QUESTION 1: HOW IS CORPORATE GOVERNANCE ASSESSED?

In order to answer the first question we investigate the nature and range of corporate governance questions raised by specialist analysts operating in the field of corporate governance and "socially responsible investing" (SRI). Boutique corporate governance and SRI analysts depend for their income on identifying alternative predictors of future value and selling their analyses to clients in the form of indices or consulting services. Their clients are typically large pension funds and other mainstream financial institutions concerned about risks to future performance as much as identifying surrogate measures for generally well-managed companies. SRI analysts often use positive screening or a "best in class" approach to select companies that will outperform their peers based on their more effective management of environmental and social risks and/or the presence of positive identifiers of more sustainable business practices. Some also use negative screens to remove ethically high-risk sectors altogether, e.g., tobacco or gambling.[8]

We contacted two high-profile large Canadian corporations in two entirely different sectors (banking and metals) and obtained copies of corporate governance rating schemes that the corporations had been requested to complete by corporate governance and SRI analysts in the previous twelve months. . . .

In comparing the corporate governance criteria of the corporate governance and SRI analysts, we noted a strong focus on the evaluation of structural questions and the control of tangible (financial) resources. The leading analysts with the most comprehensive assessments of corporate governance were GMI, ISS, and Standard and Poor's. All three evaluators examined board composition, board accountability for the financial assets of the firm, financial disclosure and internal controls, ownership, and shareholder rights in considerable depth. Assessments relating to these factors represented up to 80 percent of the total criteria examined.

Governance factors relating to the management and development of intangible and relational resources had a more minor presence in the surveys we examined, with board training and remuneration, and risk minimization (to protect the firm's reputation and brand) emerging as the more common themes.

. . . Analysts that conduct detailed evaluations of social and environmental criteria (Michael Jantzi Research Associates, EthicScan, and SAM) had some focus on the efficient stewardship of stakeholder relations and human and environmental resources. The common factors that were examined in these areas included employee training and career management, workplace safety, and social and environmental management systems.

QUESTION 2: CAN IN-DEPTH CORPORATE GOVERNANCE RANKINGS PREDICT PERFORMANCE?

SRI and governance analysts' ranking schemes are proprietary. Thus, although we can describe how criteria are applied to companies for the purposes of information gathering, we cannot necessarily judge how those criteria are ranked and modeled and/or what correlations may be claimed (or not) in private advice provided to clients.

However, in October 2002, the *Globe and Mail* newspaper's Report on Business (ROB) section published a comprehensive ranking of 270 companies listed on the Toronto Stock Exchange S&P/TSX index. The rankings were based on "a tough set of 'best practices' culled from the corporate governance guidelines and recommendations of US and Canadian regulators, as well as major institutional investors and associations."[9] Similar to our observations above, the criteria related largely to structural questions and issues relating to accountability for investors' money. The criteria were grouped in terms of board composition (ten criteria representing 40 percent of total score), shareholding and compensation issues (four criteria representing 23 percent of total score), shareholder rights issues (four criteria representing 22 percent of total score), and disclosure issues (five criteria representing 15 percent of total score).

The governance rankings ranged from a low of 36 for film and media company Alliance Atlantis Communications through to 96 for Manulife Financial Corporation. Our two governance/SRI analyst target companies (see p. 225) scored 87 and 77, placing both in the upper quartile of good governance according to the ranking.

We selected companies from the ROB list that were also present in the top sixty of the Toronto Stock Exchange on October 1, 2002 (total fifty-six firms). We then calculated the changes in market capitalization for the subset from October 1, 2002, to October 1, 2003. Share prices were obtained from TD Newcrest S&P/TSX index breakdowns with number of shares outstanding estimated from float shares data.

Given the clear lack of any correlation between one-year market capitalization shifts and the corporate governance rankings, we then excluded two outliers: Nortel Networks and Kinross Gold, companies that had annual gains of more than 600 percent and 200 percent, respectively. In both cases, special factors might be deemed to have been at play. Exclusion of these two companies improved the r^2 statistic (from 0.0057 to 0.028) but not close to anything that might denote significance. These observations tell us two things:

(1) Current approaches to measurement of good governance are varied but tend to be based largely on structural and process issues; and

(2) current measures that focus on structure and accountability for tangible (financial) assets do not necessarily predict short-term performance.

A STAKEHOLDER APPROACH TO GOOD GOVERNANCE

To summarize our arguments so far, it seems we have ended up with a somewhat paradoxical set of observations:

(1) We have made an empirical and theoretical case for stakeholder-mediated "goodwill" (social capital) and associated intangible assets being linked to market valuation of firms and thus to the creation of shareholder value.

(2) We have made a theoretical case for there being no necessary contradiction between pragmatic versions of agency theory and stakeholder theory in the context of good corporate governance.

(3) We have noted the difficulties of quantifying novel risks to tangible resources and the largely socially constructed nature of intangible resources and thus the practical challenge of measuring the economic value of both tangible and intangible resources.

(4) We have postulated that good governance might be conceptualized as stewardship of tangible and intangible resources and that effective stewardship might be associated with future performance of firms.

However, we have been unable to provide compelling evidence that currently applied measures of good governance are predictive of future firm performance. And thus we must conclude that:

(a) Our theoretical reasoning is faulty; or

(b) current measures of good governance are inadequate to capture phenomena associated with good stewardship and future performance; or

(c) timescales over which good governance is manifested in firm performance are simply too long to allow their detection in studies conducted to date; or

(d) good governance (as currently measured) is irrelevant to performance; or

(e) a combination of two or more of these factors is at play.

For the purpose of this discussion we will focus on points (b), (c), (d), and (e) and invite others to comment on point (a) on a future occasion.

Our favored explanation for the lack of clear association between current assessments of good governance and firm performance is that we have yet to define the characteristics of good governance in sufficiently useful terms to allow them to be measured and correlated with economic outcomes within relevant timescales. This explanation encompasses points (b), (c), and (e). We also believe that if good governance were to be adequately defined, it would necessarily be done in the context of firm performance, thus eliminating (d) as a *non sequitur*. So this leaves us with the fundamental question as to how we might define good governance.

As noted above, if we look at the way in which good governance practices are currently measured ... we observe that measures are largely concerned with structural and process issues. Typically, the measures relate to the duties of the board and their agents . . . their independence of each other, the oversight of their compensation and other incentives and various other mechanisms for assuring accountabilities for shareholders' wealth. In that sense, it is perfectly consistent with what normative agency theorists would prescribe.

It is as though the firm were a farm owned by an absent landlord and the agents responsible for it have simply to glare at each other with sufficient vigilance (presumably with the option of resorting to bare knuckles if necessary) in order to ensure that none of them make off with the farm machinery or that year's produce. Meanwhile . . . no one is thinking about next year's crops, and no one is making sure that everyone gets along or is indeed competent to do their jobs. Stewardship theory would go some way to mitigating some aspects of this model, but not all.

For example, stewardship theory would not address behavioral and cultural questions (do the farm agents have complementary styles and mindsets?), and it would not necessarily recognize plurality and diversity of stakeholder definitions of value (do the farm customers want organic produce, meat, dairy, or grain?). If we know anything about organizational performance, it is that achieving alignment between external (market) opportunity and strategy and internal culture, behaviors, and capabilities is a key characteristic of successful, high-performing businesses;[10] however, relatively little work has been conducted on where boards and senior management teams figure in this happy alignment when it occurs.[11]

One of the most significant barriers to research in this area is that, as noted by Daily et al., it is notoriously difficult to gain access to boards and senior management teams for the purpose of exploring their culture, behaviors, and capabilities. One notable exception to this is the recent work of Leblanc and Gillies. . . . Their ground-breaking conclusions focused on the crucial importance of aligning board structure, membership, and process, and they identified five optimal and five dysfunctional archetypes for directoral behaviors. Finally, without claiming an *a priori* link to financial performance, their prescription for designing effective (i.e., nondysfunctional) boards was almost entirely concerned with relational factors: explicitly to ensure alignment between board competences, behaviors, strategy, and recruitment.

These observations . . . take us back to the question of goodwill and social capital. In the same way that social capital can never be entirely or satisfactorily understood from simply a structural perspective,[12] neither, it would seem, can good governance. Culture (including beliefs, behaviors, and norms) and the quality of relationships are important. If business objectives are to be achieved with low transaction costs, then the firm and its stake-holders must engage in reciprocal behaviors with a common vision of what is to be achieved.

Thus we can postulate the challenge as one of bringing a "stakeholder approach" . . . to corporate governance. In the same way that ensuring inclusivity in firm processes for the purpose of building social capital and delivering value to the firm and its stakeholders requires the development of an appropriate culture together with specific capabilities,[13] so might the development of an effective board.

There is another key question to address, which is the importance of how confidence is established between the firm and its stakeholders; in particular, the confidence of capital markets. This takes us into the realm of reputation, legitimacy, and "prestige." Suchman distinguishes between moral and practical legitimacy consistent with established regulations, norms, and beliefs and describes the cognitive nature of how firms' actions are deemed appropriate. Clearly there is a high degree of social construction involved in what is deemed legitimate by different stakeholders in their various discourses with the firm and with each other and how this impacts on firm reputation.[14] And consistent with a pragmatic approach to stakeholder theory, it would be inappropriate to separate the normative from the instrumental in this regard. . . .

Another way of conceptualizing legitimacy and the confidence (or lack of confidence) this inspires in stakeholders is the question of prestige. According to the work of Certo,[15] a key contribution of boards is the signaling of prestige (as defined by D'Aveni) to external stakeholders: "board prestige results from the subjective evaluations that individuals associate with the board's objective characteristsics. . . ." Certo goes on to propose that: "perceptions of board prestige are derived from the board's aggregate human capital and social capital." Whilst especially important in the context of an IPO where a firm seeks capital investment, Certo makes a more general point (consistent with resource dependency theory), that prestigious boards and their associated networks may help mobilize information, talent, and other intangible resources of direct value to the firm.

This reasoning . . . may help us understand why we are currently unable to detect such links and it does suggest where we might want to commence our search for better measures of board effectiveness. In order to establish new criteria for measuring good governance, we might need to develop direct or surrogate measures for both:

(i) the capabilities and cultural characteristics (beliefs, behaviors, and norms) of boards and their individual members; and

(ii) the legitimacy and prestige that boards and senior teams confer and how this may link to the effective mobilization of resources.

... [W]e have constructed a simple model (see figure 1) for describing how boards and senior management teams might begin to think about their roles. ...

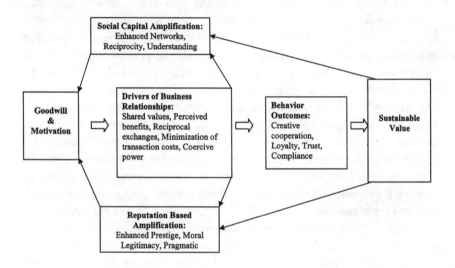

Figure 1: Proposed model linking goodwill to sustainable value creation (developed from MacMillan et al., 2000)

One implication of the model is that goodwill in the absence of a motivation (e.g., shared objectives) or indeed social capital in the absence of reputational reenforcement, may not be sufficient to maintain the virtuous cycles. ... This should be uncontroversial, as every honest market analyst would attest: "If we are confident the firm will enhance shareholder value, we recommend its stock; if our peers and clients follow suit the firm's market value increases, which in turn increases shareholder value and further reinforces our confidence." There are obvious dangers in this circular reasoning, but at least the process should be clear.

APPLICATIONS OF THE MODEL
AND IMPLICATIONS FOR RESEARCH

By way of further illustration of our model, and in order to propose some promising directions for future research, we might describe two publicly quoted Canadian companies with positive records in the fields of governance, reputation, and sustainable value creation. Suncor is an oil and gas company with the majority of its tangible resources associated with the oil sands of Alberta. Dofasco is a steel company with its roots firmly embedded in the community of Hamilton, Ontario. . . . Both companies are committed to a vision of "sustainability," both take an explicitly stakeholder-inclusive approach to strategy, and both have significantly out-performed their peers in economic terms in recent years. Both also invest significantly in human and social capital as part of their normal approach to business. In the case of Dofasco this is encapsulated in their deep roots in the community of Hamilton and their corporate identity expressed as "our product is people, our strength is steel." In the case of Suncor, a company that depends on a high level of stakeholder support for its pursuit and exploitation of natural resources, the company has achieved significant competitive advantage through its superior relationships with First Nations groups, environmentalists, and regulators, and the high level of motivation of its employees.[16]

These two companies seem to have established the virtuous cycles described in our model and consequently—to date at least—have driven value more sustainably than the majority of their peers. They are also astute enough to recognize that the goodwill and motivation they mobilize through their social networks and reputational reinforcement helps them maintain the confidence of capital markets. . . .

IMPLICATIONS OF MODEL FOR GOVERNANCE CODES,
CORPORATE LAW, AND PUBLIC POLICY

. . . Our arguments do support the logic of ensuring the right blend of stakeholder inclusive capabilities and cultures on corporate boards and in senior management teams. Whether stakeholder networks and social capital resources are mobilized for the purpose of raising capital, obtaining new market insights, securing managerial talent, or simply for procuring contacts or information, our arguments would lend force to the need for diversity, networking skills, shared beliefs, and decent behaviors and norms among those who are asked to govern corporations. Board members and senior management team members should also be capable of signaling legitimacy or "prestige" to various networks of stakeholders (including capital markets and investors), and this legitimacy—moral and practical—should be recognized as an important firm resource.

IMPLICATIONS FOR BOARDS AND SENIOR MANAGEMENT TEAMS

. . . We propose that director training in the recognition of novel risks and the stewardship of intangible resources could do no harm and might actually help. In addition, recruitment processes might take greater account of the need for board and senior management team capabilities in relationship building and stakeholder approaches more generally.

We suggest that directors of companies challenge their own beliefs and then reconsider their espousal of the narrow ideas of the normative agency theorists. In their well-intended support of "shareholder value" as the overriding purpose of the firm, these theorists have overlooked how that value is created in the real world and paradoxically may have contributed to the problems of practitioners and investors alike. The simplistic application of agency theory to corporate governance, long dominant in North American business and academic discourse, seems not to have prevented scandal or improved board director or senior management effectiveness; it might therefore be time to try something new.

Finally we suggest that boards of directors talk more frequently about their own behaviors and norms. Do they work as a challenging, engaging, and yet supportive team dedicated to their own high performance as well as that of the firm; or do they operate as a politicized, dysfunctional, or disengaged group only concerned with the performance of others?

NOTES

1. M. I. Lengnick-Hall and C. A. Lengnick-Hall, "HR's Role in Building Relationship Networks," *Academy of Management Executive* 17, no. 4 (2003): 53–63; *Human Resource Management in the Knowledge Economy. New Challenges, New Roles, New Capabilities* (San Franciso: Berrett-Koehler, 2002).

2. P. S. Adler and S. W. Kwon, "Social Capital Prospects for a New Concept," *Academy of Management Review* 27, no. 1 (2002): 17–40.

3. J. Nahapiet and S. Ghoshal, "Social Capital, Intellectual Capital, and the Organizational Advantage," *Academy of Management Review* 23, no. 2 (1998): 242–66.

4. See by way of comparison the experience of Shell in Nigeria, in Wheeler et al., "Paradoxes and Dilemmas for Stakeholder Responsive Firms in the Extractive Sector: Lessons from the Case of Shell and the Ogoni," *Journal of Business Ethics* 39, no. 3 (2002): 297–318.

5. See, for example, P. Diekmeyer, "Auditor Independence Is under Fire: The Heat Is On," *CAMagazine* 133, no. 8 (2000): 20–26.

6. For an early paper on some of the emerging challenges in accounting for intangibles see, for example, Bell, Marrs, Solomon, and Thomas (1997). For a more recent example of practical attempts by the profession to reflect broader risks in accounting and reporting, see CICA(2002). For more theoretical discussions see also Ratnatunga, Gray, and Balachandrang (2004); Grascnick and Low (2004).

7. For a forthright analysis of the urgency for corporate governance reform and the importance of addressing the problem of excessive compensation for senior management, see Monks and Sykes (2002) and Martin (2003).

8. M. Mansley, *Socially Responsible Investment: A Guide for Pension Funds and Institutional Investors* (Sudbury, UK: Monitor Press, 2000).

9. J. McFarland et al., "Board Games," *Globe and Mail Report on Business* (October 7–8, 2002); J. McFarland, "How ROB Created the Rating System," *Globe and Mail Report on Business* 6 (October 7, 2002).

10. For perspectives on organizations and performance with a focus on corporate culture as a resource, see Schein (1985); Prahalad and Hamel (1990); Kotter and Heskett (1992); Collins and Porras (1994); O'Reilly and Pfeffer (2000).

11. For discussions of what board culture may mean to corporate boards, see Cascio (2004), Letendre (2004).

12. Nahapiet and Ghoshal, "Social Capital, Intellectual Capital, and the Organizational Advantage," pp. 242–66.

13. For discussions of capabilities, culture, and stakeholder inclusion see, for example, D. Wheeler and M. Sillanpää, 1998; D. Wheeler in R. Burke and C. Cooper, eds., 2003.

14. See, for example, Rao (1994) and Deephouse (2000).

15. S. T. Certo, "Influencing Initial Public Offering Investors with Prestige: Signaling with Board Structures," *Academy of Management Review* 28, no. 3 (2003): 432–46.

16. K. McKague et al., "Growing a Sustainable Energy Company: Suncor's Venture into Alternative and Renewable Energy," *Schulich School of Business Case* (Toronto: York University Press, 2001).

19.

A STAKEHOLDER MODEL FOR IMPLEMENTING SOCIAL RESPONSIBILITY IN MARKETING

Isabelle Maignan, O. C. Ferrell, and Linda Ferrell

● ● ● A new emerging logic of marketing is that it exists to provide both social and economic processes, including a network of relationships to provide skills and knowledge to all stakeholders.[1]

This logic is captured in the new definition of marketing developed by the American Marketing Association (2004), which states that:

> Marketing is an organizational function and a set of processes for creating, communicating, and delivering value to customers and for managing customer relationships in ways that benefit the organization and its stakeholders.

. . . The reconceptualization of the marketing concept based on a long-term, multiple stakeholder approach has also been suggested as a prescriptive model for organizational responsibility in marketing.[2]

. . . Even though some leading businesses—including Shell, Beyond Petroleum, and Starbucks—have introduced innovative corporate social responsibility (CSR) initiatives, many organizations have failed to implement a solid CSR program that truly integrates and balances their responsibilities to various stakeholder groups. Instead, most companies have a tendency to adopt uncoordinated initiatives that address only specific stakeholder issues (e.g., policies against child labor, green marketing, equal opportunity programs). . . .

. . . This paper adopts an encompassing view of stakeholder orientation

Excerpts from Isabelle Maignan, O. C. Ferrell, and Linda Ferrell, "A Stakeholder Model for Implementing Social Responsibility in Marketing," *European Journal of Marketing* 9/10 (2005): 956–77. © Emerald Group Publishing, Ltd. Reprinted by permission.

and describes a step-by-step methodology that can be used to implement a well-integrated CSR program in marketing to consolidate, coordinate, and integrate with existing initiatives at the organizational level of analysis.

CSR FROM A MARKETING PERSPECTIVE

Shared Stakeholder Norms and Values

Major stakeholders may have different needs and a fine-grained approach may be needed to ascertain even differences within major stakeholder groups, such as customers, employees, suppliers, and investors.[3] . . . Some of them choose to join formal communities dedicated to better defining, and to advocating, these values and norms. For example, some investors choose to play a role in SocialFunds.com, an organization that provides information about socially responsible investing and stimulates shareholder activism in favor of CSR. Similar communities can also be found among employees (Employee's Advocacy Group), consumers (Consumer Federation of America), suppliers (Covisint in the automobile industry), competitors (Better Business Bureau), the geographical areas where the firm operates (Alaska Wilderness League), and the media (National Association of Broadcasters). Individual stakeholders may embrace and discuss issues on a collective basis even when they do not join a formal organization. For instance, customers do not need to be members of Greenpeace . . . to discuss environmental issues with others, and to incorporate this concern in their voting and purchasing decisions. Accordingly, stakeholders can be regrouped into formal or informal communities that share a certain number of values and norms about desirable business behaviors. . . .

Stakeholder Issues in Marketing

Stakeholder values and norms apply to a variety of marketing issues such as sales practices, consumer rights, environmental protection, product safety, and proper information disclosure.[4] . . . Consumers may worry not only about product safety, but also about child labor, an issue that does not impact them directly. We define stakeholder issues as the concerns that stakeholders embrace about organizational activities and the residual impact. Within the context of marketing, Social Responsibility (SA) 8000 registration/certification addresses customer concerns about child labor, worker rights, discrimination, compensation, and other issues that could impact marketing activities.[5] . . .

Stakeholder Pressures

. . . In spite of disparities across communities, stakeholders conform to broad and abstract norms that define acceptable behavior in society. Home Depot requires that an independent firm check the promoted environmental practices of the products and materials provided by its suppliers. In particular, the retailer requires wood products be certified through the independent Forest Stewardship Council. Hence, Home Depot imposes its norms and concerns regarding the natural environment on its suppliers. . . .

Stakeholder Values and Norms

. . . [O]rganizations may be driven to commit to a specific cause independently of any stakeholder pressure. Businesses may also want to exceed stakeholder expectations. Thus, organizational values and norms can dictate modes of behavior that are more stringent than those demanded by more various stakeholder communities. For example, Starbucks engages in recycling, employee-friendly policies, and fair trade initiatives that go beyond what stakeholders might require. Organizations such as Home Depot engage in strategic philanthropy, tying their business goals to their social mission. When employees volunteer to erect Habitat for Humanity homes, they are applying their skills and improving their expertise as sales associates for the company.

Clear organizational values and norms are also needed to select among conflicting stakeholder demands. . . . For example, while customers may demand environmentally friendly products, shareholders may question green investments because of their high costs and uncertain returns. . . .

Organizational values and norms are most likely to actually pervade decisions and practices when they are clearly formalized and well-communicated to employees and business partners. The formalization of CSR norms can be accomplished in many ways such as:

- Presenting the stakeholder issues viewed as most important in official organizational communications (mission statement, values statement, annual reports).
- Clarifying the nature of desirable and undesirable behaviors in a code of ethics and associated training programs.
- Openly endorsing environmental, ethical, or social charters . . .
- Actively benchmarking achievement of CSR goals and establishing revised expectations annually.

Noticeably, even though strong organizational values and norms are important, . . . they may fail to account for the evolving norms and issues valued by powerful stakeholder communities. . . . Businesses must be capable of defining their values and norms while concurrently keeping abreast of those of their stakeholders.

Stakeholder Issues and Processes

Important stakeholder issues. Given limited organizational resources, businesses cannot possibly address all stakeholder issues. The nature of the most important stakeholder issues is determined by considering simultaneously:

- the priorities dictated by organizational values and norms (urgency);
- the relative power of different stakeholder groups; and
- the legitimacy of the issues presented.[6]

. . . As earlier mentioned, organizational values and norms can be more stringent than those of stakeholders; therefore, addressing relevant stakeholder issues is seen as a strict minimum to show commitment to CSR.

CSR processes. Two main types of CSR processes can be recommended to bring organizational norms into practice and to properly address relevant stakeholder issues. First, stakeholder intelligence generation processes help the firm keep abreast of the nature of powerful stakeholder communities along with their main norms and concerns. A second type of CSR processes consists of implementing concrete initiatives aimed at tackling relevant stakeholder issues. These initiatives can take many different forms. For example, processes aimed at addressing some employee issues could include a health and safety program, the development of a career management program, or work schedules that facilitate the coordination of personal and professional lives. With respect to customers, concrete CSR implementation processes could consist of product quality and safety programs, or of procedures aimed at responding to individual customer complaints. Initiatives aimed at the community include philanthropic and volunteerism programs along with environmental protection efforts.

It has been suggested that a stakeholder management approach systematically integrates managers' concerns about organizational strategy with the interests of marketing and other functional areas of business.[7] By assessing each stakeholder's potential to threaten or to cooperate with the organization it is possible to identify supportive, nonsupportive, and marginal stakeholders.[8] The next section uses this conceptual framework as a basis to develop a solid plan to manage CSR.

HOW TO IMPLEMENT CSR IN MARKETING

Step 1: Discovering Organizational Values and Norms

In order to enhance organizational fit, a CSR program must align with the values, norms, and mission of the organization. . . . Very often, relevant organizational values and norms can be found in corporate documents such as the mission statement, annual reports, sales brochures, or Web sites.

Formal documents may not be sufficient to elicit how the organization envisions its relationships and contributions to stakeholders. Interviews of leading and senior organizational members may yield fruitful insights to begin the management process. While they clarify the stakeholders and issues they stand for, businesses must also understand which corporate practices and impacts are of greatest concern to their stakeholders. While limited attention has been given to processes for identifying alternatives based on stakeholder values, Gregory and Keeney (1994) . . . support an approach to guide stakeholder trade-off decisions that uses a logical methodological framework. First, with mutual understanding of the decision context, each stakeholder articulates objectives. Stakeholders then, based on a list of objectives, identify alternatives with the understanding that objectives should be linked to values. Then a balanced compromise is developed from the objectives of competing stakeholders through negotiations.[9] . . . Organizations that embrace a stakeholder orientation need to generate intelligence identifying stakeholders and understanding their needs.

Identifying CSR issues and problems is the first step in determining the stakeholder groups that have an interest in organizational participation and solutions. When addressing marketing issues, consumer surveys have been used as a key input for decision making, especially in shaping public policy through agencies such as the Federal Trade Commission and the Food and Drug Administration.[10]

Step 2: Identifying Stakeholders

In managing this stage, it is important to recognize stakeholder needs, wants, and desires. There are many important issues that gain visibility because key constituencies such as consumer groups, regulators, or the media express an interest.[11] When agreement, collaboration, or even confrontations exist on an issue, there is a need for a decision-making process. . . . Altman and Petkus (1994) suggest that there will be conflicting needs that require:

- consulting, accommodation, and involvement;
- formulation of alternatives;
- communication and leadership; and
- policy implementation that is monitored and adjusted.

. . . Stakeholders have some level of power over a business because they are in the position to withhold, or at least threaten to withhold, organizational resources.[12] To assess the power of a given stakeholder community, it is useful to rate the extent to which:

- the firm depends on the resources of this stakeholder community for its continued survival; and
- the welfare of the stakeholder community depends on organizational success.[13]

Stakeholders have the most power when their own survival is not really affected by the success of the organization, and when they have access to vital organizational resources. . . .

The proper assessment of the power held by a given stakeholder community also requires an evaluation of the extent to which that community can collaborate with others to pressure the firm. The more ties that exist or can easily be developed between stakeholder communities with similar norms, the more vulnerable the organization. . . .

Step 3: Identifying Stakeholder Issues

. . . Step 3 consists . . . in understanding the nature of the main issues of concern to . . . stakeholders. Conditions for collaboration exist when problems are so complex that multiple stakeholders are required to resolve the issue and the weaknesses of adversarial approaches are understood.[14] Some of this knowledge is often partially in-house, but has not been systematically integrated and analyzed. Boundary spanners (e.g., sales representatives, customer service representatives, purchasing managers, public relations, and advertising specialists) may be especially knowledgeable about the main norms and concerns shared by customers, suppliers, and the public opinion. Relevant information can also be found in secondary documents published by stakeholder organizations such as professional associations, governmental agencies, NGOs, or competitors. In spite of this existing knowledge, it may still be useful to conduct panel discussions or interviews with stakeholders to better understand their specific expectations. . . .

Step 4: Assessing the Meaning of CSR

. . . Step 4 brings these three first stages together to arrive at a concrete definition of CSR that specifically fits the organization of interest. This general definition will then be used to evaluate current practices and to select concrete CSR initiatives. Functional areas such as marketing should be able to use this definition for CSR activities that address stakeholder concerns. Ideally, this chosen definition is then formalized in official documents such as annual reports, Web pages, or company brochures. The definition should at least clarify two main points:

(1) The motivation underpinning the commitment to CSR.
(2) The stakeholders and issues that are perceived as priority by the organization.

The first element . . . therefore places CSR in the context of the broader organizational objectives and mission. When a CSR issue and mandate for a solution exists, there is a shift to exploring alternatives with constituencies such as consumer groups, trade associations, regulatory agencies, as well as others to develop a CSR definition and policy.[15] . . .

The second element of a CSR definition pinpoints the stakeholders and issues that are the main targets of CSR initiatives. The formation of voluntary collaborations is related to organizational commitments in their values and objectives to participate in solutions that result in improved CSR.[16] For instance, the global bank ABN AMRO defines its social responsibilities as follows:

> Being an active and responsible member of the societies and communities in which we operate is very important to us, morally as well as financially. Whether creating new products designed to promote sustainable development, spelling out the principles on which we conduct our business or supporting sports and the arts, we believe that being a good corporate citizen creates value for all stakeholders—employees, clients, investors, communities and others.[17]

In this definition, ABN AMRO identifies key stakeholders along with stakeholder issues that are considered as most important including sustainable development, integrity, and sponsorships of sports and arts. . . .

Step 5: Auditing Current Practices

The use of social auditing to identify stakeholder issues is important to demonstrating a firm's commitment to social responsibility. Social auditing is a process of assessing and reporting business performance and fulfilling social responsibilities expected by its stakeholders.[18] Without reliable measurements of the achievement of social objectives, a company has no concrete way to verify its importance, link to organizational performance, or justify expenditures to stakeholders.[19] The social audit should provide regular, comprehensive, and comparative verification of stakeholder feedback, especially key issues and concerns.

Two main questions can guide an audit of current CSR practices:

(1) What does the organization already have in place to address important stakeholder issues?
(2) Which practices need improvement?

The first part of this inventory is necessary because most organizations do not have a good overview of the various processes already in place to tackle each specific stakeholder issue. . . .

The second part of the audit consists essentially in identifying which organizational practices need to be modified. . . . A systematic review of all organizational processes along with surveys of different stakeholders could be conducted to perform the second part of this audit. Objective indicators of the organizational impacts on specific stakeholder issues can also be used. Businesses can rely on standardized audits such as those offered by the Global Reporting Initiative and the Social Accountability Institute. These standards provide a listing of issues to be surveyed, along with recommended indicators of impacts. These standardized audits implicitly assume that all companies share similar values and face about the same stakeholder communities and issues. As a result, they are most adequate for large companies that confront a wide range of issues and can afford to tackle this variety. Regardless of size, businesses should make sure that their audit centers on the stakeholders and issues favored in their own definition of CSR. Such a focus best enables businesses to concentrate their efforts and to establish a clear profile in the eyes of stakeholders. . . .

Step 6: Implementing CSR Initiatives

. . . The levels of financial and organizational investments required by different actions should be considered. In particular, one could distinguish between the challenges that require:

- Only small adaptations of current processes. For instance, philanthropic donations could be reorganized to systematically target one specific strategic issue . . .
- The creation of new external marketing processes. Examples would include the development of a supplier selection program based on environmental criteria . . .
- The development of new products to enhance green marketing. For instance, businesses could attempt to lower the nonrecyclable content of products . . .

A second criterion to consider when prioritizing CSR challenges is urgency. When the challenge under consideration corresponds to a point listed in the definition of CSR, and when stakeholder pressures on the issue could be expected, then the challenge can be considered as urgent. . . . Once a depiction and schedule of CSR challenges have been established, it is essential to allocate responsibility both to individual initiatives, and to the CSR implementation process as a whole. Even though it is often neglected, the designation of an individual or committee in charge of overseeing all CSR efforts is the only way to ensure the coherence of diverse initiatives, along with their fit with the stated definition of CSR.

Step 7: Promoting CSR

. . . Given that one aspect of CSR consists in addressing stakeholder issues, it is essential that businesses keep internal and external stakeholders aware of the initiatives undertaken to address these issues. Public relations including environmental and social reports constitute an increasingly popular means of keeping some stakeholders informed (mainly shareholders, investment funds, business partners, and employees). An increasing number of companies seem to also use Web sites to communicate their achievements.[20]

Traditional advertising can also be used to enhance awareness of CSR initiatives. For instance, Shell has been conducting for several years a campaign on the theme: "Profits and principles: is there a choice?" This campaign emphasizes Shell's commitment to social responsibility and environmental sustainability. Given that the successful management of CSR requires the continuous generation of intelligence about stakeholders, communications on CSR should not flow solely from businesses to stakeholders. Instead, businesses should strive not only to create awareness of CSR, but also to establish bonds to stakeholders and invite them to participate in their CSR initiatives.

. . . One approach to stimulating a sense of bonding to the firm consists in emphasizing the fact that the business and its stakeholders share similar concerns. For example, Wal-Mart advertises on store displays and on its Web site the thank-you letters . . . received by its employees during the working hours they spent as volunteers in the community. . . .

Overall, step 7 is intended first and foremost to encourage the exchange and interaction of ideas to gain stakeholder engagement. Meanwhile, promotion adopted during this phase may provide important information to stakeholders to secure increased support for their activities. . . . Even though these findings need confirmation, they suggest that businesses may be able to enjoy concrete rewards from their investments in CSR. Even though such benefits may be real, businesses should not be tempted to use step 7 only for promotional spin rather than focusing on stakeholder expectations. . . .

Step 8: Gaining Stakeholder Feedback

The different activities mentioned in step 7 help stimulate a dialogue with stakeholders. Other instruments can be employed to keep abreast of stakeholders' views of the firm and of their evolving issues.[21] Additional stakeholder feedback can be generated through a variety of means. First, stakeholders' general assessment of the firm and its practices can be obtained through satisfaction or reputation surveys. Second, in order to gauge stakeholders' perceptions of the firm's contributions to specific issues, more qualitative methods may be desirable. . . .

. . . [S]takeholders' feedback can be used as an input to reassess the first three steps of the CSR management process in the long run (approximately every four years). Stakeholder surveys and interviews could indeed highlight a new and important stakeholder group, or could reveal emerging stakeholder issues. . . . Since social responsibility practices are aimed in large part at addressing stakeholder issues, it is essential that businesses continuously gauge the evolution of these concerns, and integrate the changes into organizational values, norms, and practices. Finally, functional areas such as marketing can assist in implementing shared values and norms relating to CSR.

NOTES

1. S. L. Vargo and R. F. Lusch, "Evolving to a New Dominant Logic for Marketing," *Journal of Marketing* 68 (January 2004): 1–17.

2. K. M. Kimery and S. M. Rinehart, "Markets and Constituencies: An Alternative View of the Marketing Concept," *Journal of Business Research* 43 (1998): 117–24.

3. J. S. Harrison and R. E. Freeman, "Stakeholders, Social Responsibility, and Performance: Empirical Evidence and Theoretical Perspectives," *Academy of Management Journal* 42, no. 5 (1999): 479–85.

4. I. Maignan and O. C. Ferrell, "Corporate Social Responsibility and Marketing: An Integrative Framework," *Journal of the Academy of Marketing Science* 32, no. 1 (2004): 19–23.

5. M. P. Miles and L. S. Munilla, "The Potential Impact of Social Accountability Certification on Marketing: A Short Note," *Journal of Business Ethics* 50, no. 1 (2004): 1–12.

6. R. K. Mitchell, B. R. Agle, and D. J. Wood, "Toward a Theory of Stakeholder Identification and Salience: Defining the Principle of Who and What Really Counts," *Academy of Management Review* 22, no. 4 (1997): 853–86.

7. G. T. Savage, T. W. Nix, C. J. Whitehead, and J. D. Blair, "Strategies for Assessing and Managing Organizational Stakeholders," *Academy of Management Executive* 5, no. 2 (1991): 61–75.

8. Ibid.

9. R. Gregory and R. L. Keeney, "Creating Policy Alternatives Using Stakeholder Values," *Management Science* 40, no. 8 (1994): 1035–48.

10. J. Hastak, M. B. Mazis, and L. A. Morris, "The Role of Consumer Surveys in Public Policy Decision Making," *Journal of Public Policy & Marketing* 20, no. 2 (2001): 170–85.

11. Ibid.

12. A. Carroll and A. Buchholtz, *Business and Society: Ethics and Stakeholder Management*, 5th ed. (Mason, OH: Thomson South-Western, 2003).

13. J. Frooman, "Stakeholder Influence Strategies," *Academy of Management Review* 24, no. 2 (1999): 191–205.

14. D. J. Lober, "Explaining the Formation of Business-Environmentalist Collaborations: Collaborative Windows and the Paper Task Force," *Policy Sciences* 20 (1997): 1–24.

15. Hastak et al., "The Role of Consumer Surveys."

16. Lober, "Explaining the Formation of Business-Environmentalist Collaborations."

17. ABN AMRO, www.abnamro.com (2004).

18. D. T. McAlister, O. C. Ferrell, and L. K. Ferrell, *Business and Society* (Boston, MA: Houghton Mifflin Company, 2005), p. 359.

19. S. Zadek, P. Pruzan, and R. Evans, eds., "Why Count Social Performance?"

in *Building Corporate Accountability: The Emerging Practices in Social and Ethical Accounting, Auditing and Reporting* (London: Earthscan Publications, 1997), pp. 12–34.

20. I. Maignan and D. A. Ralston, "Corporate Social Responsibility in Europe and the USA: Insights from Businesses' Self-Presentations," *Journal of International Business Studies* 33, no. 3 (2002): 497–614.

21. S. Sen and C. B. Bhattacharya, "Does Doing Good Always Lead to Doing Better? Consumer Reactions to CSR," *Journal of Marketing Research* 38 (2001): 225–43.

20.

CORPORATE SOCIAL RESPONSIBILITY COMMUNICATION

Stakeholder Information, Response, and Involvement Strategies

Mette Morsing and Majken Schultz

INTRODUCTION

To increase our understanding of how managers can develop and maintain an ongoing awareness toward themselves and their environment, we argue in line with other research,[1] that the theory of sensemaking is a fruitful method for better understanding communication processes. Sensemaking is inherently social,[2] as we "make sense of things in organizations while in conversation with others, while reading communications from others, while exchanging ideas with others,"[3] implying that no manager or organization makes sense in splendid isolation.[4] But, the extent to which an individual—or an organization—is able to integrate the sensemaking of others will influence the individual's—or the organization's—ability to enact strategically a productive relationship.[5] This implies that managers need to develop a sense of the organization's internal and external environments[6] and thereafter be willing to define a revised conception of the organization. This process is what Gioia and Chittipeddi refer to as "interpretive work" under the label "sensemaking,"[7] i.e., trying to figure out what the others want and ascribe meaning to it. However, Gioia and Chittipeddi expand the notion of sensemaking by introducing the concept of "sensegiving," putting a special focus on the managerial processes facilitating sensemaking in organizations. According to Gioia and Chittipeddi, sensemaking is followed by action in terms of articulating an abstract vision that is then disseminated and championed by corporate management to stakeholders in a process labeled "sensegiving,"[8] i.e., attempts to influence the way another party understands or makes sense. In contrast to Gioia and Chittipeddi, who have an internal focus on sensegiving and sensemaking processes among managers and employees, we add an external focus as we suggest that by involving external stakeholders in CSR efforts, managers and employees will also engage in the sensegiving and sensemaking processes. Building on Gioia and Chittipeddi's terminology, we suggest that not only managers but also external stakeholders may more strongly support and contribute to CSR efforts if they engage in progressive iterations of sensemaking and sensegiving processes, as this enhances awareness of mutual expectations.

THREE CSR COMMUNICATION STRATEGIES

Based on Grunig and Hunt's (1984) characterization of models of public relations, we unfold three types of stakeholder relations in terms of how companies strategically engage in CSR communication *vis-à-vis* their stakeholders: the stakeholder information strategy; the stakeholder response strategy; and the stakeholder involvement strategy.

STAKEHOLDER INFORMATION STRATEGY

In the "stakeholder information strategy," similar to Grunig and Hunt's public information model, communication is always one-way, from the organization to its stakeholders. Communication is basically viewed as "telling, not listening,"[9] and therefore the one-way communication of the stakeholder information strategy has the purpose of disseminating information, not necessarily with a persuasive intent, but rather to inform the public as objectively as possible about the organization. Companies adopting a stakeholder information model engage in active press relations programs and concurrently produce information and news for the media, as well as a variety of brochures, pamphlets, magazines, facts, numbers, and figures to inform the general public. Governments, nonprofit organizations, and many businesses primarily use the public information model. The company "gives sense" to its audiences.

The stakeholder information model assumes that stakeholders are influential as they can either give support in terms of purchasing habits, showing loyalty, and praising the company, or they can show opposition in terms of demonstrating, striking, or boycotting the company.[10] Therefore, the company must inform stakeholders about its good intentions, decisions, and actions to ensure positive stakeholder support.

STAKEHOLDER RESPONSE STRATEGY

The stakeholder response strategy is based on a "two-way asymmetric" communication model, as opposed to the two-way symmetric model of the stakeholder involvement strategy. In both models, communication flows to and from the public. But there is a conspicuous difference between the two models in that the two-way asymmetric assumes an imbalance from the effects of public relations in favor of the company, as the company does not change as a result of the public relations. Rather, the company attempts to change public attitudes and behavior. As such, the company needs to engage stakeholders by making the corporate decisions and actions relevant for them because the company needs the external endorsement from external stakeholders. The corporate communication department will typically conduct an opinion poll or a market survey to make sense of where the company has—hopefully—improved and can improve its CSR efforts. Communication is perceived as feedback in terms of finding out what the public will accept and tolerate. This is an evaluative mode of measuring whether a particular communication initiative has improved stakeholder understanding of the company—and vice versa. Corporate management will champion and "give sense" to its decisions according to the market survey results in which managers "make sense." . . .

STAKEHOLDER INVOLVEMENT STRATEGY

The stakeholder involvement strategy, in contrast, assumes a dialogue with its stakeholders. Persuasion may occur, but it comes from stakeholders as well as from the organization itself, each trying to persuade the other to change. Ideally, the company as well as its stakeholders will change as a result of engaging in a symmetric communication model, i.e., progressive iterations of sensemaking and sensegiving processes. Because the stakeholder involvement strategy takes the notion of the stakeholder relationship to an extreme, companies should not only influence but also seek to be influenced by stakeholders, and therefore change when necessary. While this could apply to Freeman's stakeholder conceptualization, it would also challenge his stakeholder concept regarding the extent to which a company should change its (CSR) activities when stakeholders challenge existing (CSR) activities, and the extent to which a company should insist on its own possibly divergent assessment.

Rather than imposing a particular CSR initiative on stakeholders, the stakeholder involvement strategy invites concurrent negotiation with its stakeholders to explore their concerns *vis-à-vis* the company, while also accepting changes when they are necessary. By engaging in dialogue with stakeholders, the company ideally ensures that it keeps abreast not only of its stakeholders' concurrent expectations but also of its potential influence on those expectations, as well as letting those expectations influence and change the company itself.

The stakeholder involvement strategy is in harmony with the stakeholder information strategy in the assumption that stakeholders are influential in terms of their support of, or opposition to, the company, and it concurs with the stakeholder response strategy in that stakeholder expectations should be investigated using opinion polls. The involvement strategy, however, further assumes that, while informing and surveying is necessary, it is not sufficient. Stakeholders need to be involved in order to develop and promote positive support as well as for the company to understand and concurrently adapt to their concerns. Therefore, the stakeholder involvement strategy suggests that companies engage frequently and systematically in dialogue with their stakeholders in order to explore mutually beneficial action. . . .

While these three CSR communication strategies have been presented to underline the increased necessity for managers to incorporate learning and techniques to support more stakeholder involvement, there is only little evidence that two-way communication processes are the norm currently being practiced. . . .

DISCUSSION

Drawing on prior research on communication, the concepts of sensegiving and sensemaking . . . we discuss how corporate managers may improve their stakeholder relations as they communicate their CSR activities in terms of (1) pointing at CSR information as a double-edged sword, (2) nonfinancial reports as a means for subtle CSR communication, and (3) involving stakeholders in CSR communication as a proactive endorsement.

CSR INFORMATION: A DOUBLE-EDGED SWORD

Reputation surveys show[11] . . . that people are uncertain with respect to how companies should communicate their CSR initiatives—in more or less conspicuous channels—and this uncertainty has been addressed in prior research, for example, by Ashforth and Gibbs's (1990) discussion on the legitimacy risks for companies that are perceived as overaccentuating their good deeds. Ashforth and Gibbs's analysis also suggests a preference for communicating CSR initiatives through minimal releases as they argue that conspicuous attempts to increase legitimacy may in fact decrease legitimacy. Ashforth and Gibbs refer to this as the challenge of the "self-promoter's paradox," in which they suggest that companies that overemphasize their corporate legitimacy run the risk of achieving the opposite effect.[12] They argue that conspicuous CSR communication often is associated with, and comes from, organizations that attempt to defend their corporate legitimacy or from companies that have experienced a legitimacy problem: "the more problematic the legitimacy, the greater the protestation of legitimacy."[13] Too much "sensegiving" regarding CSR efforts may be counterproductive. It is argued that companies already perceived as legitimate constituents do not need to communicate their CSR efforts loudly. With reference to impression management, Ashforth and Gibbs indicate that individuals who believe that others will become aware of their desirable qualities tend to be less self-aggrandizing than individuals who do not. If companies are not granted positive recognition from their stakeholders, they tend to find it necessary not only to exemplify desirable qualities but also to promote them. Thus, the promotion of desirable qualities such as CSR will tend to evoke skepticism if a company is stigmatized beforehand with a bad reputation or if a company is experiencing a legitimacy threat such as a corporate scandal. While Ashforth and Gibbs take this argument to one extreme by pointing at companies with a legitimacy problem, we build on their argument and suggest that contemporary companies increasingly need to prepare for potential legitimacy problems.

. . . Some years ago, CSR had narrower and more well-defined limits, whereas today any company may in principle be associated with the violation of human rights as supplier and customer actions are increasingly seen as a corporate responsibility by stakeholders. Any contemporary company may in fact encounter legitimacy problems at some point. On the one hand, informing about CSR initiatives may be a means of preparing to avoid such a legitimacy problem by concurrently informing stakeholders about CSR initiatives. On the other hand, CSR communication may in fact provoke a legitimacy problem if a company encounters a stakeholder concern about its legitimacy. Information on CSR initiatives may then retrospectively be perceived as a means of covering up or accommodating the legitimacy problem, which in turn reinforces stakeholder skepticism toward CSR initiatives and corporate legitimacy. Thus, a straightforward "stakeholder information strategy" turns out to have a double edge.

A MEANS TOWARD SUBTLE COMMUNICATION: NONFINANCIAL REPORTS

Reputation surveys[14] suggest the increasing importance of minimal releases such as annual reports and Web sites as a preferred means of CSR communication by stakeholders on behalf of corporate advertising or corporate releases. Prior research has argued that implicit forms of communication (e.g., organizational rituals and folklore) are perceived to be more credible than explicit forms, e.g., press releases and policy statements.[15] This argument suggests that CSR communication will be perceived as more plausible if it is indirect and subtle, such as, for example, in the presentation of more objective data in nonfinancial reports,[16] which supports the tendency shown in reputation surveys that many stakeholders prefer more subtle forms of CSR communication. . . . Nevertheless, while nonfinancial reports may be used as a type of "subtle CSR communication," they are still predominantly designed as a means to "give sense" to potentially critical stakeholders. They are produced to inform and convince public audiences about corporate legitimacy and, as such, they are framed within a one-way communication perspective. In addition they may be illusory as they may possibly lead managers to conclude that they control meanings and perceptions among stakeholders.[17]

Nonfinancial reports may seem an appropriate response and sensegiving tool for making stakeholders aware of CSR efforts, but they also raise the potential risk of organizational self-absorption. Organizational communication research has pointed out that one of the major risks for communication in practice is that corporate managers publish the information that they themselves find important, taking pride in what is presented, and therefore also believe it is what other stakeholders want to hear.[18] Even with market analysis as an analytical tool to collect data to understand stakeholder concerns, prior research has pointed to the risk of self-fulfilling prophecies in market surveys and opinion polls.[19] In the case where managers are to communicate issues of social responsibility to stakeholders, managers may be tempted to reinforce information on issues they themselves identify with and take a pride in regardless of stakeholder concerns, because social responsibility often implies a personal moral designation for managers.[20] The risk is that in deciding what CSR issues to communicate and how to do it, managers become what Christensen and Cheney (2000) refer to as "self-seduced and self-absorbed," not realizing that other stakeholders may be uninterested in the information presented, and more importantly, that other stakeholders may not find it appropriate for companies to publish information on how good they are. To avoid this trap of CSR communication, close collaboration with stakeholders on the relevance of what CSR issues to emphasize and report on may possibly increase organizational awareness regarding stakeholder expectations. This dialogue contributes to the identification of potentially critical issues of importance for corporate legitimacy and a company's reputation. . . .

INVOLVING STAKEHOLDERS IN CSR COMMUNICATION: PROACTIVE ENDORSEMENT

We suggest that communicating messages that claim to represent a true image of corporate initiatives such as CSR will benefit from a proactive third-party endorsement, i.e., that external stakeholders express their support of CSR initiatives. This implies that managers need to understand how to enact carefully the dynamic processes of sensegiving and sensemaking in order to develop the endorsement in practice. Further, we suggest that this happens during the development of CSR efforts, and for this purpose, some companies have demonstrated how nonfinancial reporting holds a potentially promising tool for managing the complexity of CSR communication. Today, however, many nonfinancial reports are still expressions of a sophisticated yet conventional "stakeholder information strategy" or "stakeholder response strategy."[21]

While these corporate nonfinancial reports on stakeholder relations demonstrate engagement in stakeholder concerns, it is most often done through a simple listing of the partners with whom the company interacts.[22] . . .

While companies (Shell, 2003; Brown & Williamson, 2001; BNFL) state how much they acknowledge the importance of stakeholder dialogue, there are no comments from stakeholders in the reports. We would like to point out the potential of exploring a more proactive commitment by external stakeholders. . . .

. . . Novo Nordisk's nonfinancial reporting is an inspiring and sophisticated example of how a company has managed to handle its CSR communication challenges in a manner that approaches the two-way symmetric model as outlined in the "stakeholder involvement strategy." In 2002, Novo Nordisk began involving stakeholders in the actual reporting. Critical and highly involved stakeholders were given a voice in the report, as they were invited to comment on and critique issues that they perceived as being of particular concern in their relations with Novo Nordisk. For example, Søren Brix Christensen of Doctors without Frontiers was given a page under the heading, "How can we improve the access to diabetes treatment by selling our products at prices affordable in the developing countries, while we maintain a profitable business?"[23] to express that he strongly believes that the medical industry needs to take responsibility and sell medicine at cost price. . . . By inviting external stakeholders inside, so to speak, Novo Nordisk opened the possibility for new issues to emerge and become integrated, hence inviting an ongoing reconstruction of the CSR efforts as stakeholder concerns develop and change. Although the communication is of course controlled from Novo Nordisk's corporate headquarters, it nevertheless allows controversial dilemmas for Novo Nordisk's core business to surface.

Another example of the proactive involvement of stakeholders is Vodafone's social report from 2004, which demonstrates how the company involves the capital market, the public, opinion makers, and customers in identifying critical issues and actions by bringing these voices into the report. Rather than being communicated to, the critical stakeholders become co-responsible for the CSR messages, as they locally articulate their shared concern regarding the company. Instead of imposing corporate norms for CSR initiatives on stakeholders, the invitation to participate and co-construct the CSR message increases the likelihood that these stakeholders and those who identify with them will identify positively with the company.

The external endorsement of CSR messages differentiates itself from other endorsement strategies in the sense that critical issues come to the surface. Rather than giving a completely positive and almost saintly impression of CSR initiatives, which may evoke skepticism, Vodafone communicates that it acknowledges that the company has a way to go yet, but that it is trying to act in a more socially responsible manner by taking stakeholder concerns into consideration. Vodafone reports on controversial issues of great importance for its business, such as electromagnetism and health, responsible marketing, inappropriate content, junk mail, and so on. In addition, Vodafone brings critical survey results. Similarly, Novo Nordisk brings issues such as obesity, the distribution of wealth, poverty, and health and hormones in its report. Many of these issues are reported and commented on by external stakeholders.

By letting critical stakeholders have their own comments in the reports, Novo Nordisk and Vodafone demonstrate that they listen to stakeholders, they dare to mention—and even openly express—stakeholder concerns in their public annual report. . . .

While we can only agree with concerns about the risks of the exploitation of stakeholders and other malfunctions connected to participation, dialogue, and stakeholder involvement—and in fact, to the whole democratic project—we also question how one is to know when stakeholders are "genuinely motivated for dialogue" and when dialogue is "instrumentally and superficially employed" as opposed to "genuinely adopted." Most importantly, and in keeping with the sensemaking perspective of constructivism . . . we argue that the ways organizations give and make sense about themselves and their practices are not neutral activities, but constitutive actions that contribute to the continuous enactment of the organizational reality.[24] From this perspective, the communicative strategies of stakeholder involvement and dialogue contribute to the enactment of such involvement, creating more awareness of the critical potential of business-stakeholder relations. It can be argued that the "stakeholder involvement strategy" is an ideal, and that neither Novo Nordisk nor Vodafone are examples of "genuine" two-way symmetric communication, and that no sustainability report can ever be an expression of real two-way symmetric communication. Yet, we contend that *striving* toward stakeholder involvement and an improved mutual understanding of stakeholder expectations toward business and vice versa are crucial elements in its enactment. In this process, CSR communication is a forceful player for all partners. . . .

NOTES

1. M. Craig-Lees, "Sense-Making: Trojan Horse? Pandora's Box?" *Psychology and Marketing* 18, no. 5 (2001): 513–26.

2. J. Cramer et al., "Making Sense of Corporate Social Responsibility," *Journal of Business Ethics* 55, no. 2 (2004): 215–22.2; K. Weick, *Sensemaking in Organizations* (Thousand Oaks, CA: Sage, 1995).

3. A. Nijhof et al., "Sustaining Competences for Corporate Social Responsibility: A Sensemaking Perspective," working paper (Enschede: University of Twente, 2006).

4. Craig-Lees, "Sense-Making."

5. D. A. Gioia et al., "Symbolism and Strategic Change in Academia: The Dynamics of Sensemaking and Influence," *Organization Science* 5, no. 3 (1994): 363–83.

6. J. B. Thomas and R. R. McDaniel, "Interpreting Strategic Issues: Effects of Strategy and the Information-Processing Structure of Top Management Teams," *Academy of Management Journal* 33, no. 2 (1990): 286–306.

7. D. A. Gioia and K. Chittipeddi, "Sensemaking and Sensegiving in Strategic Change Initiation," *Strategic Management Journal* 12, no. 6 (1991): 434.

8. Ibid., p. 443.

9. J. E. Grunig and T. Hunt, *Managing Public Relations* (Fort Worth, TX: Harcourt Brace Jovanovich College Publishers, 1984), p. 23.

10. C. Smith, "CSR: Whether or How?" *California Management Review*, 45, no. 4 (2003): 52–76.

11. See M. Morsing and M. Schultz, "Corporate Social Responsibility Communication: Stakeholder Information, Response, and Involvement Strategies," *Business Ethics: A European Review* 15, no. 4 (2006), for full survey results and data.

12. B. E. Ashforth and B. W. Gibbs, "The Double-Edge of Organizational Legitimation," *Organization Science* 1, no. 2 (1990): 188.

13. Ibid., p. 185.

14. See note 11.

15. J. Martin, *Cultures in Organizations: Three Perspectives* (New York: Oxford University Press, 1992).

16. S. J. Tan, "Can Consumers' Scepticism Be Mitigated by Claim Objectivity and Claim Extremity?" *Journal of Marketing Communications* 8, no. 1 (2002): 45–64.

17. A. Crane and L. Livesey, "Are You Talking to Me? Stakeholder Communication and the Risks and Rewards of Dialogue," in *Unfolding Stakeholder Thinking: Relationships, Communication, Reporting and Performance*, ed. J. Andriof, S. Waddock, B. Husted, and S. S. Rahman (Sheffield: Greenleaf, 2003), pp. 39–52.

18. A. Morgan, *Eating the Big Fish. How 'Challenger Brands' Can Compete against Brand Leaders* (New York: John Wiley, 1999); L. T. Christensen and G.

Cheney, "Self-Absorption and Self-Seduction in the Corporate Identity Game," in *The Expressive Organization*, ed. M. J. Hatch, M. Schultz, and M. H. Larsen (Oxford: Oxford University Press, 2000), 256–70.

19. L. T. Christensen, "Marketing as Auto-communication," *Consumption, Markets and Culture* 1, no. 3 (1997): 197–227.

20. J. M. Lozano, "Ethics and Management: A Controversial Issue," *Journal of Business Ethics* 15, no. 2 (1996): 227–36; P. Pruzan, "From Control to Values-Based Management and Accountability," *Journal of Business Ethics* 17, no. 13 (1998): 1379–94.

21. See, for example, the SAS Group's Annual Report and Sustainability Report; KMD's Strategic Report 2004; and Novozymes' Annual Integrated Report 2004.

22. See, for example, Danisco Sustainability Report (Copenhagen: Danisco, 2004), Danisco.com; and SAS Sustainability Report (Copenhagen: SAS, 2004), SAS.com.

23. Novo Nordisk, Sustainability Report (2002), p. 27, novonordisk.com.

24. K. Weick, *The Social Psychology of Organizing* (Reading, MA: Addison-Wesley, 1979).

21.

THE BODY SHOP VALUES REPORT

Towards Integrated Stakeholder Auditing

Maria Sillanpää

THE BODY SHOP APPROACH TO SOCIAL AUDITING

The methodology development work for The Body Shop social audit first commenced in 1993 and was formalized for the first audit cycle of 1994/95. . . . The commitment to social auditing followed successful experience in implementing audit programs for environmental protection and health and safety at work, as well as ingredient monitoring programs for animal protection. In the case of environmental audits, The Body Shop elected in 1991 to follow the European Union Eco-management and Audit Regulation (EMAS) as the most rigorous framework available.[1] Since 1992, the company has published five independently verified environmental statements (The Body Shop International 1992, 1993, 1994, 1996, 1998).

In January 1996, The Body Shop published its first integrated document of its ethical performance called the Values Report 1995. The report was comprised of three statements on the company's performance on environmental, animal protection, and social issues. Each statement had an element of independent verification in line with established best practice. The publication also included a paper—"The Body Shop Approach to Ethical Auditing"—describing the methods underpinning the three reports. In January 1998, the company published its second integrated Values Report.

Maria Sillanpää, "The Body Shop Values Report—Towards Integrated Stakeholder Auditing," *Journal of Business Ethics* 17 (1998): 1443–56. Copyright Kluwer Academic Publishers, 1998. Copyright © 1998 Kluwer Academic Publishers. Reprinted with the kind permission of Springer Science and Business Media.

... The audit cycle consists of ten key components, namely: policy review, determination of audit scope, agreement of performance indicators, stakeholder consultation, internal management systems audit, preparation of accounts, agreement of strategic and local targets, verification, publication of statement and internal reports, and follow-up dialogue with stakeholders.

The following describes each step briefly in general terms and provides examples on how these steps relate to the company's first two audit cycles of 1994/95 and 1995/97.

COMMITMENT AND LEADERSHIP

The Body Shop committed itself to a formal social audit process in 1993. This followed publication of Anita Roddick's autobiography in 1991 in which she wrote: "I would love it if every shareholder of every company wrote a letter every time they received a company's annual report and accounts. I would like them to say something like, 'OK, that's fine, very good. But where are the details of our environmental audit? Where are the details of your accounting to the community? Where is your social audit?'"[2]

There is no doubt that had it not been for the commitment of the founders of the company and the development of an "accountability ethos" within The Body Shop in the early 1990s, the company would not have been in a position to publish a statement of its social performance in 1996.

POLICY REVIEW

In every company there will be a variety of formal and nonformal policies which prescribe the organization's intentions with respect to its stakeholders. These may range from occupational safety and health at work for employees (usually very well documented) to customer service (frequently expressed more through a company's culture than through any formalized system). There may be dividend policies for shareholders, payment terms for suppliers, codes of ethics for company representatives working overseas, and so on. Clear policies help provide a framework for assessing the quality of a company's relationships with its stakeholders. Before any assessment or audit of social relationships, a company should be aware of its explicit and implicit intentions with respect to each stakeholder group.

For The Body Shop's first social audit, the main policies against which performance was judged were the company's mission statement and trading charter. More specific policies and guidelines existed for health and safety at work, human resources (managers' and employees' handbooks) and Fair Trade (Community Trade program). These were also used as the basis for assessing the ability of management systems to deliver on policy commitments.

DETERMINATION OF AUDIT SCOPE

Because parallel systems exist at The Body Shop for auditing and reporting on ethical performance with respect to animal protection and the environment, the subject area of the social audit was restricted to people: human stakeholders who may affect or be affected by The Body Shop. The number of individual stakeholders groups could theoretically be quite large, . . . The Body Shop took the view that in the first cycle, the net should be cast as wide and as deep as possible. . . .

Another important factor in the scoping of a social audit . . . is the level to which indirect stakeholders may be embraced. For The Body Shop this required a decision about whether, for example, staff of franchisees or nongovernmental organizations in franchised markets should be consulted. It was decided that such stakeholders were better consulted directly at such a time when franchisees were able to conduct their own audit processes.

The stakeholder groups for The Body Shop's first social audit included:

- Directly employed staff . . .
- International head franchisees
- . . . Local franchisees
- . . . Customers
- Suppliers
- Community trade suppliers
- Shareholders
- Local community . . .
- . . . Nongovernmental organizations
- Foundation applicants

AGREEMENT OF PERFORMANCE INDICATORS

There are three types of performance measurement in The Body Shop's approach to social auditing. They are:

1. **Performance against** *standards* **(performance indicators).** These should reflect nationally and internationally available information on best practices for activities and policies that describe the organization's social performance. . . .
2. **Stakeholder perception of performance against** *core values* **(i.e., The Body Shop mission statement and trading charter).** These core values are essentially defined by the organization itself. Each stakeholder group is consulted to establish their perception of how closely the organization's performance matches its stated aspirations.
3. **Stakeholder perception of performance against specific** *needs of stakeholders.* These needs are particular to individual stakeholder groups. They are identified as salient through consultation with stakeholders in focus groups and measured in anonymous and confidential surveys of opinion.

STAKEHOLDER CONSULTATION

. . . Engaging stakeholders in direct dialogue is one of the most important and sensitive processes in social auditing. It is especially important to identify salient issues for each group in face-to-face conversation before conducting wide-scale surveys of opinion. The Body Shop's first social audit engaged stakeholder groups in focus groups to explore specific stakeholder needs and to allow stakeholder views and concerns to be expressed. To ensure open dialogue in the discussion, it was considered important, especially for the initial stages of the process, that the verifiers had access to the process as observers.

Following the focus groups, when specific issues had been identified as salient or of particular interest to stakeholders, questionnaires were designed to measure more wide-scale opinion. . . .

Questionnaires were designed with professional assistance to avoid inadvertent introduction of bias. Space was also allowed on the questionnaires themselves for open-ended commentary on the company's performance.

Surveys were done using the largest manageable sample size; respondents completed the questionnaires anonymously and returned them to an independent organization for confidential analysis. Only summary information and lists of comments were submitted to The Body Shop for inclusion in the audit process.

Following publication of the results of the social audit, it was considered vital to obtain feedback from stakeholders and engage them in follow-up dialogue about how they reacted to the findings presented in the social statement. . . .

THE INTERNAL MANAGEMENT SYSTEMS AUDIT

There were three main sources of information for The Body Shop's first audit process: i) the results of the focus groups and surveys described above; ii) the documentary information provided by departments which had agreed on quantitative and qualitative standards; and iii) the output from confidential internal audit interviews with staff and managers. This latter source of information was based on the kind of "management systems" structured interviews used in environmental and quality management auditing. Checklists were developed specifically for the purpose of the interviews and results used to build up a dynamic picture of departmental handling and knowledge of issues and company policies relevant to social performance.

During 1996/97 the internal management systems audit was further developed toward an integrated methodology whereby individual departments were audited on management systems relating to the company's policies on environment, animal protection, human resources, communications, occupational health and safety, information management, and other relevant ethical issues.

The audits result in time-framed action plans prioritizing recommendations for proposed improvements. The audit reports as well as documentation relating to the auditing procedures are made available to external verifiers. The management systems audits are conducted by a semi-independent audit team which reports directly to the company's executive committee.

Management audits are sometimes based on professional codes and standards; this is especially true of financial audits. With stakeholder relationships and social performance there are as yet no professional or accredited international standards, although groups such as the Institute for Social and Ethical Accountability are working toward them.

PREPARATION OF ACCOUNTS—THE SOCIAL STATEMENT

The format chosen for The Body Shop's first social statement was based on a stakeholder model, with each group given its own section within the report. . . . Each stakeholder section then followed a common format:

1. The basis for the company's approach and aims for each stakeholder group . . . as well as basic information about the stakeholder group. . . .
2. The methodology used for each consultation process. . . .
3. The results of stakeholder consultation with perception surveys described in as even-handed and neutral a way as possible so as to avoid premature interpretation, together with direct quotations from stakeholders selected in an independent fashion.
4. Quantitative and qualitative standards of performance where these existed.
5. A company response in the form of a quote from a board member or senior manager setting out their reaction to the audit results and noting where progress is already being made and/or where improvements were clearly required ("Next Steps").

The above format was based on the assumption that by setting out the accounts in this way promotes the dialogue process and allows stakeholders to take a view on the adequacy or otherwise of the company response. In order to make the follow-on dialogue process efficient, stakeholders receiving the social statement were encouraged to complete a response card and attend a discussion with representatives of the company.

The final components of The Body Shop's first social statement were a verification statement and a summary chapter on those stakeholders who could not be included in the cycle, but should be in future cycles. The external verification process should have an influence on the tone, format, and style of the social statement. The extent of this influence is guided by the verifier.

The Values Report 1995 consisted of three separate statements on the company's social, environmental, and animal protection–related performance, respectively. In an attempt to develop the companies reporting toward greater integration, the 1997 report comprises of a single document, structured throughout in a stakeholder-driven way, each stakeholder section reporting on those aspects of environmental, animal protection, and social performance most salient to a particular stakeholder group. . . .

AGREEMENT OF STRATEGIC AND LOCAL OBJECTIVES

As with environmental auditing and reporting, a very important part of the process is to set strategic objectives for the business which can help clarify the future priorities of the company and unite all stakeholders behind a common purpose. . . .

Strategic objectives must also be underpinned by subsidiary or localized objectives which apply more specifically to individual stakeholder groups. The latter are in some ways simpler to negotiate because they involve fewer decision makers at the corporate level. However, the endorsement and support of the company board and central management committee are essential if more localized objectives are to be executed speedily and efficiently and kept in line with wider business goals.

As mentioned earlier, the social statement for 1995 included a response from the relevant board member or senior manager to each stakeholder section. All in all, eighty-nine specific "Next Step" commitments were made together with seven company-wide strategic targets. The Values Report 1997 reports on progress toward these targets. The external verifiers assessed the company's claims toward these targets. The 1997 statement includes ninety-seven new targets relating to the company's stakeholder/social performance as well as ten integrated targets where stakeholder/social performance forms a component part.

VERIFICATION

. . . Based on The Body Shop's experience, [independent verification] is also of enormous value in assessing and improving the quality of relationships with stakeholders. Organizations such as the United Kingdom–based think tank New Economics Foundation have pioneered techniques of "social audit" verification with some success. It involves, for instance, documentation review, testing the veracity of numerical accounts, examining the integrity of internal management and audit systems, and ultimately signing off on the accuracy of published reports as "true and fair" accounts. It has also proven useful for the verifiers of a social/stakeholder audit to convene advisory panels of experts in particular stakeholder perspectives to comment on the scope and adequacy of draft public accounts.

PUBLICATION OF STATEMENT

The social statement needs to be a true and fair picture of the social impacts of the organization, in so far as the defined scope of the audit allows. It needs to be comprehensive and systematic, but above all, understood. Because of the complex nature of a social audit and because of the variety of stakeholder needs for information, a multi-tier approach was adopted for the publication of The Body Shop's first social statement. The full statement was published based on the approved, verified accounts and made available to all stakeholder groups.

In addition, more detailed information was provided to employees on specific results relevant to them and their part of the company. A summary document of all the ethical statements was produced for wider-scale distribution alongside even briefer material appropriate for customers and other large audiences. In each case readers were made aware of how they could obtain more detailed information. The full Values Report was also launched on the Internet.

Similarly, in 1997 a summary report—The Road Ahead—was published, aimed mostly at general audiences. A special broadsheet has also been produced for employees on the social audit results relating to them.

FOLLOW-UP DIALOGUE AND INTERNAL REPORTS

Following publication of the results of the company's first social audit, stakeholders were invited to engage in follow-up dialogue in order to obtain feedback on how they reacted to the findings presented in the social statement. The aim of this process is to help shape future audit cycles, enable indicators and data presentation to be fine-tuned for future cycles, and help set priorities for future action by the company. . . .

CONCLUSION

. . . The Body Shop has found that its social auditing has led to an increased understanding of the company's identity, with massive votes of confidence by stakeholders in its values and mission. Greater understanding of stakeholder needs and aspirations is already leading to improved communication and business decision making by those departments responsible for looking after individual stakeholder groups. The Body Shop also believes that, in the future, fewer mistakes will be made and less effort and resources expended on inappropriate business and stakeholder-specific initiatives. In short, social auditing and reporting is not just an ethically desirable activity, it is also a driver for improved effectiveness for the organization and enhanced inclusion and thus support from stakeholders.

NOTES

1. D. Wheeler, "Memorandum by The Body Shop International," in *A Community Eco-audit Scheme*, 12th Report of the Select Committee on The Body Shop International, the European Communities, House of Lords Paper 42 (London: HMSO, 1992), pp. 58–59.

2. A. Roddick, *Body & Soul* (London: Ebury Press, 1991).

SUGGESTIONS FOR FURTHER READING

Alkhafaji, A. *A Stakeholder Approach to Corporate Governance: Managing in a Dynamic Environment*. New York: Quorum Books, 1989.

Ayuso, S., M. Rodriguez, and J. Ricart. "Using Stakeholder Dialogue as a Source for New Ideas: A Dynamic Capability Underlying Sustainable Innovation." *Corporate Governance* 6, no. 4 (2006): 475.

Baron, S., N. Hill, and S. Sundaram. "An Empirical Test of Stakeholder Theory Predictions of Capital Structure." *Financial Management* 2 (1989): 36–44.

Berman, S., A. Wicks, S. Kotha, and T. Jones. "Does Stakeholder Orientation Matter? The Relationship between Stakeholder Management Models and Firm Financial Performance." *Academy of Management Journal* 42, no. 5 (1999): 488–506.

Bowie, N., and P. Werhane. *Management Ethics*. New York: Blackwell Publishing, 2004.

Carroll, A., and A. Buchholtz. *Business and Society: Ethics and Stakeholder Management*. Belmont, CA: Thomson Southwestern, 2006.

Clarkson, M. *The Corporation and Its Stakeholders*. Toronto: Toronto Press, 1998.

———. *Principles of Stakeholder Management*. Toronto: Clarkson Centre for Business Ethics, 1999.

———. "A Stakeholder Framework for Analyzing and Evaluating Corporate Social Performance." *Academy of Management Review* 20, no. 1 (1995): 92–117.

Cornell, B., and A. Shapiro. "Corporate Stakeholders and Corporate Finance." *Financial Management* 16 (1987): 5–14.

Culpan, R., and J. Trussel. "Applying the Agency and Stakeholder Theories to the Enron Debacle: An Ethical Perspective." *Business and Society Review* 110, no. 1 (2005): 59.

Freeman, R. E., and D. Gilbert. "Managing Stakeholder Relationships." In *Business and Society: Dimensions of Conflict and Cooperation*, ed. S. Sethi and C. Falbe. Lexington, MA: Lexington Books, 1987.

Frooman, J. "Stakeholder Influence Strategies." *Academy of Management Review* 24, no. 2 (1999): 191–205.

Gao, S., and J. Zhang. "Stakeholder Engagement, Social Auditing, and Corporate Sustainability." *Business Process Management Journal* 12, no. 6 (2006): 722.

Harting, T., S. Harmeling, and S. Venkataraman. "Innovative Stakeholder Relations: When 'Ethics Pays' (and When It Doesn't)." *Business Ethics Quarterly* 16 (2006): 43–68.

Kolk, A., and J. Pinkse. "Stakeholder Mismanagement and Corporate Social Responsibility Crises." *European Management Journal* 24, no. 1 (2006): 59–72.

Lampe, M. "Mediation as an Ethical Adjunct of Stakeholder Theory." *Journal of Business Ethics* 31, no. 2 (2002): 165.

Maak, T. "Responsible Leadership, Stakeholder Engagement, and the Emergence of Social Capital." *Journal of Business Ethics* 74, no. 4 (2007): 329–44.

Maak, T., and N. Pless. "Responsible Leadership in a Stakeholder Society—A Relational Perspective." *Journal of Business Ethics* 66, no. 1 (2006): 99.

Maranville, S. "You Can't Make Steel without Some Smoke: A Case Study in Stakeholder Analysis." *Journal of Business Ethics* 8 (1989): 57–63.

Pedersen, E. "Making Corporate Social Responsibility (CSR) Operable: How Companies Translate Stakeholder Dialogue into Practice." *Business and Society Review* 11, no. 2 (2006): 137.

Preble, J. "Toward a Comprehensive Model of Stakeholder Management." *Business and Society Review* 110, no. 4 (2005): 407–31.

Preston, L., and T. Donaldson. "Stakeholder Management and Organizational Wealth." *Academy of Management Review* 24, no. 4 (1999): 619.

Preston, L., and H. Sapienze. "Stakeholder Management and Corporate Performance." *Journal of Behavioral Economics* 19 (1990): 361–75.

Reynolds, S., F. Schultz, and D. Hekman. "Stakeholder Theory and Managerial Decision-Making: Constraints and Implications of Balancing Stakeholder Interests." *Journal of Business Ethics* 64, no. 3 (2006): 285.

Roberts, R. "Determinants of Corporate Social Responsibility Disclosure: An Application of Stakeholder Theory." *Accounting, Organizations and Society* 17, no. 6 (1992): 595–612.

Scott, S. G., and V. R. Lane. "A Stakeholder Approach to Organizational Identity." *Academy of Management Review* 25, no. 1 (2000): 43–62.

Steurer, R., M. Langer, A. Konrad, and A. Martinuzzi. "Corporations, Stakeholders, and Sustainable Development I: A Theoretical Exploration of Business-Society Relations." *Journal of Business Ethics* 61, no. 3 (2005): 263.

Winn, M. "Building Stakeholder Theory with a Decision Modeling Methodology." *Business and Society* 40, no. 2 (2001): 133.

PART 6.

APPLICATIONS 2: EXTENDING STAKEHOLDER THEORY

The benefits of applying stakeholder theory to management decisions in publicly owned corporations have inspired many to extend the application of stakeholder theory to other less typical domains. In this chapter, we examine attempts to apply stakeholder analysis to more diverse business contexts and to domains outside of the publicly owned corporation, which is where stakeholder theory was initially generated. Although the application of stakeholder theory to nonstandard subject areas is too vast to represent fully here, we do attempt to provide a representative sampling of the more recent and various applications. This includes the applications of stakeholder theory to specialized business endeavors, notably the management of healthcare organizations. We also examine the ways in which stakeholder theory has been used to manage nonprofit organizations (e.g., parks and conservation projects) as well as how stakeholder theory can impact curriculum in business education. Furthermore, we explore the inherent challenges of applying stakeholder theory in a global context where companies are often expected to pick up some of the moral slack for governments around the world that either do not or cannot adequately attend to the needs of both their people and native ecosystems. While companies cannot and should not try to do the jobs of government, they do need to find ways to act responsibly among peoples of diverse cultures and in a context of often lax enforcement of government regulation. This is especially difficult given the vastly disproportionate power wielded by transnational corporations as compared to the individuals, governments, and community groups in poorer nations around the globe.

The first article in this section deals with the application of stakeholder theory to organizations that must be mindful of the bottom line, but whose ultimate function is to provide healthcare. In "Business Ethics, Stakeholder Theory, and the Ethics of Healthcare Organizations," Patricia H. Werhane argues that stakeholder theory can help healthcare organizations better to meet their goals as institutions. Some might worry that Milton Friedman's overly libertarian perspective on business might prove that business structure is antithetical to the demands of healthcare because business must always put profit before all else, including the health of individuals. This is morally repugnant. Werhane argues that the objection is premised upon a false dichotomy between business and healthcare. Business has never solely been in the business of making profits and healthcare has never been completely disconnected from business interests. Werhane points to the example of several visionary companies to show that many of the most profitable businesses over the long term rarely have the maximization of profit as their first priority. Second, she points out that even doctors traveling by horse and buggy still had to make a living from their profession. Given that business and healthcare must work together on some level, Werhane argues that since stakeholder theory sees business as functioning in the context of a moral community that must also be mindful of the bottom line, it is especially well suited to the analysis of management for healthcare organizations. Werhane goes on to discuss a series of structural elements that mark the management of healthcare organizations as having distinct duties and facing distinctive difficulties not likely faced by managers of other organizations.

Stakeholder theory may be applied not just to professionally based organizations but also to fundamentally nonprofit organizations. Thanakvaro Thyl De Lopez, an economic advisor to the Ministry of Environment in Cambodia, explores the application of stakeholder theory to the management of conservation projects in his piece, "Stakeholder Management for Conservation Projects: A Case Study of Ream National Park, Cambodia." De Lopez points out the difficulty of protecting nature in poor countries where conservation is seen as a luxury. By using stakeholder theory, the managers of the Ream National Park were better able to bring relevant stakeholders into the discussion; this enabled them to find strategies that were both mutually acceptable and most likely to result in better protection of the park. The managers of Ream National Park faced a crisis situation in which the state, community members, rangers, local villagers, commercial loggers, fishermen, the navy, the police, tourists, and land speculators all had various competing and often conflicting stakes in the management of the park. By identifying various stakeholders and working on garnering commitments from each to endorse an effective overall management strategy, De Lopez believes that the committee charged with strengthening the integrity of the park was able to effectively meet its goals.

The next article in this section also deals with the application of stakeholder theory to management decisions in a globalized economy. Grahame Thompson and Ciaran Driver explore efforts to develop corporate social responsibility internationally in "Stakeholder Champions: How to Internationalize the Corporate Social Responsibility Agenda." While Thompson and Driver are not yet convinced that sufficient evidence is available to show that companies with a strong corporate social responsibility agenda are able to turn a higher profit than their less morally responsible competitors, they believe that the moral case for corporate social responsibility is clear. Creating a context of corporate social responsibility internationally is challenging not only because most calls for corporate accountability are voluntary rather than obligatory, but also because of the complex political interaction between global governing bodies that are themselves less than fully democratic. This makes it increasingly difficult for companies to navigate a complex array of economic, political, social, and moral expectations. Since companies must also deal with the moral value attached to local ecosystems and future generations of humans who cannot speak for themselves, the task is further complicated. In order to remedy this last problem, Thompson and Driver argue that companies ought to appoint champions to ensure that companies will be able to meet stewardship obligations in their attempts to apply stakeholder theory with as much transparency as possible. They also suggest the creation of an independent commission of experts, possibly drawn from business schools that teach corporate social responsibility and from a set of corporate social responsibility champions involved in the nonprofit sector, to examine the records of CEOs after they retire. In this way, management might be better motivated to leave a legacy of social responsibility that extends beyond mere profits.

The last article in this section relates the stakeholder concept to higher education. In "Re-engineering the Business Curriculum: A Stakeholder Paradigm," Jeff Heinfeldt and Fran Wolf describe a stakeholder-orientated approach to developing a core business school curriculum. In developing their position, the authors lay out specific recommendations for integrating stakeholder theory into traditional functional areas (e.g., accounting, finance, marketing, and management) and for developing more innovative methods to business education, such as cross-disciplinary and team-taught courses. The advantages of a stakeholder-based curriculum are argued to include: pro-

viding a common hermeneutic (i.e., the stakeholder) for addressing and integrating functional area concepts, presenting a more illustrative or "big-
picture" representation of stakeholder issues across disciplines, and offering
a sound framework in which ethical and societal issues can be raised in a
meaningful and constructive manner.

22.

BUSINESS ETHICS, STAKEHOLDER THEORY, AND THE ETHICS OF HEALTHCARE ORGANIZATIONS

Patricia H. Werhane

• • • [I] n this paper I will make four points. First, I will argue that the misidentification of business ethics with a libertarian Milton Friedman perspective can be reinterpreted to contribute to the thinking about the ethics of healthcare organizations. Second, I will suggest that it is not the profitability of healthcare organizations that is the danger, it is the prioritizing of profits as the first order of business in healthcare organizations that is questionable. . . . Third, one prevalent theory in business ethics, stakeholder theory, has much to contribute to organization ethics for healthcare delivery organizations. . . . Stakeholder theory assumes that the organization and all its stakeholders form a shared moral community, and it appeals to moral minimums or principles of fairness when evaluating organizational decisions. I will conclude, however, that even though business ethics contribute to our thinking about the ethics of healthcare organizations, these organizations have distinguishing characteristics that make them worth considering apart from other business or charitable enterprises.

To facilitate these arguments I will make the following assumptions. By healthcare organizations (HCOs) I will mean medium- and large-sized provider organizations that have a defined management structure. I will also make the rash assumption that the purpose or mission of healthcare organizations is, by definition (because they are called *healthcare* organizations), patient or patient population healthcare or well-being. . . . I will assume it

---

makes sense to say that organizations are moral agents and can be held morally responsible, although they are not moral agents in the same sense as, say, individuals.[1]

FRIEDMAN ECONOMICS

. . . There is a myth that business ethics is primarily focused on libertarian views defending laissez faire capitalism and competitive, unfettered free markets except in cases of egregious harms, particularly harms to liberties. This myth is perpetuated by a reading of the Nobel Prize–winning economist Milton Friedman,[2] who some time ago declared:

> There is one and only one social responsibility of business—to use its resources and engage in activities designed to increase its profits so long as it stays within the rules of the game, which is to say, engages in open and free competition without deception or fraud.[3]

This often misquoted statement does not advocate that "anything goes" in commerce. Law and common morality should guide our actions in the marketplace just as they guide our actions elsewhere. Nevertheless . . . Friedman places primary importance on profit maximization as the role of business. Thus managers' first duties and fiduciary duties are to owners or shareholders. Ordinarily, these duties are to maximize return on investment. . . .

Friedman's conclusion is based on a neoclassical economic model of rational choice theory. Rational choice theory is grounded in the assumption that human beings act primarily . . . in their own self-interests, broadly conceived.

According to most proponents of this view, it is rational to maximize your interests, even when these are interests in oneself. When one acts rationally (and no economist assumes that any of us do most of the time), one acts to maximize one's interests, or long-term chosen preference, all things considered.[4]

. . . The assumption by economists such as Friedman is that what is in the "interest" of a commercial enterprise is maximization of profit. If we understand business organizations on this model, what is ethical is the maximization of shareholder interests since shareholders are the owners of the enterprise. . . . Despite this alleged introverted organizational focus on itself and its interests, it is further argued that in a climate of free enterprise, when the playing field is relatively level, competition among businesses may act to regulate economic interests, increasing well-being by producing competitively qualitative goods and services at low cost.

Rational choice theory, and Milton Friedman's version in particular, has been influential in changing the model of contemporary healthcare delivery. The promise of managed care has been that self-interested commercial competition between providers and insurers will be a sufficient mechanism to improve the efficiency and reduce the cost of healthcare, without imperiling quality. Yet there are a number of difficulties with this argument even as it applies to the practice of commerce or business, and even greater difficulties when applied without qualification to healthcare delivery.

The difficulty when applied to business is that, in fact, many of the best for-profit corporations do not operate under Friedman's philosophy. A case in point was the reaction of Johnson & Johnson in 1982 to the poisoning of Tylenol capsules. The CEO of J&J, James Burke, decided to discontinue the marketing of the capsules, despite the absence of correlation between the J&J manufacturing process and poisonings, against the best advice of marketers and even the FBI. . . . Citing J&J's credo, the first line of which states, "We believe our first responsibility is to the doctors, nurses and patients, to mothers and all others who use our products and services," Burke withdrew the capsules from the shelves and Tylenol capsules were never again manufactured or sold.[5] This act alone cost J&J more than ten million dollars.

There is further evidence that the action of this company is not a moral anomaly. In a six-year project, James Collins and Jerry Porras, professors of management at Stanford University, set out to identify and systematically research the historical development of a set of what they called "visionary companies," to examine how these companies differed from a carefully selected control set of comparison companies.[6] Collins and Porras's interest lay in explaining the enduring quality and prosperity of these visionary companies, but in the course of their research they dispelled a number of myths, including the myth that insists that the most successful companies exist first and foremost to maximize profits. . . .

Each of the visionary companies identified by Collins and Porras faced setbacks, that is, each has made mistakes. Nevertheless, each has displayed a resiliency, an ability to bounce back from adversity. The long-term financial performance of each has been remarkable. A dollar invested in a visionary company stock fund on January 1, 1926, with dividends reinvested and making appropriate adjustments for when the companies became available on the stock market, would have grown by December 31, 1990, to $6,356. That dollar invested in a general market fund would have grown to $415.[7]

The comparison companies chosen by Collins and Porras are by no means sluggards. . . . But that dollar invested in a comparison stock fund composed of these companies would have returned $955—more than twice the general market but less than one-sixth of the return provided by the visionary companies.[8] . . . Collins and Porras state:

> Contrary to business school doctrine, "maximizing shareholder wealth" or "profit maximization" has not been the dominant driving force or primary objective through the history of the visionary companies. Visionary companies pursue a cluster of objectives, of which making money is only one—and not necessarily the primary one. Yes, they seek profits, but they are equally guided by a core ideology—core values and a sense of purpose beyond just making money. Yet, paradoxically, the visionary companies make more money than the more purely profit-driven comparison companies.[9]

Having dispelled Friedman's edict as the only acceptable normative framework for organizations, there is one sense in which Milton Friedman's version might be useful in thinking about HCOs. HCOs are, at least in theory, created for one purpose: to minister to the health of patients and patient populations. If their mission is patient or population health, then as rational agents they should act so as to maximize the treatment and well-being of their designated populations. . . .

One of the "rules of the game" in the present economic climate might be the proviso that an HCO . . . must break even or create the ability to pay its debts. Even HCOs that depend on charitable contributions or state funds are under such economic constraints. Another "rule" would be the practice of following legal and regulatory mandates. This formulation puts in perspective and focuses the unique feature of HCOs that distinguishes them from other types of organizations, including for-profit, nonhealth-related corporations, while appealing to a Friedmanesque rationale and justification for their actions. Actions of an HCO that do not maximize patient or population treatment would, on this account, be irrational and indeed morally wrong, given the mission of the HCO. Efficiency, productivity, profitability, economic stability, needs, and interests of healthcare professionals, and interests of insurers, government, or the community, are important goals only insofar as they contribute to the primary aim of the HCO.

STAKEHOLDER THEORY

What Milton Friedman sometimes neglects to consider in his description of a manager's fiduciary responsibility to shareholders is an organization's obligations to other stakeholders, in particular, in business, to employees, managers, customers or clients, and the community. . . . These groups of individuals (and there are others), are important, not merely because one could not exist or achieve profits without them, but also because they are individuals or groups of individuals—human beings with rights and interests.

An approach to business ethics that takes into account the rights and interests of the broad range of individuals and organizations who interact with and are affected by business decision making is stakeholder theory. Widely defined, stakeholders are "groups or individuals who benefit from or are harmed by, and whose rights are violated or respected by, corporate actions."[10] In a modern business corporation the primary or most important stakeholders commonly include employees, management, owners/shareholders, and customers, and, usually, suppliers and the community.

. . . One way to prioritize stakeholder claims is to examine an organization's purpose and mission, ranking stakeholders in terms of who has legitimate or appropriate claims, and who is essential to that mission and to the survival and flourishing of the organization.

A finer-grained analysis of stakeholder identification identifies and prioritizes stakeholders in terms of, "[(1)] the stakeholder's *power* to influence the firm, (2) the *legitimacy* of the stakeholder's relationship with the firm, and (3) the *urgency* of the stakeholder's claim on the firm."[11] By power the authors mean, most obviously, coercive power, such as that derived from legislation or regulation. But power can also be in the form of utility, for example, access to resources. So an HCO with a large capital base has more power just because it has financial flexibility. Normative power is a third dimension.[12] The recognition of a physician as a professional backed by a strong professional association and a code of ethics gives to that person or group of professionals normatively grounded power.

Legitimacy does not merely refer to legally mandated relationships. Legitimacy also includes relationships or structures that are socially expected or accepted. For example, healthcare organizations are expected to provide patient care, and in some communities provide it to the whole community, including the indigent. The third criterion, urgency, is more situational. A patient in intensive care requires more attention, ordinarily, than an outpatient with an earache.

The instrumentality of the prioritization deals only with part of what is important in stakeholder relationships. It does not take away from the normative claim of stakeholder theory that each stakeholder's interest has intrinsic value. . . .

The descriptive accuracy of the theory presumes the truth of the core normative conception, insofar as it presumes that managers and others act [*or
should act*] as if all stakeholders' interests have intrinsic value. In turn,
recognition of these ultimate moral values and obligations gives stakeholder management its fundamental normative base.[13]

The normative core of stakeholder theory has three aspects: the purpose
of the firm, the relationships between the firm and its stakeholders, and, at
least in healthcare organizations, the interrelationships among stakeholders.
Challenging the position that a manager's primary responsibility is to maximize profits . . . stakeholder theory argues that the *goal* of any firm and its
management is, *or should be*, the flourishing of the firm and *all* its primary
stakeholders. That purpose is identified with stakeholder interests.

The very purpose of a firm [and thus its managers] is to serve as a vehicle
for coordinating stakeholder interests. It is through the firm [and its man-
agers] that each stakeholder group makes itself better off through voluntary
exchange. The corporation serves at the pleasure of its stakeholders, and
none may be used as a means to the ends of another without full rights of
participation of that decision. . . . Management bears a fiduciary relationship to its stakeholders and to the corporation as an abstract entity.[14]

Let us assume for our purposes that all stakeholders in question are individuals or groups (including institutions) made up of individuals. If stakeholder
interests have intrinsic value, then, according to R. Edward Freeman, the
"father" of stakeholder theory, in every stakeholder relationship, the "stakes
[that is, what is expected and due to each party] of each are reciprocal,
[although not identical], since each can affect the other in terms of harms and
benefits as well as rights and duties."[15] Therefore stakeholder relationships are
normative reciprocal relationships for which each party is accountable. . . .

Obligations between stakeholders and stakeholder accountability notions
are derived on two grounds. First and obviously, stakeholder relationships are
relationships between persons or groups of persons. So the firm and each of
its stakeholders are reciprocally morally accountable to each other just
because they are people. One is obligated to treat individuals with respect,
play fairly, avoid gratuitous harm, and so forth. What is distinctive about
stakeholder relationships, however, is that these relationships entail additional obligations because of the unique and specific organizationally defined
and role-defined relationships between the firm and its stakeholders. For
example, an organization has obligations to its employees because they are

human beings *and* because they are employees of the organization.[16] Conversely, because of their organizationally defined roles, employees have role obligations to the organization that employs them and to its other stakeholders, *as well as* ordinary moral obligations to that organization and its other stakeholders.

In HCOs these obligations become more complex. For example, an HCO has obligations to its employee-professionals (a) because they are moral agents, (b) because they are employees, and (c) because they are professionals and hired *as professionals*. Conversely, healthcare professionals have role obligations to the HCO that employs them and role obligations to patients, to their profession, and to their professional associations. They may also have role obligations to the communities they serve and to healthcare payers, and they have ordinary moral obligations to all of these populations by the simple fact of their existence in the community.[17]

. . . [T]here is a simple method for prioritizing stakeholder importance in HCOs. First, by the fact of being a *healthcare* organization, the primary stakeholders in any HCO are its patients or the patient population it serves. Because the primary value-creating activity of an HCO is excellence in patient care, and because survival in the healthcare industry requires offering professionally excellent service, healthcare professionals are the second most important stakeholders. . . . [L]ong-term organizational viability that includes financial stability is necessary for the continuation of an HCO and the quality of its services. Finally, because health is considered a public good, community, community access, and public health are part of the stakeholder equation.

. . . According to some stakeholder theorists, stakeholder theory is descriptive, instrumental, internally normative, and has another normative dimension as well. In evaluating stakeholder claims, Evan and Freeman, two of the initiators of stakeholder theory, initially took a Kantian approach, arguing that because stakeholder relationships are between individuals or groups of individuals, any decision must be one that affords equal respect to persons and their rights, valued for their own sake. A decision or action that used people as means for other objectives would not meet this Kantian criterion. Such prioritization leads to judgments that value corporate material goals over persons, a valuation that would violate this kind of stakeholder approach. In addition to autonomy and respect for individuals, procedural fairness, informed consent, and respect for contractual agreements are means tests for stakeholder relationships. And in a properly constructed stakeholder arrangement, stakeholders should have viable avenues for self-governance and recourse.

Some thinkers, such as Robert Phillips, develop a standard of fairness as the normative basis for stakeholder relationships.[18] This principle, derived from Rawls's theory of justice, argues that

> Whenever persons or groups of persons voluntarily accept the benefits of a mutually beneficial scheme of co-operation requiring sacrifice or conurbation on the parts of the participants and there exists the possibility of free-riding, obligations of fairness are created among the participants in the co-operative scheme in proportion to the benefits accepted.[19]

These formal considerations of such a fairness standard should provide a set of externally derived minimum guidelines or moral minimums for evaluating organizations and stakeholder decisions: for judging some of them morally acceptable and some morally problematic. Decisions that affect various stakeholders must meet these minimum standards of respect for individuals, fairness of procedures and outcomes, informed consent, and availability of recourse.[20] . . .

BUSINESS ETHICS AND HEALTHCARE ORGANIZATIONS

Given the reformulated edict of Milton Friedman and the normative contributions of stakeholder theory to the ethics of healthcare organizations, can we simply subsume HCOs under the philosophical umbrella of business ethics? Several characteristics of the HCO complicate our understanding of the organizational aspects of healthcare and therefore complicate or even preclude such a move. They are the following.

1. *Mission*: Few corporations define their mission solely in terms of profitability, as we discussed earlier. . . . [T]he best organizations integrate other missions with the aim of profitability, and that the best (longest-surviving, most responsible, and most profitable) business organizations are those that do not focus on profitability as their primary mission. Still, whatever the mission, a goal of any for-profit business firm is the economic flourishing of its shareholders, or of its primary stakeholders. In an HCO there is no such tight relationship between the rationale of the organization's existence and the condition for its economic survival. The difference between garden variety corporations and any HCO (whether a for-profit organization or not) is the primary mission of HCOs, which is always the provision of health services to individuals and populations. This constitutive goal stands in an uneasy relation to economic ends. What is strange is not that an HCO is concerned with

efficiency, profitability, or at least sustainability. The trouble begins when an HCO realigns its mission or creates an organizational culture in which efficiency, productivity, and/or profitability become the first priorities.

2. *Patient priority*: In any organization, how one prioritizes value-creating activities determines the nature of stakeholder relationships. Patients, the consumers of the healthcare services provided by HCOs, have a privileged status among the stakeholders. It is true that in many excellent companies profitability is only one of a number of goals, such as integrity, customer satisfaction, employee well-being, respect for community, and so forth. Nevertheless, no for-profit entity can stay in business very long if it loses money. So while customers may be a set of important stakeholders, they are not the only primary stakeholders. This is not the case in HCOs.

3. *Separation of customer/payer and consumer/patient*: In HCOs, recipients of healthcare services are usually not the payers. . . . Various forms of insurance, employer-sponsored health plans, or government agencies purchase health coverage for the individuals and patient groups who are the actual and potential patients for a given HCO. This three-way relationship complicates accountability among the parties affected in healthcare delivery. Unlike the typical consumer, the patient may have no choice to go elsewhere or to change providers. Even in those cases where the recipient is also the payer, the consumer/patient is often ill and vulnerable. So, unlike ordinary consumers, patients are not always able to exercise their choices coherently.

4. *Central role of professionals in HCOs*: Healthcare professionals—physicians, nurses, members of other allied health professions—play key roles in the capacity of an HCO to deliver the services central to its definition and mission. It is the healthcare professional, not the manager, who is responsible for delivering care. One cannot gloss over, trade off, or subordinate professional commitments to patient health. Not only is this morally irresponsible for obvious reasons, it imperils the mission of any HCO. . . . Many if not all professionals consider themselves primarily bound by the ethical prescriptions of their profession, preeminent among which are their duties to their patients. The necessity of professionals in HCOs complicates stakeholder relationships, particularly when the professional is also an employee of the HCO.

5. *Community and public health*: Despite the ability of HCOs to define and restrict the patient population they will serve, community access and public health are always part of the accountability equation, because of the simple societal expectation that healthcare organizations *should* serve health needs.

6. *Healthcare markets*: There are a number of factors that complicate healthcare markets. There is an obvious information asymmetry between managers and healthcare professionals, and between professionals and customers or patients. Coupled with patient vulnerability, an HCO's healthcare customers are never "fully informed" customers. If "buyer beware" was ever an appropriate slogan, it clearly does not apply to HCOs. There is also an information asymmetry between healthcare organizations. Competitive healthcare organizations do not have access to customer (i.e., patient) information in ways in which they have access to market information in other business enterprises. So ordinary competitive relationships are not possible in the healthcare market. Additionally, there is a supply/demand asymmetry. Healthcare organizations cannot respond to all market demands, in particular, to the demands of the uninsured. Along with that is a pricing asymmetry. Some patients or patient groups cannot pay for what they consume while others pay for more than they consume.

These six factors (and there are others) give ample evidence that the distinguishing features of healthcare organizations warrant their separate study as a particular set of organizations. Business ethics provides some tools for that study, but this does not merit merely conflating HCOs with other business organizations.

NOTES

1. There is an enormous literature on this subject. See, for example, T. Donaldson, 1982; P. French, "The Corporation as a Moral Person," *American Philosophical Quarterly* 16 (1979): 207–15; M. Keeley, *A Social-Contract Theory of Organizations* (Notre Dame, IN: Notre Dame University Press, 1988); J. Ladd, "Morality and the Ideal of Rationality in Formal Organizations," *Monist* 54 (1970), pp. 488–516; L. May, *The Morality of Groups* (Notre Dame, IN: Notre Dame University Press, 1987); M. Velasquez, "Why Corporations Are Not Morally Responsible for Anything They Do," *Business and Professional Ethics Journal* 2 (1982): 1–18; P. H. Werhane, *Persons, Rights, and Corporations* (Englewood Cliffs, NJ: Prentice Hall, 1985).

2. M. Friedman, "The Social Responsibility of Business Is to Increase Its Profits," *New York Times Magazine* (September 1, 1970), pp. 122–26.

3. Ibid., p. 126.

4. D. M. Hausman and M. S. McPherson, *Economic Analysis and Moral Philosophy* (Cambridge: Cambridge University Press, 1996); A. Sen, *On Ethics and Economics* (Oxford: Basil Blackwell, 1987).

5. W. K. Smith and R. S. Tedlow, "James Burke: A Career in American Busi-

ness," Harvard University Graduate School of Business Administration Case No. 9-389-177 (Boston: Harvard Business School Press, 1989).

6. J. C. Collins and J. I. Porras, *Built to Last* (New York: Harper Business, 1994), p. 2.

7. See note 6, Collins and Porras, *Built to Last*, pp. 4–5.

8. Ibid., p. 5.

9. Ibid., p. 8.

10. R. E. Freeman, "Stakeholder Theory and the Modern Corporation," *Ethical Issues in Business*, 6th ed., ed. T. Donaldson and P. H. Werhane (Upper Saddle River, NJ: Prentice Hall, 1999), pp. 247–57.

11. R. K. Mitchell, B. Agle, and D. Wood, "Toward a Theory of Stakeholder Identification and Salience: Defining the Principle of Who and What Really Counts," *Academy of Management Review* 22 (1997): 853–86.

12. A. Etzioni, *Modern Organizations* (Englewood Cliffs, NJ: Prentice Hall, 1964), p. 59.

13. T. Donaldson and L. Preston, "The Stakeholder Theory of the Corporation: Concepts, Evidence, and Implications," *Academy of Management Review* 20 (1995): 74.

14. W. Evan and R. E. Freeman, "A Stakeholder Theory of the Modern Corporation: Kantian Capitalism," in *Ethical Theory and Business*, 4th ed., ed. T. Beauchamp and N. Bowie (Englewood Cliffs, NJ: Prentice Hall, 1988), p. 104.

15. See note 10, Freeman, "Stakeholder Theory and the Modern Corporation," p. 250.

16. R. Phillips, "Normative Stakeholder Theory: Toward a Conception of Stakeholder Legitimacy," forthcoming.

17. An HCO has different obligations to a healthcare professional who is hired to clean rooms than it does to a healthcare professional who is hired as a professional. In the former case the obligations are to the person as a moral agent and as an employee, not as a professional.

18. R. Phillips, "Stakeholder Theory and a Principle of Fairness," *Business Ethics Quarterly* 7 (1997): 51–66; original emphasis deleted.

19. See note 18, Phillips, "Stakeholder Theory and a Principle of Fairness," p. 57.

20. D. Luben, *Lawyers and Justice* (Princeton, NJ: Princeton University Press, 1988).

23.

STAKEHOLDER MANAGEMENT FOR CONSERVATION PROJECTS

A Case Study of Ream National Park, Cambodia

Thanakvaro Thyl De Lopez

STAKEHOLDER APPROACH IN CONSERVATION

The concept of stakeholder appears more recently in conservation literature. In the field of conservation in developing countries, the emphasis has been on participation and on the development of a framework for the resolution of conflicts.[1] This parallels a more general trend toward the development of participative management of natural resources.[2] . . .

The main difference between the concept of stakeholders in conservation projects and the stakeholder theory of the firm is the emphasis on participation of all the stakeholders of conservation, rather than on the management of those stakeholders by an organization. . . . A comprehensive stakeholder management framework would involve an analysis of all stakeholders and the formulation of strategies to ensure that the objectives of a conservation project are met. The following definition of stakeholder is suggested for the broader context of natural resources management projects: "a stakeholder is any group or individual who can affect the achievement or is affected by the achievement of a conservation project's objectives."

APPLYING A STAKEHOLDER MANAGEMENT FRAMEWORK TO CONSERVATION PROJECTS

... A wide range of individuals and organizations has competing stakes in natural resources management. Conflicts are inevitable and consensus may not be possible in situations characterized by complex social interactions.

Stakeholder management recognizes that a conservation project has a wide variety of stakeholders with differing objectives and values. The role of the managers of the project is to see that the objectives of the primary stakeholders are achieved and that other stakeholders, where possible, are also satisfied. ... Stakeholder management essentially consists of understanding and predicting the behavior and actions of stakeholders and devising strategies to ethically and effectively deal with them. ...

DEVELOPING A STAKEHOLDER MANAGEMENT FRAMEWORK FOR REAM NATIONAL PARK

Three decades of war have left Cambodia's society, economy, and natural environment deeply scarred. ... With a gross national product of US$260 per capita, Cambodia remains one of the poorest countries in the world.[3] Severe pressure on natural resources has resulted in the rapid deforestation of the country over the past twenty years.[4]

The Cambodian system of protected areas was established in 1993 by a royal decree. The total area under protection covers 3,568,100 ha, or 19.7 percent of the country's total area.[5] The Ministry of Environment (MoE) is responsible for the management of protected areas. Inadequate funding severely constrains the effectiveness of management of these protected areas.

Preah Sihanouk "Ream" National Park ... is located 194 kilometers southwest of Phnom Penh. Ream is a coastal park of 21,000 ha and encompasses a variety of marine and terrestrial habitats. Particular features include mangrove forests, lowland and evergreen forests, beaches, rocky shores, and islands. A freshwater river, the Preah Toek Sap flows through the park into the ocean.

Ream National Park was officially inaugurated in March 1995. MoE presence remained minimal until July 1997, when the Environmental Technical Advisory Programme (ETAP), a component of the United Nations Development Programme (UNDP) in Cambodia, started a thirty-six-month demonstration project of training and management. Operating expenses, not including investment in infrastructure and equipment, were budgeted at around US$30,000 a year. The park is divided into four zones: (1) a core zone in which all resource use is prohibited, (2) a general conservation zone in which limited resource use is permitted, (3) a resource management zone that includes some farmland and degraded forest, and (4) a community development zone with villages and rice fields.

DEVELOPMENT OF THE FRAMEWORK: A CRISIS SITUATION

The formalization of the framework itself took place only in late 1997, after initial attempts at implementing a participatory approach of all the stakeholders of Ream had failed. . . . Representatives of the principal stakeholders included: MoE, UNDP, rangers, local villagers, commercial loggers, commercial fishermen, the navy, the police, the Department of Fisheries, and land speculators. Commercial fishermen, loggers, and land speculators refused to collaborate in park management. Local communities were reluctant to sit at the same table as individuals they considered to be criminals with little respect for subsistence activities. Rangers were confused about their own mandate over the park and the respective roles of the navy and the Department of Fisheries. . . . Despite investments in equipment and training, illegal activities were reaching a climactic peak. A broader framework that would take into account the specifics of each stakeholder group was called for. Some stakeholders would have to be excluded from park management, while others would require the reallocation of available resources. . . .

The stakeholder management team comprised the UNDP project coordinator, the UNDP senior trainer, the park director, the head ranger, and an independent researcher (the author). This team acted as the stakeholder management team and will be referred throughout the paper as the management team. The project coordinator was himself a civil servant with MoE, which gave him direct access to the higher levels of the ministry. The senior trainer . . . was able to have access to higher UNDP officials. This proved crucial to the building of a stronger coalition between the two organizations, and the gathering of institutional support. The management framework was entirely developed by park managers and other field staff, with little involvement from senior levels of either organization. . . .

KEEPING IMPLEMENTATION IN MIND: USING A SIMPLE METHODOLOGICAL FRAMEWORK

Step 1: Stakeholder Analysis

The analysis of stakeholders was based on a combination of two sources. The first source was the actual observed behavior of stakeholders. This had been documented by park staff in periodical management reports. The second source relies on direct interviews and more informal day-to-day communication during which stakeholders expressed their views on the natural resources of Ream. The interviews were conducted in early 1998 by park staff for the specific purpose of stakeholder management. The interviews started with very general questions about the environment and gradually focused on the natural resources of the park. . . . Stakeholders will not readily admit to engaging in illegal activities. This creates a strategic bias, since some stakeholders may want to appear as conservationist, whereas in fact they have harvesting goals for the park. For violators and armed groups, observed behavior remains the main source of information. The stakeholder analysis was a learning exercise for park staff. A workshop was organized to answer the following questions about stakeholders: What did the different stakeholders want to do with the park? What strategies were they going to adopt? Which people could we count on for help? Who were our main opponents? What would we do about it? The analysis reflects the perceptions, experience, and personal understanding of each member of the park staff.

MoE. With 0.17 percent of the budget of the Royal Government of Cambodia, or less than US$520,000 in 1997, the management capacity of the MoE was severely limited. Cambodia almost entirely relied on foreign assistance for capital expenditures and the financing of daily operations in the environmental sector.

UNDP/ETAP. UNDP's stated mission was to help Cambodia build national capacity and to achieve development through poverty. UNDP's Environmental Technical Advisory Programme (ETAP) essentially focused on the development aspects of conservation and on the contribution of natural resources management to the Cambodian economy. The functions of ETAP included strengthening the institutional capacity of MoE, promoting environmental awareness, and monitoring environmental change. The Management Plan of Ream National Park (1997), approved by the Council of Ministers, defined the primary objective of management as: "to restore, maintain and enhance the biodiversity, habitats and conservation values of the Park." This general objective was broken down into three operational goals: (1) to enhance the capacity of government and local communities to effectively manage the park for conservation of its natural values; (2) to increase the options for sustainable livelihoods and income generation in local communities living in and around the park; and (3) to enhance the access and use of the park for tourism, recreation, and environmental education.

Rangers. The first twelve rangers were recruited in July and August 1997 in the communities adjoining the park. The staff had no prior experience in conservation. . . . Their awareness of environmental issues and conservation was low. The management capacity of rangers was further limited by a lack of park infrastructure and equipment. Their main tasks included controlling illegal activities and guiding visitors.

Local communities. Twenty-three villages were located in proximity to Ream National Park. These villages contained 20,840 people; 58 percent of the residents were less than sixteen years old. The population was predominantly Khmer (82 percent) and Cham (17 percent), and 30 percent of the population was illiterate. . . . The main occupations included farming, fishing, wood cutting, charcoal production, and contract laboring; 65 percent of villagers lived a hand-to-mouth existence. Average income was . . . equivalent to less than US$1.[6] Much agricultural land was of limited productivity because of the poor quality of soils, problems with salinity, and a general lack of resources. . . .

Commercial loggers. Commercial logging for the production of charcoal and timber had been the principal cause of deforestation in the park. The 1996–1997 level of harvest would have resulted in the loss of all trees larger than ten centimeters in diameter in a period of five to ten years. Commercial loggers were harvesting trees directly from the park. . . . In 1997, there were sixty-eight known charcoal kilns and three sawmills in the park. Most kilns and sawmills were operated by entrepreneurs from other provinces, some were under military protection. Local communities strongly disapproved of commercial logging.

Commercial fishermen. Push-nets were introduced at the beginning of the 1990s by Vietnamese fishermen. . . . Push-nets rake the ocean floor for crustaceans and fish and have been documented to cause destruction of fish habitats. . . . The use of push-net boats was thus strictly forbidden in the park, particularly in shallow waters where they can cause considerable damage to spawning grounds. Push-net boats were operated in Ream by commercial fishermen under the protection of the navy and the police. Local fishermen had complained to park authorities that the use of push-net boats would result in a gradual depletion of the fish stock. Villagers had also reported abuse and intimidation by police and navy units operating push-nets.

Navy. The Cambodian navy had its largest base in the southeastern corner of Ream National Park. Several thousand men and their families were stationed at Ream. The navy regularly patrolled the coastline and the Preah Toek Sap... . For several years, personnel from the Ream Naval Base had played a major role in commercial logging and wildlife hunting. The gradual extension of park rangers' patrols resulted in armed confrontations with soldiers. It appeared very quickly that rangers were outgunned and outnumbered.

Police. There was a widespread failure to enforce civil and criminal codes in Cambodia. The situation was particularly acute in rural areas. . . . Off-duty policemen, dressed in civilian clothes, were acting as bodyguards for push-net boats or were operating push-net boats themselves.

Land speculators. There had been a great deal of land speculation in the area surrounding the city of Kompong Som. The boom of the tourist industry in the early 1990s provided investment opportunities for commercial developers. Investors included government officials in Kompong Som and Phnom Penh and foreign nationals. . . . Land tenure in the buffer zone was allowed, since it pre-dated the creation of the park. However, land transactions that occurred after 1995 had been retrospectively declared invalid by the Council of Minister.[7] Speculators had been acquiring land from local communities. Villagers then encroached upon the national park to clear additional land for cultivation.

Department of Fisheries. The Department of Fisheries (DF) had . . . delivered fishing permits for push-net boats to operate in Ream at a cost varying between five hundred and a thousand dollars. These permits were not legally valid on two accounts: (1) the DF did not have any authority over the management of the park[8] and (2) the use of push-nets in coastal areas con-travened Cambodian fisheries law.

Tourists and tourism industry. Ream national park is located eighteen kilometers from the provincial capital of Sihanoukville, also known as Kom-pong Som. . . . Kompong Som had been a seaside resort popular with Phnom Penhners and foreigners since the 1960s. . . .

Step 2: Stakeholder Mapping

. . . The objective was to design a simple workable model that could generate strategic guidelines for conservation projects. Stakeholders were divided according to a two-dimensional matrix. The first dimension assessed the potential of stakeholders for the conservation of natural resources. The second dimension measured the influence or power of stakeholders on the project . . .

Step 3: Generic Strategies and Development of Workplan by Stakeholder Management Team

Stakeholder management at Ream was essentially proactive: it involved planning and implementing strategies to meet the stated objectives of the conservation project. At any given time, stakeholders could be located on the classification matrix. However, the matrix was not a static picture, but a map that evolved through time. The insight given by management theorists is that stakeholders ought to be actively managed to ensure the success of the conservation project. . . . Stakeholders could be moved from one quadrant to another in the following ways: (1) Coalition between conservationists—no shift; (2) Marginalization—shift from developer to marginal developer; (3) Involvement—shift from developer to conservationist; (4) Conversion—shift from marginal developer to marginal conservationist; and (5) Empowerment—shift from marginal conservationist to conservationist.

Strategies 2–5 resulted in either a decrease or increase in a stakeholder's influence or in an increase in a stakeholder's potential for conservation. Marginalization decreased the influence of nonsupportive stakeholders, involvement increased the potential for conservation of nonsupportive stakeholders, conversion increased the potential for conservation of marginal opponents, and empowerment increased the influence of marginal supporters.

Generic strategies provided the general direction for the development of a more specific workplan. It was important at this step to systematically examine and discuss all available strategies. The team tried not to have any bias on alternative management options. All strategies had to be considered, and rejected or adopted. Given budgetary and human resources constraints, it was impossible for the park to develop and implement strategies for all stakeholders. The workplan for 1998 focused on the immediate and direct threats to the integrity of the park. Management resources were allocated to the implementation of strategies that dealt with stakeholders with the highest combination of influence and potential for exploiting natural resources, and the establishment of a strong coalition between conservationists.

Step 4: Presentation of Workplan to Park Staff and Local Communities

The management team presented the workplan to rangers and to local communities in simple straightforward terms. . . . A certain amount of "command and control" could be used with rangers, who after all were civil servants. The major obstacle was that rangers were uncertain about the commitment from all "the big lords in the capital city," as one of them put it. In truth, the stakeholder management team was also uncertain about this. As for the villagers, their attitude could be characterized as wait and see. The park had to gain credibility by tackling the navy, the police, and the commercial loggers and to show commitment to the community forestry program. At this stage the management team decided not to present the workplan to the navy base, as its willingness to participate in the protection of the park was uncertain.

Step 5: Implementation of the 1997–1998 Workplan

. . . All those who implemented the stakeholder strategies were those who participated in their design. UNDP and MoE had provided general management objectives. Within these boundaries, the design and implementation of strategies were entirely left to park authorities. . . . Every month, the workplan was reviewed and readjusted. Management of the stakeholders of the park was not a one-time annual exercise, but rather an ongoing process. As new data became available and new behaviors were observed, the management team had to adapt its own set of strategies. . . .

MoE and ETAP. With its limited budget, MoE depended heavily on external financing. The ETAP project provided funding for operating expenses, equipment, infrastructure, and staff training at Ream. The management team extended seminars and workshops to staff from other protected areas and MoE departments. The goal was to involve a broad range of individuals throughout the conservation sector. . . .

Rangers. An essential component of the project was training the park rangers in law enforcement, community extension, and environmental interpretation for visitors. This paralleled the construction of a park headquarters with living quarters, a ranger station on the Preah Toek Sap, and the acquisition of motorbikes and boats. Rangers were all recruited in local communities. As villagers gained a better understanding of the national park, more suitable candidates applied for positions.

Local communities. The contribution of local communities to the management of natural resources has been essential to maintaining the integrity of the park. The stakeholder strategy toward the local community focused on environmental education, community forestry, and law enforcement. Three community forestry projects were initiated. . . . The initial skepticism of villagers gradually decreased. At the beginning of 1999, an estimated four hundred households had joined community forestry programs. . . .

Commercial loggers. The intensification of ranger patrols resulted in systematic confiscation of equipment and impounding of harvest. . . . By the third quarter of 1998, seventy sacks of charcoal and six hundred trees had been confiscated. Two-thirds of the known charcoal kilns and all sawmills in the park had been destroyed. By the end of 1998, with the gradual involvement of the navy in patrols, commercial logging had been put to an end.

Land speculators. The environmental education campaign helped clarify the land-use system within the park. Farming was allowed only on the land that villagers had already owned prior to the establishment of the park. . . . This, in effect, restrained legal land tenure to local communities. By the third quarter of 1998, few outside investors were attempting to acquire land within the park, since they were generally aware that private ownership of land within the park is not recognized.

Department of Fisheries. Once MoE asserted its management jurisdiction over the park, the Department of Fisheries reassigned its patrols to surrounding areas. . . . Rangers gradually took over the inspection of fishing activities in the estuary.

Tourists and tourism industry. From mid-1998, visitors were able to enjoy ranger-led boat tours and walks. . . . A monthly average of forty to fifty foreign visitors have been visiting the park. . . .

By the end of 1998, with the successful implementation of a broad stakeholder management framework, the situation of the park had considerably improved. The support of local communities had strengthened the influence of the conservationist coalition, both over other ministries and over local stakeholders. The combined pressure of UNDP/ETAP, MoE, and local communities made it very difficult for the navy or the police to continue to exploit natural resources within the park. . . .

CONCLUSIONS: LEARNING FROM REAM'S EXPERIENCE

The conservation literature has too often focused on participation and conflict resolution. Worldwide, park managers have shown creativity in implementing specific strategies for their stakeholders. The Ream management team has attempted to develop a formalized stakeholder management framework that recognizes this creativity. Stakeholder management consists in understanding and predicting the behavior of stakeholders and in formulating adapted strategies to effectively deal with them. . . . .

The stakeholder management framework is about understanding a specific set of groups or individuals and dealing with them. The framework is useful as a tool that forces people to think systematically about other stakeholders and to examine all management alternatives. . . . However, the framework is neither a recipes book nor about blindly applying strategies developed for one park to another park. Managers of other protected areas need to go through the same process of understanding their own stakeholders and thinking about specific ways to manage them.

NOTES

1. IUCN and C. Lewis, *Managing Conflicts in Protected Areas* (Gland, Switzerland: ICUN, 1995); Warner, "'Consensus' Participation: An Example for Protected Areas Planning," *Public Administration and Development* 17, no. 4 (1997): 413–32.

2. B. Mitchell, ed., *Resource Management and Development* (Toronto: Oxford University Press, 1990); R. E. Grumbine, "What Is Ecosystem Management?" *Conservation Biology* 8, no. 1 (1994): 27–38; M. A. Moote et al., "Theory in Practice: Applying Participatory Democracy Theory to Public Land Planning," *Environmental Management* 21, no. 6 (1997): 877–89; R. D. Margerum, "Integrated Environmental Management: The Foundations for Successful Practice," *Environmental Management* 24, no. 2 (1999): 151–66.

3. UNDP (United Nations Development Programme), *United Nations Development Programme in Cambodia* (Phnom Penh, Cambodia: UNDP, 1998); World Bank, *Cambodia Public Expenditure Review* (Washington, DC: World Bank, 1999).

4. Global Witness, *Corruption, War and Forest Policy: The Unsustainable Exploitation of Cambodia's Forests* (London: Global Witness, 1996); World Bank, *The World Bank Participation Source-Book* (Washington, DC: World Bank, 1996); World Bank, *Forest Policy Assessment—Cambodia* (Washington, DC: World Bank, 1996); MoE (Ministry of Environment), *National Environmental Action Plan 1998–2002* (Phnom Penh, Cambodia: Ministry of Environment, 1998).

5. MoE, *National Environmental Action Plan.*

6. Ream Commune unpublished data, 1997.

7. Council of Minister, Order 53 (January 1995).

8. As declared by Royal Decree, 1993.

24.

STAKEHOLDER CHAMPIONS

How to Internationalize the Corporate Social Responsibility Agenda

Grahame Thompson and Ciaran Driver

CHARACTERISTICS AND FORMS OF STAKEHOLDING

Current Influential Views: Shareholder Activism

In recent years, public concern with "stakeholding" in Anglo-American economies has narrowed down to a concern with ensuring a voice for shareholder activism. In particular, there is a concern to encourage greater activity by institutional investors like pension funds in the composition of the board and in setting standards for such aspects as executive pay.[1] . . . However, this increased involvement has been accompanied by widening disparities between the pay of CEOs and senior managers and others within the corporation, along with (at least perceived) increased incidence of corporate fraud. It is thus hard to claim that the process has been effective and many regard the exercise as cosmetic. . . . Moreover, the focus on shareholder power is likely to entrench short-termist thinking.[2]

. . . A broader stakeholding approach has some attractions over the shareholder activist model. In particular, this may involve oversight by alternative players with significant inside information on the firm's performance, such as employees. . . .

*   *   *

Excerpts from Grahame Thompson and Ciaran Driver, "Stakeholder Champions: How to Internationalize the Corporate Social Responsibility Agenda," *Business Ethics: A European Review* 14, no. 1 (2005): 56–66. Copyright © Blackwell Publishing, 2005. Reprinted by permission of Wiley-Blackwell.

Stakeholding may also bring gains in terms of efficiency and in terms of equity. The efficiency arguments, while forceful, are not, however, completely compelling. There may be other ways to incentivize those with hold-up power, such as efficiency wages. . . . In general, there may be a concern that too much monitoring and oversight may cripple managerial autonomy to the point where it weakens managerial creativity and the potential for growth.[3] . . .

So while the ethical case for stakeholding can certainly be argued, it is too early to say if the efficiency argument for it can be supported or how stakeholding would best be implemented. In an international context, the implications of this need to be considered further. On the one hand, governmental constraints on firms may be less effective in the international context (because of the "race to the bottom" that pits state against state). This strengthens the ethical argument for other forms of institutional checks on the activities and forms of operation of both foreign and domestic firms in such countries. However, it must also be recognized that the costs of enforcing regulatory control may be higher in these countries because of a lack of skills and established institutions.

THE INTERNATIONAL DIMENSION

Supra-National Regulation

. . . Democratic control is weak or nonexistent when corporations are operating beyond their national territories, i.e., outside the country where they are legally registered. First, such companies may disregard the wishes of their home state or global citizens, e.g., by failing to comply with ethical standards in regard to corruption or simply by evading taxation. Second, these companies may operate abroad in ways that disadvantage weak stakeholders, particularly in less-developed countries where such states are constrained by competing states' offers of light-touch corporate regulation. The relative importance of these two concerns . . . is not always obvious *a priori*. For example, the environment should not *simply* be viewed as a problem of exporting dirty industries to poor countries but also as affecting advanced countries. Thus, while it is true that outward foreign direct investment (FDI) by the US chemical industries and non-OECD-based firms is sensitive to environmental regulation, it is also the case that inward FDI to the United States involves more pollution-intensive industries than outward FDI from the United States.[4]

The first issue above is a main concern of the cooperative institutions that have emerged as supra-national regulators. Increasingly, a vast array of institutions and instruments are being fashioned to impose order on global players. The institutions include the UN, WTO, G8, G20, OECD, World Bank, IMF, ILO (International Labour Organization), BIS, NAFTA (North American Free Trade Agreement), EU, and the various offshoots of these organizations (e.g., UNCTAD, UNCHR). . . . The key underlying rationale for global regulation is the "tragedy of the commons," i.e., the inability to secure a "win-win" outcome to global games without cooperative frameworks.

A clear problem with this drive for global order is the lack of accountability and true representative nature of the main organizations charged with designing and implementing the new rules.[5] A fundamental question that is often skirted in discussions of global governance is the nature of the power relation when the international agencies themselves have been captured by the interests of global capital.[6] Certainly, US multinationals were behind the drive to increase intellectual property protection that led to the Uruguay Round agreement on this (TRIPs). . . .

The role of the G8 is increasingly being challenged on democratic grounds. . . . The accountability issue has proved highly controversial in the case of the WTO and in particular the debate on the new agreements in respect of services and intellectual property. . . .

In addition to these supra-national examples, there have been further "unilateral" national governmental initiatives in respect of "corporate responsibility." The most notable of these was the recent US Sarbanes-Oxley Act (2002) that established new financial reporting disclosures and board-room structure and committee requirements, not only for US companies operating in the United States but for US companies operating abroad. It extended this to foreign companies operating in the United States, or just listed in the United States, and even to companies not listed there but which do business there.[7] This legislation significantly extends the reach of United States extraterritoriality, and it adds to the power of nonexecutive directors and shareholders at the expense of CEOs in boardroom affairs. The question is, however, whether other countries could act like the United States even if they wished to, and whether such unilateral action is for the long-term benefit of the international trading system and regulatory regime as a whole.

The second issue for supra-national regulation concerns the activities of multinational corporations (MNCs) and how these may be regulated so as to defend weak stakeholders, especially those operating in weak states. Again, there has been an institutional response. The Global Corporate Governance Forum is a joint initiative sponsored by the OECD and the World Bank. . . .

This body monitors corporate governance initiatives in different countries and presses for best practice based upon the OECD principles. . . . The OECD principles press for the *legal recognition* of stakeholder interests, something not often found in declarations of this kind, and its approach goes well beyond the voluntary codes suggested by other bodies. Other initiatives include activities by the ILO, which is in regular and close discussion with the Chinese and other emergent market governments about constructing specific legally backed domestic corporate responsibility regimes in connection to worker rights in those countries.

In respect of non-OECD countries, a particular problem arises with the application of unitary rules in respect, say, of labor or environmental standards or even corporate governance when applied to heterogeneous conditions: different circumstances might require different rules. Put bluntly, the imposition of common standards may retard growth in non-OECD economies. . . . It may still be possible to devise and comprehensively implement rules that are sensitive to local conditions, but the pattern today seems to have developed more in the direction of a patchwork of voluntary corporate codes of social responsibility.[8]

VOLUNTARY REGULATION

Institutions of global governance generally act cautiously to consolidate best practice and extend it to countries or regions where it is not yet approved or applied. This judicious approach is necessary for the same reason that we earlier argued for a balanced view of stakeholder involvement generally: there are gains and losses involved in any application of rules, and different circumstances provide more or less scope for progressive application of the rules. However, in many cases individual firms may be persuaded or may simply decide to press ahead with guidelines and practices that are in advance of what is currently regarded as the standard.[9] . . . The attraction for companies in signing up to such initiatives is not only in terms of their CSR image but also relates to the assurance that they can cooperate with other companies that have so committed themselves. Compliance may also confer an option to be able to prepare for regulatory changes that might require compliance. . . . Compliance with international standards may also be necessary to do business in some markets. For example, certification by the International Standards Organisation (ISO) is necessary to trade in the EU and several thousand firms have certification ISO 14001, which relates to CSR. . . .

In the case of the UN's Global Compact, for instance, the ILO—plus several INGOs like Amnesty International, Oxfam, and the International Union for the Conservation of Nature—have cooperated in fostering a new initiative.[10] The compact stresses nine areas of corporate responsibility. . . . At the last count (February 2004), there were some 1,690 participants who had voluntarily signed up to this compact, and in as much as they take their involvement seriously, this locks them into an ambitious program of social responsibilities.[11] Other initiatives of a voluntary nature include industry-specific ones such as the Chemical Manufacturers Association and the "Equator Principles" for international banks. . . .

Two of the most significant campaigning bodies are the International Council on Human Rights Policy (ICHRP) (2002) and Christian Aid (CA) (2004), both of which call for supplementing the current voluntary approach with a newly established international legal regime to govern CSR issues. A useful service provided by these bodies is that they show how there have been successes in converting voluntary code building into a statutory framework at the international level. Christian Aid (2004), for instance, documents how since 1997 thirty-five rich countries of the OECD have signed up to a convention that outlaws bribery of foreign public officials by businesspeople. . . . Both the ICHRP and CA want to extend such regimes to encompass the responsibility for "duty of care" to company directors for communities and the environment, making them legally accountable for the actions of their companies overseas. This advocates a move beyond CSR to *corporate social accountability*.

These firm-centered approaches are backed by their own set of organizations and bodies that register company commitments, disseminate best practice, monitor developments on a voluntary basis, and so forth—like the Global Reporting Initiative (GRI), the International Business Leaders Forum, Corporate Sustainability Reporting, and many others. . . . [T]he World Economic Forum's Global Corporate Citizenship's (GCC) . . . particular concerns are signaled in the following passage:

> Rarely have businesses found such a complex and challenging set of economic pressures, political uncertainties and societal expectations. Regardless of their industry sector, country of origin, or corporate ownership structure, they are under growing pressure to demonstrate outstanding performance not only in terms of competitiveness and market growth, but also in their corporate governance and their corporate citizenship.[12]

The World Economic Forum (WEF) encourages companies to commit voluntarily to "good corporate governance" protocols and to pay close attention to their social responsibilities, all in the name of their becoming proper global corporate *citizens*. This has to do with what has come to be termed "reputation capital," which firms are assumed to want to foster and preserve.[13]

But . . . [t]he purely voluntary nature of these initiatives means they have problems discriminating in terms of whom they allow to "sign up" to their protocols. The UN Global Compact suffers from this problem: for example, Royal Dutch Shell was a founder signatory of the Global Compact but has recently been heavily criticized for its environmental record. The problem here is that the UN cannot be very selective about membership—something that undermines its wider legitimacy as an international governance mechanism operating in many fields. . . .

TOWARD A NEW INSTITUTIONAL FORM

. . . Even the most progressive of companies that have embraced the full CRS agenda enthusiastically do not talk much about corporate democracy. *In large part, then, voluntary CRS may be a substitute process and a less-threatening one for corporate reform than corporate democracy, hence, to some extent at least, its enthusiastic embrace by the corporate world.*

Company reform to increase internal democratic decision making is a complex issue, made even more so by the progressive internationalization of business activity as mentioned above. But suppose there was a dramatic change in the sentiment associated with CSR and GCC among companies and governments alike so that they were eager to embrace radical reform. How could this be practically organized and implemented?

Elsewhere we have addressed this issue in more detail.[14] The main problem, as we see it, is exemplified by the case of treating something like the environment or the unemployed as a stakeholder. In the national context, there may well be a case for identifying these concerns as the business of central government, but in the international context there is a void in this regard. How could these be constituted into viable and convincing "entities" able to be involved in any direct decision-making activity? And these examples, while extreme ones perhaps, are illustrative of the wider difficulty of constituting all stakeholders as decision-making entities for MNCs as the international bases of their activities spread.

So far we have avoided using much of the traditional language of "political representation." The normal language used in these situations would be to consider this precisely as a problem of the *representation of an interest*. But the difficulty is clear in the case of the environment. How could this be constituted as an interest? One way around this is to abandon the language—and indeed, the conception—of both representation and interest. Instead, it is a former language of politics that is invoked here: that of *championing and stewardship.* ... However champions were elected or appointed, they would simply act as "decision makers," not as representatives of an interest. They would operate in an organization to champion a cause, nurture it, and act as a steward of that cause through the decision-making and implementation processes.

Clearly, this approach raises all sorts of difficulties of its own, not least as to the mechanism of how such champions would be appointed or how they would be made accountable. One way forward would be to strengthen the non-executive directorship role via this route. ... The suggestion here would be much more radical and would strengthen the role of the nonexecutive directorship by making it the job of such directors to champion the cause of the unemployed, the environment, the community, the employees, the customer, and so on, and even the shareholder. And this would put these various considerations at the very heart of the organizational decisionmaking processes.

But from where would such champions be found and how would they be appointed? Here we might think of the formation of a pool of such persons from which could be drawn suitable individuals to serve on different company boards or senates, or who were "elected" to do so. But by whom? Here we would suggest that already existing global governance organizations, national bodies and governments, NGOs, trade and professional associations, trade unions, pressure groups, and even other companies in completely different sectors, and so forth, that already address these separate issues could constitute themselves into "quasi-constituencies" around their existing concerns and provide "expert lists" of such acceptable personnel as potential candidates. They could then either elect or appoint as suits their purpose, but operating in an open and transparent manner. The champions so produced by such a process would then have to "report back" to such accredited bodies on their stewardship: their accountability would be addressed to these new "civil associations" as we would term them.[15] In a sense, then, what is being promoted here is a form of "indirect democracy," where the legitimacy of the process relies upon the legitimacy of the organizations that support it and feed personnel into it.[16]

One issue of some importance in the foregoing scheme is the legitimacy of the bodies from which the pool of monitoring talent is drawn. ... It is our suggestion that to gain such legitimacy the new civic associations outlined above might have to be accredited by existing international representative organizations and perhaps lists of the candidates proposed by them as appointed champions would be allocated in proportion to rules established by those representative bodies. . . .

No one can pretend that the appointment of nonexecutives to champion particular interests of global concern will solve the problem of the void created by the inability to rely fully on supra-national institutions of governance because of their lack of accountability. Both systems have their merits and drawbacks. The inherent flaw in the notion of champions is that such individuals cannot weigh up the relative competing claims of different stakeholders in any meaningful way. What is to be done, for example, when the interests of the environment clash with the interests of development and employment? Perhaps companies will use differences between competing champions as a way of justifying what they would have done anyway. But at least the system has the merit of transparency in that champions will be free to make their case publicly.

Thus the principle of stewardship can go some way toward nudging companies in the direction of a more progressive stance that takes into account the interests of broad stakeholders. In addition, here we would like to tentatively propose another suggestion in the same mold. . . . Our proposal is for an independent commission of experts—perhaps partly drawn from business school staff teaching CSR and partly from the pool of CSR champions—to examine ex-post the performance of CEOs after they have retired. The posting of such a considered report in the public domain could act as a serious incentive to managers who seem to care much about their reputation and image. Such a practice was common in medieval Venice, where an audit of the Doge's rule was drawn up on completion of his office.[17]

NOTES

1. In the United Kingdom, initial "New Labour" support for a broader stakeholding agenda faded on taking office. In the United States, where the subject was more seriously discussed in policy circles as an answer to reduced US competitiveness, it was knocked off the agenda by the dot-com bubble and improved productivity growth later in the 1990s and reemerged as shareholder activism in the wake of the widely publicized accounting scandals.

2. E. Stockhammer, "Financialisation and the Slowdown of Accumulation," *Cambridge Journal of Economics* 28, no. 5 (2004): 719–41; C. Driver and D. Shepherd, "Capacity Utilization and Corporate Restructuring: A Comparative Study of the US, UK and Other EU Countries," *Cambridge Journal of Economics* 29, no. 1 (2005): 1–22.

3. J. Kay and A. Z. Silberston, "Corporate Governance," *National Institute Economic Review* (August 1995): 84–95.

4. V. Fitzgerald, "Regulatory Investment Incentives," working paper QEHWPPS80 (University of Oxford, 2002).

5. D. Held, *Global Covenant* (Cambridge: Polity, 2004).

6. J. Stiglitz, *Globalization and Its Discontents* (New York: Norton, 2002).

7. More extensive reforms such as compulsory rotation of audit firms or breakup of investment banks did figure in the US debate but they were not enacted in the Sarbanes-Oxley Act. This turned out to be an umbrella act including reforms of corporate governance and associated changes in accounting and law partnerships. The act mandates the change of lead audit partner every five years (although not the rotation of audit firms) and decided that accounting firms should not provide consultancy services (which most of them were in any case jettisoning) while allowing the same accounting firms to continue to provide lucrative tax services. Thus, this act could be considered as rather minimalist in character despite many of its radical features.

8. A. Singh and A. Zammit, "Globalisation, Labour Standards and Economic Development," in *The Handbook of Globalisaton*, ed. J. Michie (Cheltenham: Edward Elgar, 2003), pp. 191–215.

9. These codes do not just involve the meeting of ISO9000 or ISO14000 standards, though these are often treated as minimum targets. In addition, there is an attempt to establish a new ISO type standard for workers' rights, sponsored by "social accountability international" (SAI)—the SA8000. This is a system which defines a set of auditable standards and an independent auditing process for the protection of workers' rights. It is based on conventions of the ILO and related international human rights instruments. As discussed elsewhere (Thompson 2005), ISO standards—to be acceptable and effective in so many different national environments—have to remain fairly open and flexible in respect to their rules, so they do not confer a very "tight" standard of compliance.

10. G. Kell, "The Global Compact: Origins, Operations, Progress, Challenges," *Journal of Corporate Citizenship* 11 (2003): 35–49.

11. The UN's Global Compact is closely supported by the IFC/World Bank Group's "Equator Principles" for international banking launched in 2003 (which was mentioned above) and the United National Environmental Programme (UNEP's) "Finance Initiative" for asset management companies (launched in July 2004), which promotes social and environmental considerations in respect of the issues of corporate governance, capital market, and investment decisions. Both of these are also voluntary initiatives.

12. World Economic Forum, *Global Corporate Citizenship: The Leadership Challenge for CEOs and Boards* (Davos: WEF, 2002), p. 2.

13. According to a report by McKinsey and Co. (2003: 1), "reputation" tops the list of CEOs' concerns over "intangible assets," and the proportion of a company's value derived from intangible assets rose from 17 percent in 1981 to 71 percent in 1998.

14. C. Driver and G. Thompson, "Corporate Governance and Democracy: The

Stakeholder Debate Revisited," *Journal of Management and Governance* 6, no. 4 (2002): 111–30.

15. This is an attempt to operationalize a form of "associationalism" in the spirit of that suggested by Hirst (1994).

16. It may be noted that there are already twenty-four hundred NGOs affiliated to the UN and these are already important in allocating the budgets of some UN agencies. The role of civil society groups in the UN has been considered recently by a high-level panel chaired by UN Secretary General Kofi Annan and its deliberations are reported in UN (2004).

17. J. Barzun, *From Dawn to Decadence* (London: Harper, 2000).

25.

RE-ENGINEERING THE BUSINESS CURRICULUM

A Stakeholder Paradigm

Jeff Heinfeldt and Fran Wolf

THE STAKEHOLDER CONCEPT

Academic Application

• • • **R**amaswamy (1992) explained that business schools satisfy expectations of three main constituencies: students, business community, and faculty. A business school fosters the personal growth and development of students. Employers require a supply of well-qualified students able to improve the performance of the entity that hires them. The scholarly interests of faculty must be supported so that new knowledge aimed at improving business competitiveness can be developed and disseminated.

Barrow (1996) noted that CEOs, politicians, and personnel specialists agree that university education must emphasize symbolic skills (as opposed to specialized disciplinary knowledge), research skills (as opposed to established knowledge), and oral and written communication skills. "Because these skills cut across traditional disciplinary boundaries, there is increasing support from government and business for the interdisciplinary programs that focus on identifiable long-term problems in the economy, society, and government, as opposed to department-based programs that focus on academically defined disciplinary paradigms."[1]

Jeff Heinfeldt and Fran Wolf, "Re-engineering the Business Curriculum: A Stakeholder Paradigm," *Journal of Education for Business* 73, no. 4 (March/April 1998). Copyright © 1998. Reprinted by permission of the Helen Dwight Reid Educational Foundation.

The 1996 Association to Advance Collegiate Schools of Business (AACSB) Continuous Improvement Symposium (9/29–10/1) in St. Louis provided two examples of interdisciplinary programs. Both the University of Idaho and the University of Oklahoma have run two-year pilot programs integrating the business core. C. Randall Byers, head of the Department of Business of the University of Idaho's College of Business and Economics, described the curriculum that commenced in fall 1994 with thirty-five volunteer students and a five-person faculty. The traditional core, which included seven required junior-level courses, was replaced by a team-taught, two-semester module block of classes. Larry Michaelsen, a professor of management in the College of Business Administration, explained the University of Oklahoma's approach. Students simultaneously attend a block of four team-taught core business courses and a lab course. The lab actually requires groups of students to start their own businesses and obtain bank loans for $4,500 or less.

The universities, their business communities, and the students were extremely pleased with the results. In fact, the University of Idaho faculty . . . adopted the integrated core as a requirement for freshmen entering in fall 1996. The University of Oklahoma also intends to eventually replace its traditional core. Both programs are team taught and entail extensive team involvement by students. The integrated core at both institutions was developed by faculty who volunteered for the project. However, the integration of the core in either program was not accomplished through the use of a common conceptual foundation or framework. The instructional approach about to be described in this article uses the stakeholder perspective of the firm as its source of course design.

STAKEHOLDER-BASED CURRICULUM

The development of a stakeholder-based curriculum is still in its early stages. However, in table 1 we provide the beginnings of a stakeholder approach that could be used within or between functional areas. The stakeholder paradigm could be introduced to the curriculum in several ways. First, the basic stakeholder concerns could be addressed within the current functional area format. For example, in an Introduction to Corporate Finance course, the impact that financial concepts and decisions have on the various stakeholders could be discussed as the more traditional topics are covered (i.e., going down a column in table 1). To be thorough, the syllabus of every functional area

Table 1.
Cross-Functional Coverage of Basic Business Concepts

STAKE-HOLDERS	AREA			
	Accounting	Finance	Marketing	Management
Customers	Receivable and bad debt losses	Credit management	Niche marketing	Quality issues
	Inventory systems	Optimal inventory levels and techniques	Distribution	Inventory levels
		Degree of debt/bankruptcy/ future services	Marketing research, quality, pricing, consumer demand	
			Product life cycle	
Employees	Pensions, benefits, and accruals	Bottom-line-powered management	Sales skills theories	Labor theory
	New FAS impact on healthcare and pensions	Financial incentives:	Customer service skills	Benefits
		ESOPs		Human resources
		Profit sharing		Empowerment
				Human relations
Suppliers	Payables	Inventory systems	Purchasing	Inventory methods
	Net versus gross methods	Financing terms	Network channels	Quality issues

Regulatory agencies	SEC, FASB, and IRS auditors Social Security Administration	SEC/IRS Social Security Efficient markets	Truth-in-advertising FDA Consumer Protection Agency	OSHA EPA
Media	Release of financial information to public (private vs. public companies)	Impact of information on stock price Pressure on BOD to replace CEOs	Advertising Perception Impact of information on sales and demand	Impact of information on treatment of employees, work conditions
Common stockholders	Reporting methods that impact financial results	Ratio/financial analysis Stock price models/issuance	Sales revenue growth Market share	Investment and asset management Agency costs
Bondholders	Retirement of debt Recording LT and ST debt Impact on ratios Leverage	Leverage Bankruptcy concerns Bond pricing	Sales revenue and cash flow to cover interest payments	Collateralize debt (assets as backing) Project substitution

would require that each stakeholder be discussed. Advantages of this method could be easier implementation and fewer disagreements among traditional functional areas. As far as specialized, upper-level coursework is concerned, it could remain unchanged.

Alternatively, an integrated, cross-disciplinary, team-teaching method could be employed. Representatives from each functional area would be required to participate in the team teaching of courses built around stakeholder parties (i.e., going across a row on table 1). This method would allow faculty from various functional areas to provide expertise while exemplifying the concept of individuals working with others from different disciplines.

As for the actual courses in this framework, the series of traditional, individually taught, introductory functional area courses could be replaced by a series of team-taught, introductory, stakeholder courses. Introductory courses in marketing, finance, accounting, and management could be replaced by a series of Introduction to Stakeholder courses. Each stakeholder displayed in the table could be covered in these various courses. For example, Introduction to Customers and the Media; Introduction to Employees, Government, and Regulatory Agencies; Introduction to Suppliers; and Introduction to Stockholders and Bondholders are potential new courses.

Though not as easy to implement, the potential advantages of the second method include (a) providing a common connection for functional area concepts through the use of a particular stakeholder, (b) presentation of the "big picture" by discussing various stakeholders across disciplines, and (c) exposure to teams, teamwork, and diverse opinions through the team-teaching format. Following completion of introductory stakeholder courses, students progress to concentrated coursework in their functional major.

TEAMS

. . . [T]he Financial Executives Research Foundation (1991) criticized current business education. They noted: "Students working on business degrees and being taught traditional American business principles face an ever more daunting challenge. The management principles that have been instilled in textbooks and classrooms over the years are becoming obsolete in today's marketplace as many firms shift from hierarchically controlled structures to entrepreneurial, team-oriented organizations."[2]

Michaelsen and Black (1994) proposed a comprehensive, integrated approach to using learning teams in higher education. In addition to presenting a framework for implementing their approach, they indicated the benefits of the method: developing students' higher-level cognitive skills, providing support for students who are at risk of dropping out, promoting the development of interpersonal and group skills, and building/maintaining faculty enthusiasm for teaching. By supplementing the team-taught, stakeholder courses with extensive team/group involvement by students, an environment for the development and reinforcement of teamwork skills could be provided.

TEACHING OF ETHICS

The new AACSB standards specifically suggest that management education "prepares students to contribute to . . . the larger society" and promotes social responsibility through the teaching of ethics.[3] The ethics component of management education might be addressed more naturally within a stakeholder paradigm. Each functional area instructor could discuss ethical and societal issues as each stakeholder is discussed.

Students may begin to understand the difficulties in trying to maintain a balance between the desires of the various stakeholders. For example, Levi Strauss has announced that it will cancel operations in China because of that government's record of human rights violations. David Schmidt, vice president for corporate marketing at Levi, stated, "There are wonderful commercial opportunities in China. But when ethical issues collide with commercial appeal, we try to ensure ethics as the trump card. For us, ethical issues precede all others."[4] These comments are a clear illustration of the difficult choices involved in balancing stakeholder desires when ethics and business opportunities are interrelated. Students could gain a sense of appreciation as to how a firm, within the context of ethics, attempts to simultaneously provide, among other things, a good return on investment for stockholders, a high-quality product for consumers, and a safe working environment with fair compensation for employees.

SUMMARY

In place of the traditional, functional area approach to business education, in this article we introduce a stakeholder methodology. Stakeholder paradigm implementation could be via current functional courses or through an integrated option. The latter approach replaces the introductory functional courses with a series of team-taught introductory stakeholder courses. With both options, students could be exposed to the various parties that have explicit and implicit contracts with the firm while still receiving the traditional, specialized, upper-level education in their major. Potential strengths of the team-taught approach include providing a common connection for functional area concepts, presentation of the "big picture," and exposure to teams, teamwork, and diverse opinions.

This particular proposal to restructure the business curriculum may seem drastic to some. However, the business community and many educators believe business education must emerge from its traditional, constraining mold. This position is supported by the following comment: "The main impediment to change is the inertia of decades-old university practices. . . . [T]oo often the curriculum planners ignore the current feedback from the market and course offerings are based on an incestuous type of duplication by new generations of business educators who find it difficult to change the basic patterns established by their predecessors."[5]

NOTES

1. C. Barrow, "The New Economy and Restructuring Higher Education," *NEA Higher Education Journal* 12 (1996): 37–54.

2. Financial Executives Research Foundation, *Educating Financial Executives* (Morristown, NJ: self-published, 1991).

3. O'Hare and Wood, "Social Responsibility and Corporate Profits: The Expense Preference Approach," *Journal of Education for Business* 69, no. 5 (1994): 278–82.

4. R. Griffin and R. Ebert, *Business* (Englewood Cliffs, NJ: Prentice Hall, 1996), pp. 132–33.

5. S. Dudley et al., "New Directions for the Business Curriculum," *Journal of Education for Business* 70, no. 5 (1995): 307.

SUGGESTIONS FOR
FURTHER READING

Atkins, M., and J. Lowe. "Stakeholders and Strategy Formation Process in Small and Medium Enterprises." *International Small Business Journal* 12, no. 3 (1993): 12–24.

Balser, D., and J. McClusky. "Managing Stakeholder Relationships and Nonprofit Organization Effectiveness." *Nonprofit Management and Leadership* 15, no. 3 (2005): 295.

Bernardi, R., and D. Bean. "Ethics in Accounting Education: The Forgotten Stakeholders." *CPA Journal* 76, no. 7 (2006): 56–57.

Blair, J., G. Savage, and C. Whithead. "A Strategic Approach for Negotiating with Hospital Stakeholder." *Health Care Management Review* 14, no. 3 (1989): 65–76.

Bouckaert, L., and J. Vandenhove. "Business Ethics and the Management of Non-Profit Institutions." *Journal of Business Ethics* 17, no. 9/10 (1998): 1073–81.

El-Gohary, N., H. Osman, and T. El-Diraby. "Stakeholder Management for Public Private Partnerships." *International Journal of Project Management* 24, no. 7 (2006): 595–604.

Gilmartin, M., and R. E. Freeman. "Business Ethics and Health Care: A Stakeholder Perspective." *Health Care Management Review* 27, no. 2 (2002): 52.

Gwin, J. "Constituent Analysis: A Paradigm for Marketing Effectiveness in the Not-for-Profit Organization." *European Journal of Marketing* 24, no. 7 (1991): 43–48.

Heather, E., S. Berman, and A. Wicks. "Ethics and Incentives: An Evaluation and Development of Stakeholder Theory in the Health Care Industry." *Business Ethics Quarterly* 12, no. 4 (2002): 413–33.

Jamali, D. "Changing Management Paradigms: Implications for Educational Institutions." *Journal of Management Development* 24, no. 1/2 (2005): 104.

Jenkins, H. "Small Business Champions for Corporate Social Responsibility." *Journal of Business Ethics* 67, no. 3 (2006): 241.

311

Jones, M., and P. Fleming. "Unpacking Complexity through Critical Stakeholder Analysis: The Case of Globalization." *Business and Society* 42, no. 4 (2003): 430.

Knox, S., and C. Gruar. "The Application of Stakeholder Theory to Relationship Marketing Strategy Development in a Nonprofit Organization." *Journal of Business Ethics* 75, no. 2 (2007): 115–37.

Lee, D. "Corporate and Public Responsibility, Stakeholder Theory and the Developing World." *Business Ethics: A European Review* 8, no. 3 (1999): 151–62.

O'Higgins, E., and J. Morgan. "Stakeholder Salience and Engagement in Political Organizations: Who and What Really Counts." *Society and Business Review* 1, no. 1 (2006): 62.

Reed, D. "Employing Normative Stakeholder Theory in Developing Countries: A Critical Theory Perspective." *Business and Society* 41, no. 2 (2002): 166–83.

Roberts, R., and L. Mahoney. "Stakeholder Conceptions of the Corporation: Their Meaning and Influence in Accounting Research." *Business Ethics Quarterly* 14, no. 3 (2004): 399.

Shelley, S. "Ethical Interpretations of Management Decision Making in Higher Education." *International Journal of Management and Decision Making* 6, no. 3/4 (2005): 284.

Zink, K. "From Total Quality Management to Corporate Sustainability Based on a Stakeholder Management Model." *Journal of Management History* 13, no. 4 (2007): 394–401.

BIBLIOGRAPHY

Aaker, D. A., and E. Joachimsthaler. *Brand Leadership*. New York: Free Press, 2000.

ABN AMRO (2004). www.abnamro.com (accessed September 29, 2004).

Abrams, F. "Management Responsibility in a Complex World." In *Business Education for Competence and Responsibility*, edited by T. Carroll. Chapel Hill: University of North Carolina Press, 1954.

Ackerman, R. "How Companies Respond to Social Demands." *Harvard Business Review* 51, no. 4 (1973): 51.

———. *The Social Challenge to Business*. Cambridge, MA: Harvard University Press, 1975.

Ackerman, R., and R. A. Bauer. *Corporate Social Responsiveness: The Modern Dilemma*. Reston, VA: Reston Publishing Company, 1976.

Ackoff, R. *A Concept of Corporate Planning*. New York: John Wiley and Sons, 1970.

———. *Creating the Corporate Future*. New York: John Wiley and Sons, 1981.

———. *Redesigning the Future*. New York: John Wiley and Sons, 1974.

Adams, J. S. "Toward an Understanding of Inequity." *Journal of Abnormal and Social Psychology* 67 (1963): 422–36.

Adler, P. S., and S. W. Kwon. "Social Capital Prospects for a New Concept." *Academy of Management Review* 27, no. 1 (2002): 17–40.

Agle, B. R., R. K. Mitchell, and J. A. Sonnenfeld. "Who Matters to CEOs? An Investigation of Stakeholder Attributes and Salience, Corporate Performance, and CEO Values." *Academy of Management Journal* 42 (1999): 507–25.

Aguilera, R. V., and G. Jackson. "The Cross-National Diversity of Corporate Governance: Dimensions and Determinants." *Academy of Management Review* 28, no. 3 (2003): 447–65.

Ahlstedt, L., and I. Jahnukainen. *Yritysorganisaatio yhteistoiminnan ohjausjaerjestelmaenae*. Helsinki: Weilin + Goeoes, 1971.

Aldrich, H., and C. M. Fiol. "Fools Rush In? The Institutional Context of Industry Creation." *Academy of Management Review* 19 (1994): 645–70.

Alkhafaji, A. *A Stakeholder Approach to Corporate Governance: Managing in a Dynamic Environment.* New York: Quorum Books, 1989.

Allan, S., B. Adam, and C. Carter, eds. *Environmental Risks and the Media.* Andover, UK: Routledge, 1999.

Altaian, J. A., and E. Petkus. "Toward a Stakeholder-Based Policy Process: An Application of the Social Marketing Perspective to Environmental Policy Development." *Policy Sciences* 27 (1994): 37–51.

Ambler, T., and A. Wilson. "Problems of Stakeholder Theory." *Business Ethics: A European Review* 4, no. 1 (1995): 30–36.

American Marketing Association. "What Are the Definitions of Marketing and Marketing Research?" www.marketingpower.com/content4620.php (accessed December 8, 2004).

Amit, R., and P. J. H. Schoemaker. "Strategic Assets and Organizational Rents." *Strategic Management Journal* 14 (1993): 33–46.

Anderson, J., J. Clement, and L. V. Crowder. "Accommodating Conflicting Interests in Forestry—Concepts Emerging from Pluralism." *Unasylva* 49, no. 194 (1997): 3–10.

Andriof, J., and S. Waddock. "Unfolding Stakeholder Engagement." In *Unfolding Stakeholder Thinking: Theory, Responsibility and Engagement,* edited by J. Andriof, S. Waddock, B. Husted, and S. S. Rahman, 19–42. Sheffield: Greenleaf, 2002.

Anon. "Flexing Their Muscle: Shareholders Hold Increased Influence in Post-Enron America." ABC News, July 8, 2004. http://www.ABCNEWS.com.

———. "Two Thirds of UK Investors Prepared to Invest 'Ethically.'" *Environmental Finance* (July 2, 2004).

Ansoff, I. *Corporate Strategy.* New York: McGraw-Hill, 1965.

Argandona, A. "The Stakeholder Theory and the Common Good." *Journal of Business Ethics* 17, no. 9/10 (1988): 1093.

Arnstein, S. R. "A Ladder of Citizen Participation." *Journal of the American Institute of Planners* 35, no. 4 (1969): 216–24.

Asher, C., and J. Mahoney. "Towards a Property Rights Foundation for a Stakeholder Theory of the Firm." *Journal of Management and Governance* 9, no. 1 (2005): 5.

Ashforth, B. E., and B. W. Gibbs. "The Double-Edge of Organizational Legitimation." *Organization Science* 1, no. 2 (1990): 177–94.

AstraZeneca International. 2004. http://www.astrazeneca.com (accessed September 29, 2004).

Atkins, M., and J. Lowe. "Stakeholders and Strategy Formation Process in Small and Medium Enterprises." *International Small Business Journal* 12, no. 3 (1993): 12–24.

Ayuso, S., M. Rodriguez, and J. Ricart. "Using Stakeholder Dialogue as a Source for New Ideas: A Dynamic Capability Underlying Sustainable Innovation." *Corporate Governance* 6, no. 4 (2006): 475.

Badaracco, C. H. "Public Opinion and Corporate Expression: In Search of the Common Good." *Public Relations Quarterly* 41, no. 3 (1996).

Baier, A. *Postures of the Mind: Essays on Mind and Morals.* Minneapolis: University of Minnesota Press, 1985.

Balser, D., and J. McClusky. "Managing Stakeholder Relationships and Nonprofit Organization Effectiveness." *Nonprofit Management and Leadership* 15, no. 3 (2005): 295.

Banerjee, S. B. "Whose Land Is It Anyway? National Interest, Indigenous Stakeholders, and Colonial Discourses: The Case of the Jabiluka Uranium Mine." *Organization & Environment* 13, no. 1 (2000): 3–38.

Bansal, P., and K. Roth. "Why Companies Go Green: A Model of Ecological Responsiveness." *Academy of Management Journal* 43, no. 4 (2000): 717–36.

Barnard, C. *The Function of the Executive.* Cambridge, MA: Harvard University Press, 1938.

Barnett, Anthony. "Towards a Stakeholder Democracy." In *Stakeholder Capitalism,* edited by G. Kelly, D. Kelly, and A. Gamble, 82–98. London: Macmillan, 1997.

Barney, J. B. "Firm Resources and Sustained Competitive Advantage." *Journal of Management* 17 (1991): 99–120.

———. *Gaining and Sustaining Competitive Advantage.* Reading, MA: Addison-Wesley, 1997.

———. "Organizational Culture: Can It Be a Source of Sustained Competitive Advantage?" *Academy of Management Review* 11, no. 3 (1986): 656–65.

Baron, S., N. Hill, and S. Sundaram. "An Empirical Test of Stakeholder Theory Predictions of Capital Structure." *Financial Management* 2 (1989): 36–44.

Barzun, J. *From Dawn to Decadence.* London: Harper, 2000.

Bateson, G. *Steps to an Ecology of Mind.* New York: Ballantine Books, 1972.

Beamish, T. "Environmental Hazard and Institutional Betrayal." *Organization & Environment* 14, no. 1 (2001): 5–33.

Becker, L. C. "Places for Pluralism." *Ethics* 102 (1992): 707–19.

———. "Property." In *Encyclopedia of Ethics,* edited by L. D. Becker and C. B. Becker, vol. 2, 1023–27. New York: Garland, 1992.

———. *Property Rights.* London: Routledge & Kegan Paul, 1978.

———. "Too Much Property." *Philosophy and Public Affairs* 21 (1992): 196–206.

Bell, T., F. Marrs, I. Solomon, and H. Thomas. *Auditing Organizations through a Strategic-Systems Lens.* Montvale, NJ: KPMG, 1997.

Bendheim, C. L., S. A. Waddock, and S. B. Graves. "Determining Best Practice in Corporate-Stakeholder Relations Using Data Envelopment Analysis." *Business and Society* 37, no. 3 (1998): 306–448.

Benedetti, M. "Cancer Risk Associated with Residential Proximity to Industrial Sites." *Archives of Environmental Health* 56, no. 4 (2001): 342–50.

Bengstsson, M., and S. Kock. "'Coopetition' in Business Networks—To Cooperate and Compete Simultaneously." *Industrial Marketing Management* 29, no. 8 (2000): 411–26.

Benhabib, S., and F. Dalimayr, eds. *The Communicative Ethics Controversy.* Cambridge, MA: MIT Press, 1990.

Bentham, J. *The Principles of Morals and Legislation.* Amherst, NY: Prometheus Books, 1988.

Berle, A., and G. Means. *The Modern Corporation and Private Property.* New York: Commerce Clearing House, 1932.

Berman, S., A. Wicks, S. Kotha, and T. Jones. "Does Stakeholder Orientation Matter? The Relationship between Stakeholder Management Models and Firm Financial Performance." *Academy of Management Journal* 42, no. 5 (1999): 488–506.

Bernardi, R., and D. Bean. "Ethics in Accounting Education: The Forgotten Stakeholders." *CPA Journal* 76, no. 7 (2006): 56–57.

Berry, M. A., and D. A. Rondinelli. "Proactive Corporate Environmental Management: A New Industrial Revolution." *Academy of Management Executive* 12, no. 2 (May 1998): 38–50.

Berry, T. *The Dream of the Earth.* San Francisco: Sierra Club Books, 1988.

Blaie, J., G. Savage, and C. Whithead. "A Strategic Approach for Negotiating with Hospital Stakeholders." *Health Care Management Review* 14, no. 3 (1989): 65–76.

Blair, M. M. *Wealth Creation and Wealth Sharing: A Colloquium on Corporate Governance and Investment in Human Capital.* Washington, DC: Brookings Institution, 1996.

Blau, P. *Exchange and Power in Social Life.* New York: Wiley, 1964.

Block, Dennis J., Nancy E. Barton, and Stephen A. Radin. *The Business Judgment Rule: Fiduciary Duties of Corporate Directors.* Englewood Cliffs, NJ: Prentice Hall Law and Business, 1989 (suppl. 1991).

Boatright, J. "Business Ethics and the Theory of the Firm." *American Business Law Journal* 34, no. 2 (1996): 217–38.

———. "Fiduciary Duties and the Shareholder-Management Relation: Or, What's So Special about Shareholders?" *Business Ethics Quarterly* 4 (1994): 393–407.

The Body Shop International: 1992, 1993, and 1994; *The Green Book* 1, 2, 3; and the Body Shop International: 1996 and 1998, *The Values Report* 1995 and 1997.

Bolin, B. "Environmental Equity in a Sunbelt City: The Spatial Distribution of Toxic Hazards in Phoenix, Arizona." *Environmental Hazards* 2, no. 1 (2000): 11–24.

Bolina, M. C., W. H. Turnley, and J. M. Bloodgood. "Citizenship Behavior and the Creation of Social Capital in Organizations." *Academy of Management Review* 27, no. 4 (2002): 505–22.

Bouckaert, L., and J. Vandenhove. "Business Ethics and the Management of Non-Profit Institutions." *Journal of Business Ethics* 17, no. 9/10 (1998): 1073–81.

Bowen, H. R. *Social Responsibilities of the Businessman.* New York: Harper & Row, 1953.

Bowie, N. "The Moral Obligations of Multinational Corporations." In *Problems of International Justice*, edited by S. Luper-Foy, 97–113. Boulder, CO: Westview Press, 1988.

Bowie, N., and R. Edward Freeman, eds., *Ethics and Agency Theory*. New York: Oxford University Press, 1992.

Bowie, N., and P. Werhane. *Management Ethics*. New York: Blackwell Publishing, 2004.

Brenner, S. N. "Stakeholder Theory of the Firm: Its Consistency with Current Management Techniques." In *Understanding Stakeholder Thinking*, edited by J. Nasi, 75–98. Helsinki: LSRJulkaisut Oy, 1995.

———. "The Stakeholder Theory of the Firm and Organizational Decision Making: Some Propositions and a Model." In *Proceedings of the Fourth Annual Meeting of the International Association for Business and Society*, edited by J. Pasquero and D. Collins, 205–10. San Diego: 1993.

Brenner, S. N., and P. L. Cochran. "The Stakeholder Model of the Firm: Implications for Business and Society Research." In *Proceedings of the Second Annual Meeting of the International Association for Business and Society*, edited by I. F. Mahon, 449–67. Sundance, UT: 1991.

Brenner, S. N., and E. Molander. "Is the Ethics of Business Changing?" *Harvard Business Review* 58, no. 1 (1977): 54–65.

Bromley, D. B. "Relationships between Personal and Corporate Reputation." *European Journal of Marketing* 35, nos. 3/4 (2001): 316–34.

Brown, L. "Challenges of the New Century." In *State of the World 2000*, edited by L. Brown, 3–21. New York: Norton, 2000.

Brown, T. J., and P. A. Dacin. "The Company and the Product: Corporate Associations and Consumer Product Responses." *Journal of Marketing* 61 (1997): 68–84.

Brown & Williamson Tobacco. "Social and Environmental Report 2001/2002." Printed by Brown & Williamson Tobacco, 2001/2002.

Brudney, Victor. "Corporate Governance, Agency Costs, and the Rhetoric of Contract." *Columbia Law Review* 85, no. 7 (1985): 1403–44.

———. "Dividends, Discretion, and Disclosure." *Virginia Law Review* 66, no. 1 (1980): 85–129.

Bruntland Commission. *The World Commission on Environment and Development: Our Common Future*. Oxford: Oxford University Press, 1987.

Bryan, L., and D. Farrell. *Market Unbound: Unleashing Global Capitalism*. London: John Wiley and Sons, 1996.

Buchholz, R. A. *Principles of Environmental Management*. Englewood Cliffs, NJ: Prentice Hall, 1993.

Burns, J., and M. Schroeder. "Accounting Firms Ask SEC for Post-Enron Guide." *Wall Street Journal*, Eastern ed., January 7, 2002.

Burton, B., and K. Dunn. "Feminist Ethics as Moral Grounding for Stakeholder Theory." *Business Ethics Quarterly* 6, no. 2 (1996): 133–47.

Byrne, John A. *Chainsaw*. New York: Harper Business, 1999.

Canadian Council of Chief Executives. *Governance, Values and Competitiveness: A Commitment to Leadership*. Ottawa: Canadian Council of Chief Executives, 2002.

Canadian Institute of Chartered Accountants (CICA). *Management's Discussion and Analysis: Guidance on Preparation and Disclosure*. Toronto: Canadian Institute of Chartered Accountants, 2002.

Cannon, T. *Corporate Responsibility*. London: FT/Pitman, 1992.

———. *Welcome to the Revolution: Managing Paradox in the 21st Century*. London: Pitman, 1996.

Carroll, A. "Corporate Social Responsibility: Evolution of a Definitional Construct." *Business and Society* 38, no. 3 (1999): 268–95.

———. "Managing Ethically with Global Stakeholders: A Present and Future Challenge." *Academy of Management Executive* 18, no. 2 (2004): 114–20.

———. "The Pyramid of Corporate Social Responsibility: Toward the Moral Management of Organisational Stakeholders." *Business Horizons* (July–August 1991): 30–48.

———. "A Three-Dimensional Model of Corporate Performance." *Academy of Management Review* 4, no. 4 (1979): 497–505.

Carroll, A., and A. Buchholtz. *Business and Society: Ethics and Stakeholder Management*. Belmont, CA: Thomson Southwestern, 2006.

Carroll, G. R., and M. T. Hannan. "Density Delay in the Evolution of Organizational Populations: A Model and Five Empirical Tests." *Administrative Science Quarterly* 34 (1989): 411–30.

Carson, R. *Silent Spring*. Greenwich, CT: Fawcett, 1962.

Carver, J., and C. Oliver. *Corporate Boards That Create Value: Governing Company Performance from the Boardroom*. San Francisco: Jossey-Bass, 2002.

Cascio, W. F. "Board Governance: A Social Systems Perspective." *Academy of Management Executive* 18, no. 1 (2004): 97–100.

Centner, T. J. "Evolving Policies to Regulate Pollution from Animal Feeding Operations." *Environmental Manager* 28, no. 5 (2001): 599–609.

Certo, S. T. "Influencing Initial Public Offering Investors with Prestige: Signalling with Board Structures." *Academy of Management Review* 28, no. 3 (2003): 432–46.

CFA Institute, Business Round Table Institute for Corporate Ethics. *Breaking the Short-Term Cycle*. Virginia: self-published, 2006.

Chandler, A. *Strategy and Structure*. Boston: MIT Press, 1970.

Chapple, S. "Laws of the Jungle." *Los Angeles Times*. August 8, 2004.

Charan, R., and R. E. Freeman. "Planning for the Business Environment of the 1980s." *Journal of Business Strategy* 1, no. 2 (1980): 9–19.

Child, J., and A. Marcoux. "Freeman and Evan: Stakeholder Theory in the Original Position." *Business Ethics Quarterly* 9, no. 2 (1999): 207.

Christensen, L. T. "Marketing as Auto-communication." *Consumption, Markets and Culture* 1, no. 3 (1997): 197–227.

Christensen, L. T., and S. Askegaard. "Corporate Identity and Corporate Image Revisited: A Semiotic Perspective." *European Journal of Marketing* 35, nos. 3/4 (2001): 292–315.

Christensen, L. T., and G. Cheney. "Self-Absorption and Self-Seduction in the Corporate Identity Game." In *The Expressive Organization*, edited by M. J. Hatch, M. Schultz, and M. H. Larsen, 256–70. Oxford: Oxford University Press, 2000.

Christian Aid. *Behind the Mask: The Real Face of Corporate Social Responsibility.* London: Christian Aid, 2004.

Chryssides, G. D., and J. H. Kaler. *An Introduction to Business Ethics.* London: Chapman & Hall, 1993.

Clark, M. "The Changing Basis of Economic Responsibility." *Journal of Political Economy* 24, no. 3 (1916): 209–29.

Clark, R. "Does the Nonprofit Form Fit the Hospital Industry?" *Harvard Law Review* 93, no. 7 (1980): 1417–89.

Clark, Robert C. "Agency Costs versus Fiduciary Duties." In *Principals and Agents*, edited by John Pratt and Richard Zeckhauser. Boston: Harvard University Press, 1985.

Clark, T. *Distance & Proximity.* Edinburgh: Pocketbooks, 2000.

Clarke, T., and S. Clegg. *Changing Paradigms: The Transformation of Management Knowledge for the 21st Century.* London: HarperCollins Business, 1998.

Clarkson, M. *The Corporation and Its Stakeholders.* Toronto: Toronto Press, 1998.

———. *Principles of Stakeholder Management.* The Clarkson Centre for Business Ethics, Joseph L. Rotman School of Management, University of Toronto, Toronto: 1999.

———. "A Risk-Based Model of Stakeholder Theory." *Proceedings of the Second Toronto Conference on Stakeholder Theory.* Toronto: Centre for Corporate Social Performance & Ethics, University of Toronto, 1994.

———. "A Stakeholder Framework for Analyzing and Evaluating Corporate Social Performance." *Academy of Management Review* 20, no. 1 (1995): 92–117.

Coase, R. "The Nature of the Firm." In *The Nature of the Firm: Origins, Evolution and Development*, edited by O. Williamson and S. Winter, 18–33. New York: Oxford University Press, 1937.

———. "The Problem of Social Cost." *Journal of Law and Economics* 3 (1960): 1–44.

Cobb, F. L. W., and C. D. Elder. *Participation in American Politics: The Dynamics of Agenda-Building.* Baltimore: Johns Hopkins University Press, 1972.

Code, L. "Second Persons." In *Science, Morality and Feminist Theory*, edited by M. Hanen and K. Nielsen. Calgary: University of Calgary Press, 1987.

———. *What Can She Know? Feminist Theory and the Construction of Knowledge.* Ithaca, NY: Cornell University Press, 1991.

Collins, James C., and Jerry I. Porras. *Built to Last: Successful Habits of Visionary Companies.* New York: HarperCollins, 1994.

Colquitt, Jason A., Donald L. Conlon, Michael J. Wesson, Christopher O. L. F. Porter, and K. Yee Ng. "Justice at the Millennium: A Meta-Analytic Review of 25 Years of Organizational Justice Research." *Journal of Applied Psychology* 86, no. 3 (2001): 425–45.

Cooper, C. L., and A. Argyris. *The Concise Blackwell Encyclopedia of Management.* Oxford: Blackwell, 1998.

Cooper, M. "A Town Betrayed." *Nation.* July 14, 1997.

Cornell, B., and A. Shapiro. "Corporate Stakeholders and Corporate Finance." *Financial Management* 16 (1987): 5–14.

Corry, D. "Macroeconomic Policies and Stakeholder Capitalism." In *Stakeholder Capitalism,* edited by G. Kelly, D. Kelly, and A. Gamble, 185–202. London: Macmillan, 1997.

Cottingham, J. "Ethics and Impartiality." *Philosophical Studies* 43 (1983): 83–99.

Cragg, W. "Business Ethics and Stakeholder Theory." *Business Ethics Quarterly* 12, no. 2 (2002): 113–41.

Craig-Lees, M. "Sense-Making: Trojan Horse? Pandora's Box?" *Psychology and Marketing* 18, no. 5 (2001): 513–26.

Crainer, S. *Key Management Ideas: Thinking That Changed the Management World.* London: Pitman, 1996.

Cramer, J., J. Jonker, and A. van der Heijden. "Making Sense of Corporate Social Responsibility." *Journal of Business Ethics* 55, no. 2 (2004): 215–22.

Crane, A., and L. Livesey. "Are You Talking to Me? Stakeholder Communication and the Risks and Rewards of Dialogue." In *Unfolding Stakeholder Thinking: Relationships, Communication, Reporting and Performance,* edited by J. Andriof, S. Waddock, B. Husted, and S. S. Rahman, 39–52. Sheffield: Greenleaf, 2002.

Crane, A., L. Livesey, D. Matten, and J. Moon. "Stakeholders as Citizens? Rethinking Rights, Participation, and Democracy." *Journal of Business Ethics* 53, no. 1/2 (2004): 107.

Cullity, C. "Moral Free Riding." *Philosophy and Public Affairs* 24, no. 1 (1995): 3–34.

Culpan, R., and J. Trussel. "Applying the Agency and Stakeholder Theories to the Enron Debacle: An Ethical Perspective." *Business and Society Review* 110, no. 1 (2005): 59.

Cyert, R. M., and J. G. March. *A Behavioral Theory of the Firm.* 2nd ed. Blackwell Business Press, 1992.

Daake, D., and W. P. Anthony. "Understanding Stakeholder Power and Influence Gaps in a Health-Care Organization: An Empirical Study." *Health Care Management Review* 25, no. 3 (2000): 94–107.

Daft, R. L., J. Sormunen, and D. Parks. "Chief Executive Scanning, Environmental Characteristics, and Company Performance: An Empirical Study." *Strategic Management Journal* 9 (1988): 123–39.

Dahl, R. A. "The Concept of Power." *Behavioral Science* 2 (1957): 201–15.

Daily, C. M., D. R. Dalton, and A. A. Cannella Jr. "Corporate Governance. Decades of Dialogue and Data." *Academy of Management Review* 28, no. 3 (2003): 371–82.

Daly, H. E., and J. B. Cobb Jr. *For the Common Good: Redirecting the Economy toward Community, the Environment, and a Sustainable Future.* Boston: Beacon Press, 1994.

————. *Beyond Growth: The Economics of Sustainable Development.* Boston: Beacon Press, 1997.

Danisco Sustainability Report. Danisco.com. Copenhagen: Danisco, 2004.

Davis, K. "The Case for and against Business Assumption of Social Responsibility." *Academy of Management Journal* 16 (1973): 312–22.

Dawkins, J., and S. Lewis. "CSR in Stakeholder Expectations: And Their Implication for Company Strategy." *Journal of Business Ethics* 44 (2003): 185–93.

Dawkins, R. *The Selfish Gene.* New York: Oxford University Press, 1976.

De Leeuw, A. C. J., and H. W. Volberda. "On the Concept of Flexibility: A Dual Control Perspective." *Omega, International Journal of Management Science* 24, no. 2 (1996): 121–39.

Deephouse, D. L. "Media Reputation as a Strategic Resource: An Integration of Mass Communication and Resource-Based Theories." *Journal of Management* 26, no. 6 (2000): 1091–1112.

Descartes, René. *The Philosophical Writings of René Descartes* (1641). Edited by John Cottingham, Robert Stoothoff, and Dugald Murdoch. Cambridge: Cambridge University Press, 1985.

Deutsch, M. *Distributive Justice.* New Haven, CT: Yale University Press, 1985.

————. "Equity, Equality, and Need: What Determines Which Value Will Be Used as the Basis for Distributive Justice." *Journal of Social Issues* 11, no. 3 (1975): 137–49.

Diekmeyer, P. "Auditor Independence Is Under Fire: The Heat Is On." *CAMagazine* 133, no. 8 (2000): 20–26.

Dill, W. "Strategic Management in a Kibitzer's World." In *From Strategic Planning to Strategic Management*, edited by I. Ansoff, R. Declerk, and R. Hayes, 125–36. New York: John Wiley and Sons, 1976.

DiMaggio, P. J., and W. W. Powell. "Introduction." In *The New Institutionalism in Organisational Analysis*, edited by W. W. Powell and P. J. DiMaggio, 1–38. Chicago: University of Chicago Press, 1991.

————. "The Iron Cage Revisited: Institutional Isomorphism and Collective Rationality in Organization Fields." *American Sociological Review* 46 (1983): 147–60.

Dimma, W. A. *Excellence in the Boardroom: Best Practices in Corporate Directorship.* Ontario: Wiley, 2003.

Dodge Bros. v. Ford, 170 N.W. 668 Mich., 1919.

Donaldson, T. *Corporations and Morality.* Englewood Cliffs, NJ: Prentice Hall, 1982.

————. *The Ethics of International Business.* New York: Oxford University Press, 1989.

————. "Making Stakeholder Theory Whole." *Academy of Management Review* 24, no. 2 (1999): 237–41.

Donaldson, T., and T. Dunfee. "Integrative Social Contracts Theory: A Communitarian Conception of Economic Ethics." *Economics and Philosophy* 11 (1995): 85–112.

———. *Ties That Bind: A Social Contracts Approach to Business Ethics.* Boston: Harvard Business School Press, 1999.

———. "Toward a Unified Conception of Business Ethics: Integrative Social Contracts Theory." *Academy of Management Review* 18, no. 2 (1994): 252–84.

Donaldson, T., and L. Preston. "The Stakeholder Theory of the Corporation: Concepts, Evidence, and Implications." *Academy of Management Review* 20, no. 1 (1995): 65–91.

Dowling, G. "Creating Corporate Reputations: Identity, Image and Performance." *European Journal of Marketing* 37, no. 7 (2003): 1144–47.

Dowling, J. B., and J. Pfeffer. "Organizational Legitimacy: Social Values and Organizational Behavior." *Pacific Sociological Review* 18 (1975): 122–36.

Driver, C., and D. Shepherd. "Capacity Utilization and Corporate Restructuring: A Comparative Study of the US, UK and Other EU Countries." *Cambridge Journal of Economics* 29, no. 1 (2005): 1–22.

Driver, C., D. Shepherd, and G. Thompson. "Corporate Governance and Democracy: The Stakeholder Debate Revisited." *Journal of Management and Governance* 6, no. 4 (2002): 111–30.

Drucker, P. *The Concept of the Corporation.* New York: Transaction Publishers, 1993.

Dudley, S., et al. "New Directions for the Business Curriculum." *Journal of Education for Business* 70, no. 5 (1995): 307.

Dunfee, T. "Business Ethics and Extant Social Contracts." *Business Ethics Quarterly* 1 (1991): 23–51.

Dunfee, T., and T. Donaldson. "Contractarian Business Ethics: Current Status and Next Steps." *Business Ethics Quarterly* 5 (1995): 173–86.

Dunham, L., R. E. Freeman, and J. Liedtka. "Enhancing Stakeholder Practice: A Particularized Exploration of Community." *Business Ethics Quarterly* 16, no. 1 (2006): 23.

Dunlap, Albert J. *Mean Business.* New York: Simon & Schuster, 1996.

Dyer, J. H., and H. Singh. "The Relational View: Cooperative Strategy and Sources of Inter-organizational Competitive Advantage." *Strategic Management Journal* 23, no. 4 (1998): 660–79.

El-Gohary, N., H. Osman, and T. El-Diraby. "Stakeholder Management for Public Private Partnerships." *International Journal of Project Management* 24, no. 7 (2006): 595–604.

Elms, Heather, and Shawn L. Berman. "Ethics and Incentives: An Inductive Development of Stakeholder Theory in the Health Care Industry." Paper presented at the Western Academy of Management Annual Meeting, 1997.

Elster, Jon. *Local Justice.* New York: Russell Sage Foundation, 1992.

ESRA. "European Sustainability Reporting Awards Report." Brussels: ESRA, 2003.

Etszioni, A. "A Communitarian Note on Stakeholder Theory." *Business Ethics Quarterly* 8, no. 4 (1998): 679.

———. *Modern Organizations.* Englewood Cliffs, NJ: Prentice Hall, 1964.

Evan, W., and R. E. Freeman. *The Moral Dimension*. New York: Basic Books, 1988.
————. "A Stakeholder Theory of the Modern Corporation: Kantian Capitalism." In *Ethical Theory and Business*, edited by T. Beauchamp and N. Bowie, 75–84. Englewood Cliffs, NJ: Prentice Hall, 1993.
Eyestone, R. *From Social Issue to Public Policy*. New York: Wiley, 1978.
Fan, J. P. H., and H. P. Lang. "The Measurement of Relatedness: An Application to Corporate Diversification." *Journal of Business* 73, no. 4 (2000): 629–60.
Fayol, H. *Central and Industrial Management*. 1916; London: Pitman, 1949.
Ferrell, O. C. "Business Ethics and Customer Stakeholders." *Academy of Management Executive* 18, no. 2 (2004): 126–29.
Financial Executives Research Foundation. *Educating Financial Executives*. Morristown, NJ: self-published, 1991.
Fitchett, J. "Consumers as Stakeholders: Prospects for Democracy in Marketing Theory." *Business Ethics* 14, no. 1 (2005): 14.
Fitzgerald, V. "Regulatory Investment Incentives." Working paper QEHWPPS80. University of Oxford, 2002.
Flood, R. L., and M. C. Jackson. *Creative Problem Solving: Total Systems Intervention*. Chichester: Wiley, 1991.
Fombrun, C., N. A. Gardberg, and J. M. Sever. "The Reputation Quotient Index: A Multistakeholder Measure of Corporate Reputation." *Journal of Brand Management* 7, no. 4 (2000): 241–55.
Fombrun, C., and M. Shanley. "What's in the Name? Reputation Building and Corporate Strategy." *Academy of Management Journal* 33, no. 2 (1990): 233–58.
Forbes, L. C., and J. M. Jermier. "Language, Organization, and Environment: An Introduction to the Symposium on the Death of Nature [Citation Classics and Foundational Works]." *Organization & Environment* 11, no. 2 (1998): 180–82.
Fort, Timothy L. "Corporate Constituency Statutes: A Dialectical Interpretation." *Journal of Law and Commerce* 15, no. 1 (1995): 257–94.
Foucault, M. *Politics, Philosophy, Culture*. New York: Routledge, 1988.
Frederick, W. C. "From CSR1 to CSR2. The Maturing of Business-and-Society Thought." *Business & Society* 33 (1994): 150–64.
————. "Moving to CSR4 What to Pack for the Trip." *Business & Society* 37, no. 1 (1998): 40–59.
————. *Values, Nature and Culture in the American Corporation*. New York: Oxford University Press, 1995.
Frederick, W. C., J. E. Post, A. Lawrence, and I. Weber. *Business and Society: Corporate Strategy, Public Policy, Ethics*. 8th ed. New York: McGraw-Hill, 1998.
Freeman, R. E. "Business Ethics at the Millennium." *Business Ethics Quarterly* 10, no. 1 (2000): 169–80.
————. "The Development of Stakeholder Theory: An Idiosyncratic Approach." In *Great Minds in Management*, edited by K. Smith and M. Hitt. Oxford: Oxford University Press, 2005.

————. "Divergent Stakeholder Theory." *Academy of Management Review* 24, no. 2 (1999): 233–36.

————. "The Politics of Stakeholder Theory: Some Future Directions." *Business Ethics Quarterly* 4 (1994): 409–21.

————. "A Stakeholder Theory of the Modern Corporation." In *Ethical Theory and Business*, edited by T. L. Beauchamp and N. E. Bowie, 66–67. 5th ed. Upper Saddle River, NJ: Prentice Hall, 1997.

————. *Strategic Management: A Stakeholder Approach*. Boston: Pitman, 1984.

Freeman, R. E., Laura Dunham, and Jeanne Liedika. "The Soft Underbelly of Stakeholder Theory: Towards Understanding Community." Darden School working paper, 2001.

Freeman, R. E., and R. Emshoff. "Stakeholder Management: A Case Study of the US Brewers and the Container Issue." In *Applications of Management Science*, edited by R. Schultz. Greenwich: JAI Press, 1981.

Freeman, R. E., and W. M. Evan. "Corporate Governance: A Stakeholder Interpretation." *Journal of Behavioral Economics* 19, no. 4 (1990): 337–59.

Freeman, R. E., and Daniel R. Gilbert Jr. "Business, Ethics, and Society: A Critical Agenda." *Business & Society* 31, no. 1 (1992): 9–17.

————. *Corporate Strategy and the Search for Ethics*. Englewood Cliffs, NJ: Prentice Hall, 1988.

————. "Managing Stakeholder Relationships." In *Business and Society: Dimensions of Conflict and Cooperation*, edited by S. P. Sethi and C. M. Falbe, 397–423. Lexington, MA: Lexington Books, 1987.

Freeman, R. E., J. S. Harrison, and M. A. Hitt, eds. *The Blackwell Handbook of Strategic Management*. Oxford: Blackwell, 2001.

Freeman, R. E., and J. McVea. "A Stakeholder Approach to Strategic Management." In *The Blackwell Handbook of Strategic Management*, edited by R. E. Freeman, J. S. Harrison, and M. A. Hitt, 189–207. Oxford: Blackwell, 2001.

Freeman, R. E., and R. Phillips. "Stakeholder Theory: A Libertarian Defense." *Business Ethics Quarterly* 12, no. 3 (2002): 331–49.

Freeman, R. E., and D. L. Reed. "Stockholders and Stakeholders: A New Perspective on Corporate Governance." *California Management Review* 25, no. 3 (1983): 88–106.

Freeman, R. E., A. C. Wicks, and B. Parmar. "Stakeholder Theory and 'the Corporate Objective Revisited.'" *Organization Science* 15, no. 3 (2004): 364–69.

French, J. R. P., and B. Raven. "The Base of Social Power." In *Group Dynamics*, edited by D. Cartwright and A. F. Zander, 607–23. 2nd ed. Evanston, IL: Row, Peterson, 1960.

French, P. "The Corporation as a Moral Person." *American Philosophical Quarterly* 16 (1979): 207–15.

Fried, C. "The Lawyer as Friend: The Moral Foundations of the Lawyer-Client Relation." *Yale Law Journal* 85 (1976): 1060–89, 1077.

Friedman, A., and S. Miles. "Developing Stakeholder Theory." *Journal of Management Studies* 39, no. 1 (2002): 1–21.

Friedman, M. *Capitalism and Freedom*. Chicago: University of Chicago Press, 1962.

———. "The Social Responsibility of Business Is to Increase Its Profits." *New York Times Magazine*. September 13, 1970.

———. "The Social Responsibility of Business Is to Increase Its Profits." In *An Introduction to Business Ethics*, edited by G. D. Chryssides and J. H. Kaler. Chapman and Hall, 1993.

———. "The Social Responsibility of Business Is to Increase Its Profits." In *Ethical Theory and Business*, edited by T. L. Beauchamp and N. E. Bowie. 5th ed. Upper Saddle River, NJ: Prentice Hall, 1997.

Frooman, J. "Stakeholder Influence Strategies." *Academy of Management Review* 24, no. 2 (1999): 191–205.

Fry, M., and M. J. Polonsky. "Examining the Unintended Consequences of Marketing." *Journal of Business Research* 57 (2004): 1303–1306.

Gao, S., and J. Zhang. "Stakeholder Engagement, Social Auditing, and Corporate Sustainability." *Business Process Management Journal* 12, no. 6 (2006): 722.

George, B. *Authentic Leadership*. San Francisco: Jossey-Bass, 2004.

———. "Managing Stakeholders vs. Responding to Shareholders." *Strategy & Leadership* 31, no. 6 (2003): 36–40.

Ghoshal, S., and P. Moran. "Bad for Practice: A Critique of the Transaction Cost Theory." *Academy of Management Review* 21, no. 1 (1996): 13–47.

Gibson, K. "The Moral Basis of Stakeholder Theory." *Journal of Business Ethics* 26, no. 3 (2000): 245–57.

Gilligan, C. *In a Different Voice*. Cambridge, MA: Harvard University Press, 1982.

Gilmartin, M., and R. E. Freeman. "Business Ethics and Health Care: A Stakeholder Perspective." *Health Care Management Review* 27, no. 2 (2002): 52.

Ginsberg, J. M., and P. N. Bloom. "Choosing the Right Green Marketing Strategy." *MIT Sloan Management Review* (Fall 2004): 79–84.

Gioia, D. A. "Practicability, Paradigms, and Problems in Stakeholder Theorizing." *Academy of Management Review* 24, no. 2 (1999): 228–32.

Gioia, D. A., and K. Chittipeddi. "Sensemaking and Sensegiving in Strategic Change Initiation." *Strategic Management Journal* 12, no. 6 (1991): 433–48.

Gioia, D. A., J. B. Thomas, S. M. Clark, and K. Chittipeddi. "Symbolism and Strategic Change in Academia: The Dynamics of Sensemaking and Influence." *Organization Science* 5, no. 3 (1994): 363–83.

Gladwin, T. N., J. K. Kennelly, and T. S. Krause. "Shifting Paradigms for Sustainable Development: Implications for Management Theory and Practice." *Academy of Management Review* 20, no. 4 (1995): 874–907.

Global Witness. *Corruption, War and Forest Policy: The Unsustainable Exploitation of Cambodia's Forests*. London: Global Witness, 1996.

Goodin, R. *Protecting the Vulnerable*. Chicago: University of Chicago Press, 1985.

Goodpaster, K. E. "Business Ethics and Stakeholder Analysis." *Business Ethics Quarterly* 1, no. 1 (1991): 53–73.

———. "Business Ethics and Stakeholder Analysis." In *The Corporation and Its Stakeholders. Classic and Contemporary Readings*, edited by M. B. E. Clarkson, 103–23. University of Toronto Press, 1998. Original work published in 1991.

Goodpaster, K. E., and Thomas E. Holloran. "In Defense of a Paradox." *Business Ethics Quarterly* 4, no. 3 (1994): 423–30.

Graafland, J., and B. van de Ven. "Strategic and Moral Motivation for Corporate Social Responsibility." *Journal of Corporate Citizenship* 22 (2006): 111–23.

Granovetter, M. "Economic Action and Social Structure: A Theory of Embeddedness." *American Journal of Sociology* 91 (1965): 481–510.

Grant, R. M. *Contemporary Strategy Analysis.* 2nd ed. Cambridge, MA: Blackwell Publishers Inc., 1995.

Grasenick, K., and J. Low. "Shaken, Not Stirred: Defining and Connecting Indicators for the Measurement and Valuation of Intangibles." *Journal of Intellectual Capital* 5, no. 2 (2004): 268–81.

Green, M. B., and R. B. McNaughton, eds. *Industrial Networks and Proximity.* Burlington, VT: Ashgate, 2000.

Greenawalt, K. *Conflicts of Law and Morality.* New York: Oxford University Press, 1987.

Greenberg, J. "Organizational Justice: Yesterday, Today, and Tomorrow." *Journal of Management* 16, no. 2 (1990): 399–432.

———. "A Taxonomy of Organizational Justice Theories." *Academy of Management Review* 12 (1987): 9–22.

Greenfield, W. "In the Name of Corporate Social Responsibility." *Business Horizons* 47, no. 1 (2004): 19–28.

Greenley, G. E., and G. R. Foxall. "Consumer and Non-consumer Stakeholder Orientation in UK Companies." *Journal of Business Research* 35 (1996): 105–16.

———. "Multiple Stakeholder Orientation in U.K. Companies and the Implications for Company Performance." *Journal of Management Studies* 34, no. 2 (1997): 259–84.

Greenley, G. E., G. J. Hooley, A. J. Broderick, and J. M. Rudd. "Strategic Planning Differences among Different Multiple Stakeholder Orientation Profiles." *Journal of Strategic Marketing* 12 (2004): 163–82.

Greer, C. R., and H. I. L. Downey. "Industrial Compliance with Social Legislation: Investigations of Decision Rationales." *Academy of Management Review* 7 (1982): 488–98.

Gregory, R., and R. L. Keeney. "Creating Policy Alternatives Using Stakeholder Values." *Management Science* 40, no. 8 (1994): 1035–48.

Griffin, R., and R. Ebert. *Business.* Englewood Cliffs, NJ: Prentice Hall, 1996.

Grimble, R., and K. Wellard. "Stakeholder Methodologies in Natural Resource Management: A Review of Principles, Contexts, Experience and Opportunities." *Agricultural Systems* 55, no. 2 (1997): 173–93.

Grimsley, Kirstin Downey. "Next for Boomers? Battles against Age Bias." *Washington Post*, February 2, 1997, p. H1.

Grumbine, R. E. "What Is Ecosystem Management?" *Conservation Biology* 8, no. 1 (1994): 27–38.

Grunig, J. E., and T. Hunt. *Managing Public Relations*. Fort Worth, TX: Harcourt Brace Jovanovich College Publishers, 1984.

Gutting, G., ed. *Paradigms and Revolutions*. Notre Dame, IN: University of Notre Dame Press, 1980.

Gwin, J. "Constituent Analysis: A Paradigm for Marketing Effectiveness in the Not-for-Profit Organization." *European Journal of Marketing* 24, no. 7 (1991): 43–48.

Habermas, J. "Discourse Ethics: Notes on a Program of Philosophical Justification." In *Moral Consciousness and Communicative Action*, translated by C. Lenhardt and S. Weber Nicholson. Cambridge, MA: MIT Press, 1990.

———. *Justification and Application: Remarks on Discourse Ethics*. Translated by C. Cronin. Cambridge, MA: MIT Press, 1993.

———. *The Theory of Communicative Action*, vol. 1. Translated by Thomas McCarthy. Boston: Beacon Press, 1984.

Hacking, I. "Our Fellow Animals." *New York Review of Books* 47, no. 11 (2000): 20–26.

Hall, J., and H. Vredenburg. "Managing Stakeholder Ambiguity." *MIT Sloan Management Review* 47, no. 1 (2005): 11–13.

Hall, R. "The Strategic Analysis of Intangible Resources." *Strategic Management Journal* 13 (1992): 135–44.

Hambrick, D. C., and P. A. Mason. "Upper Echelons: The Organization as a Reflection of Its Top Managers." *Academy of Management Review* 9 (1984): 193–206.

Hammer, Michael, and James Champy. *Reengineering the Corporation*. New York: Harper Business, 1991.

Handelman, J. M., and S. A. Arnold. "The Role of Marketing Actions with a Social Dimension: Appeals to the Institutional Environment." *Journal of Marketing* 63 (1999): 33–48.

Handy, Charles. "Balancing Corporate Power: A New Federalist Paper." *Harvard Business Review* (November–December 1992): 59–67.

Hansmann, H. "The Role of Nonprofit Enterprise." *Yale Law Journal* 89, no. 5 (1980): 835–901.

Hardin, Russell. *Morality within the Limits of Reason*. Chicago: University of Chicago Press, 1988.

Hargreaves, J., and J. Dauman. *Business Survival and Social Change*. New York: John Wiley and Sons, 1975.

Harrison, J. S., and R. E. Freeman. "Stakeholders, Social Responsibility, and Performance: Empirical Evidence and Theoretical Perspectives." *Academy of Management Journal* 42, no. 5 (1999): 479–85.

Harrison, J. S., and C. H. St. John. "Managing and Partnering with External Stake-holders." *Academy of Management Executive* 10, no. 2 (1996): 46–58.

Hart, H. L. A. "Are There Any Natural Rights?" *Philosophical Review* 64, no. 4 (1955): 175–91.

Hart, S. L. "A Natural Resource–Based View of the Firm." *Academy of Management Review* 20 (1995): 986–1014.

Hart, S. L., and G. Ahuja. "Does It Pay to Be Green? An Empirical Examination of the Relationship between Emission Reduction and Firm Performance." *Business Strategy and the Environment* 5 (1996): 30–37.

Hart, S. L., and M. B. Milstein. "Creating Sustainable Value." *Academy of Management Executive* 17, no. 2 (2003): 56–67.

Hart, S. L., and S. Sharma. "Engaging Fringe Stakeholders for Competitive Imagination." *Academy of Management Executive* 18, no. 1 (2004): 7–18.

Harting, T., S. Harmeling, and S. Venkataraman. "Innovative Stakeholder Relations: When 'Ethics Pays' (and When It Doesn't)." *Business Ethics Quarterly* 16 (2006): 43–68.

Hasnas, J. "The Normative Theories of Business Ethics: A Guide for the Perplexed." *Business Ethics Quarterly* 8, no. 1 (1998).

Hastak, J., M. B. Mazis, and L. A. Morris. "The Role of Consumer Surveys in Public Policy Decision Making." *Journal of Public Policy & Marketing* 20, no. 2 (2001): 170–85.

Hattori, April. "General Motors Agrees to Seek New Use for Shuttered Plant in Ypsilanti, Mich." *Bond Buyer*, April 15, 1994.

Hausman, D. M., and M. S. McPherson. *Economic Analysis and Moral Philosophy.* Cambridge: Cambridge University Press, 1996.

Heath, J. "Business Ethics without Stakeholders." *Business Ethics Quarterly* 16, no. 4 (2006): 533–57.

Heather, E., S. Berman, and A. Wicks. "Ethics and Incentives: An Evaluation and Development of Stakeholder Theory in the Health Care Industry." *Business Ethics Quarterly* 12, no. 4 (2002): 413–33.

Heid, V. "Feminism and Moral Theory." In *Women and Moral Theory*, edited by E. Kittay and D. Meyers. Savage, MD: Rowman and Littlefield, 1987.

Heinfeldt, J., and F. Wolf. "Re-engineering the Business Curriculum: A Stakeholder Paradigm." *Journal of Education for Business* 73, no. 4 (1998): 198.

Heintzman, A., and E. Solomon. *Fueling the Future. How the Battle over Energy Is Changing Everything.* Toronto: Anansi Press, 2003.

Held, D. *Global Covenant.* Cambridge: Polity, 2004.

Hendry, John. "Missing the Target: Normative Stakeholder Theory and the Corporate Governance Debate." *Business Ethics Quarterly* 11, no. 1 (2001): 59–176.

———. "Economic Contracts versus Social Relationships as a Foundation for Normative Stakeholder Theory." *Business Ethics: A European Review* 1, no. 3 (2001): 223–32.

Herman, S. L., A. C. Wicks, S. Kotha, and T. M. Jones. "Does Stakeholder Orientation Matter? The Relationship between Stakeholder Management Models and Firm Financial Performance." *Academy of Management Journal* 42, no. 5 (1999): 488–506.

Heuer, M. A., and M. Starik. "Multidirectional Stakeholder Networks: Specifying Capability, Turbulence, and Reputation." Presented at the Academy of Management Meetings, Denver, CO, August 2002.

Hill, C. W. L., and T. M. Jones. "Stakeholder-Agency Theory," *Journal of Management Studies* 29, no. 2 (1992): 131–54.

Hirschman, A. *Exit, Voice and Loyalty.* Cambridge, MA: Harvard University Press, 1970.

Hirst, P. Q. *Associative Democracy: New Forms of Economic and Social Governance.* Cambridge: Polity, 1994.

Holliday, C., S. Schmidheiny, and P. Watts. *Walking the Talk: The Business Case for Sustainable Development.* Sheffield, UK: Greenleaf, 2002.

Homburg, C., H. Krohmer, and J. P. Workman. "A Strategy Implementation Perspective of Market Orientation." *Journal of Business Research* 57 (2004): 1331–40.

Homer-Dixon, T. "Environmental Scarcities and Violent Conflict: Evidence from Cases." *International Security* 19, no. 1 (1994): 5–40.

Honore, A. M. "Ownership." In *Oxford Essays in Jurisprudence*, edited by A. G. Guest. Oxford: Clarendon Press, 1961.

Hutton, Will. *The State We're In.* London: Jonathan Cape, 1995.

Hybels, R. C. "On Legitimacy, Legitimation, and Organizations: A Critical Review and Integrative Theoretical Model." Best Paper Proceedings of the Academy of Management, 1995, pp. 241–45.

Industrial Society. *Empowerment: Managing Best Practice*, no. 8. London: Industrial Society, 1995.

Intergovernmental Panel on Climate Change. "Emissions Scenarios 2000: Special Report of the Intergovernmental Panel on Climate Change." Edited by N. Nakicenovic and R. Swart, 570. Cambridge: Cambridge University Press, 2000.

International Council on Human Rights Policy. *Beyond Voluntarism: Human Rights and the Developing International Legal Obligations of Companies.* Geneva: ICHRP, 2002.

IUCN (World Conservation Union) and C. Lewis. *Managing Conflicts in Protected Areas.* Gland, Switzerland: IUCN, 1995.

Jagger, A. M. "Love and Knowledge: Emotion in Feminist Epistemology." In *Women, Knowledge and Reality*, edited by A. Garry and M. Pearsall. Boston: Unwin Hyman, 1989.

Jamali, D. "Changing Management Paradigms: Implications for Educational Institutions." *Journal of Management Development* 24, no. 1/2 (2005): 104.

Jardim, Anne. *The First Henry Ford: A Study in Personality and Business Leadership.* Cambridge, MA: MIT Press, 1970.

Jawahar, L. M., and G. L. McLaughlin. "Toward a Descriptive Stakeholder Theory: An Organizational Life Cycle Approach." *Academy of Management Review* 26, no. 3 (2001): 397–414.

Jenkins, H. "Small Business Champions for Corporate Social Responsibility." *Journal of Business Ethics* 67, no. 3 (2006): 241.

Jennings, D., and P. A. Zandbergen. "Ecologically Sustainable Organizations: An Institutional Approach." *Academy of Management Review* 20, no. 4 (1995): 1015–52.

Jensen, M. C. "Value Maximization, Stakeholder Theory, and the Corporate Objective Function." *Business Ethics Quarterly* 12, no. 2 (2002): 235.

———. "Value Mazimization, Stakeholder Theory, and the Corporate Objective Function." In *Corporate Governance at the Crossroads. A Book of Readings*, edited by D. H. Chew and S. L. Gillan, 7–20. Irwin, New York: McGraw-Hill, 2005.

———. "Value Maximization and the Corporate Objective Function." In *Breaking the Code of Change*, edited by M. Beer and N. Nohria, 37–58. Boston: Harvard Business School Press, 2000. Reprinted as "Value Maximization, Stakeholder Theory, and the Corporate Objective Function." *Business Ethics Quarterly* 12, no. 2 (2002): 235–56.

Jensen, M. C., and W. F. Meckling. "The Nature of Man." In *Corporate Governance at the Crossroads. A Book of Readings*, edited by D. H. Chew and S. L. Gillan, 87–102. Irwin, New York: McGraw-Hill, 2005.

———. "Theory of the Firm: Managerial Behavior, Agency Costs, and Capital Structure." *Journal of Financial Economics* 3 (October 1976): 305–60.

Johnson-Cramer, M. E., S. L. Berman, and J. E. Post. "Re-examining the Concept of "Stakeholder Management." In *Unfolding Stakeholder Thinking: Relationships, Communication, Reporting and Performance*, edited by J. Andriof, S. Waddock, B. Husted, and S. S. Rahman, 145–61. Sheffield: Greenleaf, 2003.

Johnston, David. *Roman Law of Trusts*. Oxford: Clarendon Press, 1988.

Jones, G. R., and C. W. L. Hill. "Transaction Cost Analysis of Strategy-Structure Choice." *Strategic Management Journal* 9 (1988): 159–72.

Jones, M., and P. Fleming. "Unpacking Complexity through Critical Stakeholder Analysis: The Case of Globalization." *Business and Society* 42, no. 4 (2003): 430.

Jones, T. M. "Corporate Social Responsibility Revisited, Redefined." *California Management Review* 22, no. 2 (1980): 59–67.

———. "Ethical Decision-Making by Individuals in Organizations: An Issue-Contingent Model." *Academy of Management Review* 16 (1993): 388–95.

———. "Instrumental Stakeholder Theory: A Synthesis of Ethics and Economics." *Academy of Management Review* 20 (1995): 404–37.

Jones, T. M., and L. Goldberg. "Governing the Large Corporation: More Arguments for Public Directors." *Academy Of Management Review* 7 (1982): 603.

Jones, T. M., and A. C. Wicks. "Convergent Stakeholder Theory." *Academy of Management Review* 24, no. 2 (1999): 206–21.

———. "Letter to AMR regarding 'Convergent Stakeholder Theory.'" *Academy of Management Review* 24, no. 4 (1999): 621–23.

Jones, Tom, and Andrew C. Wicks. "Unified Stakeholder Theory in Management Research." Paper presented at the 1996 Society for Business Ethics Annual Meeting.

Kaler, J. "Morality and Strategy in Stakeholder Identification." *Journal of Business Ethics* 39, no. 1/2 (2002): 91.

———. "Positioning Business Ethics in Relation to Management and Political Philosophy." *Journal of Business Ethics* 24, no. 3 (2000): 257–72.

Kant, I. *Groundwork of the Metaphysic of Morals.* New York: Harper Torchbooks, 1964.

Kaufman, A. "Managers' Double Fiduciary Duty: To Stakeholders and to Freedom." *Business Ethics Quarterly* 12, no. 2 (2002): 189.

Kay, J., and A. Z. Silberston. "Corporate Governance." *National Institute Economic Review* (August 1995): 84–95.

Keeley, M. *A Social-Contract Theory of Organizations.* Notre Dame, IN: Notre Dame University Press, 1988.

Kell, G. "The Global Compact: Origins, Operations, Progress, Challenges." *Journal of Corporate Citizenship* 11 (2003): 35–49.

Kelly, Gavin, Dominic Kelly, and Andrew Gamble, eds. *Stakeholder Capitalism.* London: Macmillan, 1997.

Kelsey, D., and F. Milne. "Externalities, Monopoly and the Objective Function of the Firm." *Economic Theory* 29, no. 3 (2006): 565–89.

Kenis, P., and D. Knoke. "How Organizational Field Networks Shape Interorganizational Tie-Formation Rates." *Academy of Management Review* 27, no. 2 (2002): 275–93.

Kenna, A. "Animal Abuse Laws That Bite." *Governing* 14, no. 2 (2000): 52–54.

Key, S. "Toward a New Theory of the Firm: A Critique of Stakeholder Theory." *Management Decision* 27, no. 4 (1999): 31–32 (2).

Kimery, K. M., and S. M. Rinehart. "Markets and Constituencies: An Alternative View of the Marketing Concept." *Journal of Business Research* 43 (1998): 117–24.

King, A. A., and M. Lenox. "Industry Self-Regulation without Sanctions: The Chemical Industry's Responsible Care Program." *Academy of Management Journal* 43, no. 4 (2000): 698–716.

Kiosko, G. "Presumptive Benefit, Fairness, and Political Obligation." *Philosophy and Public Affairs* 16 (1987): 241–59.

———. *The Principle of Fairness and Political Obligation.* Lanham, MD: Rowman & Littlefield, 1992.

Klein, T. A. *Social Costs and Benefits of Business.* Englewood Cliffs, NJ: Prentice Hall, 1977.

Kohlberg, L. *The Philosophy of Moral Development.* San Francisco: Harper & Row, 1981.

Kolk, A., and J. Pinkse. "Stakeholder Mismanagement and Corporate Social Responsibility Crises." *European Management Journal* 24, no. 1 (2006): 59–72.

Kotter, J. P., and J. L. Heskett. *Corporate Culture and Performance.* New York: Free Press, 1992.

Kreiner, P., and A. Bhambri. "Influence and Information in Organization-Stakeholder Relationships." *Research in Corporate Social Performance and Policy,* no. 12 (1991): 3–36.

Kuhn, T. *The Structure of Scientific Revolutions.* Chicago: University of Chicago Press, 1970.

Ladd, J. "Morality and the Ideal of Rationality in Formal Organizations." *Monist* 54 (1970): 488–516.

Lakatos, I., and A. Musgrave, eds. *Criticism and the Growth of Knowledge.* Cambridge: Cambridge University Press, 1970.

Lampe, M. "Mediation as an Ethical Adjunct of Stakeholder Theory." *Journal of Business Ethics* 31, no. 2 (2002): 165.

Langtry, B. "Stakeholders and the Moral Responsibilities of Business." *Business Ethics Quarterly* 4 (1994): 431–43.

Laverty, K. J. "Economic 'Short-Termism': The Debate, the Unresolved Issues, and the Implications for Management Practice." *Academy of Management Review* 21, no. 3 (1996): 825–60.

Lawrence, A. T. "The Drivers of Stakeholder Engagement: Reflections on the Case of Royal Dutch/Shell." In *Unfolding Stakeholder Thinking: Theory, Responsibility and Engagement,* edited by J. Andriof, S. Waddock, B. Husted, and S. S. Rahman, 185–200. Sheffield: Greenleaf, 2002.

Lea, D. "The Imperfect Nature of Corporate Responsibilities to Stakeholders." *Business Ethics Quarterly* 14, no. 2 (2004): 201.

Leap, T., and M. L. Loughry. "The Stakeholder-Friendly Firm." *Business Horizons* 47, no. 2 (2004): 27–32.

Leblanc, R., and J. Gillies. *Building a Better Board: What Directors, Investors, Managers and Regulators Must Know about Boards of Directors.* Chichester: Wiley & Son, 2005.

Lee, D. "Corporate and Public Responsibility, Stakeholder Theory and the Developing World." *Business Ethics: A European Review* 8, no. 3 (1999): 151–62.

Lee, R. M., and S. B. Robbins. "Understanding Social Connectedness in College Women and Men." *Journal of Counseling and Development* 78, no. 4 (2000): 484–91.

Lengnick-Hall, M. I., and C. A. Lengnick-Hall. "HR's Role in Building Relationship Networks." *Academy of Management Executive* 17, no. 4 (2003): 53–63.

———. *Human Resource Management in the Knowledge Economy: New Challenges, New Roles, New Capabilities.* San Francisco: Berrett-Koehler, 2002.

Leopold, A. *A Sand County Almanac with Essays on Conservation from Round River.* New York: Ballantine, 1970. Original work published in 1949.

Letendre, L. "The Dynamics of the Boardroom." *Academy of Management Executive* 18, no. 1 (2004): 101–104.

Leventhal, G. S. "The Distribution of Reward and Resources in Groups and Organizations." In *Advances in Experimental Social Psychology*, vol. 9, edited by L. Berkowitz and E. Walster, 91–131. New York: Academic Press, 1976.

Lieber, James. *Friendly Takeover: How an Employee Buyout Saved a Steel Town*. New York: Viking Press, 1995.

Lind, E. A., and T. Tyler. *The Social Psychology of Procedural Justice*. New York: Plenum, 1988.

Lindbloom, C. *Politics and Markets*. New York: Basic Books, 1977.

Lingaard, T. "Creating a Corporate Responsibility Culture. The Approach of Unilever UK." In *Corporate Social Responsibility. Reconciling Aspiration with Application*, edited by A. Kakabadse and M. Morsing, 86–104. London: Palgrave Macmillan, 2006.

Lober, D. J. "Explaining the Formation of Business-Environmentalist Collaborations: Collaborative Windows and the Paper Task Force." *Policy Sciences* 20 (1997): 1–24.

Lorsch, Tay W. *Pawns or Potentates: The Reality of America's Corporate Boards*. Boston: Harvard Business School Press, 1989.

Lovins, A. B., L. H. Lovins, and P. Hawken. "A Road Map for Natural Capitalism." *Harvard Business Review* (May–June 1999): 145–58.

Lozano, J. M. "Ethics and Management: A Controversial Issue." *Journal of Business Ethics* 15, no. 2 (1996): 227–36.

Luben, D. *Lawyers and Justice*. Princeton, NJ: Princeton University Press, 1988.

Lynall, M. D., B. R. Golden, and A. J. Hillman. "Board Composition from Adolescence to Maturity: A Multi-theoretic View." *Academy of Management Review* 28, no. 3 (2003): 416–31.

Maak, T., and N. Pless. "Responsible Leadership in a Stakeholder Society—A Relational Perspective." *Journal of Business Ethics* 66, no. 1 (2006): 99.

MacMillan, K., and S. Downing. "Governance and Performance: Goodwill Hunting." *Journal of General Management* 24, no. 3 (1999): 1–11.

Macy, Jonathan, and Jeffrey Miller. "Corporate Stakeholders: A Contractual Perspective." *University of Toronto Law Journal* 63, no. 3 (1993): 401–24.

Maignan, I., and D. A. Ralston. "Corporate Social Responsibility in Europe and the USA: Insights from Businesses' Self-Presentations." *Journal of International Business Studies* 33, no. 3 (2002): 497–614.

Maignan, I., and O. C. Ferrell. "Corporate Social Responsibility and Marketing: An Integrative Framework." *Journal of the Academy of Marketing Science* 32, no. 1 (2004): 19–23.

———. "Nature of Corporate Responsibilities: Perspectives from American, French, and German Consumers." *Journal of Business Research* 56, no. 1 (2003): 55–67.

Maignan, I., O. C. Ferrell, and L. Ferrell. "A Stakeholder Model for Implementing Social Responsibility in Marketing." *European Journal of Marketing* 39, no. 9/10 (2005): 956.

Maignan, I., O. C. Ferrell, and G. T. M. Hult. "Corporate Citizenship: Cultural Antecedents and Business Benefits." *Journal of the Academy of Marketing Science* 27, no. 4 (1999): 455–69.

Maitland, I. "Distributive Justice in Firms: Do the Rules of Corporate Governance Matter?" *Business Ethics Quarterly* 11, no. 1 (2001): 129–43.

Mansley, M. *Socially Responsible Investment: A Guide for Pension Funds and Institutional Investors*. Sudbury, UK: Monitor Press, 2000.

Maranville, S. "You Can't Make Steel without Some Smoke: A Case Study in Stakeholder Analysis." *Journal of Business Ethics* 8 (1989): 57–63.

Marcoux, A. "Balancing Act." In *Contemporary Issues in Business Ethics*, edited by J. R. DesJardins and J. J. McCall Wadsworth, 92–100. 4th ed. Belmont, CA: Wadsworth/Thompson Learning, 2000.

———. "A Fiduciary Argument against Stakeholder Theory." *Business Ethics Quarterly* 13, no. 1 (2003): 25.

Marens, R., and A. Wicks. "Getting Real: Stakeholder Theory, Managerial Practice, and the General Irrelevance of Fiduciary Duties Owed to Shareholders." *Business Ethics Quarterly* 9, no. 2 (1999): 273–93.

———. "Getting Real: Stakeholder Theory, Managerial Practice, and the General Irrelevance of Fiduciary Duties Owed to Shareholders." In *Business, Institutions, and Ethics: A Text with Cases and Readings*, edited by J. W. Dienhart. New York: Oxford University Press, 2000.

Margerum, R. D. "Integrated Environmental Management: The Foundations for Successful Practice." *Environmental Management* 24, no. 2 (1999): 151–66.

Margolis, J. O., and J. P. Walsh. "Misery Loves Companies—Rethinking Social Initiatives by Business." *Administrative Science Quarterly* 48 (2003): 268–305.

Martin, J. *Cultures in Organization: Three Perspectives*. New York: Oxford University Press, 1992.

Martin, R. "The Problem with Corporate Governance." Working paper. Toronto: Rotman School of Management, 2003.

Matten, D., and J. Moon. "A Conceptual Framework for Understanding CSR." In *Corporate Social Responsibility across Europe*, edited by A. Habisch, J. Jonker, M. Wegner, and R. Schmidpeter, 335–56. Berlin: Springer Verlag, 2004.

Matter of Heilman's Estate, 37 Ill.App.3d 390, 345 N.E.2d 536, 540.

Maury, M. "A Circle of Influence: Are All the Stakeholders Included?" *Journal of Business Ethics* 23, no. 1 (2000): 117–21.

May, L. *The Morality of Groups*. Notre Dame, IN: Notre Dame University Press, 1987.

Mayo, E. *The Human Problems of an Industrial Civilization*. New York: Macmillan, 1933.

McAlister, D. T., O. C. Ferrell, and L. K. Ferrell. *Business and Society*. Boston, MA: Houghton Mifflin Company, 2005.

McFarland, J. "How ROB Created the Rating System." *Globe and Mail Report on Business*, October 7, 2002, p. 6.

McFarland, J., E. Church, and L. Nguyen. "Board Games." *Globe and Mail Report on Business*, October 7, 2002, pp. i, 8.

McKague, K., D. van der Veldt, and D. Wheeler. "Growing a Sustainable Energy Company: Suncor's Venture into Alternative and Renewable Energy." Schulich School of Business Case. Toronto: York University Press, 2001.

McKinsey and Co. *The Business Case for Corporate Citizenship.* Davos: World Economic Forum, 2003.

Mendieta, E., ed. *Take Care of Freedom and the Truth Will Take Care of Itself: Interviews with Richard Rorty.* Stanford, CA: Stanford University Press, 2006.

Mennell, Robert L. *Wills and Trusts in a Nutshell.* St. Paul: West Publishing Co., 1994.

Mercuro, N., ed. *Taking Property and Just Compensation.* Boston: Kluwer, 1992.

Metcalfe, C. E. "The Stakeholder Corporation." *Business Ethics: A European Review* 7, no. 1 (1998): 30–36.

Meyer, J. W., and B. Rowan. "Institutional Organizations: Formal Structures as Myth and Ceremony." *American Journal of Sociology* 80 (1977): 340–63.

Meyer, Stephen. *The Five Dollar Day: Labor Management and Social Control in the Ford Motor Company.* Albany: SUNY Press, 1981.

Michaelson, L., and R. Black. *Collaborative Learning: A Sourcebook for Higher Education.* State College, PA: National Center for Teaching, Learning, and Assessment, 1994.

Miles, M. P., and L. S. Munilla. "The Potential Impact of Social Accountability Certification on Marketing: A Short Note." *Journal of Business Ethics* 50, no. 1 (2004): 1–12.

Mill, J. S. *On Liberty.* Cambridge: Cambridge University Press, 1989. Oxford University Press, 1976. Reprinted Indianapolis, IN: Liberty Classics, 1982.

Miller, R. L., and W. F. Lewis. "A Stakeholder Approach to Marketing Management Using the Value Exchange Models." *European Journal of Marketing* 25, no. 8 (1991): 55–68.

Mills, R. "Accounting and Finance: Life after Enron." *Manager Update* 13, no. 4 (Summer 2002): 35.

Mitchell, B., ed. *Resource Management and Development.* Toronto: Oxford University Press, 1990.

Mitchell, Lawrence E. Book review of *The Economic Structure of Corporate Law.* *Texas Law Review* 71, no. 1 (1992): 217–42.

Mitchell, Lawrence E., Lawrence A. Cunningham, and Lewis Solomon. *Corporate Finance and Governance: Cases, Materials, and Problems.* Durham, NC: Carolina Academic Press, 1996.

Mitchell, R. K., B. R. Agle, and D. J. Wood. "Toward a Theory of Stakeholder Identification and Salience: Defining the Principle of Who and What Really Counts." *Academy of Management Review* 22, no. 4 (1997): 853–86.

MoE (Ministry of Environment). *National Environmental Action Plan 1998–2002.* Phnom Penh, Cambodia: Ministry of Environment, 1998.

Monks, R., and N. Minow. "The Director's New Clothes (or the Myth of Corporate Accountability)." In *Corporate Governance at the Crossroads. A Book of Read-*

ings, edited by D. H. Chew and S. L. Gillan, 151–57. New York: McGraw-Hill, 2005.

———. *Power and Accountability*. New York: Harper Business, 1991.

Monks, R., and A. Sykes. *Capitalism without Owners Will Fail—A Policymaker's Guide to Reform*. New York: Centre for the Study of Financial Innovation, 2002.

Moote, M. A., M. P. McClaran, and D. K. Chickering. "Theory in Practice: Applying Participatory Democracy Theory to Public Land Planning." *Environmental Management* 21, no. 6 (1997): 877–89.

Morello-Frosch, R., M. Pastor, and J. Sadd. "Environmental Justice and Southern California's 'Riskscape': The Distribution of Air Toxins, Exposures and Health Risks among Diverse Communities." *Urban Affairs Review* 36, no. 4 (2001): 551–78.

Morgan, A. *Eating the Big Fish. How 'Challenger Brands' Can Compete against Brand Leaders*. New York: John Wiley, 1999.

Morgan, R. M., and S. D. Hunt. "The Commitment-Trust Theory of Marketing." *Journal of Marketing* 58 (2000). Cited in K. MacMillan, K. Money, and S. Downing, "Successful Business Relationships," *Journal of General Management* 26, no. 1 (2000): 69–83.

Morsing, M., and M. Schultz. "Corporate Social Responsibility Communication: Stakeholder Information, Response, and Involvement Strategies." *Business Ethics: A European Review* 15, no. 4 (2006): 323–38.

Mosakowski, E., and P. C. Earley. "A Selective Review of Time Assumptions in Strategy Research." *Academy of Management Review* 25, no. 4 (2000): 796–812.

Munzer, S. R. *A Theory of Property*. New York: Cambridge University Press, 1992.

Nader, R., and M. I. Green, eds. *Corporate Power in America*. New York: Grossman, 1973.

Nadler, David A., and Michael L. Tushman. *Competing by Design: The Power of Organizational Architecture*. New York: Oxford University Press, 1997.

Nahapiet, J., and S. Ghoshal. "Social Capital, Intellectual Capital, and the Organizational Advantage." *Academy of Management Review* 23, no. 2 (1998): 242–66.

Nash, R. *The Rights of Nature*. Madison: University of Wisconsin Press, 1987.

Nasi, J. "What Is Stakeholder Thinking? A Snapshot of a Social Theory of the Firm." In *Understanding Stakeholder Thinking*, edited by J. Nasi, 19–32. Helsinki: LSR-Julkaisut Oy, 1995.

Nasi, J., S. Nasi, N. Philips, and S. Zyglidopoulos. "The Evolution of Corporate Social Responsiveness: An Exploratory Study of Finnish and Canadian Forestry Companies." *Business and Society* 3, no. 6 (1997): 296–321.

Nasi, J., S. Nasi, and G. T. Savage. "A Stubborn Entrepreneur under Pressure of a Union and the Courts: An Analysis of Stakeholder Strategies in a Conflict Process." In *Proceedings of the Fifth Annual Meeting of the International Association for Business and Society*, edited by S. Wartick and D. Collins, 228–34. Hilton Head, SC: 1994.

National Academy of Sciences, 2002. www.nationalacademies.org/news.nsf/isbn/ 0309075742?Open Document (accessed August 1, 2002).

National Parks and Conservation Association. *Our Endangered Parks.* San Francisco, CA: Foghorn Press, 1994.

Nijhof, A., O. Fisscher, and H. Honders. "Sustaining Competences for Corporate Social Responsibility: A Sensemaking Perspective." Working paper. Enschede: University of Twente, 2006.

Noddings, N. *Caring: A Feminine Approach to Ethics & Moral Education.* Berkeley: University of California Press, 1984.

Nonaka, I., and H. Takeuchi. *The Knowledge-Creating Company: How Japanese Companies Create the Dynamics of Innovation.* New York: Oxford University Press, 1995.

Novo Nordisk. Sustainability Report, 2002. novonordisk.com.

———. "What Does Being There Mean to You?" Sustainability Report, 2003. novonordisk.com.

Oakland, J. S. *Total Quality Management: Text with Cases.* Oxford: Butterworth-Heinemann, 1996.

O'Hare, S., and W. Wood. "Social Responsibility and Corporate Profits: The Expense Preference Approach." *Journal of Education for Business* 69, no. 5 (1994): 278–82.

O'Higgins, E., and J. Morgan. "Stakeholder Salience and Engagement in Political Organizations: Who and What Really Counts." *Society and Business Review* 1, no. 1 (2006): 62–76.

Oldenquist, A. "Loyalties." *Journal of Philosophy* 79 (1985): 173–93.

Oliver, C. "Strategic Responses to Institutional Processes." *Academy of Management Review* 16, no. 1 (1991): 145–79.

O'Neill, O. "Duty and Obligation." In *Encyclopedia of Ethics*, vol. 1, edited by L. C. Becker and C. B. Becker, 273–78. London: St. James Press, 1992.

O'Neill, Terry A. "Employees' Duty of Loyalty and the Corporate Constituency Debate." *Connecticut Law Review* 25, no. 3 (1993): 681–716.

O'Reilly, C. A., and J. Pfeffer. *Hidden Value. How Great Companies Achieve Extraordinary Results with Ordinary People.* Boston: Harvard Business School Press, 2000.

Orts, Eric W. "Beyond Shareholders: Interpreting Corporate Constituency Statutes." *George Washington Law Review* 61, no. 1 (1992): 14–135.

———. "A North American Legal Perspective on Stakeholder Management Theory." *Perspectives on Company Law* 2 (1997): 165–79.

Orts, Eric W., and Alan Strudler. "The Ethical and Environmental Limits of Stakeholder Theory." *Business Ethics Quarterly* 12, no. 2 (2002): 215–33.

Pacelle, W. "Battle of the Ballots: A Guide to State Voter Initiatives in 2000." *Animals' Agenda* 20, no. 5 (2000): 44–45.

Paine, L. S. *Value Shift: Why Companies Must Merge Social and Financial Imperatives to Achieve Superior Performance.* New York: McGraw-Hill, 2001.

Palmer, D. "Upping the Stakes: A Response to John Hasnas on the Normative Viability of the Stockholder and Stakeholder Theories." *Business Ethics Quarterly* 9, no. 4 (1999).

Park, S. "Industry Clustering for Economic Development." *Economic Development Review* 12, no. 2 (1994): 26–38.

Parkinson, J. "Company Law and Stakeholder Governance." In *Stakeholder Capitalism*, edited by G. Kelly, D. Kelly, and A. Gamble, 142–54. Basingstoke: Macmillan, 1997.

Parsons, T. *Structure and Process in Modern Societies*. New York: Free Press, 1960.

Patagonia. Company Web site, 2002. http://www.patagonia.com/sports/surf.shtml (accessed August 4, 2002).

Paul, K. "The Impact of U.S. Sanctions on Japanese Business in South Africa: Further Developments in the Internationalisation of Social Activism." *Business & Society* 31 (1992): 51–58.

Pava, M. L., and J. Krausz. *Corporate Responsibility and Financial Performance: The Paradox of Social Cost*. London: Quorum Books, 1996.

Pedersen, E. "Making Corporate Social Responsibility (CSR) Operable: How Companies Translate Stakeholder Dialogue into Practice." *Business and Society Review* 11, no. 2 (2006): 137–63.

Pejovich, S. *The Economics of Property Rights: Towards a Theory of Comparative Systems*. Dordrecht: Kluwer Academic Publishers, 1990.

Perraton, Jonathan. "The Global Economy." In *Stakeholder Capitalism*, edited by G. Kelly, D. Kelly, and A. Gamble, 226–37. Basingstoke: Macmillan, 1997.

Perrow, C. *Complex Organisations: A Critical Essay*. 3rd ed. New York: Random House, 1986.

Peters, T. *Liberation Management. Necessary Disorganization for the Nanosecond Nineties*. New York: Knopf, 1992.

Peters, T. J., and R. H. Waterman. *In Search of Excellence*. New York: Harper & Row, 1982.

Pfeffer, J. *Managing with Power: Politics and Influence in Organizations*. Boston: Harvard Business School Press, 1992.

———. *Power in Organisations*. Marshfield, MA: Pitman, 1981.

Pfeffer, J., and Gerald R. Salancik. *The External Control of Organizations: A Resource Dependence Perspective*. New York: Harper & Row, 1978.

Phillips, R. "Stakeholder Legitimacy." *Business Ethics Quarterly* 12, no. 1 (2003): 25–41.

Phillips, R. A. "Stakeholder Theory and a Principle of Fairness." *Business Ethics Quarterly* 7, no. 1 (1997): 51–66.

Phillips, R. A., and J. M. Margolis. "Toward an Ethics of Organizations" *Business Ethics Quarterly* 9, no. 4 (1999): 619–38.

Phillips, R. A., and J. Reichart. "The Environment as Stakeholder? A Fairness-Based Approach." *Journal of Business Ethics* 23, no. 2 (2000): 185–97.

Phillips, R., R. E. Freeman, and A. Wicks. "What Stakeholder Theory Is Not." *Business Ethics Quarterly* 13, no. 4 (2003): 479.

PNC, 2004. www.pnc.com (accessed September 29, 2004).

Pollock, T. G., and V. P. Rindova. "Media Legitimation Effects in the Market for Initial Public Offerings." *Academy of Management Journal* 46, no. 5 (2003): 631–42.

Porter, M. "Capital Choices: Changing the Way America Invests in Industry." In *Studies in International Corporate Finance and Governance Systems*, edited by D. H. Chew, 5–17. New York: Oxford University Press, 1997.

Porter, M., and M. R. Kramer. "The Competitive Advantage of Corporate Philanthropy." *Harvard Business Review* 80, no. 12 (2002): 56–68.

Post, J. E., L. E. Preston, and S. Sachs. *Redefining the Corporation, Stakeholder Management and Organizational Wealth.* Palo Alto, CA: Stanford University Press, 2002.

Prahalad, C. K., and G. Hamel. "The Core Competence of the Corporation." *Harvard Business Review* 68, no. 3 (1990): 79–91.

Preble, J. "Toward a Comprehensive Model of Stakeholder Management." *Business and Society Review* 110, no. 4 (2005), 407–31.

Preston, L., and T. Donaldson. "Stakeholder Management and Organizational Wealth." *Academy of Management Review* 24, no. 4 (1999): 619.

Preston, L., and H. Sapienze. "Stakeholder Management and Corporate Performance." *Journal of Behavioral Economics* 19 (1990): 361–75.

Pruzan, P. "From Control to Values-Based Management and Accountability." *Journal of Business Ethics* 17, no. 13 (1998): 1379–94.

Purser, R. E., C. Park, and A. Montuori. "Limits to Anthropocentrism: Towards an Ecocentric Organization Paradigm?" Special topic forum on ecologically sustainable organizations, *Academy of Management Review* 20 (1995): 1053–89.

Quinn, Dennis P., and Thomas M. Jones. "An Agent Morality View of Business Policy." *Academy of Management Review* 20, no. 1 (1995): 22–42.

Rao, H. "The Social Construction of Reputation: Certification Contents, Legitimation, and the Survival of Organization in the Automobile Industry." *Strategic Management Journal* 15 (1994): 29–44.

Rasche, A., and D. Esser. "From Stakeholder Management to Stakeholder Accountability." *Journal of Business Ethics* 65, no. 3 (2006): 251–67.

Ratnatunga, J., N. Gray, and K. R. Balachandrang. "CEVTTA. The Valuation and Reporting of Strategic Capabilities." *Management Accounting Research* 15, no. 1 (2004).

Rawls, J. "Legal Obligation and the Duty of Fair Play." In *Law and Philosophy*, edited by S. Hook. New York: New York University Press, 1964.

———. *Political Liberalism.* New York: Columbia University Press, 1993.

———. *A Theory of Justice.* Cambridge, MA: Belknap Press of Harvard University Press, 1971.

"Redefining the Corporation." 2000. http://www.mgmt.utoronto.ca/~stake/Principles .htm (accessed January 31, 2002).

Reed, D. "Employing Normative Stakeholder Theory in Developing Countries: A Critical Theory Perspective." *Business and Society* 41, no. 2 (2002): 166–83.

———. "Stakeholder Management: A Critical Theory Perspective." *Business Ethics Quarterly* 9, no. 3 (1999): 453–83.

Renner, M. "Creating Jobs, Preserving the Environment." In *State of the World* 2000, edited by L. Brown, 162–83. New York: Norton, 2000.

Reuters. "Tourism Must Respect Environment, Pope Says." June 25, 2002, www.cnn.com/2002/TRAVEL/NEWS/06/25/environment.pope.reut/index.html (accesssed July 5, 2002).

Reynolds, S., F. Schultz, and D. Hekman. "Stakeholder Theory and Managerial Decision-Making: Constraints and Implications of Balancing Stakeholder Interests." *Journal of Business Ethics* 64, no. 3 (2006): 285–301 (17).

Rhenman, E. Foeretagsdemokrati och foeretagsorganisation. Stockholm: Thule, 1964.

———. *Industrial Democracy and Industrial Action*. London: Tavistock Publishing, 1968.

Ring, P. S. "Fragile and Resilient Trust and Their Roles in Cooperative Interorganizational Relationships." In *Proceedings of the Fourth Annual Meeting of the International Association for Business and Society*, edited by J. Pasquero and D. Collins, 107–13. San Diego: 1994.

Roberts, R. "Determinants of Corporate Social Responsibility Disclosure: An Application of Stakeholder Theory." *Accounting, Organizations and Society* 17, no. 6 (1992): 595–612.

Roberts, R., and L. Mahoney. "Stakeholder Conceptions of the Corporation: Their Meaning and Influence in Accounting Research." *Business Ethics Quarterly* 14, no. 3 (2004): 399.

Roddick, A. *Body & Soul*. London: Ebury Press, 1991.

Rolston, H. *Conserving Natural Value*. New York: Columbia University Press, 1994.

Ross, W. D. *The Right and the Good*. Oxford: Oxford University Press, 1930.

Rowley, T. "Moving beyond Dyadic Ties: A Network Theory of Stakeholder Influences." *Academy of Management Review* 22, no. 4 (1997): 887–910.

———. "A Normative Justification for Stakeholder Theory." *Business and Society* 37, no. 1 (1998): 105.

Ruddick, S. *Maternal Thinking: Toward a Politics of Peace*. Boston: Beacon Press, 1984.

Rustin, Mike. "Stakeholding and the Public Sector." In *Stakeholder Capitalism*, edited by G. Kelly, D. Kelly, and A. Gamble, 72–81. Basingstoke: Macmillan, 1997.

Ryland, E. "Gaia Rising: A Jungian Look at Environmental Consciousness and Sustainable Organizations." *Organization & Environment* 13, no. 4 (2000): 381–402.

Salancik, G. R., and J. Pfeffer. "The Bases and Use of Power in Organizational Decision Making: The Case of Universities." *Administrative Science Quarterly* 19 (1974): 453–73.

SAS Sustainability Report, SAS.com. Copenhagen: SAS, 2004.

Savage, G. T., T. W. Nix, C. J. Whitehead, and J. D. Blair. "Strategies for Assessing and Managing Organizational Stakeholders." *Academy of Management Executive* 5 (1991): 61–75.

Schaefer, R. T. *Sociology: A Brief Introduction*. 4th ed. Boston: McGraw-Hill, 2002.

Schein, F. *Organizational Culture and Leadership*. San Francisco: Jossey-Bass, 1985.

Schmidheiny, S., and F. J. L. Zorraquin. *Financing Change: The Financial Community, Ecoefficiency, and Sustainable Development*. Cambridge, MA: MIT Press, 1996.

Schumacher, E. F. *Small Is Beautiful: Economics as If People Mattered*. New York: Harper & Row, 1973.

Schwartz, M. "God as a Managerial Stakeholder?" *Journal of Business Ethics* 66 (2006): 291–306.

Schweikhardt v. Chessen, 161 N.E. 118, 123, 329 111. 637.

Schwenk, C. R. "Cognitive Simplification Processes in Strategic Decision-Making." *Strategic Management Journal* 5 (1984): 111–28.

Sciarelli, S. "Corporate Ethics and the Entrepreneurial Theory of 'Social Success.'" *Business Ethics Quarterly* 9, no. 4 (1985): 639–49.

Scott, S. G., and V. R. Lane. "A Stakeholder Approach to Organizational Identity." *Academy of Management Review* 25, no. 1 (2000): 43–62.

Scott, W. R. *Organizations: Rational, Natural, and Open Systems*. Englewood Cliffs, NJ: Prentice Hall, 1987.

Sen, A. *On Ethics and Economics*. Oxford: Basil Blackwell, 1987.

Sen, S., and C. B. Bhattacharya. "Does Doing Good Always Lead to Doing Better? Consumer Reactions to CSR." *Journal of Marketing Research* 38 (2001): 225–43.

Senge, P. M. *The Fifth Discipline: The Art and Practice of the Learning Organization*. New York: Doubleday, 1990.

Shankman, N. "Reframing the Debate between Agency and Stakeholder Theories of the Firm." *Journal of Business Ethics* 19, no. 4 (1999): 319–34.

Sharplin, A., and L. D. Phelps. "A Stakeholder Apologetic for Management." *Business and Professional Ethics Journal* 8, no. 2 (1989): 41–53.

Shein, James B. "A Limit on Downsizing: *Varity Corp. v. Howe*." *Pepperdine Law Review* 24, no. 1 (1996): 1–35.

Shelley, S. "Ethical Interpretations of Management Decision Making in Higher Education." *International Journal of Management and Decision Making* 6, no. 3/4 (2005): 284.

Shleifer, A., and R. W. Vishny. "A Survey of Corporate Governance." Working paper 5554. National Bureau of Economic Research, 1996.

Shrivastava, P. "CASTRATED Environment: GREENING Organization Studies." *Organization Studies* 15, no. 5 (1994): 705–26.

———. "Ecocentric Management for a Risk Society." *Academy of Management Review* 20, no. 1 (1995): 118–37.

————. "The Role of Corporations in Achieving Ecological Sustainability." *Academy of Management Review* 20, no. 4 (1995): 936–60.

Simmons, J. *Moral Principles and Political Obligations*. Princeton, NJ: Princeton University Press, 1979.

Simon, H. A. *Administrative Behavior*. New York: Macmillan, 1958.

Sinclair, S. "The WTO and Its GATS." In *The Handbook of Globalisaton*, edited by J. Michie, 347–57. Cheltenham: Edward Elgar, 2003.

Singer, Joseph. "Jobs and Justice: Rethinking the Stakeholder Debate." *University of Toronto Law Journal* 63, no. 3 (1993): 475–510.

Singh, A., and A. Zammitt. "Globalisation, Labour Standards and Economic Development." In *The Handbook of Globalisaton*, edited by J. Michie, 191–215. Cheltenham: Edward Elgar, 2003.

Sirgy, M. J., and D. Lee. "Setting Socially Responsible Marketing Objectives." *European Journal of Marketing* 30, no. 5 (1996): 20–34.

Slater, S. F., and J. C. Narver. "Market-Oriented Is More Than Being Customer-Led." *Strategic Management Journal* 20 (1999): 1165–68.

Smith, A. *The Wealth of Nations*, 1776. D. D. Raphael & A. L. Macfie, eds. Oxford: Oxford University Press, 1976. Reprinted Indianapolis, IN: Liberty Classics, 1982.

Smith, C. "CSR: Whether or How?" *California Management Review* 45, no. 4 (2003): 52–76.

Smith, D. M. "Proximity: Locality and Community." In *Moral Geographies: Ethics in a World of Difference*, edited by D. M. Smith. Edinburgh: Edinburgh University Press, 2000.

Smith, F. L. "Guess Your Liability! Full Disclosure Gone Berserk." *Forbes*, July 26, 2004.

Smith, J., ed. *The Daily Globe: Environmental Change, the Public, and the Media*. London: Earthscan, 2000.

Smith, W. K., and R. S. Tedlow. "James Burke: A Career in American Business." *Harvard University Graduate School of Business Administration Case No. 9-389-177*. Boston: Harvard Business School Press, 1989.

Sollars, G. G. "An Appraisal of Shareholder Proportional Liability." *Journal of Business Ethics* 32, no. 4 (2001): 329–45.

Solomon, J., and R. Solomon. *Corporate Governance and Accountability*. Chichester, UK: Wiley, 2004.

Sonnefeld, J. A. "What Makes Good Boards Great." *Harvard Business Review* (September 2002): 106–13.

Soskice, David. "Stakeholding Yes; The German Model No." In *Stakeholder Capitalism*, edited by G. Kelly, D. Kelly, and A. Gamble, 219–25. Basingstoke: Macmillan, 1997.

Soukhanov, A. H., ed. *Webster's II New Riverside Dictionary*. Boston: Houghton Mifflin, 1984.

Spence, L., A. Coles, and L. Harris. "The Forgotten Stakeholder? Ethics and Social Responsibility in Relation to Competitors." *Business and Society Review* 106, no. 4 (2001): 331.

Spurgin, E. "Do Shareholders Have Obligations to Stakeholders?" *Journal of Business Ethics* 1, no. 4 (2001): 287.

Srikantia, P., and D. Bilimoria. "Isomorphism in Organization and Management Theory." *Organization & Environment* 10, no. 4 (1997): 384–406.

Starik, M. "Is the Environment an Organizational Stakeholder? Naturally!" In *Proceedings of the Fourth Annual Meeting of the International Association for Business and Society*, edited by J. Pasquero and D. Collins, 466–71. San Diego: 1993.

———. "Should Trees have Managerial Standing? Toward Stakeholder Status for Nonhuman Nature." *Journal of Business Ethics* 14, no. 3 (1995): 207–17.

———. "What Is a Stakeholder?" Essay by Mark Starik, pp. 89–95 of "Toronto Conference: Reflections on Stakeholder Theory." *Business & Society* 33 (1994): 82–131.

Starik, M., and G. P. Rands. "Weaving an Integrated Web: Multilevel and Multisystem Perspectives of Ecologically Sustainable Organizations." *Academy of Management Review* 20, no. 4 (1995): 908–35.

Stead, J. G., and W. E. Stead. "Ecoenterprise Strategy: Standing for Sustainability." *Journal of Business Ethics* 24, no. 4 (2000): 313–29.

———. *Management for a Small Planet.* 2nd ed. Thousand Oaks, CA: Sage, 1996.

Sternberg, E. *Corporate Governance: Accountability in the Marketplace.* London: Institute of Economic Affairs, 1998.

———. "The Defects of Stakeholder Theory." *Corporate Governance: An International Review* 5, no. 1 (1995): 3–10.

———. *Just Business.* New York: Oxford University Press, 2000.

———. "Stakeholder Theory: The Defective State It's In." In *Stakeholding and Its Critics*, 70–85. London: Institute of Economics Affairs, 1997.

———. "The Stakeholder Concept: A Mistaken Doctrine." *Foundation for Business Responsibilities.* 2001.

Steurer, R., M. Langer, A. Konrad, and A. Martinuzzi. "Corporations, Stakeholders, and Sustainable Development I: A Theoretical Exploration of Business-Society Relations." *Journal of Business Ethics* 61, no. 3 (2005): 263.

Stiglitz, J. *Globalization and Its Discontents.* New York: Norton, 2002.

Stinchcombe, A. L. *Constructing Social Theories.* Chicago: University of Chicago Press, 1968.

Stockhammer, E. "Financialisation and the Slowdown of Accumulation." *Cambridge Journal of Economics* 28, no. 5 (2004): 719–41.

Stone, C. *Should Trees Have Standing? Towards Legal Rights for Natural Objects.* Los Altos, CA: William Kaufmann, 1974.

Stone, Katherine V. Wezel. "Employees as Stakeholders under State Nonshareholder Constituency Statutes." *Stetson Law Review* 21, no. 1 (1991): 45–72.

Stoney, C., and D. Winstanley. "Stakeholding: Confusion or Utopia? Mapping the Conceptual Terrain." *Journal of Management Studies* 38, no. 5 (2001): 603–26.

Suchman, M. C. "Managing Legitimacy: Strategic and Institutional Approaches." *Academy of Management Review* 20 (1995): 571–610.

Summers, Clyde. "Worker Dislocation: Who Bears the Burden? A Comparative Study of Social Values in Five Countries." *Notre Dame Law Review* 70, no. 5 (1995): 1033–78.

Sundaram, A., and A. Inkpen. "The Corporate Objective Revisited." *Organization Science* 15, no. 3 (2004): 350–63.

Sturdivant, F. *Business and Society: A Managerial Approach.* Illinois: R. D. Irwin, 1977.

———."Executives and Activists: A Test of Stakeholder Management." *California Management Review* 22, no. 1 (1979): 53–59.

Suzuki, D. *The Sacred Balance: Rediscovering Our Place in Nature.* Vancouver: Greystone Books, 1997.

Szwajkowski, E. "Simplifying the Principles of Stakeholder Management: The Three Most Important Principles." *Business & Society* 39, no. 4 (2000): 379–96.

Takala, T., and P. Pallab. "Individual, Collective and Social Responsibility of the Firm." *Business Ethics: A European Review* 9, no. 2 (2000): 109–18.

Tan, S. J. "Can Consumers' Scepticism Be Mitigated by Claim Objectivity and Claim Extremity?" *Journal of Marketing Communications* 8, no. 1 (2002): 45–64.

Taylor, B. "The Future Development of Corporate Strategy." *Journal of Business Policy* 2, no. 2 (1971): 22–38.

———. "Managing the Process of Corporate Development." In *Corporate Strategy and Planning,* edited by B. Taylor and J. Sparkes. New York: John Wiley and Sons, 1977.

Taylor, F. *Principles of Scientific Management.* New York: Harper & Row, 1911.

Thomas, J. B., and R. R. McDaniel. "Interpreting Strategic Issues: Effects of Strategy and the Information-Processing Structure of Top Management Teams." *Academy of Management Journal* 33, no. 2 (1990): 286–306.

Thomas, T., J. R. Schermerhorn, and J. W. Dienhart. "Strategic Leadership of Ethical Behavior in Business." *Academy of Management Executive* 18, no. 2 (2004): 56–66.

Thompson, G. F. "Is the Future 'Regional' for Global Standards?" *Environment and Planning A* 37, no. 1 (2005): 2053–71.

Thompson, J. *Organizations in Action.* New York: McGraw-Hill, 1967.

Thompson, J. K., S. L. Wartick, and H. L. Smith. "Integrating Corporate Social Performance and Stakeholder Management: Implications for a Research Agenda in Small Business." *Research in Corporate Social Performance and Policy* 12 (1991): 207–30.

Tong, R. *Feminine and Feminist Ethics.* Belmont, CA: Wadsworth Publishing, 1993.

Topalian, A. "Experienced Reality: The Development of Corporate Identity in the Digital Era." *European Journal of Marketing* 37, no. 7 (2003): 1119–32.

Tsai, W. "Social Capital, Strategic Relatedness, and the Formation of Intraorganizational Linkages." *Academy of Management Journal* 21, no. 9 (2000): 925–39.

Ulrich, W. *Critical Heuristics of Social Planning. A New Approach to Practical Philosophy.* Chichester: Wiley, 1983.

————. "Systems Thinking, Systems Practice, and Practical Philosophy: A Program of Research." *Systems Practice* 1, no. 2 (1988): 137–63.

UNDP (United Nations Development Programme). *United Nations Development Programme in Cambodia.* Phnom Penh, Cambodia: UNDP, 1998.

United Nations. *We the Peoples: Civil Society, the United Nations and Global Governance.* United Nations, 2004. www.un.org.

Uzzi, B. "Social Structure and Competition in Interfirm Networks: The Paradox of Embeddedness." *Administrative Sciences Quarterly* 42, no. 1 (1997): 35–67.

Van Buren, H. "If Fairness Is the Problem, Is Consent the Solution? Integrating ISCT and Stakeholder Theory." *Business Ethics Quarterly* 11, no. 3 (2001): 481.

Van de Ven, B. "Human Rights as a Normative Basis for Stakeholder Legitimacy." *Corporate Governance* 5, no. 2 (2005): 48–59.

Van Riel, C. B. M. *Principles of Corporate Communication.* London: Prentice Hall, 1995.

Vargo, S. L., and R. F. Lusch. "Evolving to a New Dominant Logic for Marketing." *Journal of Marketing* 68 (January 2004): 1–17.

Velamuri, S. R. "Entrepreneurship, Altruism, and the Good Society." *Ethics and Entrepreneurship*, Ruffin Series 3 (2002): 125–43.

Velasquez, M. "Why Corporations Are Not Morally Responsible for Anything They Do." *Business and Professional Ethics Journal* 2 (1982): 1–18

Vira, B., O. Dubois, S. E. Daniels, and G. B. Walker. "Institutional Pluralism in Forestry: Considerations of Institutional and Analytical Tools." *Unasylva* 49, no. 194 (1997): 35–48.

Volcker, P. A. "A Litmus Test for Accounting Reform." *Wall Street Journal*, May 21, 2002, Eastern ed.

Von Stange, Gary. "Corporate Social Responsibility through Constituency Statutes: Legend or Lie?" *Hofstra Labor Law Journal* 11, no. 2 (1994): 461–97.

Vos, J. "Corporate Social Responsibility and the Identification of Stakeholders." *Corporate Social Responsibility and Environmental Management* 10, no. 3 (2003): 141–52.

Waddock, S. A., C. Bodwell, and S. B. Graves. "Responsibility: The New Business Imperative." *Academy of Management Executive* 16, no. 2 (2002): 132–49.

Warner, M. "'Consensus' Participation: An Example for Protected Areas Planning." *Public Administration and Development* 17, no. 4 (1997): 413–32.

Wartick, S. L., and I. M. Mahon. "Toward a Substantive Definition of the Corporate Issue Construct: A Review and Synthesis of the Literature." *Business & Society* 33 (1994): 293–311.

Waxenberger, B., and L. Spence. "Reinterpretation of a Metaphor: From Stakes to Claims." *Strategic Change* 12, no. 5 (2003): 239–49.

Weaver, G. R., L. K. Trevino, and P. L. Cochran. "Integrated and Decoupled Corporate Social Performance: Management Commitments, External Pressures, and Corporate Ethics Practices." *Academy of Management Journal* 42, no. 5 (1999): 539–52.

Weber, M. *The Theory of Social and Economic Organization*. New York: Free Press, 1947.

Weick, K. *Sensemaking in Organizations*. Thousand Oaks, CA: Sage, 1995.

———. *The Social Psychology of Organizing*. Reading, MA: Addison-Wesley, 1979.

Wempe, J. *Market and Morality. Business Ethics and the Dirty and Many Hands Dilemma*. Delft: Eburon, 1998.

Werhane, P. H. *Persons, Rights, and Corporations*. Englewood Cliffs, NJ: Prentice Hall, 1985.

Wernerfeld, B. "A Resource-Based View of the Firm." *Strategic Management Journal* 5 (1984): 171–80.

Wheeler, D. "Memorandum by The Body Shop International." In *A Community Eco-audit Scheme*. 12th Report of the Select Committee on The Body Shop International, the European Communities. House of Lords Paper 42. London: HMSO, 1992.

———. "The Successful Navigation of Uncertainty: Sustainability and the Organization." In *Leading in Turbulent Times*, edited by R. Burke and C. Cooper, 182–207. Oxford: Blackwell, 2003.

Wheeler, D., B. Colbert, and R. E. Freeman. "Focusing on Value: Reconciling Corporate Social Responsibility, Sustainability and a Stakeholder Approach in a Network World." *Journal of General Management* 28, no. 3 (2003): 1–28.

Wheeler, D., H. Fabig, and R. Boele. "Paradoxes and Dilemmas for Stakeholder Responsive Firms in the Extractive Sector. Lessons from the Case of Shell and the Ogoni." *Journal of Business Ethics* 39, no. 3 (2002): 297–318.

Wheeler, D., and M. Sillanpää. "Including the Stakeholders: The Business Case." *Long Range Planning* 31, no. 2 (1998): 201–10.

———. *The Stakeholder Corporation: A Blueprint for Maximizing Stakeholder Value*. London: Pitman, 1997.

Wheeler, D., and J. Thomson. "The New Bottom Line: Energy and Corporate Ingenuity." In *Strategy: Process, Content, Context*, edited by B. de Wit and R. Meyer. London: Thomson, 2003.

———. "Sustainability and a Stakeholder Approach to Corporate Governance." In *The Accountable Corporation*, edited by M. J. Epstein and K. O. Hanson. Greenwood: Praeger Publishers, 2005.

Whitbeck, C. "The Maternal Instinct." In *Mothering: Essays in Feminist Theory*, edited by J. Trebilcot. Totawa, NJ: Rowan and Allanheld, 1984.

White, R. P., P. Hodgson, and S. Crainer. *The Future of Leadership: A Whitewater Revolution*. London: Pitman, 1996.

Whiteman, G. "Poems from James Bay [Poetry]." *Organization & Environment* 10, no. 2 (1997): 186–93.

Wicks, A. C., D. R. Gilbert Jr., and R. E. Freeman. "A Feminist Reinterpretation of the Stakeholder Concept." *Business Ethics Quarterly* 4 (1994): 475–97.

Wijnberg, N. "Normative Stakeholder Theory and Aristotle: The Link between Ethics and Politics." *Journal of Business Ethics* 25, no. 4 (2000): 329–42.

Williams, B. *Ethics and the Limits of Philosophy*. Cambridge, MA: Harvard University Press, 1985.

Williamson, O. *Markets and Hierarchies: Analysis and Antitrust Implications*. New York: Free Press, 1975.

Williamson, O. E. *The Economic Institutions of Capitalism*. New York: Free Press, 1985.

Williamson, O. E., and S. G. Winter, eds. *The Nature of the Firm: Origins, Evolution, and Development*. New York: Oxford University Press, 1991.

Williams v. Griffin, 35 Mich.App. 179, 192 N.W.2d 283, 285.

Wilson, E. O. *The Diversity of Life*. Cambridge, MA: Belknap Press of Harvard University Press, 1992.

————. *Ecology, Evolution and Population Biology: Readings from Scientific American*. San Francisco: W. H. Freeman, 1974.

Windsor, D. "Corporate Social Responsibility: Three Key Approaches." *Journal of Management Studies* 43, no. 1 (2006): 93–114.

————. "Stakeholder Management in Multinational Enterprises." In *Proceedings of the Third Annual Meeting of the International Association for Business and Society*, edited by S. N. Brenner and S. A. Waddock, 121–28. Leuven, Belgium: 1992.

————. "Stakeholder Responsibilities: Lessons for Managers." In *Unfolding Stakeholder Thinking: Theory, Responsibility and Engagement*, edited by J. Andriof, S. Waddock, B. Husted, and S. S. Rahman, 137–54. Sheffield: Greenleaf, 2002.

Winn, M. "Building Stakeholder Theory with a Decision Modeling Methodology." *Business and Society* 40, no. 2 (2001): 133.

Wood, D. J. *Business and Society*. 2nd ed. New York: HarperCollins, 1994.

————. "Corporate Social Performance Revisited." *Academy of Management Review* 16, no. 4 (1991): 691–718.

Wood, D. J., and R. E. Jones. "Stakeholder Mismatching: A Theoretical Problem in Empirical Research on Corporate Social Performance." *International Journal of Organizational Analysis* 3, no. 3 (1995): 226–29.

World Bank. *Cambodia Public Expenditure Review*. Washington, DC: World Bank, 1999.

————. *Forest Policy Assessment—Cambodia*. Washington, DC: World Bank, 1996.

————. *The World Bank Participation Source-Book*. Washington, DC: World Bank, 1996.

World Economic Forum. *Global Corporate Citizenship: The Leadership Challenge for CEOs and Boards*. Davos: WEF, 2002.

Worldwatch Institute. 2000. http://www.worldwatch.org (accessed December 29, 2000).

World Wildlife Fund. 2002. http://www.panda.org/resources/publications/climate/Health_Issue/page9.htm (accessed June 23, 2002).

Yamak, S., and O. Suer. "State as a Stakeholder." *Corporate Governance* 5, no. 2 (2005): 111.

Yoshihashi, Pauline. "Lockheed Ordered to Pay $30 Million to NL Industries." *Wall Street Journal*, December 8, 1992, p. A10.

Zadek, S., P. Pruzan, and R. Evans, eds. "Why Count Social Performance?" In *Building Corporate Accountability: The Emerging Practices in Social and Ethical Accounting, Auditing and Reporting*, 12–34. London: Earthscan Publications, 1997.

Zeller, S. "Counsel for a Menagerie of Clients." *National Journal* 32, no. 10 (2000): 714–15.

Zimmerman, M. A., and G. J. Zeitz. "Beyond Survival: Achieving New Venture Growth by Building Legitimacy." *Academy of Management Review* 27, no. 3 (2002): 414–31.

Zinkin, J. "Strategic Marketing: Balancing Customer Value with Shareholder Value." *Marketing Review* 6, no. 2 (2006): 163–81.

Zyglidopoulos, S. C. "The Social and Environmental Responsibilities of Multinationals: Evidence from the Brent Spar Case." *Journal of Business* 36, nos. 10–12 (2002): 141–51.

LIST OF CONTRIBUTORS

Frank W. Abrams was chairman of the board of directors at Standard Oil Company and was memorialized by the Exxon Education Foundation through the Abrams Lecture Series at Syracuse University.

Russell L. Ackoff is the Anheuser-Busch Professor Emeritus of Management Science at the Wharton School of Business, University of Pennsylvania, and a pioneer in the area of management science.

Bradley R. Agle is associate professor of business administration and serves as director of the David Berg Center for Ethics and Leadership at the University of Pittsburgh.

Brian K. Burton is associate professor of management and director of the MBA program at Western Washington University.

Rachel Davies is an MBA graduate from the Schulich School of Business, York University, Toronto, Canada, where she specialized in business, sustainability, and finance.

Thanakvaro Thyl De Lopez is a member of the Environment, Development, and Society Group, Department of Geography, University of Cambridge.

William R. Dill is the former dean of the Graduate School of Business at New York University and professor emeritus and former dean at Babson College.

Thomas Donaldson is the Mark O. Winkleman Professor of Legal Studies and Business Ethics at the Wharton School of Business, University of Pennsylvania.

Cathy Driscoll is associate professor in the Department of Management at Sobey School of Business, Saint Mary's University, Halifax, Canada.

Ciaran Driver is professor of economics at Imperial College London.

Craig P. Dunn is associate professor of management at San Diego State University, specializing in business and society issues.

Linda Ferrell is associate professor of marketing at the Robert O. Anderson Schools of Management at the University of New Mexico.

O. C. Ferrell is professor of marketing at the Robert O. Anderson Schools of Management at the University of New Mexico.

R. Edward Freeman is the Elis and Signe Olsson Professor of Business Administration at the Darden School of Business, University of Virginia, and director of the Olsson Center for Applied Ethics.

John Hasnas is associate professor at the McDonough School of Business, Georgetown University.

Jeff Heinfeldt is associate professor of finance at Ohio Northern University.

John Kaler is a senior lecturer in business ethics and governance at Plymouth Business School, University of Plymouth, United Kingdom.

Isabelle Maignan is associate professor of marketing at Nijmegen School of Management, the Netherlands.

Alexei M. Marcoux is associate professor of business ethics at the School of Business Administration, Loyola University, Chicago.

Richard Marens is assistant professor in the Department of Organizational Behavior and Environment at the College of Business Administration at Sacramento State University.

Ronald K. Mitchell is professor of entrepreneurship at the University of Victoria Faculty of Business, is head of the Entrepreneurship Program, and holds the Francis G. Winspear Chair in Public Policy and Business.

Mette Morsing is professor in the Department of Intercultural Communication and Management at the Copenhagen Business School.

Daniel Palmer is associate professor of philosophy at Kent State University, Trumbull Campus.

Robert A. Phillips is associate professor of management at San Diego State University and visiting associate professor of management at the Robbins School of Business, University of Virginia.

Lee E. Preston is professor emeritus in business management at the Robert H. Smith School of Business, University of Maryland.

David L. Reed coauthored the groundbreaking article entitled "Stockholders and Stakeholders: A New Perspective on Corporate Governance" with R. Edward Freeman, included in this volume.

Majken Schultz is professor of management at the Copenhagen Business School, where she also serves as associate dean for the full-time MBA program.

Maria Sillanpää is the director of the Sustainability Advisory Group in Brighton, United Kingdom.

Mark Starik is department chair and professor of strategic management and public policy at the George Washington University School of Business.

Grahame Thompson is professor of political economy in the Department of Politics and International Studies at the Open University, United Kingdom.

Janita F. J. Vos teaches at the Faculty of Management and Organization at the University of Groningen, the Netherlands.

Patricia H. Werhane is the Wicklander Chair of Business Ethics in the Department of Philosophy and serves as the executive director of the Institute for Business and Professional Ethics at DePaul University with a joint appointment as the Peter and Adeline Ruffin Professor of Business Ethics and a senior fellow of the Olsson Center for Applied Ethics at the Darden School of Business, University of Virginia.

David Wheeler is the Erivan K. Haub Professor of Business and Sustainability at the Schulich School of Business, York University, Toronto, Canada.

Andrew C. Wicks is associate professor of business administration at the Darden School of Business, University of Virginia, as well as a codirector of the Olsson Center for Applied Ethics.

Fran Wolf is professor in the Department of Accounting and Finance at the Williamson College of Business Administration at Youngstown State University.

Donna J. Wood holds the David W. Wilson Chair in Business Ethics at the University of Northern Iowa.